PEVSNER ARCHITECTURAL GUIDES

Founding Editor: Nikolaus Pevsner
Advisory Editor: John Newman
Editor: Bridget Cherry

Manchester
CLARE HARTWELL

THE PEVSNER ARCHITECTURAL GUIDES

comprising the four series, *The Buildings of England,
Ireland, Scotland* and *Wales*, were founded by the
architectural historian Sir Nikolaus Pevsner (1902–
83). *The Buildings of England* county volumes, largely
written by Pevsner himself, began to appear in 1951;
his *South Lancashire*, published in 1969, was the starting point for this guide to Manchester.
The research undertaken for this book will be incorporated in a wider-ranging volume: *Manchester and
South-East Lancashire*, in preparation.

THE BUILDINGS BOOKS TRUST

is a registered charity established 1994. It promotes
the appreciation and understanding of architecture
by supporting and financing the research needed to
sustain new and revised volumes of *The Buildings
of England, Ireland, Scotland* and *Wales*.

THE SAINSBURY FAMILY CHARITABLE TRUSTS
have made a generous contribution toward the work
of revision and the extension of the series to all the
countries of the British Isles.

The Building Books Trust gratefully acknowledges:
Grants towards the costs of research, writing and
illustrations for this volume from:
HERITAGE LOTTERY FUND
ENGLISH HERITAGE
THE PILGRIM TRUST
THE AMBERSTONE TRUST
TRAFFORD METROPOLITAN BOROUGH COUNCIL

Assistance with photographs from
ENGLISH HERITAGE

Manchester

CLARE HARTWELL

PEVSNER ARCHITECTURAL GUIDES

PENGUIN BOOKS

PENGUIN BOOKS

Published by the Penguin Group
Penguin Books Ltd, 80 Strand, London WC2R ORL, England
Penguin Putnam Inc., 375 Hudson Street, New York, New York 10014, USA
Penguin Books Australia Ltd, Ringwood, Victoria, Australia
Penguin Books Canada Ltd, 10 Alcorn Avenue, Toronto, Ontario, Canada M4V 3B2
Penguin Books India (P) Ltd, 11 Community Centre, Panchsheel Park, New Delhi – 110 017, India
Penguin Books (NZ) Ltd, Private Bag 102902, NSMC, Auckland, New Zealand
Penguin Books (South Africa) (Pty) Ltd, 5 Watkins Street, Denver Ext 4, Johannesburg 2094, South Africa

Penguin Books Ltd, Registered Offices: 80 Strand, London WC2R ORL, England

On the World Wide Web at: www.penguin.com

First published 2001

Set in 9/11.25 pt PostScript Adobe Minion
Typeset by Cambridge Photosetting Services, Cambridge
Colour origination and printing by Saxon Photolitho Ltd, England

In memory of my mother

Contents

How to use this book

The book is designed as a practical guide for exploring the buildings of central Manchester and its inner suburbs. Each section starts with a map which indicates the area covered and, where relevant, shows the route of the walk to be followed. The first two sections describe major buildings in the central area and academic institutions. The section on central streets is arranged alphabetically; for other parts of the inner areas the account is in the form of a Walk. Walks are also provided for most of the outer areas, which are described more selectively. The last chapter suggests some excursions to outstanding buildings further afield. These outer areas will all be treated in more detail in the forthcoming Buildings of England volume: *Manchester and South-East Lancashire*.

Within each section, certain topics are singled out for special attention and presented in separate boxes:

Manchester history: Manchester's Lost Churches p. 11, Principal Manchester Estates Developed from the Late C18 p. 12, Population p. 17, Peterloo p. 183, The Romans in Manchester p. 269

Cathedral: Chantry Chapels p. 46, The Stanley Family and Ecclesiastical Patronage p. 51, Misericords p. 56–7, The Lathom Legend p. 58, The West Windows p. 59, Further Reading p. 61

Town Hall: Sculpture p. 79, The Murals of the Great Hall p. 81, Further Reading p. 84

Waterways and transport: Hanging Ditch p. 235, The Irwell Navigation p. 255, The Bridgewater Canal p. 259

Trade and industry: Cast-iron Technology p. 15, The Commercial Warehouse p. 24, Early Transport Warehouses in Manchester p. 262, Fireproof Construction p. 278, The Marsland and Birley Families p. 315, Macintosh's Waterproof Fabric p. 317

Domestic building: Hall Houses p. 6, Workshop Dwellings p. 227, Early C19 Housing p. 320, Community Architecture in Hulme p. 328

Styles, materials and sculpture: Venetian Gothic p. 143, Greek Revival Architecture in Manchester p. 165, Terracotta p. 170, Assize Courts Statuary p. 248

Parks: Cathedral Gardens p. 239

Acknowledgements

Nikolaus Pevsner visited Manchester in 1967 as part of his research for *South Lancashire* (1969). His account of the city and its buildings was the starting point for this book, which expands on its predecessor to include much new information made available by recent research, and to encompass the many changes which have transformed Manchester over the last thirty years.

Manchester could not have been published without a grant from the Heritage Lottery Fund to support the research, nor without the generosity of English Heritage which included provision of most of the photographs through Bob Skingle and his team. Trafford Metropolitan Borough Council was generous in their support of the project, and thanks also go to Trafford Conservation Officer Alexandra Fairclough. The University of Manchester and its Field Archaeology Centre provided office facilities for which I am extremely grateful. Dr Peter Arrowsmith of the Centre ably assisted with aspects of the research, and Norman Redhead of the Sites and Monuments Record was unfailingly helpful. Officers of Manchester City Council assisted in many ways and I am particularly grateful to Mike Pilkington, Photographer, and to David Hilton, Plankeeper, who made so many investigations on my behalf and generously gave me the benefit of his wide-ranging knowledge of the city's Victorian architecture.

John H. G. Archer is owed a major debt as the author of the entries on Manchester Town Hall, the John Rylands Library, Deansgate, and the Free Trade Hall. I am also personally indebted to him for his encouragement and support over many years. I am grateful to Julian Holder who contributed the entries on the Central Library and Town Hall extension and advice on the city's post-war architecture; to Rory O'Donnell who assisted with the entry on the Holy Name of Jesus and advised on other Manchester R.C. churches; and to Frank Kelsall who has been an unfailing supporter of the project. Particular thanks go to Dr Michael Powell and staff of Chetham's Library who offered me every assistance in my work on the building and other aspects of my research.

Many others have given me the benefit of their expertise: Terry Wyke of Manchester Metropolitan University, Matthew Hyde contributed to descriptions of several city centre buildings, Mike Williams of English

Heritage on cotton mills, Dr Sharman Kadish on Manchester's Jewish heritage, David George of the Manchester Region Industrial Archaeology Society, and Steve Little on Ancoats and other subjects. I am indebted to the English Heritage buildings team in York, especially Simon Taylor, Marion Barter of the Regional Office in Manchester, and Emma Whinton and Alyson Rogers at Swindon. Also generous with information and advice have been E. Alan Rose who gave me access to Methodist archives, Dr Christa Grössinger of the University of Manchester, and Carol Gausden of the Manchester Early Dwellings Research Group. Useful information has been offered by the committee of the Portico Library and Gallery, Dr Paul Crossley, Elain Harwood and W. J. Smith, and I am grateful also to Peter Ferriday, Peter Barnes, J. Holt and T. H. Cowle. Karen Evans is owed special thanks for her thorough and prompt assistance on various research topics. Research of this sort could never be done without the co-operation of the staff of libraries, record offices and repositories: I am grateful to all of them, and I am especially appreciative of the patience and professionalism of the staff of the local history and archive sections of Manchester Central Reference Library. I must also thank Gill Barry of Manchester Metropolitan University for making library facilities available to me.

Several architects and artists kindly gave time to discuss projects with me, including Ken Moth, John Sheard, Harry M. Fairhurst, Antony Hollaway and William Mitchell. Owners, custodians, clergy and staff were helpful in giving me access to their buildings and assisting me with my enquiries. I must thank particularly Dr J. Patrick Greene, Director of the Museum of Science and Industry in Manchester, and his staff; Philip White of the Co-operative Insurance Company; Francis Law of Manchester Crown Court; Father Dennis Clinch of St Mary; Geoffrey Robinson of Manchester Cathedral; Father Matus of the Holy Name of Jesus; and the Sisters of the Presentation Convents in Manchester and Clonmel.

This book would not have been possible without the help and advice of Bridget Cherry and Simon Bradley who were responsible not only for assistance on all aspects of the text but also for many useful suggestions and valuable insights. All the staff of the Pevsner Architectural Guides have been supportive, and special thanks go to Fleur Richards who was a thorough and tenacious picture and illustrations researcher. The production of the book involved many people including Andrew Henty, Alan Fagan who drew the maps, Andrew Barker who designed the layout, Stephany Ungless who painstakingly checked the text and graphics and Judith Wardman who prepared the indexes. Thanks also go to Anthony J. Pass, J. Y. Lee of Stephenson Bell, Chris Mawson of Aerofilms, Wayne Ankers of the *Manchester Evening News* and Michael Dyer Associates.

Introduction

Introduction

Manchester is one of England's great cities, outstanding for its combination of Victorian architecture and industrial heritage. It lies on the banks of the River Irwell near the s w foothills of the Pennines, less than 40 m. (24 km.) from the w coast; a topographical position blamed for the damp climate but responsible for economic advantages in communications and trade long before the industrial revolution. The local stone is purplish-red sandstone from worked-out quarries to the n of the centre in Collyhurst, but by the c19 the predominant building materials were well-made red brick and buff sandstone. These dominate most of the city centre, despite waves of redevelopment, a process which still continues. The centre of town lies between two tributaries of the Irwell, the Irk to the n and the Medlock to the s, though they have largely been culverted, and only the Irwell, which divides Manchester from Salford to the w, survives as a visual boundary. Grand civic and commercial architecture in the centre gives way on the s side to some of the most

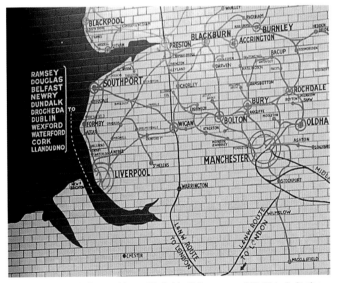

1. Detail from the tiled Lancashire and Yorkshire Railway map within Victoria Station.

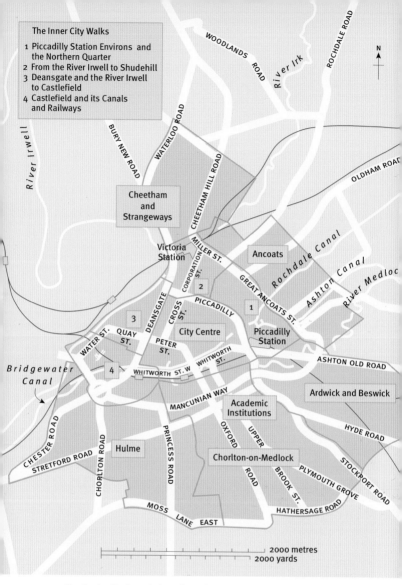

Manchester. The boundaries refer to the areas addressed in this book and do not reflect the full extent of the outlying townships.

memorable streetscapes of the city, where C19 and early C20 commercial warehouses line the streets and the Rochdale Canal can be glimpsed. Pre-C19 Manchester is recalled on the N side of the centre in the medieval buildings of the collegiate church (now the cathedral) and little pockets of late C18 buildings amongst the C19 warehouses and C20 offices. Beyond the centre this book also includes parts of immediately neighbouring townships whose character and appearance reflect their individual histories. Ancoats, on the NE side, was the world's first industrial suburb, and still retains some of Manchester's famous cotton mills. Cheetham and Strangeways, to the N, was the centre of the city's C19 Jewish community, and the area to the SE in Chorlton-on-Medlock is largely the province of the academic quarter. Canals and railways dominate the landscape to the SW in Castlefield, today a tourist attraction, but once the hub of the industrial transport network. To the S is the residential suburb of Hulme, rebuilt in the mid C20, now the site of some of the most innovative new housing schemes in the city.

Early and Medieval History

South Lancashire was occupied in the Iron Age by the Brigantes, or a sub tribe the Setantii, though evidence for their presence in Manchester is restricted to the discovery of a single pottery vessel. The Romans established a fort at Castlefield in AD 79 close to the confluence of the rivers Medlock and Irwell, but if the associated civilian settlement survived the end of Roman rule there is little evidence for it. Probably the only lasting legacy was part of the route from Chester to Ribchester and Carlisle, approximately on the line of Deansgate, Victoria Street and Bury New Road. Little else is known of pre-Conquest Manchester, though a fleeting reference in the Anglo-Saxon Chronicle suggests that an existing Saxon *burh* may have been repaired in the C10 as part of Edward the Elder's attempts to contain the incursions of the Norsemen. A naturally defensible bluff at the confluence of the rivers Irwell and Irk about 1 m. (.66 km.) N of the Roman fort was the site of the manor house of the Grelley family by the C13, and probably also their castle, recorded in 1184. Three concentric ditches encircling the promontory have been identified, two of them related to the line of Long Millgate and Hanging Ditch, close to the present cathedral, and one running through the yard of Chetham's School and Library. The origins and exact course of each are open to conjecture though it has been suggested that they may relate to the Norman castle or even the Saxon *burh*.

Of the medieval town which grew up around the manor house almost nothing earlier than the C15 survives, though there are a number of impressive timber-framed halls further afield, of which the C14 Baguley Hall is one of the earliest and most interesting (*see* Excursions, and topic box on next page). The parish church (made a cathedral in 1847) lies within the line of Hanging Ditch, possibly on the site of one of the two churches mentioned in Domesday, though there is little evidence for fabric earlier than the C13. It was made collegiate in 1421 and almost completely rebuilt thereafter. It is one of the largest and most lavish medieval collegiate churches in England, with notable furnishings of the late C15 to early C16. The priest's college with its great hall (now Chetham's School and Library) which was erected on the site of the Grelley manor house is the best and most intact example of its type in the country (*see* topic box). If we add Hanging Bridge, which crosses

Hall Houses

Chetham's School and Library (*see* Major Buildings) and Baguley Hall (*see* Excursions) are good examples of large medieval houses with a principal room in the form of a ground-floor hall open to the roof. Although there are variations over time and according to locality and social status, buildings of this type tend to share the same basic form, with a strongly defined spatial hierarchy. The upper end of the hall was reserved for senior members of the household who presided over meals and other communal activities from a table which could be elevated on a low platform or dais furnished with a canopy. Before the adoption of chimneys there would be a hearth in the centre of the room, with the smoke vented through a louvre, an opening at the ridge with a lantern over. Behind the dais private rooms, a parlour and upper chamber, afforded a degree of comfort which contributed to the gradual abandonment of public dining in the hall by the family except on special occasions. Services were reached from the lower end of the hall from a cross passage with doorways leading off to buttery (for storage of drinks etc.), pantry and kitchen. The passage was usually screened from the hall by a spere, a timber partition designed to reduce draughts, with two openings giving to the cross passage. This is more or less the arrangement at Chetham's School and Library, where the standard domestic plan was adapted for institutional use by the college of priests. At Baguley Hall, which survives in more fragmentary form, there is a spere truss, a common feature of timber-framed halls in the North and West of England. This is a roof truss on two free-standing posts marking the division between cross passage and hall with fixed partitions at each end, which would have had a screen between.

3. Typical timber-framed hall house looking towards the cross-passage. The dotted line indicates the position of the screen.

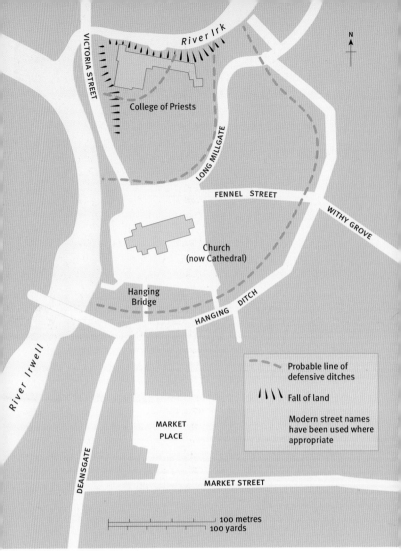

Key:
- - - - Probable line of defensive ditches

\\\\ Fall of land

Modern street names have been used where appropriate

100 metres
100 yards

4. Layout of the late medieval town.

Hanging Ditch beside the church, we have named all that survives architecturally of Leland's 'fairest, best builded, quickest and most populus tounne of al Lancastreshire'. Of the houses, market buildings, grammar school and bridge over the Irwell with its 'praty litle chapel', there when he visited *c.* 1538, no physical evidence survives.

The Seventeenth Century

By the end of the C16 the importance of the town as a centre of trade is reflected by the fact that the cloth market in London at Blackwell Hall had a separate department called the Manchester Hall. It was a leading

5. Chetham's Library. The original bookcases were made by Richard Martinscrofte (*c.* 1655).

cloth trader and former Lord Mayor of London Nicholas Mosley who bought the lordship of his native Manchester in 1595. In the early C17 the production of pure woollens in s Lancashire declined in favour of fabrics incorporating linen, classed as smallwares and fustians, which were being exported to w and s Europe by 1620. Cotton, most of it imported from the Levant, became increasingly popular for use in mixed cloths, and at the end of the C17 Manchester was firmly established at

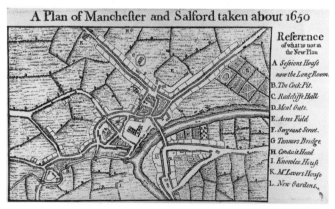

6. C18 copy of a plan of Manchester and Salford (*c.* 1650). The map is oriented with s at the top, rather than N.

the centre of a network of s Lancashire towns that specialized in the production of cloth containing cotton.

Manchester came under siege during the Civil War in 1642, but Royalist forces were repelled and the town went on to play a leading role in the war as a Parliamentarian headquarters. Trade came to a standstill during this period and the situation was worsened by a serious outbreak of bubonic plague, which claimed at least 931 lives in 1645. The effects were disastrous in the short term, but recovery came quickly as merchants resumed their activities and inward migration renewed the population.

It is no coincidence that the cloth trade formed the basis for the fortune of Humphrey Chetham, whose bequest founded a bluecoat school and free library in the college of priests in 1654–8. The institution, which still occupies the building, is the custodian of the C17 fittings and remarkable library furnishings which, apart from two Mosley family brasses and one or two other memorials in the cathedral, are all that have come down to us from that century. Of the wealth of timber-framed buildings nothing has survived except the fragmentary re-erected remains of the C17 Old Wellington Inn on Cateaton Street.

The Eighteenth Century

The establishment of the church of St Ann in 1709 and laying out of St Ann's Square in 1720 to the s of the old town centre was the first major planned development outside the medieval town, though a dissenters' meeting house, the predecessor of the present Cross Street Chapel, had already been built nearby in 1693–4. Apart from two mutilated houses on King Street slightly to the s, the church is the sole surviving architectural representative of the early C18. It has the expected auditory plan and retains the original pulpit. It can scarcely claim anything but local significance architecturally, yet the fluted pilasters of the exterior, tall apse, and lofty proportions of the interior betray obvious ambitions towards urbane sophistication, matched by some of the long-demolished houses illustrated in the margins of Casson & Berry's 1741 map.

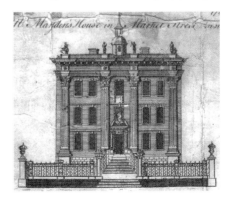

7. Detail of Marsden's
House (demolished)
from Casson & Berry's
1741 map.

By the end of the C18 the congregation of the dissenting chapel on Cross Street had moved towards a Unitarian position. The chapel was to remain at the centre of liberal and tolerant intellectual circles in the town throughout the C19. Several other independent chapels are also shown in the town centre on Green's 1794 map. In 1780–1 the Wesleyans replaced their old meeting house with a showy Gothic chapel on Oldham Street which rivalled their New Chapel in City Road, London, in size and which resembled the Established Church in liturgical arrangements. Manchester Quakers and Baptists had meeting houses by the end of the century, and the Roman Catholics built their first church in 1794, where St Mary, Mulberry Street, now stands. C18 Jewish traders probably met in rented premises off Deansgate in the area of John Dalton Street, where a Synagogue Alley is recorded in the 1740s. A warehouse on Withy Grove was used as a synagogue in 1796 and the first to be purpose-built was erected on nearby Halliwell Street in 1825. New churches were built, and by the end of the C18 there were eight in addition to the medieval parish church.

Increase in trade was accompanied by better communications. The roads to Stockport, Oldham and Ashton-under-Lyne were all turnpikes by the early 1730s and links to Liverpool and the w were improved when the Irwell and Mersey Navigation was completed in 1736. The first Exchange was built in the market place in 1729 and the erection of the Manchester Infirmary in Piccadilly followed in 1755. By the second half of the C18 Manchester had become a provincial town of the first rank. Trade was burgeoning and by 1750 pure cottons were being produced. Production was mainly in domestic workshops but manufacture of smallwares such as tapes and garters using Dutch looms, of which around 1,500 existed in the town by the mid C18, was in some cases concentrated in workshops containing a dozen machines or more.

Rapid expansion towards the end of the C18 was facilitated by sales of large parcels of land in and around the centre (*see* topic box, p. 12). Terraces in the s part of the town on Byrom Street, Quay Street and St John Street indicate the character of **housing** of the middle classes at the turn of the C18 and C19. Cobden House on Quay Street, of the 1770s, boasts the best domestic interior, but there is nothing in Manchester to

8. Hand-coloured engraving by Robert Whitworth (1734).

Apart from St Ann, the only legacy of Manchester's c18 churches is one or two open spaces in the centre and *William Peckitt*'s glass from St John, now in St Ann. The most accomplished was *James Wyatt*'s St Peter (*see* ill. p. 202), started in 1788, with its Greek portico, the only one for which an architect is known. Others did not lack ambition. St John, of 1768–9, was an early example of the Gothic Revival which had galleries supported by slender Gothic cast-iron columns. It was built for local landowner and businessman Edward Byrom whose choice of style may

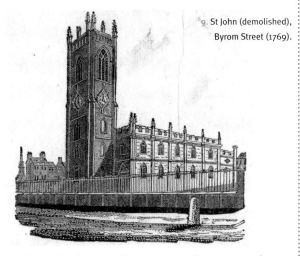

9. St John (demolished), Byrom Street (1769).

be explained by the fact that he was, according to Aston's 1804 *Manchester Guide*, 'a zealous churchman, and much attached to all its ceremonies'. St Mary, w of Deansgate (1753–6), was conventional apart from the extraordinary tower. The Gothic third stage was copied from the medieval parish church, and topped by an approximation of the rotunda and steeple of James Gibbs' St Martin-in-the-Fields in London (1722–6). Dr Joan Lane attributes the addition to *Timothy Lightoler*.

Dates of consecration and demolition (dem.) are given, unless otherwise stated.

St Mary, Parsonage, 1756, dem. 1928
St Paul Turner Street, 1765, rebuilt 1878, dem. 1984
St John Byrom Street, 1769, dem. 1931
St Michael Angel Meadow, 1789, dem. *c.* 1951
St Peter St Peter's Square, 1794, dem. 1907
St Clement Stevenson Square, 1793, dem. *c.* 1878
St George Rochdale Road, started 1778, consecrated 1818, dem. 1977

1. Byrom Estate between Water Street, Quay Street and Deansgate. Laid out by 1788, but only around half built-up by 1820.

10. Late c18 houses in Byrom Street.

2. Chorlton Hall Estate, owned by the Minshulls, SE of Piccadilly. Roger Aytoun, who married the Minshull heiress in 1769, laid out and sold land between Piccadilly, Portland Street, Princess Street and the Medlock during the 1770s.

3. Lever Estate N of Piccadilly, disposed of by Sir Ashton Lever from the 1770s. In 1780 a 25-acre (10-hectare) block was acquired by William Stevenson who laid out a grid of streets centring on Stevenson Square, bounded by Oldham Street, Great Ancoats Street, Back Piccadilly and Newton Street.

4. Mosley Street, core of the development by the Mosley family, Lords of the Manor. They disposed of some holdings in the town centre in 1783. The street became one of the most fashionable parts of town.

5. Legh family holdings in the angle of Great Ancoats Street and Oldham Road in Ancoats, laid out from the 1770s onwards.

This account is based on C. W. Chalklin, *Provincial Towns of Georgian England*, 1974.

compare with the elegance of the late Georgian terraces of Liverpool. Emigration to the suburbs had already begun before 1800, and although little survives from the c18 some early c19 houses and terraces can still be seen around Chester Road in Hulme, near Ardwick Green, and scattered through Chorlton-on-Medlock. The early c19 villas of

11. Houses with attic workshops illustrated in *The Builder* (1862).

Cheetham Hill have almost all disappeared. In the centre occasional dwellings further down the social scale survive, with a concentration in the streets N of Piccadilly Gardens and in Castlefield, where houses of artisans and skilled workers include examples with attic workshops.

During the 1770s to early 1790s large parcels of land near the centre of Manchester were sold for development in response to increasing demand and soaring land values. With the striking exception of Ancoats, where evidence exists for sales unencumbered by the usual restrictive covenants designed to prevent nuisances, the promotions were mainly for residential development. It was common practice for owners to survey and stake out roads and building plots themselves before selling to developers who acted as middlemen between original landlord and builder. Developers played a greater role in Manchester and Liverpool than in Birmingham, for example, where land usually passed directly from owner to builder. The interlocking grids are still discernible in the modern streets, which in many cases preserve names of owners and developers.

The Industrial Revolution in the Early Nineteenth Century

At the end of the C18 Manchester was poised to move on to the world stage as urban and industrial expansion gathered pace. SE Lancashire and Manchester became the first industrial economy and society in the world, but the precise reasons for the astonishing transformation have remained unclear. Long experience of textile production and trade and the absence of restrictive practices associated with a corporation and craft guilds played a part. It has been suggested that the humidity of the climate, which made cotton easier to manipulate, could have been significant. Perhaps the most important factor was the regional specialization in producing cotton-using cloths and the high level of expertise acquired in the purchasing, marketing and handling of the material, which had made s E Lancashire the national centre for the production of cotton and mixed-cotton cloth well before the end of the c18.

The first cotton mill had been built for Richard Arkwright on Miller Street in the early 1780s, and the first to be powered by a rotary steam engine was erected for Peter Drinkwater on Auburn Street in 1789. The boom followed. The number of cotton-spinning firms doubled from 51 in 1799 to 111 in 1802 and their rateable values trebled.* The town had by then an important asset in the country's first **canal** (1759–65) of the industrial era, built by the third Duke of Bridgewater, with its terminal basin at Castlefield, s of the centre. By 1776 it was extended w to Runcorn, giving Manchester efficient links with international trade routes and bringing coal and raw cotton into the town. The Manchester-

12. Skewed aqueduct, Store Street, by Benjamin Outram (c. 1794–9).

Bury-Bolton, Manchester-Ashton-Oldham and Manchester-Rochdale canals followed between 1790 and 1806. The surviving warehouses of the Rochdale and Bridgewater canal basins are of considerable interest, while *Benjamin Outram*'s skewed aqueduct (*c.* 1794–9) on the Ashton Canal is the earliest surviving example of its type. The transport revolution continued with the coming of the **railways**. The terminus of the world's first passenger railway, the Liverpool and Manchester, with the original station and warehouse of 1830, survives near the Bridgewater Canal Basin in Castlefield.

The application of steam power to textile processing was accom-

* The figures are based on research by A. J. Bailey quoted in M. Williams with D. A. Farnie, *Cotton Mills in Greater Manchester*, 1992.

Cast-iron Technology

The use of structural cast iron in building took off in the late C18 and became increasingly popular in the C19 until it was replaced by steel. There was some early success in the design of bridges and fireproof factories (*see* Fireproof Construction p. 280), but the physical properties of the material were not at first well understood. Early C19 Manchester, with its atmosphere of intellectual enquiry, its brilliant circle of scientists centred on John Dalton, and its pool of experienced founders and engineers, offered the ideal conditions for innovation. *Eaton Hodgkinson*, a former pupil of Dalton, began working on the design of cast-iron beams with the help of the engineer *William Fairbairn* in the 1820s. Beams were made and tested in Fairbairn's (demolished) Ancoats works. The key was the correct analysis of tensile stresses. Hodgkinson devised a beam which was lighter, more efficient and cheaper than its predecessors. His findings, which were published by the Manchester Literary and Philosophical Society in 1830, formed the basis for all future C19 structural cast-iron design. The new beam became standard in iron-framed buildings, but the first known application was in *George Stephenson*'s (demolished) Liverpool and Manchester Railway Water Street bridge of 1829–30 (*see* Inner City, Walk 4, p. 266) where the superior qualities of the beams facilitated the construction of a flat, level bridge, the prototype for the most common type in use today, the level beam or girder bridge.

Hodgkinson beams can be seen on the UMIST campus (*see* Academic Institutions, p. 124) where part of the cast-iron frame of the 1840s Havelock Mills has been erected.

Further Reading: T. Bannister, 'The First Iron Framed Buildings', *Architectural Review*, 107, 1950; A. W. Skempton & H. R. Johnson, 'The First Iron Frames', *Architectural Review*, 121, 1962; R. S. Fitzgerald, 'Development of the Cast Iron Frame in Textile Mills to 1850', *Industrial Archaeology Review*, 10, 1988.

panied by rapid development of technological expertise, bringing improved mill buildings, machines and machine tools, foundations that led to the city becoming by the end of the C19 a world centre of engineering. Manchester is one of the best places to study early experiments in fireproof construction and iron framing, with two concentrations of large **cotton mills** close to the centre.* The powerful visual effect of the mills registered by so many early C19 visitors was due partly to their unusual height, probably a consequence of high land values, and also because the buildings could be sited right next to one another, since

---

* The surviving mills are not representative as the record is biased by the better survival rate of fireproof and fire-resistant structures and of the buildings of larger owner-occupied firms whose size shielded them from the worst effects of economic recession.

Population

Manchester's growth in the first half of the c19 was prodigious. London's population doubled between 1801 and 1841; during the same period Manchester's trebled in size. The figures from 1801 are based on census returns for the 1838 borough. Earlier figures are for the Manchester Township, of which only those for 1773 are based on a reliable census.*

1717	c. 10,000	1811	89,068	1851	303,382
1757/8	c. 17,000	1821	126,066	1871	351,189
1773	22,481	1831	182,016	1901	347,495
1801	75,281	1841	235,507		

* I am grateful to Terry Wyke for supplying these figures.

steam power freed them from the need to harness a head of water. Proximity brought economic advantages in shared infrastructure and access to a pool of labour. The group in Ancoats which includes Murrays Mills and McConnel & Kennedy's Mills on Redhill Street, and Beehive Mill on Radium Street illustrates development in design and construction techniques from the 1790s to the opening of the c20. The other group, Chorlton New Mills in Chorlton-on-Medlock, includes the oldest surviving fireproof mill (1813–15) in Manchester and the remains of the Macintosh Works, one of the earliest manufactories of rubber for commercial applications.

Rapid growth was accompanied by seemingly unprecedented levels of poverty, deprivation and squalor. As early as the mid 1780s increased mortality from fever was attributed to the 'crowded and uncleanly manner in which the poorer people have been lodged'.* Cyclical trade depressions and the casual or seasonal nature of many branches of employment made many working-class lives precarious and unpredictable, while lack of regulation encouraged the proliferation of overcrowded insanitary housing. A much-altered row of late c18 back-to-back houses can be seen on Portugal Street in Ancoats, but even these were vastly superior to the miserable houses and shacks of the worst slums. The conditions of the poorest city-dwellers were highlighted by men like James Kay whose *Moral and Physical Conditions of the Working Classes* appeared in 1832. This and Edwin Chadwick's *Report on the Sanitary Condition of the Labouring Population* of 1842 were more influential than Engels' latterly better-known *The Condition*

* T. Henry, 'Observations on the Bills of Mortality for the towns of Manchester and Salford', *Memoirs of the Literary and Philosophical Society of Manchester*, 3, 1795.

13. McConnel & Kennedy's Mills, Redhill Street, alongside the Rochdale Canal (1818–1913).

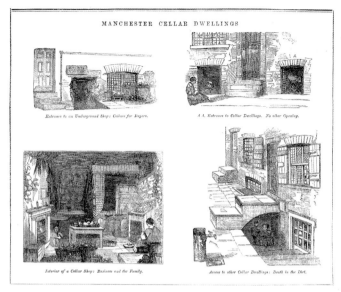

MANCHESTER CELLAR DWELLINGS

Entrance to an Underground Shop: Cellars for Eggers.

A A. Entrance to Cellar Dwellings. No other Opening.

Interior of a Cellar Shop: Business and the Family.

Access to other Cellar Dwellings: Death in the Dirt.

14. Cellar dwellings as illustrated in *The Builder* (1862).

of the Working Class in England of 1844 which was not published in Britain until 1892. Poverty, urbanization and class differences in Manchester are themes in the novels of Elizabeth Gaskell, such as *Mary Barton* (1848). A little later other authors created a sub genre of Victorian fiction which has been styled Manchester *Bildungsroman*. This variant usually emphasizes local and regional identity with themes of rapprochement between the social classes and the doctrine of self help. Typically the stories chart the social and moral progress of a child from one of Manchester's notorious slums, Angel Meadow, Lower Deansgate, Ancoats or Shudehill, who escapes from poverty through diligence to win worldly success and spiritual maturity.

The Early Nineteenth-century Town

The **public buildings**, **clubs** and **institutions** of the early C19 town illustrate the ambitions of the town's middle classes and belie their reputation as hard-headed Manchester men who had to learn their manners from Liverpool gentlemen. Liverpool was undoubtedly an influence, but Manchester was quick to adopt the fashionable Greek Revival style and fortunate in obtaining the services of one of its best practitioners, *Thomas Harrison* of Chester. Of his three Manchester buildings, the Exchange (1806–9), Theatre Royal (1803), and Portico Library (1802–6) on Mosley Street, only the last survives, an advanced building for its day with a sophisticated Soane-inspired interior. *Francis Goodwin* designed the first town hall (1819–34, demolished) using the decorative Ionic of the Erechtheum in Athens. *Charles Barry*'s Royal

15. Portico Library, Mosley Street, by Thomas Harrison (1802–6).

Manchester Institution of 1824–35 (now the City Art Gallery), Mosley Street, is a major early work of that architect and one of great accomplishment, which successfully married the Greek-inspired exterior to its impressive interior. The chief local practitioner of the style was *Richard Lane*, who trained in Paris before settling in the town *c.* 1820. His buildings have neither the authority of Harrison's work nor the individuality of Barry's but they are good, scholarly examples of provincial Greek Revival style. Many of them have disappeared, including a large club on Mosley Street and an ornate concert hall on Peter Street, but the surviving façade of the Chorlton-on-Medlock Town Hall and Dispensary (now part of the Grosvenor Building, Manchester Metropolitan University) is typical of his style.

Religious Buildings

The grants of the national Church Building Commission (established 1818) were directed at Manchester's populous hinterland and suburbs rather than the centre. Of these *Francis Goodwin*'s florid Gothic St George (1826–8) survives in Hulme, but *Barry*'s St Matthew in Castlefield (1822–5) was demolished in 1951. The intriguing tradition established by *William Hayley*'s rather clumsy experiments in neo-Norman and Italianate style (*see* the tower of St Thomas, Ardwick, of 1836 and All Souls, Ancoats, a Commissioners' church of 1839–40) must await further analysis of his work in the region. *Barry*'s Unitarian Chapel of 1836–9 on Upper Brook Street is sparer and more mature than his earlier Gothic efforts, while of other early C19 Nonconformist chapels only *Richard Lane*'s Grecian Friends Meeting House (1828–31) on Mount Street in the centre and the classical Independent Chapel of *c.* 1840 in Cheetham Hill survive.

In 1838 H. N. Humphreys noted in J. C. Loudon's *Architectural Magazine* that Manchester's public buildings 'bespeak a lavish munificence highly creditable to the place'. He described 'noble ranges of warehouses' and houses on Market Street where 'in some instances a whole range is made to form one architectural design, after the manner of Regent Street or Regent's Park'. Although this comparison is dubious so far as architectural quality is concerned, his account does something to balance others, which dwelt almost exclusively on the horrors and marvels of the industrial city. For all the stark mill chimneys and squalid slums, the pre-Victorian town had more architectural distinction than is sometimes realized.

Victorian Manchester *c.* 1840–80

Manchester on the threshold of Victoria's accession had become an urban and industrial colossus, with industries such as iron-founding, engineering, bleaching and dyeing as well as cotton spinning, though commerce and trade were already more important than manufacturing; the Exchange, which was extended in 1847, had to be rebuilt in 1869–74. The system of local government, however, had changed little in centuries. The Manchester Court Leet was essentially the manorial court which chose unpaid officers to administer a limited range of services such as day police, market inspectors, etc. The Manchester and Salford Police Act of 1765 set up cleansing and lighting commissioners but little changed until the Manchester and Salford Police Commissioners were set up by another Act of 1792. They had the power to light and cleanse the streets and maintain a night police force. They enterprisingly established one of the earliest municipal gas companies for which a gasworks was built in 1817. The profits were used to pay for expenses such as paving and refuse disposal. Despite these improvements the old system could not cope with the levels of expansion or resist the challenge of middle-class Nonconformist reformers led by Richard Cobden.

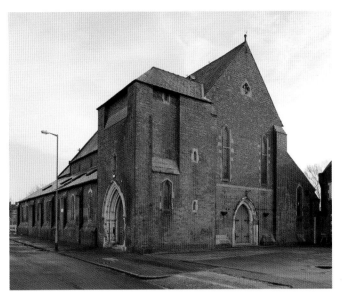

16. St Wilfrid (R.C.), St Wilfrid's Street, by A. W. N. Pugin (1842).

It was these men who secured a municipal corporation in 1838 under the Municipal Reform Act of 1835 which provided for the creation of new boroughs with elected councils. The manorial rights were bought by the Corporation ten years later, and in 1853 Manchester became administratively a city.

As Victoria's reign began *Charles Barry*'s palazzo-style Athenaeum on Princess Street (1836–7) and the new Gothic principles of *A. W. N. Pugin*'s church of St Wilfrid in Hulme of 1842 pointed to the future. It was Manchester-based architects who were to dominate the middle decades of the century. The mantle passed from Richard Lane to men such as *Edward Walters* who came from London, *J. E. Gregan* of Dumfries, and most notably *Alfred Waterhouse* who came from a Liverpool family and trained in Lane's Manchester office. The legacy of the Greek Revival is represented by *Charles Cockerell*'s cerebral Branch Bank of England in King Street of 1845, but apart from *Irwin & Chester*'s Theatre Royal in Peter Street, built in the same year, this had no other C19 repercussions and the architecture of the High Victorian decades is dominated by Gothic and Italianate styles.

The palazzo style was adopted enthusiastically for commercial buildings and for one of the city's chief monuments, *Walters' chef d'œuvre*, the Free Trade Hall (1853–6) on Peter Street. It commemorates the success of the Manchester based Anti-Corn Law League and the campaign for free trade of the 1830s–40s. Nikolaus Pevsner described it as 'perhaps the noblest monument in the Cinquecento style in England'. The superb Manchester and Salford Bank (1862, now the Royal Bank of

17. Britannia Hotel (formerly Watts Warehouse), Portland Street, by Travis & Mangnall (1851–6).

Scotland) on Mosley Street, also by *Walters*, is an example of the willingness of Manchester bankers to invest in good architecture, as is Benjamin Heywood's bank of 1848 (now the Royal Bank of Scotland) on St Ann's Square by *J. E. Gregan*.

It was trade more than industry that shaped the centre of the Victorian town. The centre was largely rebuilt from the 1820s onwards in response to the demand for commercial premises, including shops and banks, as the middle-class emigration to the suburbs speeded up. Manchester in the 1840s was the central market for the 280 cotton towns and villages within 12 m. (19 km.) of the centre, and a larger population beyond. The advantages conferred by having a warehouse near the Exchange was another trigger for redevelopment, and it was *Walters* who initially adopted the palazzo style for Manchester's most archetypal Victorian building. In the hands of an architect of his calibre a high degree of architectural subtlety could be obtained, illustrated by the ranges of warehouses along the N end of Portland Street and the s side of Charlotte Street. *Charles Barry*'s Athenaeum (completed in 1837) is often cited as the example which started the trend, and while his was the first to be built in the city, Walters had visited Italy and had first-hand experience of the palazzi of the c15 and c16 which were his model. *Travis & Mangnall*'s Watts Warehouse (the Britannia Hotel) of 1851–6 on Portland Street shows how quickly diverse architectural styles and motifs were incorporated into the basic framework. The work of firms such as *Clegg & Knowles* illustrates development of a flexible vocabulary, with gradual abandonment of architectural expression of a piano nobile and the incorporation of European Gothic forms from the late 1860s, at first using polychrome combinations of brick and stone dressings, later adopting the stone facing and more muted tones of the town hall. The quality of the city's warehouses attracted the continuing attention of the architectural press. *The Builder* in 1848 noted 'in many cases they display not only sound construction ... but good taste', while according to the *Building News* in 1870 'if a collection of even the doorways of these buildings were to be published, it would put to shame ... the commercial buildings and speculating builders of the Metropolis'.

Ruskinian Gothic, the other main strand in the architecture of Victorian Manchester, was introduced by *Alfred Waterhouse*, but his two early buildings in this style, the Binyon & Fryer Warehouse of 1855–6 and the Manchester Assize Courts of 1859–64 have been demolished. The latter was a milestone in the history of the Gothic Revival which won Ruskin's approval. The style was adopted for some of the city's most prominent buildings by leading Manchester men such as

18. Manchester Assize Courts (demolished), Cheetham and Strangeways, by Alfred Waterhouse (1859–64).

The Commercial Warehouse

Typical warehouses of the mid C19 were of brick with stone dressings, of five or six storeys, with high basements housing hydraulic presses powered by steam engines, and steps up to the front door. Cast-iron columns and timber floors were the norm; fireproof forms of construction were not generally used throughout until the end of the century. A loading bay with hydraulic wall cranes would be located at the side or rear of the building. Circulation was strictly controlled so that staff and customers were segregated. Only the largest and most successful traders built their own warehouses and speculative developments offered flexible space, including suites for merchants and agents who did not need to store quantities of goods on the premises.

Specialization in trade and distribution led to the development of different warehouse types. The **home trade warehouse** served the home market and retailers visited the premises to inspect the goods and make orders. Emphasis was on display and good lighting for viewing the goods, and there would usually be an impressive hall or foyer and showrooms with mahogany counters beneath the windows where goods could be inspected. The industry encompassed made-up clothing, haberdashery and a wide range of fancy goods. **Shipping warehouses** proliferated with the opening up of foreign trade after 1815. Goods would be received, examined, stored and packed for export. Although outward display might be important there was not the same need for impressive interiors. A refinement of the function of the shipping warehouse emerged with the **packing warehouse**, solely concerned with packing and despatching goods, seen in its most developed form in the early C20 Lloyds Packing Warehouses on Whitworth Street.

Edward Salomons (Reform Club, King Street, 1870–1) and *Thomas Worthington* (Memorial Hall, Albert Square, 1863–6; Minshull Street Courts 1867–73), as well as by many lesser architects.

The Free Trade Hall and the Assize Courts were used as exemplars by the opposing sides in the parliamentary debate of 1861 on the appropriate architectural style of the Government and Foreign Offices: an indication of the stature of the city's mid-Victorian architecture. The crowning achievement was *Alfred Waterhouse*'s town hall (1867–77), a monument to the civic pride and confidence of a city at the height of its powers. Here the Gothic style is more muscular than at the Assize Courts, and lacks external polychromy (which became obscured so quickly by Manchester soot). It is one of the major works of Victorian architecture, the more precious because it retains its original interior fittings and decorative schemes. *The Builder* in 1896 wrote: 'In after years it will probably be accounted one of the most excellent works which the

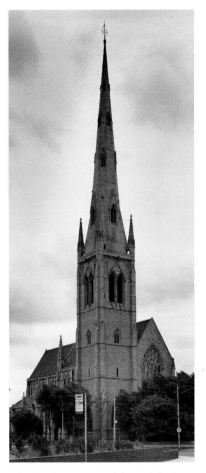

19. St Mary, St Mary's Street, Hulme, by J. S. Crowther (1856–8).

nineteenth century has bequeathed to its successors'. 'We of the later twentieth century have no hesitation in subscribing to this statement' was the rejoinder of Nikolaus Pevsner writing in *South Lancashire* in 1969. There can be few of the early C21 who would disagree.

So far as **religious buildings** are concerned, the best Anglican Victorian churches lie outside the centre and so beyond the scope of this volume (but *see* Excursions for *G. F. Bodley*'s St Augustine, Pendlebury). *J. S. Crowther* was one of Manchester's most serious students of Gothic and his high and noble churches are amongst the best in Manchester of their day. It was he who undertook repairs to the cathedral during the 1870s and wrote the first detailed architectural analysis of the building (*see* topic box, p. 61). His St Benedict, Ardwick (1880), and St Mary, Hulme (1856–8), survive although St Alban in Cheetham and Strangeways (1857–64) was demolished in the 1990s, one of the city's most grievous recent losses. Of Roman Catholic churches

J. A. Hansom's daring Holy Name of Jesus in Chorlton-on-Medlock retains an unusually good range of contemporary furnishings, while the idiosyncratic St Mary on Mulberry Street (*Weightman & Hadfield*, 1845) and *E. W. Pugin*'s St Francis, Gorton (*see* Excursions), are both of more than local interest. The first Armenian Church in England was built on Upper Brook Street in Chorlton-on-Medlock in 1869–70, a reflection of the diverse character of the city's business communities. Manchester in the late C19 was the home of the largest Jewish community in Victorian England, London excepted, concentrated in the streets around Cheetham Hill, where the former Sephardic Synagogue of 1889 by *Edward Salomons* survives as the chief treasure of an architectural legacy which has been decimated.

The Art Treasures Exhibition of 1857 confirmed the city's cultural credentials. Held at Old Trafford in a temporary cast-iron pavilion by *Edward Salomons* with interior decoration by *J. G. Crace*, it was an internationally important event which attracted over one million visitors and royal patronage. In spite of this a permanent art gallery was not established until 1882 when the premises of the Royal Manchester Institution became the City Art Gallery. The Regional College of Art got its own premises in 1881 (now part of the Grosvenor Building, Manchester Metropolitan University), designed by *G. T. Redmayne*.

The most important example of Victorian **public art** in the city is *Ford Madox Brown*'s town hall **murals** (completed between 1878 and 1893), one of the city's treasures and an example of enlightened civic patronage. There is also an extensive range of **public statuary**. The *Building News* in 1870 said that Manchester could be 'justly proud of, not only the number, but the quality of her statues'. Piccadilly, the main public space until Albert Square was created in 1863, was laid out by *Joseph Paxton* in 1854 with an esplanade where national figures are commemorated. They include Peel (*William Calder Marshall*, 1853) and Wellington (*Matthew Noble*, 1856), later joined by *E. Onslow Ford*'s seated figure of Queen Victoria (unveiled 1901).* In Albert Square the Albert Memorial, designed in 1862 by *Thomas Worthington*, came first, with a statue of the prince by *Matthew Noble*. He and *William Theed* were favourite sculptors who repeatedly won Manchester commissions in the middle of the C19. Later work mainly commemorates local dignitaries such as Bishop Fraser, by *Thomas Woolner*, 1887.

Much sculpture was placed in the town hall to commemorate civic dignitaries and leading figures from the Free Trade movement. Statues, mainly by *Theed*, were incorporated into key architectural positions on the main stair and in the Great Hall, while the Sculpture Hall houses a large collection of marble busts. The entrance vestibule has two of the city's finest examples of Victorian sculpture in *Chantrey*'s Dalton (1837) and *Alfred Gilbert*'s Joule (1893), while in the cathedral *E. H. Baily*'s

* It is not clear if this group will be retained in the new layout of the gardens.

20. Queen Victoria, Piccadilly Gardens, by E. Onslow Ford (1901).

Thomas Fleming (1851) and *W. Theed*'s seated statue of Humphrey Chetham (1853) are the best of the Victorian monuments.

Architectural sculpture is generally of a good standard. The best examples are from *Waterhouse*'s demolished Assize Courts from which statues by *Thomas Woolner* and some capitals by the *O'Shea* brothers are preserved in the Crown Court, Crown Square. The rich sculptural scheme of the Free Trade Hall is by *John Thomas*, while *Earp & Hobbs* is one of the better known firms of architectural sculptors at work in the city, responsible for schemes at Minshull Street Crown Court (*Thomas Worthington* 1867–73) and elsewhere. Less accomplished, but rewarding nevertheless, are *Henry Bonehill*'s scenes of fishermen at work, incorporated into the former Wholesale Fish Market on High Street (*Speakman, Son & Hickson*, 1873). *J. J. Millson*'s figures for *Woodhouse, Willoughby & Langham*'s London Road police and fire station (1901–6) and *W. J. Neatby*'s delightful scheme for *J. Gibbons Sankey*'s extension to the Regional College of Art (by then the Municipal School of Art, now part of the Grosvenor Building, Manchester Metropolitan University) of 1897 are notable examples of terracotta sculpture from the very end of the C19.

The 1870s and 1880s saw the virtual rebuilding of several city streets, with the next generation of warehouses along Princess Street and Portland Street, and new shops and offices along Deansgate and the lower part of King Street. Italianate and Gothic styles continued, seen

21. Detail from police and fire station (former), London Road, by Woodhouse, Willoughby & Langham (1901–6).

22. Capitals at the Crown Court, Crown Square (from the demolished Manchester Assize Courts), carved by the O'Shea brothers (1859–64).

in the architecture of some of the better local firms such as *Clegg & Knowles*, *Pennington & Bridgen*, and *G. T. Redmayne*. The Queen Anne style did not enjoy great popularity in the centre, though the School Board Offices (*Royle & Bennett* 1878, now Elliott House) on Deansgate is a prominent example of the style. Nearby the cast-iron and glass Barton Arcade (*Corbett, Raby & Sawyer*, 1871) is one of the loveliest Victorian shopping arcades in the country. North European Renaissance styles became more popular from the end of the 1880s, seen for example in *Alfred Waterhouse*'s former National Provincial Bank on Spring Gardens of *c.* 1890 and the Municipal School of Technology (now the University of Manchester Institute of Science and Technology) on Sackville Street by *Spalding & Cross*, 1895–1902.

The legacy of the city's thriving cultural and intellectual life includes the Hallé Orchestra, the *Manchester Guardian* (now the *Guardian*) and the Victoria University of Manchester, the first and still one of the foremost of the redbrick universities. This started as Owens College in 1851. Its buildings in Chorlton-on-Medlock are a product of *Alfred Waterhouse*'s maturity, erected between 1870 and 1902 (later parts by *Paul Waterhouse*) in the practical modern Gothic of the town hall. They make a grand gesture on Oxford Road and created a collegiate atmosphere in the quadrangle behind.

Educational initiatives such as the Mechanics' Institute, founded in 1824, whose premises from 1855 were *Gregan*'s noble palazzo on Princess Street, and the Free Library in 1852, which had branches in residential areas, demonstrate commitment to the ideal of self-improvement but they reached only a minority of the working classes. Manchester played an important role in the campaign for state education. The Lancashire (later National) Public Schools Association was formed in 1847 to promote a locally controlled non-sectarian education system, a campaign which finally bore fruit with the 1870 Education Bill. Thirty-nine board

23. Barton Arcade, Deansgate, by Corbett, Raby & Sawyer (1871).

schools were erected in Manchester after 1870, the commissions awarded to a variety of mainly local firms, at first executed in Gothic, later adopting loosely Queen Anne and Renaissance styles (for the survivors *see Manchester and South-East Lancashire*, forthcoming). The austerity of the schools built in the centre after the 1902 Education Act is a reflection of financial stringency; rooftop playgrounds were made necessary by the overcrowded sites, as in the school of 1912 on Atherton Street.

The problem of housing remained acute. There were few parallels in Manchester to the charitable trusts set up elsewhere to provide decent cheap accommodation and well-intentioned organizations such as the Manchester and Salford Workmen's Dwellings Association made little impact. The city's first municipal housing was the flats of Victoria Square and the associated terraces, built 1894–9 by *Spalding & Cross* in Ancoats, an area which also has examples of late Victorian night shelters, model lodging houses and servants' homes designed to offer an alternative to the street or the common lodging house. The Methodists had two large halls in the centre by 1910, both with social-work facilities, as well as men's and women's lodging houses and night shelters, reflecting the

24. Methodist Women's Night Shelter, Great Ancoats Street, by W. R. Sharp (1899).

size and strength of Methodist commitment in Manchester in the face of the failures of the state system.

The close of the c19 saw the erection of two buildings, the Whitworth Art Gallery and the John Rylands Library, major educational institutions both financed by the bequests of Nonconformist magnates who made their fortunes in engineering and cotton respectively. The difference in scale and emphasis of each project lies in the particular circumstances of the commissions (the art gallery a product of a competition and a committee, the library a personal choice by the benefactor's widow), but they make an interesting comparison. They both use historicist styles, but in ways which could hardly be more different. The Whitworth Art Gallery by *J. W. Beaumont & Sons*, erected between 1894 and 1908, is executed in a solid Jacobean, which suits its purpose but is resolutely unexciting. With the John Rylands Library (1890–9) no expense was spared, and the high drama of *Basil Champneys'* Art-for-Art's-sake Gothic is an example of historic style used freely as a medium for individual expression.

The Early Twentieth Century

At the opening of the c20 Manchester was reaping the benefits of one of the most ambitious municipal undertakings of the c19, the Manchester Ship Canal, which opened in 1894. It was a remarkable engineering achievement, making Manchester a port of international stature and diversifying the economic base of the region as industry concentrated in the canal-side Trafford Park Industrial Estate. Ultimately it cushioned the city from the worst effects of interwar recession. Its success is reflected in the proliferation of commercial buildings of the early c20, amongst the most conspicuous of which are the huge Lloyds Packing Warehouses on Whitworth Street designed by *Harry S. Fairhurst*. He

25. The opening of the Manchester Ship Canal (21 May 1894).

26. Royal Infirmary, Oxford Road, by E.T. Hall (1905–8), painted by L. Roberts.

and other local architects such as *Charles Heathcote* (later joined by his sons), *Charles Clegg*, *J. Gibbons Sankey*, *Percy Scott Worthington* and *Bradshaw & Gass* were some of the beneficiaries as new offices, banks and insurance company premises swallowed up their humbler predecessors.

The significance of Manchester as the financial centre of the North is reflected in huge commercial buildings such as the Refuge Assurance Offices (now the Palace Hotel) on Oxford Street, built in stages between 1891 and 1912 by *Alfred Waterhouse* and *Paul Waterhouse* (and extended again in the 1930s), and banks which outstripped even those in London for display. The capacity of the Royal Exchange had been successively extended through the C19, yet swelling numbers forced another rebuild by 1914, by *Bradshaw, Gass & Hope*.

Charles Heathcote was the foremost local practitioner of Baroque and creator of the most opulent of the surviving bank interiors, seen for example in his Parrs Bank on Spring Gardens (1902). Baroque was the favoured style for some of the most conspicuous municipal buildings from the early C20, for example *Woodhouse, Willoughby & Langham*'s police and fire station of London Road (1901–6). Greenwich Baroque was the predictable choice when the Royal Infirmary was rebuilt 1905–8 on a new site in Chorlton-on-Medlock by *E. T. Hall* and *J. Brooke*. Freer styles are seen in the former telephone exchange of 1909 on York Street by *Leonard Stokes* and the YMCA (now St George's House) on Peter Street, 1907–11 by *Woodhouse, Corbett & Dean* (a relatively early example of reinforced-concrete construction on the *Kahn* system). One of the

most original buildings of its day, *Edgar Wood*'s extraordinary First Church of Christ, Scientist (1903–4), is tucked away in the suburbs (*see* Excursions). It is a brilliant work of great individuality which speaks for the spirit of an age searching for an alternative to historical precedent.

Increased prosperity encouraged retail, leisure and entertainment ventures. There is an interesting range of theatres and cinemas, still concentrated on the Oxford Street-Peter Street-Quay Street axis which was established as the theatre and entertainment quarter in the early C19. The classicism of *Richardson & Gill*'s New Theatre of 1912 (now the Opera House) on Quay Street picks up where Cockerell left off more than half a century before, while the Palace Theatre (*Alfred Darbyshire*, 1891, altered by *Bertie Crewe* 1913) on Oxford Street hides a splendid interior behind the bland mid-C20 tiles. One of the first purpose-built cinemas was opened in 1911 on Oxford Street (the Picture House by *Naylor & Sale*) and the former Regal Twins (now the Dancehouse Theatre) of 1929–30 on Oxford Road by *Pendleton & Dickenson* is a proto-multiplex with a good Art Deco interior. Few good late C19 or early C20 pub or shop interiors survive. For an Edwardian shop there is Manchester Metropolitan University's Righton Building, and for pubs the Castle on Oldham Street and the Peveril of the Peak on Great Bridgewater Street.

Interwar Years

After the First World War the major civic undertaking in the centre was the Central Library and town hall extension, by *Vincent Harris*, erected 1930–8. The town hall extension successfully makes the transition from *Waterhouse*'s Gothic town hall to the circular form and grandiose classicism of the library which dominates St Peter's Square. This was the crowning achievement of the free library system in Manchester and it remains one of the finest public libraries in the country. The Midland Bank on King Street by *Edwin Lutyens*, designed in 1928, is easily the best example of interwar classicism in the city, which experienced a mini boom in large, mainly Portland stone office blocks before the

28. First World War Memorial, 'The Sentry', by C. S. Jagger (1921), within the Britannia Hotel, Portland Street (1851–6).

Depression set in. By far the best of these is the extension to the offices of Tootal Broadhurst, Lee & Co., Lee House, by *Harry S. Fairhurst & Son* with *J. H. Sellers* on Great Bridgewater Street, the base of a proposed skyscraper notable for its sophisticated interplay of materials, texture and form. The severely stripped classicism of the Kendal Milne's store on Deansgate, a most uncharacteristic work of *J. S. Beaumont* (1939), remains, with the Barton Arcade, the best example of retail architecture in the city. The Modern Movement is represented only by the Daily Express in Ancoats by *Sir Owen Williams* (1936–9), as good as anything of its day in England. It lacks the splendid interior of the paper's Fleet Street offices in London but enjoys a better site. Apart from *Lutyens'* Cenotaph in St Peter's Square of 1924, which Manchester cannot call her own since it is based on the Whitehall one, and *C. S. Jagger's* expressive sculpture of 1921, in the foyer of the Britannia Hotel, which was a private commission commemorating employees of Watts Warehouse, Manchester's war memorials are disappointing; especially when compared with the moving monuments of small towns in the North West such as Stalybridge. The first half of the c20 saw the demolition of religious buildings in central Manchester, although some interesting ones were built in the growing suburbs: *see* Excursions for *N. F. Cachemaille-Day's* St Michael (1935–7) in Northenden, notable for Continental influences and its star-shaped plan.

After the First World War expansion of the suburbs, mainly to the s of the centre, were composed partly of owner-occupied housing, but more of the new accommodation was provided by the Corporation or by private contractors with financial assistance from the Corporation.

More than 27,000 council houses were erected between 1924 and 1938, but council rents were still out of reach of the poorest. Housing conditions were appalling in the older inner suburbs like Ancoats, Chorlton-on-Medlock, Hulme and Angel Meadow, where only three per cent of the houses had baths. A limited programme of slum clearance took place but in 1945 it was estimated that 68,000 houses were unfit for human habitation.

Postwar

Trafford Park was kept busy by the Second World War, but a slow inexorable decline in manufacturing industry and the city's economic well-being followed soon after. The cotton industry, which had been in decline since the 1930s, had collapsed by the 1950s, and the most dramatic period of industrial decline began in the late 1960s. Housing problems remained, despite the creation of a satellite town at Wythenshawe for which *Barry Parker* had produced plans in 1927 (*see Manchester and South-East Lancashire*, forthcoming). Although some of the housing was completed, Parker's scheme, like the ambitions of the City of Manchester Plan of 1945 to create new council estates of largely low-rise housing with cultural and community facilities, foundered on the rocks of expediency. The high-rise and deck-access solutions of the 1960s and 70s resulted in poorly built schemes and social problems were exacerbated by widespread unemployment. Even when newly built they failed to convince. Nikolaus Pevsner wrote of Manchester in 1969: 'industrial housing … remains visually indifferent, and, even where much care has been taken on designing the façades, socially dubious. Do we really want these towers of flats everywhere? Do tenants want them? … Will they not be the slums of fifty years hence?' In the event

29. Mathematics and Social Sciences Building, UMIST campus, by W. A. Gibbon of Cruickshank & Seward (1966–8).

the problems started to manifest themselves in less than a decade, and the response to the failures of social housing is now unfolding in the regeneration of Hulme.

The universities and colleges were a beneficiary of the optimism of the early 1960s, but the UMIST campus is the only one with real cohesion. Here *W. A. Gibbon* of *Cruickshank & Seward* designed impressive Brutalist edifices of Corbusian influence, and *H. M. Fairhurst* designed his best university building, the Chemical Engineering Pilot Plant. The buildings of the University of Manchester of these years, with only a few exceptions, are disappointing but *Bickerdike, Allen, Rich & Partners'* Royal Northern College of Music (1968–73) is expressive and acts incidentally as a potent reminder of the unrealized 1960s ambitions of creating a network of upper-level walkways to link the buildings of the Manchester Educational Precinct.

In the centre the emphasis was at first on rebuilding war-damaged and run-down areas. Some of the city's finest buildings were badly damaged; of these the cathedral and the Free Trade Hall were painstakingly repaired, while the Assize Courts were eventually demolished. The new building was not, on the whole, a success. With the exception of *Yorke, Rosenberg & Mardall's* Magistrates' Court of 1969–72 (due for demolition) the buildings of Crown Square and the tower blocks on Portland Street are architecturally undistinguished and have never become absorbed into the grain of the city. In contrast Albert Bridge House (*E. H. Banks*, 1958–9) on Bridge Street is one of the better early multi-storey office blocks which makes intelligent use of its riverside site. Best of them all and still one of the best c20 buildings of the city is the group of Co-operative Insurance Society and Co-operative Wholesale Society buildings on Miller Street (by *G. S. Hay* and *Sir John*

30. Albert Bridge House, Bridge Street, by E. H. Banks (1958–9).

Burnet, Tait & Partners 1959–62). The twenty-five storey CIS tower remains the tallest in the city and is successfully related to the single-storey hall and fourteen storeys of the other elements. The three elements of the Piccadilly Plaza (*Covell, Matthews & Partners*, 1959–65, to be remodelled 2001) on the other hand lack real unity though they share a common podium. Despite the appeal of their brash confidence they completely fail to take account of their surroundings, unlike *Casson, Conder & Partners'* former District Bank (1966–9) and *Brett & Pollen's* Pall Mall Court (1969), both on King Street, which are carefully related to the street scene. For the rest, *R. Seifert & Partners'* Gateway House (1967–9) on Piccadilly Station Approach and *Ralph Tubbs'* Granada offices (1960–2) on Atherton Street have stood the test of time, but 111 Piccadilly by *Douglas Stephen & Partners* (1963–6) suffers from the poor quality of the finish, an illustration of the effects of the Manchester atmosphere on concrete surfaces. One of the most interesting and innovative buildings of the period was a product of the public sector. Oxford Road Station was built in 1960 by the staff architects of British Rail, project architect *Max Clendinning* with *Hugh Tottenham* of the Timber Development Association. It is the most ambitious example in the country of conoid timber shell roofing.

A few churches were built during the 1960s, of which *Maguire & Murray's* Church of the Ascension in Hulme, 1968–70, and *Desmond Williams & Associates'* Roman Catholic St Augustine in Chorlton-on-Medlock (1967–8) reflect the new liturgy of that decade.

From the Late Twentieth Century

The battle to preserve the best of the city's Victorian architecture came to a peak in the 1970s when conservation groups were successful in their campaign to save the Albert Memorial. Their activities did much to increase public awareness and appreciation of the city's historic architecture. New building of the 1970s was less ambitious than in the previous decade, except in terms of scale. *Levitt, Bernstein Associates'* high-tech Royal Exchange Theatre pod of 1976 is an example of creativity in a period which is memorable mainly for the erection of the ugly inward-looking Arndale Centre (*Wilson & Womersley*, 1972–80) while the scattering of undistinguished 1980s Postmodernist buildings in the centre have done little to enhance its appearance. Although the materials and palette changed, office blocks featuring dislocated columns and broken pediments were still going up in the second half of the 1990s. More interesting is the work in the modernist tradition of firms such as *Mills Beaumont Leavey Channon, Hodder Associates, Ian Simpson Architects* and *Stephenson Architecture* whose 15 Quay Street (1991–2) was influential. The firm's successor was *Stephenson Bell*, whose International Convention Centre (due for completion 2001) on Windmill Street is crisp, expressive and carefully related to its site, where it forms part of a striking group with the arched shed of former

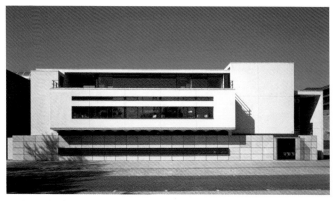

31. Career Services Unit, Booth Street East, by Hodder Associates (1995).

Central Station (G-Mex exhibition centre) and the glazed prow of the Bridgewater Hall (*RHWL Partnership*, 1993–6) in Barbirolli Square. The latter has an impressive auditorium and structural interest for the use of isolation units developed for earthquake zones. Elsewhere the uplifting Trinity Bridge by *Santiago Calatrava* of 1993–5 was actually a City of Salford initiative. Some of the best recent architecture has been commissioned by, or is associated with, the higher education sector, of which *Mills Beaumont Leavey Channon*'s Aytoun Library on Aytoun Street for Manchester Metropolitan University, *Hodder Associates*' Career Services Unit and *Short & Associates*' quirky Contact Theatre, both in Chorlton-on-Medlock, deserve mention.

The past few decades have seen some exemplary conservation schemes, such as the preservation of the Liverpool and Manchester Railway terminus buildings as part of the Museum of Science and Industry in Manchester, the creation of a Jewish Museum in the Sephardic Synagogue on Cheetham Hill Road and the relocation of the National Museum of Labour History in a hydraulic pumping station off Bridge Street. One of the earlier large-scale initiatives was the restoration and conversion of Central Station, Windmill Street, as the G-Mex exhibition centre, opened in 1986. There have been drawbacks and losses as well. The early C19 Havelock Mills, the last group of mills in the city centre, were demolished after a public inquiry in 1991, and it is quite shocking that buildings of the quality of *Percy Scott Worthington*'s Skin Hospital (1903–5) on Quay Street should have disappeared as recently as 1999. *Cockerell*'s Branch Bank of England was reduced to the status of a foyer of an office block in 1995, while the integrity of *Walters*' Free Trade Hall is to be sacrificed to a hotel conversion.

Attempts to improve the quality of the urban environment have met with some success, although it should have been possible to avoid the unsightly clutter associated with the Metrolink tram system. The overhaul of Piccadilly Gardens is long overdue, but the final outcome of

Tadao Ando's scheme and the fate of the c19 statuary there remains to be seen. Having said this, traffic management and pedestrian schemes have made the city much more congenial for those on foot, as well as improving the setting of buildings such as the town hall, where the paving of Albert Square has been a success. In the past few years trees have appeared in some city-centre streets and squares, but this sort of soft landscaping is not suited to the character of former industrial areas like Castlefield. 'Heritage' bollards and street lamps (inexplicably used to replace the stylish 1960s street lights outside the Granada offices on Atherton Street) seen in Castlefield and elsewhere illustrate typical late c20 responses to historic environments. More recently the treatment of parts of the town centre reflect attempts to create distinctive character for particular areas, but the spherical bollards and fanciful fountain in St Ann's Square have little connection with the character of its buildings. The slick street furniture of New Cathedral Street, though, is satisfyingly urban and modern. The street, which links St Ann's Square to Exchange Square, was laid out as part of the post-bomb developments (*see* p. 40, below). Here the response to the historic environment is a curving water feature meant to echo the line of the ancient watercourse of Hanging Ditch. If the giant grey children's windmills (*John Hyatt*, 1999) come into this category, the square is also the site of some of the city's recent **public art**, which is mostly of a lamentable standard. Some of the small-scale work in the Northern Quarter (various artists, 1996–8) provides engaging incident in the streetscape, but, with few exceptions such as *Kan Yasuda*'s Touchstone in Barbirolli Square, most examples are uninspired, or worse, whimsical.

Castlefield was the first of the run-down areas on the fringes of the centre to be rehabilitated, starting in the early 1980s. This was the result of private initiatives, grants from the European Union and regeneration schemes promoted by the Central Manchester Development Corpora-

32. Touchstone, Barbirolli Square by Kan Yasuda (1996).

tion. This marked the beginning of the restoration of the canal system for its townscape qualities and for leisure use. The establishment of the Museum of Science and Industry in Manchester made the area a tourist attraction and this was followed by the creation of an outdoor arena and other visitor facilities in the mid 1990s. The standard for office conversions was set by *Stephenson Architecture*'s Eastgate (1992) and *Ian Simpson Architects*' Merchants' Warehouse (1995–7), while the quality of new building varies from the intelligent individualism of the Quay Bar (*Stephenson Bell*, 1998) to the excesses of the Visions Centre (*M. Seddon*, 1999–2000). Further afield the regeneration of the Salford Docks, apart from *Michael Wilford*'s Lowry centre (completed 2000), has been more of a commercial than an architectural success. The Trafford side of the Ship Canal meanwhile is being transformed by *Daniel Libeskind*'s sculptural Imperial War Museum in the North, which is now approaching completion (for this and the Lowry *see* Excursions).

During the late 1980s and 1990s the city was reputed to have the best clubs in Europe, attracting people from all over the country as part of a phenomenon which has taken its place in the history of popular music and youth culture. The huge student population and the city's gay community contributed to the enormous success of the music and entertainment industry, and increasing numbers of clubs, restaurants and café bars opened in the centre during these years, most of them reusing existing buildings. This produced some interesting, though probably ephemeral, examples of interior design, but nothing to match conversions such as *OMI Architects*' Fourth Church of Christ, Scientist on Peter Street (1998) and *Hodder Associates*' CUBE gallery (1998) on Portland Street. The real boom is in residential conversion, which started in the 1980s with early C20 warehouses in the Whitworth Street neighbourhood. In 1991 fewer than a thousand people were resident in the central area. By 1998 this had risen to 4,550, and the projected figure for

33. Chorlton New Mills, Cambridge Street, loft conversion by developers Space Group (2000–1).

2002 is over 10,000. This trend has given a new lease of life to many older buildings, probably saving some from dereliction and demolition, but at the price of the loss of some impressive internal spaces such as could be seen in the MS&LR London Warehouse (*see* illus. 154). Conversions include *Stephenson Bell*'s Smithfield Building (1997–8) which fits well into the streetscape and knits the original buildings on Oldham Street into a coherent whole. The number of residential schemes started or planned in the period 2000–1 suggests that saturation point must soon be reached, but confidence seems boundless as more and more are proposed, reusing c20 office buildings and retail premises as well as c19 warehouses and mills. Purpose-built apartment blocks are beginning to emerge from their scaffolding. Better examples include the well-composed schemes of architects such as *Glenn Howells* and *Stephenson Bell*; some of the others are poorly detailed and formulaic. *Mills Beaumont Leavey Channon*'s Homes for Change in Hulme (1999–2000) is the most interesting, though this was not a product of the private sector, but designed with the input of prospective tenants.

The most dramatic changes of the recent past were brought about by a completely unforeseen event, a terrorist bomb which exploded near the s end of Corporation Street in the town centre on 15 June 1996 causing severe damage to surrounding buildings. This area and that to the n around the cathedral are undergoing a transformation, with new pedestrian streets and squares, new buildings and refurbishments. It is not yet clear if the ambitions of *Ian Simpson Architects*' Urbis building will make it a good neighbour to the medieval buildings, but the completion of *Building Design Partnership*'s Cathedral Gardens should create a better setting for them. The Marks & Spencer store by *Building*

34. Manchester city centre before the 1996 bomb. Manchester Cathedral can be seen to the bottom right.

35. Manchester city centre in February 2000, partially rebuilt after the 1996 bomb. Manchester Cathedral can be seen to the bottom right.

Design Partnership (completed 2000) is decent retail architecture but the main interior space of the nearby Printworks entertainment centre, completed 2000, is a disappointing pastiche. Repairs to the Royal Exchange Theatre on the other hand were accompanied by an impressive refurbishment using modern lighting and bold colour schemes to enhance the Edwardian interior.

The rebuilding after the bomb seemed to unleash a tidal wave of development which has sent ripples all over the city. The most typical structure of the past few years in the centre is the giant crane, and the most typical new buildings are retail and leisure outlets, hotels, and, most recently, purpose-built apartment blocks. Part of the stimulus is the 2002 Commonwealth Games, for which a new stadium is being constructed in E Manchester (*see Manchester and South-East Lancashire*, forthcoming), but it remains to be seen if the 3,000 or so extra hotel rooms planned for completion by that time can remain viable afterwards. Future schemes will affect neglected parts of the centre such as the Rochdale Canal Basin on Dale Street, where there are two early C19 canal warehouses, and the former Smithfield Market area in the part of town now known as the Northern Quarter, N of Piccadilly Gardens. Here the Thomas Street neighbourhood retains a late C18 street pattern with related groups of modest late C18 and early C19 buildings, and the challenge will be in the treatment and setting of the historic fabric. Some of Ancoats's more important buildings have already been stabilized and there are signs that the future of others, including some of the huge cotton mills, will be secured, while parts of this area too have been earmarked for residential development. The design of new buildings and treatment of the streetscapes and canal sides will need to respect the tough industrial character of the area.

Manchester has responded to the opportunities and challenges of recent decades with imagination and energy. In spite of this the contrast between the glittering new buildings, exclusive apartment blocks and café bars of the centre, and the decaying inner suburbs, run-down 1960s and 1970s estates and bleak clearance areas remains stark. Is there not a danger that the city-centre communities will be a monoculture of affluent childless young professionals? Can the achievements of community architecture in Hulme be matched in other inner-city suburbs? Will the proposed Millennium Village in Ancoats and planned rejuvenation of E Manchester have a lasting effect?

With these fundamental questions of life and environment unanswered we must leave this survey of the development of Manchester.

Major Buildings

*Other public buildings will be found under the City Centre
street entries, for example Bridgewater Hall under Barbirolli
Square, Royal Exchange under Exchange Street, and so on.*

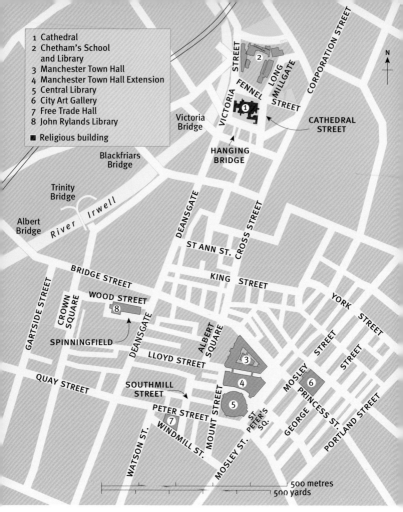

1 Cathedral
2 Chetham's School
  and Library
3 Manchester Town Hall
4 Manchester Town Hall Extension
5 Central Library
6 City Art Gallery
7 Free Trade Hall
8 John Rylands Library

■ Religious building

CORPORATION STREET

N

VICTORIA STREET

FENNEL STREET

LONG MILLGATE

Victoria Bridge

CATHEDRAL STREET

HANGING BRIDGE

Blackfriars Bridge

Trinity Bridge

River Irwell

Albert Bridge

DEANSGATE

CROSS STREET

ST ANN ST.

KING STREET

BRIDGE STREET

GARTSIDE STREET

CROWN SQUARE

WOOD STREET

YORK STREET

SPINNINGFIELD

DEANSGATE

LLOYD STREET

ALBERT SQUARE

MOSLEY STREET

GEORGE STREET

PRINCESS ST.

QUAY STREET

SOUTHMILL STREET

PETER STREET

MOUNT STREET

ST. PETER'S SQ.

PORTLAND STREET

WATSON ST.

WINDMILL ST.

MOSLEY ST.

GEORGE STREET

500 metres
500 yards

36. Major Buildings.

Cathedral

Cathedral Street

Manchester has one of the most impressive examples in England of a late medieval collegiate church, a reflection of the significance of the town as a regional centre by this time. The church stands N of the modern town centre, on a sandstone bluff between the River Irwell and the culverted River Irk, with an ancient watercourse on the s (*see* Hanging Bridge, Inner City, Walk 2); its originally prominent defensive position now obscured by later buildings. This was also the site of Manchester's medieval manor house which lay slightly to the N, and the church may well occupy the site of one of the two Manchester churches mentioned in Domesday. The present church dates essentially from after the foundation of the college in 1421, although its predecessor was probably of similar length by the C14, and evidence for C13 and C14 work was found during restorations. The regular plan of aisled nave and aisled chancel, each of six bays, was expanded piecemeal by additional chapels to N and s to reach its present exceptional width in the early C16, under Warden James Stanley II, later Bishop of Ely, who was also part-donor of the magnificent set of choir stalls, the cathedral's chief treasure. The elaborately decorated exterior with its lofty w tower and the general uniformity of the Perp style also impresses, although so much of the fabric has been renewed that it is not easy to distinguish what is genuinely medieval from the work that took place in the flurry of building activity after the church was elevated to cathedral status in 1847. For the same reasons the relative dating of the different parts is also problematic.

History

In 1421 Thomas de la Warre, Lord of the Manor, obtained a licence from Henry V to transform the church into a collegiate foundation. It was essentially a chantry college, as masses were to be said every day for Henry V, the Bishop of Coventry and Lichfield, Thomas de la Warre, and their progenitors. The church was dedicated to St Mary, St George and St Denys, the last perhaps chosen because Henry's claim to the throne of France had been strengthened by his marriage in 1420 to the daughter of the French King, Charles VI. The domestic premises by some good fortune survive; they were built on the site of the manor house and became the Chetham Hospital and Library in the C17 (*see*

Chantry Chapels

A chantry was a kind of insurance policy for the after life – an endowment provided for one or more priests to say masses for the benefit of a named person after his or her death. The concept of purgatory as an intermediary resting place for the souls of the dead encouraged the belief that their progress to heaven could be assisted by prayer. The practice was general by the later C13 but particularly popular in the later Middle Ages, until suppressed at the Reformation. A chantry could be established at an existing altar or in a separate chapel built for the purpose, often housing the tomb of the founder. The most prestigious site was at the E end, to the N of the high altar. At Manchester, not surprisingly, this area was reserved for the Stanleys, but there were also an unusually large number of chantry chapels added by wealthy local families to both choir and nave, giving the church its exceptional breadth. The screens that once divided them off have now largely been removed, so that in the nave these once separate spaces now appear as outer aisles. The original tombs have disappeared, but a brass to Bishop Stanley remains in St John the Baptist Chapel.

1. St Nicholas Chapel (traditionally of ancient foundation, possibly rebuilt when the chantry was conveyed to the Traffords from the Booths in 1470)
2. Holy Trinity Chapel (William Radcliffe of Ordsall. 1498)
3. Jesus Chapel (Richard Beswick. 1506)
4. St James Chapel (Warden Huntingdon left lands for erection and endowment in his will, but it was not built until 1507)
5. St George Chapel (William Galley, *c.* 1503. There was also a Chetham chantry at this altar and possibly another founded by the Guild of St George)
6. St John the Baptist Chapel (begun by James Stanley II, Bishop of Ely, *c.* 1513, completed by Sir John Stanley after 1515)
7. Ely Chapel (demolished, built by Sir John Stanley to commemorate James Stanley II, Bishop of Ely d. 1514–15)

Chetham's School and Library, p. 63). The building history of the church has yet to be satisfactorily resolved. The documents suggest that the first warden John Huntingdon (incumbent 1422–58) rebuilt the choir. His will, dated 1454, refers to 'edificacion, expences, costes, and bygging of the newe work begonen by me in the Chauncell' and the inscription on his restored brass (based on a transcript of 1650) states that he built the chancel 'de novo'. The nave is traditionally attributed to the third warden Ralph Langley (1465–81) but there is no documentary evidence to support this. The fifth warden James Stanley (1485–1506,

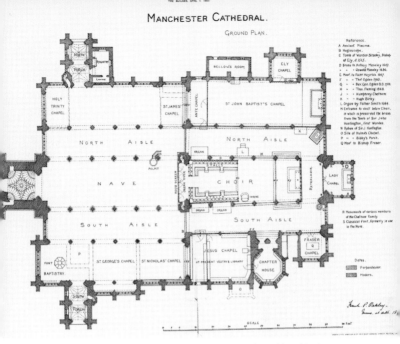

MANCHESTER CATHEDRAL.
GROUND PLAN.

37. Manchester Cathedral, Cathedral Street as illustrated in *The Builder*. This plan was drawn before Champneys' additions on the w and se, and before war damage removed the Ely Chapel.

subsequently Bishop of Ely, d. 1514), is known to have contributed a chantry chapel and the choir furnishings. His will, dated 20 March 1514/15, shows that he had started work on the St John the Baptist Chapel (now the Regimental Chapel) N of the chancel. His badge appears on the s choir stalls; on the N stalls is the badge of the merchant Richard Beswick, who also founded the Jesus Chapel on the s side, given a licence for worship in 1506.

c19 restoration started with disastrous alterations by *John Palmer*, who rebuilt the NW corner between the tower and chapel of St James, covered the nave interior with Roman cement and rebuilt the galleries added after the Reformation. By the mid c19 the soft Collyhurst sandstone which had not already been replaced was in a parlous condition, patched up by Roman cement. The exterior was repaired and refaced during the 1850–70s, and the nave arcades rebuilt by *J. S. Crowther*; the w tower, having been declared unsafe, was largely rebuilt by *J. P. Holden* in 1862–8. *Basil Champneys* added porches and vestries in 1898, and a large s annexe in 1902–3, and after the Second World War *Sir Hubert Worthington* restored and rebuilt what was necessary, working with the woodcarving firm *James Brown* of Wilmslow.

38. Manchester Cathedral, Cathedral Street, from an engraving of 1893.

Exterior

The general impression is of a large, lavishly decorated Perp church, although as a result of late C19 refacing and the C20 rebuilding of much of the NE corner, little or no exterior stonework is medieval. The original work was largely followed in outline though older views suggest there was some invention in the detail, for example the parapet carving and pinnacles. The rebuilt w tower is sheer below but richly appointed at the top. Crowther believed that the lower stages of the original were Dec, and Palmer's drawings of the original w door seem to confirm this. At the upper level are Perp two-light transomed bell openings with panelling above. Openwork battlements (as on the rest of the church), grouped pinnacles at the corners, above set-back buttresses decorated with canopied tracery. Holden's design is based upon what he found, but the detail was not followed precisely and the height was increased by 20 ft (6 metres). The elaborate w porch added in 1898 is by *Basil Champneys*. *G. F. Bodley*, the consultant architect, curbed Champneys' ambitions to create a version of the Rylands Library's front here (*see* p. 96).* The nave outer walls are those of the medieval chantry chapels added beyond the aisles, though in some cases this was achieved by rebuilding aisle walls on a new line.

The tour starts from the sw. Adjoining Champneys' ornate s porch of 1898, two four-light windows to the slightly projecting St George Chapel (*c.* 1503). Then two five-light windows to the Chapel of St Nicholas, dated variously 1470–86 (both windows are C19 restorations after work of 1809 had destroyed the originals). Further E the view is obscured by

---

*Information from John Maddison.

Champneys' vestries and annexe (1902–3), excellent, as one would expect, subdued in contrast to his porches, yet charmingly varied in the grouping and with felicitous decorative passages such as the bay windows to the s. On *Percy Scott Worthington*'s extension of 1933–4, over the Dean's entrance, is a beautiful relief panel of the Christ Child with St Mary, St Denys and St George, by *Eric Gill*, 1933. The Jesus Chapel (1506), its windows with heavy supertransoms, is next in the main sequence. The small octagonal Perp chapter house (its exterior a casualty of the Second World War) is attached, and the window to the E is of the same design as those to the Jesus Chapel. Another example, reset, appears in the adjacent Fraser Chapel of 1890.

The E view is impressive, thanks chiefly to *Hubert Worthington*'s bare E wall, part of a rebuilding of the whole of the NE corner, including the outer walls of the Lady Chapel after the 1940 bomb. In a niche a gilded Mother and Child by *Charles Wheeler*. Above it is the seven-light choir E window. To the N, the E window to the Chapel of St John the Baptist (now Regimental Chapel), started in 1513, has the same tracery pattern and four-centred arch as the windows of St Nicholas Chapel but whether this is its authentic medieval form is unclear. It had been heavily restored in 1803 before its destruction in 1940, so Worthington may have been forced to improvise. On the N side the chapel has four-light windows with stilted arches, possibly reused, it has been suggested, from the mid-C15 aisle wall. Further w the five-light window lit the Chapel of St James, where the altar was hallowed *c.* 1507. The remaining windows on this side were all rebuilt and altered in the early C19 to light the galleries inside so it is unlikely that the next generation of restorers had anything reliable to go on. Alteration and rebuilding of the w end also took place in the early C19. The clerestory windows are of five lights but in the C19 restorations the differing treatment between nave and chancel was not followed. The nave formerly had uncusped lights; possibly as a result of

39. Relief panel of the Christ Child with St Mary, St Denys and St George, by Eric Gill (1933).

work of 1815. The roofline detail is wholly of the 1870s and is unlike the parapet and finialed buttresses shown in early C19 views. At the junction of nave and choir are two prominent rood-stair turrets, restored to a more ornate design than early C19 engravings suggest.

Interior

Six bays to the choir arch; six bays for the choir; there are no transepts, but the semblance of outer aisles provided by the remains of the chantry chapels gives an impression of great width to both nave and choir. Detailed examination should start at the E end with the small **Lady Chapel**. Only the inner w wall and entrance arch survived the 1940 bomb. Its round shafts rise from polygonal bases to polygonal banded caps. A narrow fillet on the fronts of the piers is carried through to the cap, the arch has broad hollows to the mouldings. The details suggest the C14, and C18 and early C19 engravings – and even Crowther's drawings – indicate Dec windows. Perhaps the chapel was retained for a special reason, such as the existence of a miracle-working statue or relic. The E wall of the choir and aisles appears to be of one phase: Perp shafts with polygonal bases and banded and battlemented polygonal capitals. The upper part shows signs of having been rebuilt, the arch above the Lady Chapel entrance has awkward stilted sections and the spandrel decorations above are similar to those of nave and choir. They must have been introduced to harmonize with the rest of the building.

The **choir** has arcades divided from the five-light clerestory windows by a crested frieze. The date is problematic. The arcades are slimmer and altogether more delicate than those elsewhere in the building.

40. Cathedral interior. Choir looking **w** (*c.* 1500).

Circular shafts rise from polygonal bases to circular banded capitals; all
the mouldings are deeply undercut. A slim shaft rising from its own
polygonal base on the front continues over the capital to the top band
of the frieze, re-emerging as the central member of a cluster of shafts
which terminate in a pretty cap with lacy edges. This supports the
wooden angels and eagles of the roof. The shaft thus draws together the
whole composition, balancing the strong horizontals of frieze and
cresting. A curious feature is the splayed plan of the arcades: the w end
is 25 ft 4 in. (7.69 metres) wide narrowing to 22 ft 1 in. (6.73 metres) at
the E end. The E responds have polygonal bases with a hollow moulding between the shafts, and polygonal banded capitals. They must have
been kept as a starting point for the new choir arcade but the junction
is awkward, as is shown by the differing heights of the stringcourses.
This suggests that only the responds and part of the E wall may remain
of Huntingdon's C15 choir, and that the arcades may be a late C15 or
early C16 rebuilding by James Stanley II, widening at the w end to allow
for the new stalls. Crowther could not believe that recently erected work
by Huntingdon would be ruthlessly swept away, and he proposed that
Stanley had taken down and re-erected his predecessor's work, splaying
the arcade to accommodate the new choir furnishings, but there is no
real evidence for this. The decorative detail supports a late C15 or early
C16 date for both choir and nave. The choir arcade spandrels have a

pattern of cusping and foiled circles containing shields, crowned by a foliage frieze. A similar scheme appears in the nave, and the window spandrels of the clerestory there. In the choir the clerestory spandrels are decorated with carved timbers in a similar style with the circles and shields, repeated in the openwork of the roof arch braces. The parallel in the region is the nave of Mold Parish Church in Flintshire, of *c.* 1500, a member of a group of Welsh churches remodelled or embellished through the patronage and benefactions of the Stanley family, though Manchester lacks the abundant Stanley badges seen at Mold. Further afield the connection is with East Anglia, where the churches of Great St Mary, Cambridge (1491), Lavenham (1495) and Saffron Walden (1497), exhibit similar treatment to the arcades, and are all the work of John Wastell,* who went on to work on King's College Chapel, Cambridge. This suggests that the chancel arcades are unlikely to be as early as the 1420s and it seems possible that Stanley was responsible, using masons from East Anglia, where he had strong connections.

The **choir roof** has camber beams with open arch braces and delicately traceried panels. There are eagles, a Stanley badge, and angels bearing shields at wall-plate level. The roof, according to Richard Hollingworth, a fellow of the college writing *c.* 1656, was taken down and repaired in 1636 (the date is carved in the roof at the E end). The date 1742 at the other end may commemorate another major repair. Greatly restored by *Crowther*, and again after serious damage in 1940. Crowther suggested Stanley remodelled the roof to fit with the realigned arcades. Huntingdon's rebus (on one side a man goes hunting, on the other he draws drink from a tun) appears on the spandrels at the w end of the roof, though this could be reset or commemorative (the rehearsal of these motifs in the entrance to the Lady Chapel is a C19 invention).

Stair-towers at the entrance to the choir gave access to the loft and on up to the roof. Outwardly they are similar, but have different diameters; could the s tower be a recased survivor from Huntingdon's time or even earlier? The choir arch must be Stanley's work. It has parallels with Mold, if Crowther's restoration can be relied upon. Between spandrels and leaf frieze are big animal carvings, and the shafts have foliated caps, both features of the Mold nave arcade.

St John the Baptist Chapel (now the Regimental Chapel), on the N side of the choir, was probably started in 1513 by James Stanley II and finished after his death by Sir John Stanley, who by some accounts was his illegitimate son or grandson. Despite rebuilding after bomb damage in 1940, part of the N wall is original, perhaps reused from Huntingdon's original choir aisle. The windows are flanked by wall brackets supported by a variety of grotesques and beasts. James Stanley II's Ely Chapel which projected from its NE end was completely destroyed by the bomb. The arcade to the choir aisle is distinguished by a very deep hollow

*Dr Paul Crossley pointed out the East Anglian parallel to me.

moulding to the arches and flared polygonal caps to the shafts. In bays one and two the hollow mould between the piers is enriched by a slim central pier, thereafter this is omitted. This change might indicate where John Stanley took over after James Stanley II's death. Hubert Worthington's replacement roof has carved angels on the principals by *Alan Durst*.

The **Jesus Chapel** on the s side was licensed in 1506. Both arcade and outer wall seem to have escaped wholesale restoration; the latter is probably the original aisle wall reused, as with St John the Baptist Chapel (Regimental Chapel). Traceried panels flank the windows; the w arcade has circular piers rising from high polygonal bases with rather crude banded and battlemented caps. A new sequence of arcades, beyond the chapel to the E, is similar in style but more crisply executed. The entrance to the chapter house has cusped panelling over the paired doorways, and there is cusped panelling too in the reveal. For the Fraser Chapel of 1890 at the end of the s aisle *see* Monuments, below.

The **nave** was almost completely rebuilt during C19 restorations, when the floor level was lowered and the arcades reconstructed by *Crowther*, who emphasized that he reproduced the original 'line for line and joint by joint', an assertion confirmed as far as it can be by Palmer's early C19 engravings. The arcades are heavier than those of the choir, although they have the same slim central pier superimposed on the main shaft. Here it is stopped by a beast's mouth in the frieze and the detail of the clustered pier above is different, with foliated mouldings – all conforming with Palmer's early C19 view of the nave. The inner face of the tower with its high arch shows the extent of the damage caused by gouging the surfaces to receive the Roman cement, though the remains of cusped panelling can be discerned. The full-height vertical channel on the right side, not repeated opposite, is another mysterious feature; possibly the tower design was compromised by earlier work. The nave arcade is offset to the N on the N side, presumably to align with the splayed choir. Crowther, on the basis of what he found when the arcades were dismantled, suggested that the N arcade had been taken down and re-erected on a new line when the choir was rebuilt, but any evidence for this was destroyed by the C19 rebuilding.

The **nave roof** is one of the glories of the building. New timbers were introduced during the restorations of the 1880s, but reusing the bosses and minstrel angels, and it purports to be an exact copy. Crowther found evidence of alteration which he interpreted as an accommodation of the moved line of the N arcade. Like the choir it is a camber beam roof, but the design differs in that each bay forms a complete compartment. The bosses, unlike those of the choir, were carved from the solid and differ in character from the choir bosses. The central bosses beneath the principals have sun designs and a figure holding a shield is set against the face of the beam on each side. The beam sides are traceried; the cresting above continues around the wall-plate. The beams are supported by braces with quatrefoils and shields similar to the arcade spandrels; beneath, a musical angel forms an ornamental supporter. The series of angel minstrels at Manchester is particularly good and complete. The figures and their instruments are largely original, although the wings have been replaced. Each of the seven angels on each side plays a different instrument, wind on the N, strings on the S (the clavicymbal on the N side was accidentally transposed with the portative organ on the S side during restoration).

Aisle roofs have been replaced, but the supporting corbels survive. The arcades between aisles and chapels were rebuilt, presumably by Crowther. Here the corbels correspond with the arcade, but the (perhaps original) corbels on the outer wall do not correspond with the openings, probably reflecting the piecemeal erection of chantries.

Furnishings

Described clockwise from the E.

Lady Chapel. **Screen**, partly original, the most elaborate of all the screens, dated *c.* 1440 by Hudson, and if so the earliest screen in the church. Statuettes survive beneath the tabernacles, although mutilated. All female: St Margaret and St Catherine, C19 replacements at each end, the rest possibly virgin martyrs and confessors flanking the central St George and dragon. Entertaining grotesques on the strip below the canopies. – Oak **reredos** no doubt to Worthington's design, and most effective. – **Piscina**, medieval, relocated, likewise the gilded **sculpture** of an angel. – **Tapestries** designed by *Austin Wright* and made by *Theo Moorman* in 1957. Attractive figures and scenes. – **Glass** in the high N and S windows by *David Peace*.

Choir. **Screens** in the E part, wrought iron, with Gothic pinnacles, and a wrought-iron **communion rail**, both delightful. They date from 1750–1. Above these the upper part of Perp wooden **screens**, thought by Hudson to be contemporary with the stalls. They were remodelled *c.* 1750 to form one large ogee arch per bay. – **Bishop's throne** 1906, by

41. James Brown's carving team repairing the choir stalls in 1947.

Sir Charles Nicholson, Perp style. – **Stalls**. Without a doubt amongst the very finest in the North of England. Installed *c.* 1500–6. Although badly damaged during the Second World War, painstaking restoration under James Brown was to an exceptionally high standard.* There is little doubt that James Stanley II, fifth warden, was responsible. The Stanley arms are prominently displayed on two of the desk ends and elsewhere there are representations of the Lathom legend (*see* topic box, below), the legs of Man and Stanley eagles. It is known that Richard Beswick, a contemporary of Stanley, paid for one side of the stalls, and his arms appear on the desk standard of the NE stall. The absence of episcopal emblems suggests the work was finished before Stanley became Bishop of Ely in 1506. The Manchester stalls can be linked with the workshop of William Brownflet or Bromflet who was responsible for the stalls at Bridlington Priory *c.* 1518–19 (demolished but fragments survive in Yorkshire churches). These are closely related stylistically to those at Ripon Minster, of *c.* 1489–94, and Beverley Minster, of 1520–4.

There are thirty stalls, twelve on each side and six returned. The exquisite canopies are intricately carved with great exuberance. The stalls of honour at the w end, the Dean's and Residentiary's, are distinguished from each other and from their fellows. The canopies both have four-sided fronts instead of the usual three, and are more ornate, with the Dean's outstripping the Residentiary's for wealth of detail. Hudson called this 'probably . . . the most elaborate structure of its kind in existence'. Above is another tier of simpler canopies, uniform in design. After the filigree below, this was necessary and it is effective. All the panels are pierced to resemble traceried windows. Crowning everything is a tester with cresting and pendant arches. It will be seen that the detail of the design is different on each side. It was a most felicitous invention, unique to Manchester (though the idea was copied at Beverley a few years later), which has the effect of unifying the whole composition and placing it within a frame. The **entercloses** are another delight, hexagonal in plan with vaulting and pierced traceried panels. The **stall desks** are set on a stone plinth with pierced quatrefoils. The desk fronts are decorated with applied tracery and the standards have poppyheads. The desk ends have projecting fronts in the form of a diagonal shaft, a feature typical of the Bromflet workshop, housed at the base in charming little tabernacles with crocketed gables and tiled roofs. The uppermost stage has open tracery and supports a bracket with animal or beast. The **handrests** are good, with well-integrated vigorous designs, mainly floral but with some animals and heads. Each bench end, including all the intricate detail described, was carved from one huge slab of oak.

A full set of **misericords**.† The designs can be linked with the Ripon misericords, dated 1489–94 and the workshop of *William Bromflet*,

*Worthington described Brown as 'one of the greatest craftsmen in the English tradition'.
†This description is based on an account by Dr Christa Grössinger.

Misericords

⇐···· SOUTH   ⬆ WEST

3. Dragon

2. Eagle with supporters; badge of Sir John Stanley

1. Eagle and Child illustrating the Lathom legend

4. Angel with shield bearing the arms of the Isle of Man

5. Elephant and castle

6. Wild Men on camel and unicorn fighting

7. Fox stealing goose with fox and fox-and-cub supporters

8. Pedlar robbed by apes

9. Bear baiting

10. Lion couchant

11. Lion and dragon fighting

12. Wild Man and dragon fighting

13. Sow playing bag-pipes and piglets dancing

14. Antelope

15. Gryphon

The scenes showing the fox running off with a goose and the apes robbing the pedlar have close parallels at Beverley, while the pig and dancing piglets is a subject found at Ripon as well as Beverley. The eagle and child seat (for the Dean, previously the warden's seat) is wider than the others.

42. Misericord, s side, wild man and dragon fighting (*c.* 1500).

though they are more sophisticated, and the relationship between the Manchester examples and those at Beverley of 1520–4 is closer, with more of the misericords sharing the same subject and a very similar carving style (*see* topic box).

    Chandeliers of brass in the chancel, given in 1690 and 1715. Fraser Chapel **screen**, partly original, brought from elsewhere. – **Painting** over the entrance to the chapter house and the inner doorway by *Carel Weight*, 1963. – **Screen** to the Jesus Chapel, partly original with charming

1. Angel bust with a shield charged with the cross of St George

2. The Pelican in her Piety

3. Two dragons fighting

4. Joshua and Caleb carrying a giant bunch of grapes (mutilated)

5. Man breaking his wife's cooking pot

6. Dragon biting its back

7. Child issuing from a whelk shell fighting a dragon

8. Two men playing backgammon

9. The fox as a hunter

10. Deer hunt

11. Hunter and stag

12. Defaced

13. Cock and cockatrice

14. Unicorn

15. The rabbit's revenge

The last scene, showing a rabbit cooking a hunter and his dog is taken from a late c14 engraving by Israhel Van Meckenem. Subjects such as the angel and shield, dragons fighting and Pelican in her Piety have parallels at Ripon. The scene with the giant grapes is common to both Beverley and Ripon.

43. Misericord, N side, two men playing backgammon (c. 1500).

design of ogee arcading. **Rood screen** or pulpitum dividing choir from nave. Four-light opening left and right of the doorway. Drastically altered through the erection of galleries, organs and other works. The loft and western face was removed in 1864, leaving only the backing of the return stalls, but it was returned to its original position and restored by *Sir G. G. Scott* in the 1870s when the parapet was added, the original having been removed many years before. At some time the side bays were altered to make doors matching the central opening. There is a

The Lathom Legend

The Lathom arms are said to have been adopted by the Stanleys when Sir John Stanley I married heiress Isobel Lathom in 1385. A pictorial representation of the eagle and child crest of the arms is the subject of three renditions on the Dean's (formerly the warden's) seat in the stalls. One appears on the side panel of the bench end, another on the misericord and a third on the left handrest. The bench carving shows a scene with trees and a castle, and an eagle at its nest in a tree with a baby in a long robe. Passing workmen look up in attitudes of wonder. The misericord rehearses the scene, but from a different viewpoint, offering the carver a chance to show off his skill. The story is linked with an ancient tradition of foundling folklore. In one well-known version an infant is discovered

in an eagle's nest and adopted by the childless Sir Thomas Lathom who believes the boy has been sent by God, and makes him his heir. He is christened Oskell and goes on to father Isobel who marries John Stanley. Other accounts describe the events as a subterfuge of Lathom, allowing him to adopt his illegitimate son without revealing the circumstances of the birth to his wife, and placing the action, more prosaically, at the foot of the tree. In fact Sir Thomas had a legitimate son, also called Thomas, as well as a daughter, Isobel, who inherited most of the Lathom estates in Lancashire on the death of her niece some time after her marriage to John Stanley.

44. Bench carving of the Lathom Legend (c. 1500).

noticeable disparity between central and flanking bays, the top of the central door opening is lower and the traceried panels wider than in the bays on each side. The screen at St Mary, Beverley, has a similar disparity in the bays. – **Sculpture**. C11 or C12, reset in nave NE respond. Small relief of an angel with wings spread in two different directions bearing a scroll with mutilated inscription. Regimental Chapel (St John the Baptist Chapel) **screen** is only very partly original. In the chapel C18 **font**, partly fluted octagonal bowl on a baluster stem.

Stained glass. – The scheme of five windows at the w end by *Antony Hollaway* was commissioned in 1971 and prepared by the artist in consultation with Cathedral Architect, *Harry M. Fairhurst*. Part of the aim was to reduce the problem of glare from the w end. Consideration was given to a scheme embracing the whole building, with careful analysis of light levels and colour, but this has not been carried out. *See* topic box. At the E end of the Regimental Chapel (St John the Baptist Chapel), the Fire Window by *Margaret Traherne* 1966, in memory of the Manchester Regiment and Sir Hubert Worthington. Badly damaged by the terrorist bomb of 1996. Traherne undertook the restoration using German glass. The E window by *Gerald Smith* was executed post 1945.

Monuments

Clockwise from the E. Fraser Chapel: Bishop Fraser d. 1885 by *J. Forsyth*. White marble recumbent effigy in a low niche in the s wall. – **Brass** in the chancel floor: Warden Huntingdon d. 1485. A 3 ft 3 in. (1 metre) figure;

The West Windows

The five w windows are a major work of *Antony Hollaway*, who was influenced by Kandinsky's theories of colour. Windows dedicated to the three patron saints of the cathedral are flanked by designs based on Genesis, the first book of the Bible, and Revelation, the last, invoking the spiritual journey from birth and baptism to the afterlife. From the s, **Creation** completed in 1991. The dynamic process of creation is suggested, with the separation of the firmaments and crystalline shapes of order emerging from chaos. **St George**, 1973, the first to be finished and the most representational. The strong forms of the cross contrast with a fragmenting dragon. **St Mary**, 1980. High and set back in the tower, at the centre of the scheme. Predomin-antly blue, with a circle pierced by a shaft representing the sword of Simeon's prophecy and themes arising from this image. Below, jumbled letters of text from the Magnificat. **St Denys**, 1976, strong forms with much red to bal-ance the St George window, on the theme of martyrdom. The window has French motifs and a depiction of St Sernin, Toulouse, at the bottom right, is a memorial to the twinning of Manchester with the abbey. Finally **Revelation** completed 1995. Big blocky shapes meant to recall the stones of the Heavenly City and an off-centre rectangle of deep blue, Kandinsky's 'pure and supernatural' colour, repre-senting Faith.

45. St Mary window by Antony Hollaway (1980).

canopy surround, heavily restored in 1907. – Nearby another **brass** to Dean Edward Maclure, 1906. SE aisle – **monument**: Thomas Ogden d. 1766. Tablet with obelisk on top, by *Christopher Moon* of Manchester. – **Brass**: Richard Heyrick, fourteenth warden d. 1667, in a C17 wooden surround. – **Monument**: Hugh Birley MP, recumbent alabaster effigy, 1886; by whom? A pair of fragmentary *ex situ* C15 brasses on the outer Jesus Chapel arcade, to the Byrom family. In the Jesus Chapel s wall, **brasses**: William Hulme d. 1691 and two Mosley family brasses: Anthony d. 1607 and son Oswald d. 1630. To the s, the site of demolished Chapels of St Nicholas and St George, two wall tablets of *c.* 1997 by *John Shaw*, one as a tribute to the work of the emergency services in the aftermath of the 1996 terrorist bomb, and the other commemorating Humphrey Booth d. 1635 whose charity helped to cover the cost of post-bomb repairs to the cathedral. **Monument**: Elizabeth Trafford d.1813; tablet surmounted by figure weeping over an urn. Attached to the s wall several brasses commemorating cathedral chapter clerks and registrars. Those to Lewis Alfred Orford d. 1948 and Lewis Hadfield Orford d. 1972 have beautiful lettering by *Donald Jackson*. **Statue** of Thomas Fleming, by *E. Baily*, 1851. – At the w end of the aisle **monument** to Dauntsey Hulme d. 1828, tablet with the Good Samaritan attributed to *Richard Westmacott*. At the w end of the N aisle free-standing seated figure of Humphrey Chetham, by *W. Theed*, 1853, a schoolboy at the foot of the base. – On the N aisle wall: simple tablets with fine lettering to Cathedral Architects Raymond Bernard Wood-Jones, d. 1982 and Hubert Worthington d. 1963. Between these a square tablet, Rawstorne

46. Humphrey Chetham monument by William Theed (1853).

Further Reading

For descriptions and histories of the fabric and furnishings *see* J. S. Crowther, *The Cathedral Church of Manchester*, 1893. Crowther was responsible for major repairs and reconstructions in the 1880s and so knew the fabric better than anyone. His theories deserve cautious attention, and the drawings are superb. Henry Hudson's *The Mediaeval Woodwork of Manchester Cathedral* of 1924 is indispensable. Hudson in the early C20 published a number of valuable articles in the *Transactions of the Lancashire and Cheshire Antiquarian Society* on the medieval glass, the brasses, early documentary sources and other subjects. Dr Christa Grössinger's leaflet *The Misericords of Manchester Cathedral*, 1980, includes a discussion of the subjects, derivations and parallels. For the work of William Bromflet *see* J. S. Purvis in *Yorkshire Archaeological Journal*, 29, 1927–9. The 1848 edition of S. Hibbert-Ware's three-volume *A History of the Foundations of Manchester* is particularly useful for a set of fine engravings of the building's exterior and interior by John Palmer executed in the 1830s. For C19 alterations and restorations *see* Thomas Locke Worthington, *Historical Account of the Cathedral Church of Manchester*, 1884.

For historical background *see* A. J. Dobbs, *Like a Mighty Tortoise, A History of the Diocese of Manchester*, 1978. F. R. Raines wrote a number of scholarly accounts including *The Rectors of Manchester and the Wardens of the Collegiate Church*, Chetham Society, 1885, and *A History of the Chantries*, Chetham Society, 1862.

For Stanley family ecclesiastical interests and architectural patronage *see* P. Hosker, 'The Stanleys of Lathom and Ecclesiastical Patronage in the North-West of England During the Fifteenth Century', *Northern History*, 18, 1982, and M. K. Jones & M. G. Underwood, *The King's Mother, Lady Margaret Beaufort Countess of Richmond and Derby*, 1992. For Stanley churches and chapels in Wales *see* E. Hubbard, *The Buildings of Wales: Clwyd*, 1986, introduction and individual entries.

Lever Gent, no date but C17 in appearance. – Tablet to Lever family children, six of them d. between 1635 and 1647, with an affecting verse. On the outer St John the Baptist (Regimental) Chapel arcade two *ex situ* fragmentary and abraded medieval brasses. They are both memorials to the Radcliffe family, one *c.* 1480 with a canopy, the other *c.* 1540. The female figure is a palimpsest, and the other side has the figure of a nun of *c.* 1450.

In the chapel N wall, **brass** to Warden James Stanley II who was Bishop of Ely at the time of his death in 1515, fragmentary, though the features can be made out, and now 29 in. (74 cm.) long. The best preserved of the medieval brasses and not over-restored like the Huntingdon brass. – Against the w wall of the chapel **monument** to Charles Lawson, 1810, by the younger *Bacon*. Tablet with the headmaster and two boys, a bust of Homer on the ground. In the Sacristy an *ex situ* brass, very badly worn, but with the date 1598 just visible.

Chetham's School
and Library

Long Millgate

The domestic premises of the collegiate church are, miraculously, almost intact, lying some distance N of the church (now Manchester cathedral). They are the best-preserved buildings of their type and date in the country. On the foundation of the college in 1421, *see* cathedral, p. 45. The establishment consisted of a master or warden, eight fellows, four clerks and six choristers. It was dissolved in 1547 and the buildings acquired by the Stanley family, Earls of Derby. The college was refounded but the buildings remained in Stanley hands until their estates were sequestered in the Civil War. They were put to a variety of uses during

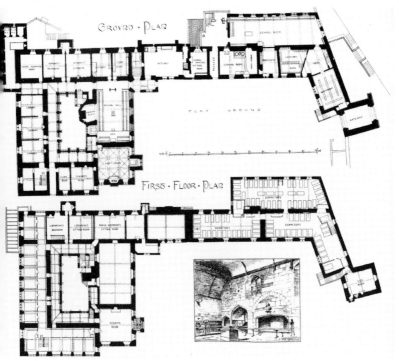

47. Chetham's School and Library, Long Millgate (C15 with C17 and later alterations). Plan by Alfred Waterhouse from *The British Architect and Northern Engineer*.

this period, and became dilapidated. They were eventually acquired by the executors of the will of the wealthy merchant Humphrey Chetham* shortly after his death in 1653 and fitted up, in accordance with his wishes, as a free library and bluecoat school. The result was the preservation of the medieval building and an exceptional early town library complete with original furnishings.

The alterations connected with the establishment of the library and school were completed over the period 1654–8 and building accounts covering the period 1656–8 shed light on how the conversion was carried out. In the C18, school and library expanded into accommodation in the original building which had formerly been rented out. There were three major phases of C19 alterations and restorations, in the 1850s by *J. E. Gregan*, in 1878 by *Alfred Waterhouse*, and in 1883–95 by *J. Medland Taylor*.† Views, measured drawings and plans produced by John Palmer *c.* 1815 provide a valuable record of the buildings before the later C19 restorations were completed. C20 expansion was largely into neighbouring C19 buildings. The school continued as a charitable institution until after the Second World War, eventually becoming a music school in 1969. The library has remained open to the public since its inception.

Now to the buildings themselves (*see* also topic box, Introduction p. 6). They are not unduly decorative, but there is some architectural display, and the accommodation for nineteen people, their servants and guests was ample and well appointed. They are of red sandstone with some (generally C19 replacement) lighter stone dressings and a stone flag roof. There is a rectangle with hall and lodgings around a cloister, then the kitchen and a series of other rooms in a long E wing with a short SE angled range, ending in the gatehouse. The buildings appear to have been erected in two or more closely spaced campaigns with the later addition of the porch and hall chimney, possibly as part of a late C15 or early C16 programme of improvements.‡ The gabled **gatehouse** on Long Millgate (refronted in the early C19) has a heated upper chamber reached from an external stair. A large archway leads into the courtyard where the main block can be viewed. All the visible windows of the range have cinquefoil lights under a four-centred arch, most with labels. The windows in the other elevations (apart from the cloister, *see* p. 67, below) are more simply treated. The **hall** is lit by three transomed two-light windows and a low window at the dais end. To the left the **wardens**

*For a study of Chetham *see* S. Guscott, 'Humphrey Chetham 1580–1653: Fortune, Politics and Mercantile Culture in Seventeenth-Century Britain', unpublished University of Sheffield PhD thesis, 2000.
†The feoffees astutely chose some of the most able and conscientious of C19 Manchester architects for the work.
‡Results of dendrochronological analysis obtained as this book goes to press suggest that hall and cloister were erected shortly after the date of foundation, with most samples giving an early to mid C15 date.

lodgings have a two-storey projecting square bay with a niche in the gable. To the right a two-storey **porch** which *J. E. Gregan* rebuilt in the 1850s to match the bay of the wardens lodgings. Palmer's drawings show it originally had a flat roof with a parapet. It is awkwardly stepped back to accommodate the hall window and there are blocked upper windows in the kitchen (*see* below) showing that it must be secondary.

Interior. Inside the porch, there are entrances to the kitchen and cellar, and then the **screens passage** with the expected paired entrances to the buttery and pantry, one of them with a medieval door, thrown into one room during the C19. The 7 ft (2 metre) high **screen** is of the spere type with two entrances. The central section was originally moveable, and it is all sturdy C15 work apart from the cresting. The stone flagged **hall** is one of the best preserved for its date in the country. Here the **roof** can be seen. It is of an unusual type for the North of England,* with arch-braced tie-beams, common rafter trusses with collars and diagonal braces, and a collar purlin. However there is no real crown-post, only a stub between the curved braces which attach the collar purlin to the principals. The soffits of the arch braces and collar purlins are moulded and the feet of the principals extend below the wall-plate. It is of one consistent design throughout the building. An additional truss joined to its neighbour by purlins indicates the position of the louvre. Windows on both sides are misaligned with bay divisions of the roof. While this can be explained on the w side by alterations to insert the chimney and C17 stair, it is difficult to account for it on the other side, though the addition of the porch would have occasioned some rebuilding. It implies that the present windows are secondary, or that they have been enlarged or repositioned.

The huge fireplace with its external stack on the w side, probably inserted in the C16 or C17, was rebuilt in 1894 by *J. Medland Taylor*. The fine original battlemented **canopy** over the dais is another remarkable survival. The alcove with bay window towards the cloister is one bay N of the high-table bay. It is followed in this direction by a doorway, which leads to a lobby with access to the upper and lower chambers of the wardens lodgings. The lower room is called the **Audit Room**, because it was used by the feoffees of Chetham's charity for their meetings and annual audits. It is fitted with C17 panelling and a plaster frieze of trails. There are similarities with the late C16 plasterwork in the Great Chamber at Speke Hall, Liverpool, but although it has charm, the work is much cruder and the design would be conservative for 1655, though that is probably when it was inserted. The remarkable oak ceiling has some affinities with the ceiling of the choir in the cathedral, though it is less elaborate. Moulded beams have carved bosses at the intersections, and the panels have diagonal ribs and central bosses. The bay is ornate

---

*But not unknown. A small family of crown-post roofs has been identified in the NW including an example at nearby Ordsall Hall in Salford.

too, with a design of stone quatrefoils in the ceiling. Panelled doors have a good collection of C17 furniture, e.g. cockshead hinges and brass latches.

The upper room, now the **library reading room**, is the most lavishly decorated of all. The bay is more elaborate than its counterpart below, with a Tudor arch with shafts rising from polygonal bases. It has a three-light principal window and two-light windows in the sides, each with the traceried outline of a third light extending to the corners of the bay. The panelling is C17. Stanley portcullis and eagle-claw badges applied to the original wall-plate and to the vaulting of the bay were added during the C19.

Above the (renewed) fireplace is a splendid timber **tympanum**. Despite a certain provincial crudeness the size and vigour of the carving are impressive. It occupies the whole width of the N wall, framed by an arched band with repeating floral motifs and raised scrolls at the edges. An array of symbolic motifs is framed by flowing acanthus leaf designs. The centrepiece is Chetham's arms with foliated mantling surmounted by a helm. Above, an eagle grasps ropes of foliage and flowers. On either side wreathed obelisks rise from piles of books and support shell lamps. Finally, flanking the obelisks, birds; on one side the Pelican in her Piety, on the other a remarkably vigorous cockerel (perhaps a restoration) grasping ears of corn, against a tree or bush which is equally remarkable for its crudeness. Paint and varnish were probably introduced in the C19. The Solomonic obelisks, lamps of learning and books speak for themselves, as does the pelican, a symbol of Christian charity. The cockerel could be a symbol of Mercury and a reference to Chetham's

48. Library reading room tympanum (*c.* early C18).

successful career as a merchant. The piece is probably the work of a local firm which had absorbed the fashions and conventions disseminated by the workshop of Grinling Gibbons. An early C18 date seems plausible, but there is no documentation and the earliest evidence for it is an engraving of *c.* 1830.

A passageway leads off to the N to a narrow room. The inner passageway door is medieval. The room is lit by a range of nine mullioned windows with pointed heads. It was originally a gallery overlooking the hall, but it was walled up – presumably at the same time as the windows to the garth were inserted – and furnished with quatrefoil openings giving views to the hall.

The **cloister** has a walk around a garth with three-light openings to only three sides, the fourth side being filled by the hall range. Along it lay the fellows' sets, much as in Oxford or Cambridge colleges, except that the cloister is two storeyed, so sets do not have individual stairs. Stepped buttresses divide the bays. Lower windows have cinquefoil heads, upper windows, in alternate bays only, trefoil heads. Pierced shutters which survive and fit the openings are said to be the precursors of the glazing. There is a camber-beam roof to the lower cloister (the upper cloister roof has been replaced). The hierarchy of spaces is indicated by the fact that cambering is discontinued in corridors extending on the S and W sides, suggesting these areas were less important. Access to the upper cloister was via a stair at the NW corner where part of the structure can be seen in the ceiling. The entrance to the garth is through a mutilated window on the W walk, the original entrance was lost when the staircase at the NE corner was inserted for the library in the C17. The S cloister range is secondary, and the cloisters may have been built in phases. The most obvious clue is the manner in which a cloister buttress sits on top of the hall plinth in the SE side of the garth. The cloister and hall plinths differ, and the entrance to the cloister from the Audit Room is not aligned with the passageway.

Fellows' sets have heated ground-floor rooms with two-centred arched entrances with continuous hollow mouldings. The upper rooms were converted to form the library, with new windows to give more light. The partitions were removed but the bay divisions are visible in the pattern of roof trusses. The upper cloister walk and the entrances from it are preserved. The sets are of a similar size, *c.* 16 ft (nearly 5 metres) square, but they are not identical. The pair on the N side shared a garderobe, but there does not seem to be evidence for garderobes serving any of the others. There are problems interpreting the S side, where we have already seen evidence that the cloister is secondary. The room adjacent to the Audit Room is larger than the others, and distinguished by a mould around the arched entrance. A doorway into the Audit Room was blocked before or at the time of the insertion of C17 panelling in that room, but there is no primary access to the upper part. This raises two possibilities: there was an internal stair or the whole of the upper

49. Cloisters (mid C15). The window on the left was altered to form an entrance to the cloister garth, probably in the mid C17.

floor of this range was one long room served by the upper doorway from the SW set. There is a tradition that there was a chapel here and the upper part of the library here is known as the Mary Chapel, though when it acquired this name is not known. Dendrochronological analysis has disposed of the theory that it was open through two floors.

Now to the **library**, an almost equally remarkable survival, described by Kelly as 'By far the most important [public] library formed in this period – indeed the greatest of all the early town libraries'. In total £1,000 was lavished on books at the outset, and the collection was augmented at regular intervals. The present entrance from the SW side of the outer courtyard was instituted by *Waterhouse*, as part of a campaign of alterations in 1876–8 which provided separate circulation for library and school. He inserted a stair into the SW set. At the same time he rebuilt and refenestrated all the ground-floor sets on the W side and made them interconnect. The C17 library entrance was from the stone **stair** beside the hall, at the NE side of the cloister, which was built in 1656. This has an oak rail, newels with finials, and shaped and pierced splat balusters, probably the work of *Richard Martinscrofte* who did the library furnishings. The stairwell is lit by two-light arched windows with cinquefoil heads, *Medland Taylor*'s 1890s reconstructions following the original pattern. They must have been salvaged from the part of the cloister and hall walls at the angle where the stair is sited.

The library is L-shaped, taking up the upper fellows' rooms on the S and W side of the cloister. The **book cases** (illus. 5), ranged at right angles to the outer walls, were constructed during *c.* 1655–8 by local joiner and surveyor *Richard Martinscrofte* and the books were chained. Originally 7 ft (2 metres) high, they were raised on two occasions. Far more light would have been admitted originally. Chaining was continued until the mid c18. After the chains were removed **gates** with wavy finials were introduced to the bays. Although it is not the custom of these volumes to describe moveable furniture, the c17 **library stools**, similar to those found at St John's College, Cambridge, deserve mention, as do the wonderful **tables** in the reading room and Audit Room.

The steps up and unadorned arched entrance into the reading room must have been created for the library, probably in 1665 when the feoffees' minute book records that the 'great chamber and closet' was 'made uniform' with the library. Here parts of a late c17 **rail** with twisted openwork balusters may connect with the tradition that the Stanleys had a chapel here, or may simply be *ex situ.*

Now for the E range. The front was largely refenestrated with replacement of the original windows which were made uniform throughout and newly furnished with trefoil heads and labels on the ground floor. The arched door openings, too, were restored and given labels. This was probably done in the 1850s as part of a substantial campaign of repair and restoration by *J. E. Gregan.* Palmer shows the ground-floor windows were then generally flat-headed, with two- and three-light mullions as some still are in the rear. The polygonal bellcote with a lead roof is shown in an engraving of 1741. It was probably put in during the c17 conversion.

The splendid **kitchen** is a huge space open to the roof with fireplaces beneath joggled lintels on two sides. The upper windows are probably authentic, albeit restored, and a light which was blocked when the porch was rebuilt in the 1850s is visible. The window rebate extends for the full width of the room, the W part was presumably blocked when the porch was erected. The huge N chimney was rebuilt in 1902 and the

50. The range containing the hall and wardens lodgings is on the left, the range to the right of the porch contains the kitchen and ancillary accommodation.

one to the E decommissioned and a stair inserted in place of the chimney in the mid or late C19. Beside this fireplace a narrow corridor leads to a room to the E. A passageway between the main courtyard and a small rear courtyard divides this room from a series of rooms further E, probably used for baking and brewing. The rear courtyard gives access to an extension of 1844 (probably by *Gregan*) and steps to the (culverted) River Irk. A stair which rose from the passage has been removed. It served two rooms, possibly accommodation for the clerks, and here there are obvious signs that there has been rebuilding, or perhaps that the room above the passageway is a later insertion. The large angled upper room beyond to the E was reached from the external stair beside the gatehouse, and must have been quarters for servants and guests, used latterly as dormitories and now as a library. Within it the roof takes the angle with a wonderfully contrived arrangement of timbers and trusses.

Two original (albeit much altered and restored) stretches of boundary walling can be seen on the s side of the gatehouse and the s side of the library entrance.

The Nineteenth-century Buildings

Alfred Waterhouse designed a new free-standing schoolroom in 1871. It was finally erected in 1876–7 to the sw of the main building. It is modest and nicely detailed, looking a little like a chapel. Perp, but the motifs of the main building have not been slavishly adopted. Red sandstone was used instead of brick at the insistence of the feoffees who presumably wanted new to harmonize with old.

Further expansion took place in the late C20 when neighbouring buildings were acquired. The buildings of the Manchester Grammar School along Long Millgate were taken over in 1955. The N part, by *Barker & Ellis*, 1869–70, has a high gatehouse motif in the centre with a high chimney towards the schoolyard. The battlements and octagonal turrets were doubtless designed to recall the medieval origins of the Grammar School (for the history and present premises of this institution *see* the forthcoming *Manchester and South-East Lancashire* volume). An extension to the s is by *Mills & Murgatroyd*, 1877. On the w side of the site the former Palatine Hotel was built in 1842–3 by *J. P. & I. Holden*. The proximity of Victoria Station was presumably the attraction. It was acquired and converted in 1969. NE of the main building two tall gabled accommodation blocks were erected in the 1980s but the bright red brick looks garish next to the soft hues and contours of the original buildings.

Manchester Town Hall

Albert Square

The building of the town hall between 1867 and 1877 gave Manchester a highly efficient building, a potent civic symbol and a distinguished work of architecture, but credit for this has to be given to the civic administration and not only to the architect. The project was conceived in 1863, and a year later the city council adopted a report showing an ambition to produce a work worthy of the city and 'equal if not superior, to any similar building in the country' at any cost 'which may be reasonably required'.* The choice of the site was thoroughly investigated and, although Piccadilly (then the city's principal public space) had its supporters, it was decided ultimately to use the near-triangular site occupied by the town's yard, which faced on to the emergent Albert Square (q.v. City Centre). Its suitability was confirmed by Edward Walters, then nearing the end of his distinguished architectural career. The design was obtained through a two-stage architectural competition, then an unusual procedure, which *The Builder* hailed as 'for the age and country, an immense innovatory stride'. In August 1867 the editor of *The Builder* was called in to assist in the selection of the finalists from the 137 entries. The eight schemes finally submitted were assessed by Professor T. L. Donaldson and G. E. Street, and *Alfred Waterhouse* was appointed on 1 April 1868.

In his initial entry Waterhouse had adopted a plan of great simplicity and effectiveness and although many changes were made in the development of the design the clarity of the plan was never compromised. The building form, a hollow triangle, fills the site, and the Great Hall required by the brief is placed in the central void perpendicular to the w side, which faces Albert Square and contains at first-floor level the civic apartments. Separate entrances were required for different functions, and these are strategically placed with the main entrance facing Albert Square. Public access is at the main angles, there is a private entrance for the lord mayor, and beneath the Great Hall was a police station with access from the s courtyard. The offices face outwards from along the sides, and concentric within the form is a corridor at each level

*The total expenditure by 1880 was £859,000. This included fees, furniture and the substantial cost of properties bought to gain additional land. The building cost was £521,357. 12s. 1d.

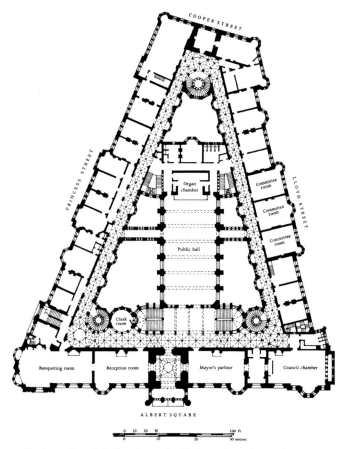

51. Manchester Town Hall, Albert Square, by Alfred Waterhouse (1867–77). Plan redrawn by Prudence Waterhouse.

which effectively serves general circulation. This arrangement provides natural light and ventilation to all rooms and the corridors. The vertical circulation is also masterly: a pair of grand staircases, located close to the main entrance, lead to the first floor and serve ceremonial purposes; other uses are served by circular staircases in each internal angle and by additional stairs located at about the mid point of the N and S corridors. A private stair links the mayor's apartments to his entrance. The building functions extremely well.

The plan and the structure are very closely integrated and the structural system is exploited architecturally. Waterhouse adopted a proprietary fireproof system of concrete vaults, the Dennet system, for use throughout the building. Large spaces are spanned by wrought-iron beams which support the vaults. In the public rooms the beams are masked by ceilings, but in offices the rhythm of beams and vaults forms

52. Manchester Town Hall by Alfred Waterhouse (1867–77), photographed from Princess Street.

an attractive feature. Rib- or groin-vaulting is used for the corridors and other circulation areas and this system enabled Waterhouse to develop the interior spaces imaginatively through the use of open arcading, so that dramatic internal views are obtained through and across spaces. Services, e.g. heating and ventilation, also are closely integrated with the plan and structure. Each circular staircase has a central open well through which heat rises from heating coils in the basement and the principles of elementary physics inform the whole service system. *G. N. Haden*, the heating engineer, and Waterhouse were personal friends, and this may partly explain the technical refinements of the design.

The architectural language of the town hall is less familiar now than it was when it was built. Several stylistic vocabularies are used and the most generally evident is the Gothic style of the c13 with its uncomplicated geometrical tracery, foliated capitals, etc. This provided a service-able vehicle but is otherwise almost incidental. Waterhouse was no historicist and carried such matters lightly. When in 1877 he delivered a paper to the RIBA, the building was referred to by Professor Donaldson as medieval: Waterhouse demurred and replied 'The learned professor spoke … as if the Manchester Town Hall were a Medieval building. On the contrary, the architecture … was essentially nineteenth-century, and was fitted to the wants of the present day' (*The Builder* 35, p. 175). Waterhouse was correct – and in more than the technical sense – but in common with other architects of his generation he was eclectic and pragmatically drew upon his architectural knowledge as a matter of convenience and without plagiarism. The main frontage owes its mas-siveness to more than the requirements of the brief. The precedents informing it are the cloth halls and *hôtels de ville* of Northern France and Belgium. Similarly, early stages of the design reveal that the hand-some circular staircases have a precursor in the famous early Renaissance staircase of the Château de Blois. The significance of Waterhouse's eclecticism is not his sources but the skill of their assimilation into a unified design.

Exterior

Massive and powerful, the exterior has four storeys and a steeply pitched slate roof. Well defined pavilions at the corners mask the acute angles with a series of obtuse ones so that instead of thinness the corners convey robustness. Towers and spires rise over the principal entrances, and the clock tower, 286 ft (87 metres) high, which dominates the w front, marks the main entrance. Waterhouse was sparing of external decoration for practical reasons, and on a very limited scale statuary (representing figures from or associated with Manchester's history) was introduced at vital points, e.g. a figure of Agricola surmounts the main entrance and a concentrated group of others, all in their contemporary dress, is on the N pavilion. All of these, by *Farmer & Brindley* of London, are competent but uninspired. Two roundels by *Thomas Woolner*, respec-tively representing spinning and weaving, are of much greater interest. These were mounted one on each side elevation, but only 'Weaving', on the Princess Street frontage, remains *in situ*. Polychromy, then highly popular, was virtually eschewed from the exterior. Practical experience had shown Waterhouse that Manchester's buildings were rapidly coated in velvety black soot from the heavily polluted atmosphere. The town hall is faced entirely in Spinkwell stone, a durable, dun-coloured, Derby-shire sandstone. The only external use of polychromy was on the roof, where the slating was patterned in two tones: it is now invisible. Although the design is severe compared with some others submitted, it received praise from the assessors for its dignity and picturesqueness. The latter stems from a varied skyline of towers and spires but is far from arbi-trary. The site, enclosed except for the w face, allows only one eleva-

53. Weaving roundel, Princess Street elevation, carved by Thomas Woolner.

tional view, but when seen from a distance the skyline is impressive and effective from many different viewpoints. An underlying rationalism relates the site, the plan and the towers, and this, together with the expression of the careful differentiation of the parts, their functions, and the nature of the material and the techniques used, derives from Pugin's rationalist principles. An example in the detailing is the alternating depths of the masonry courses, which express their toothing into the brick backing: the narrow faces are the bonding courses.

The deliberate play on asymmetry owes much to Ruskin. It is developed from the observation of nature, in which a dominant form provides a strong focal point that is unaffected by variety in the related details. This concept pervades the design, beginning with the main frontage, which flouts the convention of mirror-image symmetry. The clock tower, the dominant feature, is approximately central but the treatment of the wall and windows on either side of it is varied and the N and S pavilions are of markedly different design. Yet the frontage remains architecturally authoritative and is often assumed to be symmetrical. The same applies to the other elevations although without such dramatic expression.

On a smaller scale the freedom of asymmetry is fully developed in the design of the N pavilion. It occupies the most public angle of the building and architecturally it serves several complex functions: it defines the corner and its own identity by breaking forward from the W and N frontages; also it provides an impressively solid face to the public by cutting across the acute angle of the site corner and carrying the three-storey scale of the main frontage into Princess Street where it meets the smaller-scaled four-storey office wing. The junction between the two is resolved by a staircase tower that terminates the pavilion and marks the significance of the Princess Street entrance. Between tower and corner an inset panel maintains the lines of the w elevation but decisively changes the scale by the introduction of smaller windows. The corner angle itself is clearly defined by changes in the wall plane and is sculpturally powerful. Two large oriels are corbelled out, one on each side of the angle, and flanked by niches containing sculptures and, on the line bisecting the angle and metaphorically supporting the whole rich edifice, is a short but massive flying buttress. This pavilion, which is as subtle as it is powerful, is almost a town hall in miniature and is a consummate illustration of successful asymmetrical design. The scale and authority of the town hall are such that many of its nuances pass unnoticed.

The emphasis on massiveness and the vigour of expression, which cannot be overlooked, also can be attributed to Ruskin's influence and especially 'The Lamp of Power', in which he admires the sublime effect of an overhanging cliff face and calls for buildings with 'a solemn frown of projection'; he also thought that power could be expressed by a 'deep thrust'. Waterhouse's design is heavy with such effects, as in the melodramatically expressive buttress on the N pavilion. Almost equally forceful is the buttress on the s face of the s pavilion which breaks through what would be otherwise an orthodox window arrangement; but the most sublime illustration of the confident and dramatic handling of powerful masses is seen looking E from Lloyd Street. It is the clashing dissonance which occurs at the junction of the wings at the apex of the plan where the bulk of the E tower apparently collides with the differently aligned face of the Lloyd Street elevation. Masterly high drama of this order is the work of an architect of great assurance.

Interior

The most memorable feature of the interior of the town hall is its spaciousness. It is not produced by the dimensions of the separate chambers but by the linking of spaces through open arcading, which gives unexpected views either into individual spaces or across a whole sequence of them. Most remarkable of all are those from the s corner staircase, revealing the main foyer and its screens and staircases. These effects arise from the command of plan, space and structure that is Waterhouse's hallmark.* Also outstanding is the manipulation of axes and cross-axes and the resolution obtained between the axis centred on the main entrance, and that of the Great Hall, offset because of the configuration of the site. Their relationship is established by the bay system common to the ground-floor cross-corridor and the adjacent four-bay entrance foyer. The entrance axis is central on the latter's most northerly

* Two changes have detracted from the spatial qualities of the building. Above the first floor an open well in the vaulting in the N corner linked the mayor's apartment to the corridor below. This has now been filled by a neatly designed timber panel. A more serious intrusion is the modern kitchen which has been inserted in the N courtyard at first-floor level, It affects the lighting of the internal corridor as well as the character of the courtyard. It has been likened to 'filling in a hole in a Henry Moore sculpture'.

bay. That to the hall is one-and-a-half bays to its s. The twin staircases flank the foyer, but the greater importance of the n staircase is signified by an arcaded spiral stair that projects above the half-landing. The ceremonial route follows the main axis to the foot of this staircase, which rises to the edge of the main foyer. From this point the user may cross to the vestibule to the public suite and enter the public rooms, or proceed to the entrance to the Great Hall, in which case, quite unconsciously, a skilful transition has been made to the new axis.

The interior is stylistically consistent with the exterior, and the design of detail and finishes shares the same values. Ruskin's influence is readily appreciable in the polychromatic nature of the internal finishes, although not in the hard, mechanistic, decorative detail of the masonry and joinery. A principal Ruskinian tenet is that on ethical grounds workmen should be freed from repetitive work and entrusted with creative craftsmanship. It is clear that Waterhouse preferred to maintain control and consistency even though this was at the price of a loss of vitality in most of the stone carving both internally and externally. All finishes are selected according to their use and location, and the richest are reserved for the ceremonial route and its related areas.

The decorative programme throughout the building illustrates two themes, Manchester's history and the nature and extent of its commerce. The first is seen in the external sculpture and the murals by *Ford Madox Brown*, and the second appears in numerous motifs incorporated in internal finishes and decorations. Where the decoration is not thematic much of it is highly innovative and reflects the contemporary modernity of the Aesthetic Movement.

55. Manchester Town Hall entrance vestibule with statues of Joule (foreground) by Alfred Gilbert (1893) and Dalton by Sir Francis Chantrey (1837).

Appropriately, the most sumptuous space in the building is the **main entrance vestibule**. From Albert Square a wide flight of steps leads through a cavernous portal into a small, glittering rib-vaulted chamber paved in white marble mosaic and enriched by fine statuary. The vaulting is similarly lined but is attractively patterned in black and gold, and in the centre is a roundel painted with the city's arms. Its equivalent in the floor is a wheel motif in porphyry and coloured marbles.

Sculpture

The town hall's collection of Victorian sculpture portrays in the main prominent local figures and includes a large collection of portrait busts and some statuary. In the latter category the best examples, amongst the finest to be found anywhere in the city, are encountered as the building is entered. Seated figures of Dalton by *Sir Francis Chantrey* (1837) and Joule by *Alfred Gilbert* (1893) face one another across the entrance vestibule, a felicitous juxtaposition in which Chantrey's dignified Neoclassicism is a foil to the relaxed lines and intimate character of Gilbert's portrait. The adjacent Sculpture Hall is lined with white marble busts. Few are memorable, some are unsigned, and all are subject to repositioning (some are at present in the corridor and foyer), so only a few indications will be given. *Matthew Noble* is well represented (e.g. Cromwell, 1861; Joseph Brotherton, 1856), and there are works by *J. Warrington Wood* (e.g. William Romaine Callender, 1880), *W. Charles May*, *H. S. Leifchild* (George Wilson, 1871), *E. G. Papworth*, *Patric Parc*, and others. One of the best is *E. Onslow Ford's* Charles Hallé (1897). Also in the hall a statue of William Fairbairn, *E. E. Geflowski* (1878), an undated bronze relief, Daniel McCabe, Lord Mayor 1913–15, and a bronze memorial to Alcock and Brown, 1921, both by *John Cassidy*. *Byron Howard's* animated triptych, Sir John Barbirolli, unveiled 1975, wood carvings by *Sol Garson* of the 1980s and a bronze bust of Gandhi by *S. D. Sathe* presented in 1995, represent the later C20. On the main stair is a statue of Bright by *William Theed* (1878). More busts line the entrance to the Great Hall, including a characterful portrait of Alderman Abel Heywood by *J. W. Swynnerton*, c. 1875. Inside the hall there are busts of Queen Victoria and Prince Albert both by *Noble* and the Prince and Princess of Wales both by *Marshall Wood*. Statues are by *Theed*: E end C. P. Villiers (1876), w end W. E. Gladstone (1879).

One side of the chamber is open-arcaded and reveals the adjacent Sculpture Hall. The richness continues to the principal foyer at first-floor level. The twin staircases from the lower foyer are each enclosed within a vaulted semicircular apse, and each is flanked by a range of tall windows lit from a courtyard. The main foyer is defined by open arcades and a panelled wagon-roof ceiling that is partly glazed. The floor, in white mosaic and patterned with bees symbolizing industry, is bordered by an interwoven motif representing ropes of spun cotton. The adjacent corridors also are highly finished. Rib-vaulted polychromatically in stone in bands of two contrasting colours, buff and blue-grey, they are lined in terracotta in matching colours above a richly patterned, tiled dado. The **Sculpture Hall**, on the ground floor, although less impressive because of its low height, is finished similarly.

56. Manchester Town Hall, groin-vaulted corridor ceiling, first floor.

Elsewhere, the corridors of the ground and first floors follow the same general pattern in simplified form. Groin-vaulted ceilings are painted and patterned and the floors are in multi-coloured mosaic with plain margins. The tiled dados are varied in colour and pattern to give individuality to the different floors and areas, as are the painted ceiling patterns, which in places show great vigour of design. Although often overlooked, decoratively, the circulation areas are as important as any individual room.

The **Great Hall**, 100 ft long by 50 ft wide (30 metres by 15 metres), is of seven bays, divided by clustered shafts and lit by tall windows. At first sight its ceiling suggests a roof constructed on the hammerbeam principle, but it is a parody, for its members are plainly too light for such a purpose. Instead it is a panelled ceiling in the form of a wagon roof. The hall's principal entrances are from the foyer, and at the opposite end is a vaulted apse and an organ. The space itself and the qualities of its decoration make the hall outstanding. The ceiling panels are emblazoned heraldically to represent the cities and nations with which Manchester traded and, to make the nature of the trade explicit, each panel is bordered by a pattern of crossed shuttles. The hall windows are set high and beneath the cills and above an oak dado are the famous **murals** (*see* topic box) by *Ford Madox Brown*, six on each side. The subjects relate, in some cases rather tenuously, to Manchester's history, giving emphasis to themes such as Christianity and Nonconformity, commercial probity, and scientific, technological and educational achievements. Brown's sympathies are illustrated by the fact that he proposed the Peterloo Massacre (*see* p. 183) and objected to the Jacobite

The Murals of the Great Hall

Ford Madox Brown commenced work on the murals in July 1878 and completed the task shortly before his death in 1893. Each mural measures 10 ft 6 in. by 4 ft 9 in. (3.2 metres by 1.45 metres) and was painted either in the studio in oils or *in situ* using the Gambier Parry method (marked GP) in which special preparation of the wall surfaces allowed them to absorb treated paint somewhat in the manner of fresco. The sequence begins from the left as the hall is entered. Numbers in brackets indicate the order of execution.

57. 'John Kay, Inventor of the Fly Shuttle'. Mural by Ford Madox Brown (1888–90). Mrs Henry Boddington, wife of Brown's patron, and her children were models.

1. The Romans Building the Fort at Mancenion AD 60 (2) GP

2. The Baptism of Edwin AD 627 (1) GP

3. The Expulsion of the Danes AD 910 (3) GP

4. The Establishment of the Flemish Weavers in Manchester AD 1363 (4) GP

5. The Trial of Wycliffe AD 1377 (7)
Completed mid 1886 GP

6. The Proclamation Regarding Weights and Measures AD 1556 (6) GP

7. Crabtree Watching the Transit of Venus AD 1639 (5) GP

8. Chetham's Life Dream AD 1640 (8)

9. Bradshaw's Defence of Manchester AD 1642 (12)

10. John Kay, Inventor of the Fly Shuttle AD 1753 (10)

11. The Opening of the Bridgewater Canal, AD 1761 (11)

12. Dalton Collecting Marsh-fire Gas (9)

rising as a subject. In the event neither was included. The murals are of added interest because members of his family and circle of friends were used as models. The Trial of Wycliffe, (5) for example, includes Frederic Shields as Wycliffe and Harold Rathbone, founder of the Birkenhead della Robbia Pottery, as John of Gaunt (centre with sword). The town hall organist sat for the seated bishop while Archbishop Sudbury (far right) was a self-portrait.

The other public rooms are the four rooms across the w front. The former Council Chamber, now used for general purposes, is the most southerly. It is separated by a vestibule from the former committee room and the Mayor's Parlour, which form a reception suite with the Banqueting Room. A second vestibule, within the tower, divides the two central rooms and is the principal reception point. All the rooms are interconnected so that large functions can be accommodated. Each room is made asymmetrical and spatially varied by at least one substantial bay.

The **Council Chamber** is second only to the Great Hall in its decorative quality. Spatially, with bays to w and s and a recess to the E beneath a public gallery, it is the most complex of the public rooms. It was designed to seat 48 councillors and aldermen who faced a low dais for the mayor and principal officers, with a gallery above for the recording clerks. Many of the original fittings and furnishings remain. Above the masonry walls is a deep frieze, painted attractively with sweeping, intertwining tendrils of cotton plants, laden with the bursting white bolls of the ripened crop. Interspersed are heraldic shields bearing the coats of arms of neighbouring cotton towns. Above, geometrically panelled ceiling in strong colours complements the more delicate ones of the frieze. This is one of the most attractive rooms of the building and heraldic pomp is less intrusive here than in the Great Hall.

In their design, the three rooms of the **reception suite** have much in common. The two reception rooms were intended to have murals but the civic nerve failed and in their place a woven-patterned fabric, now replaced by a facsimile, was inserted. Their ceilings are of great interest. Light in tone and effect, their colours and patterns introduce the Aesthetic Movement and the advanced taste of the 1870s. This is common also to the chimneypieces of all three rooms.

The **Banqueting Room**, in addition to a bay, has the two oriels of the N pavilion and a musicians' gallery. Its ceiling is panelled in oak and decorated by gilt suns. Its furnishings included curtains, made by the *Royal School of Art Needlework*, South Kensington, and have a place in the history of Victorian design.

The decoration of the town hall is an important aspect of the design. It has survived through the use of polychromy and because, fortunately, the original decoration in the public rooms has been maintained. It shows that Waterhouse was committed to the modern design of the day and participated actively in its development. It is not known who

58. Manchester Town Hall, the s vestibule, ceiling detail.

designed the textiles but three firms were responsible for the design and execution of the painted decoration. *Heaton, Butler and Bayne*, of London, decorated the Great Hall, *Best & Lea*, of Manchester, decorated the Council Chamber, and the s reception room, and *Pollitt & Coleman*, of Manchester, the Mayor's Parlour. The designs in the front suite show a consistency which suggests that the work was closely co-ordinated. Waterhouse personally designed the painted decoration for the corridor vaulting, which varies greatly in character and colour, presumably because the patterns were meant to be seen in rapid sequence. Notable decoration occurs also in the vestibules in the public suite. The central one is now more conventional but has a fine original ceiling. The s one is a brilliant example of Japonaiserie, a major element in the vocabulary of the Aesthetic Movement. In another respect also Waterhouse's taste is revealed only from within the building. In all of the windows most of the quarry glazing is white, but the margins are in subtle and seemingly infinitely varied tones of grey and wine colours from claret to rosé. Its simplicity is unusual and it is noteworthy that at the turn of the century C. R. Mackintosh used a similar palette.

Waterhouse's hand can be seen everywhere in the building. He designed the furniture for the public rooms, the alphabet used in the etched glass, the fire-irons, the dinner service, and he was consulted even about the inscriptions for the bells. It was suggested that some Greek or Latin tag would be fitting, but he suggested that it would be sufficient to refer to contemporary literature. Tennyson's 'In Memoriam' was selected and each bell is inscribed with a line from the stanza opening 'Ring out the false, ring in the true ...'. The inscription on the clock tower also is fitting: 'Teach us to number our days'.

59. Mosaic bee, a Mancunian emblem and symbol of industry.

Manchester Town Hall has the complexity, imagination and invention of a great work of architecture and, like other outstanding creative achievements, its richness is not revealed immediately. It is widely known as a classic of its age, but now, a century after that age, it justly transcends that limit.

JHGA

Further Reading

For contemporary descriptions *see* W. E. A. Axon, ed., *An Architectural and General Description of the Town Hall, Manchester*, 1878, and A. Waterhouse, 'A Description of the New Town Hall at Manchester', *RIBA Transactions*, 1876–7.

Recent publications: *see* John H. G. Archer, 'A Civic Achievement: the Building of Manchester Town Hall. 1. The Commissioning', *Transactions of the Lancashire and Cheshire Antiquarian Society*, vol. 81, 1982; also, in John H. G. Archer, ed *Art and Architecture in Victorian Manchester*, 1985, for references to sculpture *see* the Introduction, for the town hall, Archer, 'A Classic of its Age', for the murals, Julian Treuherz, 'Ford Madox Brown and the Manchester Murals'. For Sculpture also *see* Benedict Read, *Victorian Sculpture*, 1982; for textiles, Barbara Morris, *Victorian Embroidery*, 1962; and for Waterhouse, Colin Cunningham & P. Waterhouse, *Alfred Waterhouse, 1830–1905: Biography of a Practice*, 1992.

Manchester Town Hall Extension

Between Lloyd Street and St Peter's Square

Built 1934–8 after *E. Vincent Harris* (1876–1971) won a competition in 1927. Pevsner viewed it as his 'best job' whilst Charles Reilly found it 'dull' and 'drab'. Conceived of as an understated link between the grandeur of the Gothic Revival town hall and the Classical bombast of the Central Library Harris's design manages to pay due deference to both whilst proclaiming its own integrity. This is essentially done by an eclectic mix of Gothic forms for the skyline, translated via more domestic stone mullion-and-transom windows to the main façades down to the more civic neo-Georgian character to the w where it faces the Central Library. Eight storeys plus attic with the seventh and eighth storeys set back behind a parapet.

The stone chosen, a rather muted and characterless Darley Dale sandstone, sits somewhere between the town hall's Yorkshire sandstone and the Portland stone of the Central Library. The whole is enlivened by ornate carved tracery grilles to the staircase bays in a late Gothic style which incorporate heraldic devices for England, Scotland, Ireland and Wales with the Lancashire cotton flower. Each of the two stair lights is surmounted by an allegorical statue carved by *Hermon Cawthra* to represent a Philosopher and a Counsellor, illustrative of the Book of Proverbs 3: 16. Beneath the windows to the top storey are decorative panels of faience by *Shaw's Glazed Brick Company*, Darwen.

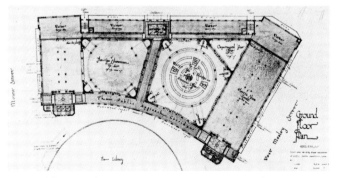

60. Ground-floor plan of the Town Hall Extension, St Peter's Square, by E. Vincent Harris (1934–8).

The ground-floor arcades were conceived of not merely as enjoyable urban spaces but as the setting for the showrooms of the Manchester Corporation Gas and Electricity Committees, the dying mouldings to their arches echoing the late Gothic ecclesiastical work of contemporaries such as Temple Moore and Walter Tapper. The concave façade linking the two sets of showrooms, and which formed an exciting new pedestrian route in the heart of the city, contained the Rates Hall with a 200-ft (61-metre) counter of Cuban mahogany. To the town hall end the extension is linked by two bronze-faced bridges at the level of the Council Chambers.

Internally the showrooms of the Gas and Electricity Committees were laid out with kitchen and bathroom displays and incorporated plaster decorations to the ceilings in a moderne manner, including the Gas logo of 'Mr Therm', and a mural painting by *A. Sherwood Edwards* entitled Progress. All have now been swept away and the clarity of the ground floor is only partially apparent in the former Rates Hall decorated by *Barry Hart*. To the Council Chamber ante-room, and Council Chamber itself are stained-glass windows, by *George Kruger Gray*, of ancient badges of the House of Lancaster, the walls faced in Hopton Wood stone with bands of Ashburton marble.

JH

Central Library

St Peter's Square

Of 1930–4, it is one of *Vincent Harris*'s most confident, assured, and bombastic essays in the Roman Imperial manner that he developed during the 1920s. Harris (1876–1971) won the commission in competition in 1925 with a scheme for a steel-framed, Portland stone clad, building of four storeys plus attic with an extensive four-storey book storage area partially below ground. Harris's Pantheon influenced design may also reflect the needs of the circular plenum heating plan for the high-voltage electrode heating plant. After he had won the competition Harris made a tour of new library buildings in the United States to understand new trends in library design, accompanied by the new Librarian, Charles Nowell, who had taken over from L. Stanley Jast. Jast had very definite views on library design which are seen in Harris's completed building though Nowell later modified them further to include a lending department.

Since it opened in 1934 it has become one of the great monuments of Manchester. A five-bay portico of Corinthian columns with round-headed arches to the returns provides a landmark entrance to the city

61. Central Library (left), St Peter's Square, by E. Vincent Harris (1930–4).

centre from the s. It also provides a Classical foil to the Gothic Revival of Manchester town hall to the N. The round arches of the portico are continued to the façade which is composed of a heavy two-storey rusticated base surmounted by a continuous Tuscan colonnaded screen to the upper storeys.

Despite the apparent weight of the exterior it is essentially more of a façade which encloses the large, top-lit and domed circular reading room in the manner of the British Museum and in which were housed subsidiary functions such as the catalogue rooms, study carrels and special collections. The ingenuity of Harris's design is seen in the way he has placed this grand space, with its Tuscan colonnade of Sienna scagliola, on top of the stacks as in the American Library of Congress and in defiance of the then fashion of creating book towers on top of reading rooms as seen at the Universities of London, Leeds and Cambridge. To the double-height entrance hall are stained-glass windows designed by *George Kruger Gray*. The original furniture throughout was designed by Harris.

JH

City Art Gallery

Mosley Street

By *Charles Barry*, 1824–35, for the Manchester Institution for the Promotion of Science Literature and the Arts, which had been founded in 1823. A competition was organized and six architects invited to enter. Barry was only 29 years old when he won, but he was known in the area for two Commissioners' churches (All Saints Stand, 1822–6, survives, *see Manchester and South-East Lancashire*, forthcoming). The building is Grecian, his only public work in this style. His success lay in his ability to make the interior fit the glove of the Greek style, partly through the use of top lighting with the consequent reduction in the number of windows and partly through his clever adaptation of designs by L. A. Dubut published in 1803. There is a debt also to Schinkel's Schauspielhaus in Berlin, of 1819–21. From these he developed the idea of a portico flanked by wings and topped by an attic. The articulation of the elements, especially as depicted in the 1824 presentation drawing, is almost Palladian, but the tightly controlled proportions of the executed design knit everything together into a compact whole.*

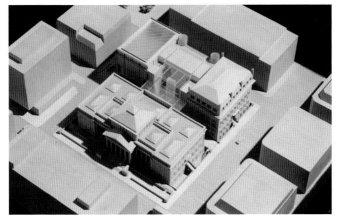

62. Model of existing buildings and extensions of the City Art Gallery and Atheneum by Michael Hopkins & Partners (2000–2).

*Marcus Whiffen suggests that the bold modelling and strong contrasts might owe something to the ancient temples Barry had seen in Egypt.

The front has six unfluted Ionic columns with a pediment, then three recessed bays with two columns *in antis*, and then three-bay solid pavilion-like ends. **Sculpture** by *John Henning Jun.* was executed in 1837. A series of metope panels in the upper part of the pavilions depicts allegorical figures with attributes and putti. Plain metope panels continue around the other sides of the building. The portico expresses the presence of the superb full-height entrance and staircase hall, which has a Greek Doric colonnade on three sides. The lofty space, with clerestory lighting all around, is mediated by a gallery, reached from a stair which rises between plinths and divides on either side of the entrance to the former lecture theatre. At ground level there is visual penetration beyond the colonnade on each side. In this way expression is given to the spaces lying on each side and above. Parts of the Parthenon frieze on the wall are casts donated by the King in 1831, and Barry altered his design to incorporate them. The colour scheme was introduced during the 1980s, with elaborate stencilling and gilding following a scheme of 1882 which claimed to be a faithful copy of the 1846 décor. Barry's own proposals were much more muted.

The building and the Institution's extensive collections were donated to Manchester Corporation in 1881, on condition that the latter would endow a trust to yield moneys for additions to the art collection. The resulting alterations included the removal of a large lecture theatre which lay immediately behind the entrance hall and can be seen in *George Strutt*'s fine 1825 model (usually on display in the gallery). Upper top-lit galleries, with a colourful decorative scheme inspired by the 1882 work, lie on three sides around the entrance hall.

63. Athenaeum (former), Princess Street, by Charles Barry (1836–7).

The gallery uses as an annexe the former **Athenaeum** in Princess Street, the premises of a club promoting adult education, which had reading and newsroom facilities. It was acquired by the Corporation in 1938. This is also by *Barry*, but it dates from 1836–7, and the design has much in common with the Reform Club in London of 1837–40. It is a stone palazzo of nine bays with pedimented piano-nobile windows. The portal with Tuscan columns is more emphatic than that of the Reform Club. The ground floor is raised high over a half basement so there are steps up to the entrance. There is an inscribed frieze, after the Palazzo Pandolfini, Florence, and there is historicism also in the big expanse of wall above the upper windows. In Italy the high ceilings above the windows helped to keep the rooms cool, hardly a requirement of the Manchester climate. The proportions are crushed by the heavy roof added after a fire in 1873, which destroyed part of the interior. (An impressive lecture theatre installed in the new attic by *Clegg & Knowles*, with vaulted and coffered ceiling and attractive plasterwork, survives.*) The newsroom took up the whole of the ground floor, the only part of the interior to survive in something like original form. It is one large hall divided by two screens of Ionic columns. This was Manchester's first palazzo, erected in the same year as the city's last major Greek revival building, Richard Lane's (demolished) Corn Exchange. It can claim to be the inspiration for a style which Manchester was to make her own as the model for commercial warehouses.

Land had been acquired in the rear angle of the two buildings in 1898, with the intention of building an extension, but a century passed before the plan came to fruition. The new work by *Michael Hopkins and Partners*, 1999–2002, is under construction at the time of writing. The original Royal Manchester Institution building is linked to the extension via a bridge at first-floor level and through doors made by extending existing windows at ground level. In this way Barry's rear elevation retains its coherence. A glass box links the buildings and leads into a transparent central part with stairs and lifts, and walkways suspended from the roof. In contrast the N part of the extension is expressed as a block matching the dimensions and solidity of the Athenaeum, clad in stone, with light brought in mainly from the roof. Treating the extension as two linked units has integrated the Athenaeum into a composition of three parts which in turn relates to the rhythms of the Institution building.

*Information from Frank Kelsall.

Free Trade Hall

Peter Street

The site of the Free Trade Hall has long-standing historical significance. As St Peter's Field in 1819 it gave its name to the infamous Peterloo Massacre, which is enshrined in the history of English radicalism (*see* topic box, p. 183), and in the 1840s it accommodated successively the two temporary public halls which were vital to Manchester's considerable role in the long campaign for the repeal of the corn laws, carried in 1846. Later a fund, ostensibly apolitical, was launched for the provision of a permanent public hall for literary, religious, musical and other purposes serving 'public amusement or instruction', and in 1853 *Edward Walters* was commissioned from five prominent Manchester architects who had been invited to submit designs for a building on the historic site. An outstanding exponent of the palazzo style, Walters had assimilated its principles and vocabulary so well from first-hand studies that he was able to use it fluently and adapt it with memorable success to a variety of projects, and on this occasion he produced a classic that belongs to the canon of historic English architecture.

The title Free Trade Hall was not used until 1855 when, much to the chagrin of Tory subscribers, it was adopted by the sponsors when they formed a joint-stock company, and from that point the building became popularly regarded as the symbol of Manchester's hour of political triumph. It gained fame also for later events, cultural and political, which brought lustre to the city. It was bought by Manchester Corporation in 1920 'so that it shall not be lost to the citizens', but in 1940 it was reduced to a shell by fire through bombing. After substantial reconstruction it reopened in 1951 and remained Manchester's principal auditorium until 1996 when it was superseded as a concert hall by the newly built Bridgewater Hall. It has now (2001) been sold for conversion to a luxury hotel.

In 1853 the task facing Walters was not simple, and only limited funds were available. The site falls sharply from E–W and S–N, is approximately trapezoidal and there were streets on three sides and a building on the w boundary. The principal requirement was for a large public hall, and to obtain this Walters filled the site with an ingenious plan that made the galleried auditorium parallel with the longest side, the rear

64. Free Trade Hall, Peter Street, by Edward Walters (1853–6).

and s boundary. The w boundary is the shortest, and to gain the maximum length the auditorium's western end was made semicircular. This
configuration left a triangle at the NE corner which Walters filled with
an assembly room, with card and coffee rooms above. The main
entrance, central on the Peter Street elevation, was gained from an open
arcade along the length of the frontage. The floor of the auditorium was
raised 10 ft (3 metres) above ground level and the basement was let for
warehousing. The architectural motif of the design, externally and
internally, was the semicircular arcade, powerfully evident in the nine-
bay front elevation. Famous as an architectural *tour de force*, it led
Pevsner in 1969 to describe the building as 'perhaps the noblest monument in the Cinquecento style in England'. In modified form the
authority of the frontage was maintained throughout the exterior.

The post-war reconstruction of the Free Trade Hall (1946–51) was
given high priority in those lean years. It was entrusted to the City
Architect, *Leonard C. Howitt*, who reinstated the interior using a C20

vocabulary, repaired or reconstructed the principal façades with consummate care and appropriately rebuilt the rear elevation in brick in a manner reminiscent of a handsome power station.

As completed by Howitt, the Free Trade Hall remained outstanding for its historic façades. Pevsner acknowledged these as 'monumental and yet amazingly refined', which is particularly true of the front elevation and its detail. In composition it is relatively simple: the slope of Peter Street is absorbed by the open arcade's pier bases, which form a datum for the immensely rich, arcaded superstructure. Massive corner piers define and bind it, and a bold cornice caps it. Within this frame the design is layered. The open, ground-floor arcade relates the building to the street; it was designed to welcome the public and provide shelter. At first-floor level a moulded, modillioned stringcourse forms a tabling for the giant arcading that expresses the piano nobile with semicircular arches carried on paired Roman Ionic columns. Within each bay is a framed and triangular-pedimented window beneath a tympanum filled with allegorical figures representing international commerce and the arts and industries. Central is the gracious, open-handed figure of Free Trade, flanked by sheaves of corn and backed by sails, masts and rigging: no message could be clearer. The artist for the architectural sculpture was *John Thomas*, a leading sculptor of the day and former superintendent of stone-carving at the new Palace of Westminster. The elevation is completed by a garlanded frieze, the cornice and a balustraded parapet. All of this substantial face is in fine ashlar Yorkshire sandstone. At the NE corner the architecture of the frontage is maintained along the E side for three bays, but from there the character is simplified.

Although the principal sculpture occurs in the tympana, elsewhere the carved detail shows great refinement and is not insignificant symbolically. Much is confined to the spandrels, which are filled with well-composed and finely cut foliage, but at different levels different features are skilfully integrated in their design. Central in the upper arcade spandrels are wreathed disks of coloured granite, which suggests possible Ruskinian influence. Beneath each a well-designed group of musical instruments reflects the liberality of the founders' purpose. More prosaically, the lower spandrels introduce the coats of arms of the towns that were related to Manchester through the cotton trade and the repeal campaign, but a final noteworthy detail occurs in the frieze of the entablature of each pier of the open arcade where, as a decorative motif, carved miniature sheaves of corn may remind all who enter or leave that the building commemorates a campaign concerned with the cost of men's daily bread.

To replace the Free Trade Hall four successive hotel schemes, all by different architects, have been proposed. All have been controversial because they have flouted the principle of finding a compatible alternative use for an outstanding historic building. All required extensive demolition except for the retention of historic façades, and all imposed a large, high, bedroom block. One was rejected after a public inquiry in 1998, but a further proposal designed by *Roger Stephenson* of the Manchester firm of *Stephenson Bell* is to be implemented. It will conserve only the main façade and the northern three bays of the E elevation. A tower of fourteen storeys will extend along the s boundary, the main entrance will remove most of the E elevation, and part of the open arcade will be glazed. The proposal cannot be commended as a conservation scheme for a major historic building but it will cause less damage to the immediate context than its predecessors.

It is extraordinary that a civic authority with such a wide range of needs and activities has chosen to sacrifice a building of such distinction that was provided originally by public subscription specifically to meet the social, spiritual and cultural needs of its citizens. Is this true regeneration or iconophobia ?

JHGA

John Rylands Library

Deansgate

The John Rylands Library was commissioned by Enriqueta Rylands (1843–1908) as a memorial to her husband John (1801–80), a Nonconformist philanthropist and an exceptionally successful textile manufacturer. It was intended to house his collection of theological books and provide a free library, but after his death Mrs Rylands added two major private collections, creating a leading scholarly library of the country. In 1890 she appointed the architect *Basil Champneys* (1842–1935), who had produced notable collegiate work including Mansfield College, Oxford, which had Nonconformist and Mancunian associations and appealed to Mrs Rylands. Little expense was spared, the library cost £230,000 and took nine years to build. Champneys gave it some of the character of a religious foundation, which Mrs Rylands resisted, and, although its design draws heavily on Gothic precedent, underlying the historicist surface are contemporary aesthetic values. These are expressed in the quiet play on asymmetry, the stress on verticality and the attenuation of forms, the studied contrasts between plain surfaces and con-

65. John Rylands
Library, Deansgate,
by Basil Champneys
(1890–9).

centrated detail, and above all in the free play of space and structure for aesthetic effect. Imagination and artistic licence rather than strict historicism or rationalism are the keys to the Rylands Library.

The site selected by Mrs Rylands was unsalubrious but highly appropriate for moral improvement. It is a long, narrow parallelogram with a short frontage to Deansgate. Narrow streets, Wood Street and Spinningfield, were to its N and S. The building is not large or showy but is distinctive through the composition of the frontage and also, as the plan is strictly rectangular and aligned to Wood Street, its face varies from the line of Deansgate and unexpectedly catches the eye.

The frontage suggests a gatehouse of three bays. Built in red sandstone, it consists of a low, two-storey block with an imposing superstructure of towers, battlements and octagonal corner turrets that rise from the leading external angles. The slightly recessed central bay of the lower block contains the sumptuously decorated main entrance. The end bays have paired windows of different design at each level. Symmetry is avoided by counterchanging the pairs, which suits the internal needs. Rising above each end bay is an octagonal tower and immediately behind each is a tall, stark rectangular tower. Deeply recessed from the street but in line with these is the end gable of the Reading Room, the very heart of the scheme. This concentrated geometry establishes the identity and character of the building. The powerful massing is complemented by an elaborate use of intricate patterning expressed in wall panelling, window tracery and open screen work of attenuated verticality. Solid battlements on the end blocks contrast with open work, and concentrated areas of detail contrast with extensive plain areas of masonry. The richest display is reserved for the reticulated tracery at the head of the window of the Reading Room, and above this the mass of the building is crowned by a spiky, open-work screen that combines the slanting lines of a conventional gable in a design that is silhouetted against the sky. This ingenious finial replaced the proposed gable of an earlier design when, because of the immense value of the book collection, Mrs Rylands insisted that the roof construction should be incombustible, and low-pitched concrete superseded a conventional trussed roof.*

The remainder of the building's external form is relatively simple. Like the nave of a double-aisled church, the Reading Room provides the main vessel, expressed by the clerestory stage; the lower stage contains the reading bays, and the lowest houses the 'cloisters' or corridors that

*Initially the clerestory was contained in the roof void and its windows were intended to transmit light from skylights in the roof pitch. Mrs Rylands' intervention incidentally improved the natural lighting of the Reading Room but exposed the brickwork clerestory, which is visible only from distant or elevated positions. There is a proposal to reinstate the original design.

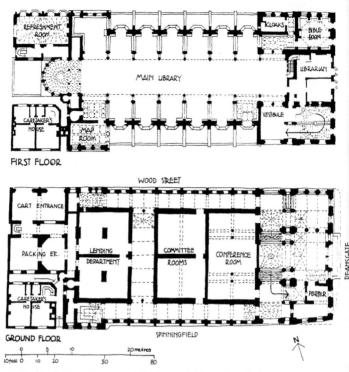

66. Vaulting is shown in representative bays only. Plan redrawn by Jane Kennedy.

give access to the core of central ground-floor rooms whose structure
supports the Reading Room. The longitudinal emphasis of this block is
halted by a tall tower, deceptively like a transept, which spans the width
of the site. On the w elevation is a central semicircular apse, now fully
masked by three extensions. Only the first of these, a NW addition of
1913–20 by *Champneys* and his son *Amian*, integrates smoothly with the
original, whereas those of 1950 and 1970 are notably misconceived.

The design of the principal element of the side elevations, i.e. the
nave-like centre piece, is now fully revealed from the s. It is the full
development of a concept that is incipient in the Mansfield College
Library. Seen from Spinningfield it terminates along the line of the
parapet above the reading bays. Buttresses and flying buttresses sub-
divide the main vessel and aisles, and each bay of the Reading Room
contains a two-storey oriel, giving a vertical stress that is further
emphasized by the slenderness of the nave buttresses and the sculptural
treatment of their counterparts to the aisles, whose exaggerated height
provides a springing point for the flying buttresses. Architecturally this
elevational treatment is an admirably lucid statement that is completed
on both the N and s sides by the return walls of the entrance block. Each
is treated individually and asymmetrically.

67. John Rylands Library, foyer.

Interior

The entrance hall, spacious and double-storeyed, together with the principal staircase on its s flank span the site's width. Both are rib-vaulted and form the most expressive architectural spaces in the building. They are designed to be seen sequentially, with a short main axis from the entrance to the cross-axis of a lateral aisle, from which the main staircase rises E. At the focal point is a heavily didactic sculpture, Theology Directing the Labours of Science and Art, by *John Cassidy* (1861–1939), which closes the axis like a reredos. The vaulting is divided into areas related to the aisles and the corner beneath the NE octagonal tower. Heavier piers define the latter space, and a row of double piers linked by ogee fretwork and carrying the weight of the E gable marks off the lateral aisle. Small vaults, narrow, steeply pitched and carried by slender, deeply moulded piers, flank the main aisle, where the bay size is increased from the entrance to a crowning tierceron vault that canopies the turning point and the symbolic sculpture. The character of the space is of lofty complexity and between the piers the two flights of the arcaded staircase can be seen rising within it. Their ascent reveals further drama, first because the hall is overlooked, then, above the half landing, an oculus penetrates the vaulting and opens into the octagonal tower and, finally, from the flight to an upper vestibule, from beneath cross-arcading it is gradually revealed that the facing wall is the soaring rear wall of the S rectangular tower. Neither the extravagance nor the drama of the design can be denied.

The Reading Room is a high, cathedral-like, tierceron-vaulted space, eight bays long, and the gable walls are filled by large, traceried windows that provide a field for stained glass. At the W end is a vaulted apse, specially designed to house a marble sculpture of John Rylands, also by *John Cassidy* as is the statue of Enriqueta Rylands at the entrance. The room is treated sculpturally, but less dramatically than the entrance hall, and it is not unlike the remarkable interior of J. L. Pearson's church of St Augustine, Kilburn (1870–80). Double-storey reading bays extend along each side and the laterally deep central piers are penetrated at gallery level by a passage. Each bay is arcaded at both levels. The lower bays are divided by central piers, the upper arcades span the full bay, and above them is the clerestory, which is the principal source of natural light to the room. The spatial character of the bays is enriched by the double-storey oriel windows, the openwork gallery fronts and the open traceried screens that separate the bays so that each forms a secluded aedicule for study.

The Reading Room is not over-richly decorated, but the gallery fronts are assertive with Victorian Dec carving, and the capitals of the mid-piers of the lower arcade provide pedestals for sculptures of literary or religious figures, selected by Mrs Rylands and carved by *Bridgeman's* of Lichfield. At the expense of the natural lighting, each gable window is panelled by two rows of figures in stained glass by *C. E. Kempe*. Those in the E window are of philosophers, writers and artists, and in the W are prophets and theologians.

Among the subsidiary rooms the two most notable are the Bible and the Aldine Rooms, which are superimposed over each other in the N octagonal tower. The former is octagonal, and the ceiling of the Aldine Room below it reflects the form above.

The wall finishes throughout the interior are red sandstone or panelled oak, and the unvaulted ceilings are of lightly modelled plaster panels designed by *George Frampton* (1860–1928), a prominent designer

68. John Rylands Library, Reading Room.

within the Arts and Crafts Movement. The vaulting of the main library is striated in two tones of sandstone, which adds a Ruskinian touch to the design.

Champneys and Mrs Rylands did not have an easy relationship and the design of the furniture, which was entrusted to the clerk-of-works, the choice of the figure sculpture, which Champneys considered to be 'tame and inartistic', the green glazing, the iconography of the stained glass, and the fine bronze railings and electrical fittings, supplied by *Singer*'s of Frome, were commissioned directly by Mrs Rylands. Singer's work is the most successful and is a notable Art Nouveau feature in its own right. However, Champneys was responsible for the highly effective design of the bookcases, which remain smooth running and dust-proof.

When completed the Rylands Library was notably advanced technically, with fire-resistant concrete construction, electric light and air conditioning. Stylistically, despite its Gothic elaboration, it illustrates an aesthetic freedom that points towards the Expressionism of the c20.

JHGA

Academic Institutions

N

Manchester
Metropolitan University
(Aytoun Campus)

Piccadilly
Station

MINSHULL ST.

AYTOUN ST.

CHORLTON STREET

OXFORD STREET

PRINCESS STREET

WHITWORTH STREET

SACKVILLE STREET

LONDON ROAD

Rochdale Canal

R. Medlock

CHARLES STREET

Oxford Road
Station

University of Manchester
Institute of Science
and Technology

MANCUNIAN WAY

GROSVENOR STREET

Manchester
Metropolitan
University

OXFORD ROAD

CAMBRIDGE STREET

Royal Northern
College of Music

BOOTH ST. EAST

UPPER BROOK STREET

BOOTH ST. WEST

University
of
Manchester

GRAFTON STREET

PENCROFT WAY

LLOYD ST. NORTH

DENMARK ROAD

1000 metres
1000 yards

69. Academic Institutions.

Introduction

Manchester has the largest urban higher-education precinct in Europe, and Chorlton-on-Medlock is the see of the majority of the academic institutions: University of Manchester, the Institute of Science and Technology (UMIST), Manchester Metropolitan University (MMU) and the Royal Northern College of Music (RNCM). They all grew from c19 institutions, but each of them has developed in its own way and there are few places where one feels that one's movements are directed by a plan. The City of Manchester Plan of 1945 envisaged expanding the educational centre from the site of the University of Manchester on Oxford Road and integrating it into a new road system in a scheme drawn up in collaboration with *Sir Hubert Worthington*. Existing poor-quality housing was to be cleared and academic, cultural and residential areas promoted. In the event clearances did not happen until the 1960s and 70s and the idea of giving the site cohesion by closing part of Oxford Road never came off. The Principal of UMIST, Lord Bowden, commissioned a plan for a student village which was drawn up by *John Sheard* of *Cruickshank & Seward c.* 1962, but in 1963 the City Council, University

70. Proposals for the University of Manchester precinct published in the *City of Manchester Plan* (1945). The original buildings are shown top centre.

of Manchester, UMIST and Manchester United Hospitals appointed *Sir Hugh Wilson* and *Lewis Womersley* to prepare a development plan for the whole of the education precinct (including the hospitals which occupy a site immediately to the s of the University of Manchester, *see* Outer Areas, Chorlton-on-Medlock). The report was published in 1967. They produced a grand design to connect the premises of the institutions and create one campus, more or less on the scale of Berkeley, California, and rather like the Smithsons' 1953 competition plan for Sheffield University. Vertical segregation of pedestrians and traffic would have been achieved by high-level walkways linking the University of Manchester campus with the College of Art and Design (now part of MMU), the Royal Northern College of Music and UMIST. With a few exceptions nothing much came of this, but several buildings put up in the wake of the plan were designed to link in with the upper walkways. Wilson & Womersley followed up the Precinct Report with a Materials and Landscape Report, recommending the use of white concrete and brown or blue brick in the UMIST complex, red brick for the University, and brown brick for the All Saints area. This was only adhered to loosely. Their review of the plan in 1974 reaffirmed the principle of high-level walkways and re-evaluated transport and infrastructure issues. The spending squeeze which followed ensured that the more ambitious elements of the scheme never came to fruition and there was little new building until the late 1990s.

The University of Manchester has from the C19 *Alfred Waterhouse*'s splendid original quad and its additions, and from the early C20 *Percy Scott Worthington*'s dignified Arts Faculty building. The only post-war contribution of real presence is the Mathematics Building by *Scherrer & Hicks*. At the Metropolitan University the oldest and best parts are the C19 Regional College of Art, now the Grosvenor Building, by *G. T. Redmayne* of 1881, as well as the extension by *J. Gibbons Sankey*. Of the post-war additions the Geoffrey Manton Building by *Sheppard Robson*, 1996–9, is more exciting than their rather bland 1970s work; otherwise only the Aytoun Library by *Mills Beaumont Leavey Channon* deserves special mention, and this is away from the main campus (*see* p. 206). The UMIST campus, which grew up close to the palatial Municipal School of Technology by *Spalding & Cross*, 1895–1902, has the most impressive of the post-war buildings, thanks mainly to the contribution of *W. A. Gibbon* of *Cruickshank & Seward*.

University of Manchester

Including the Federal School of Business and Management

The University of Manchester started as Owens College in 1851 under the will of John Owens who directed that members should not be required to subscribe to the Anglican creed. It was reorganized in 1870, incorporated the Royal Manchester School of Medicine in 1872, and moved to the present site in 1873. It became the first college of the new Victoria University in 1880, with Liverpool joining in 1884 and Leeds in 1887. In 1904 it achieved independence and autonomy. There was expansion up until the First World War, then a gap until the burst of building in the 1960s and 70s. Financial restraint which followed reduced new building to a trickle. The architectural development since the Second World War is a sad record. If the University of Liverpool asked too many architects to design their buildings and the result was lack of unity, the University of Manchester showed too little initiative, too easy a sense of satisfaction, and the result was lack of architectural interest. There is too much that is just run-of-the-mill. Most of the buildings are by local firms, but they did not produce the most innovative buildings, this distinction going to outsiders *Scherrer & Hicks* and *Building Design Partnership* (though by this time BDP had a Manchester Office). Of the local firms *Cruickshank & Seward*'s contribution does not match the confidence and style of their UMIST buildings and *Harry S. Fairhurst*

71. University of Manchester, w range of the quadrangle, the first buildings to be completed by Alfred Waterhouse (1869–74).

& *Son*'s carefully planned engineering, science and medical buildings are more notable for incorporating original artwork than for architectural interest. These contribute to the fairly representative range of 1960s and 70s public art to be seen in the precinct. The buildings of *J. S. Beaumont* are on the whole deplorably weak and unimaginative. The most significant new buildings, the School of Management by *ORMS* and *Hodder Associates'* Career Services Unit, are not really University buildings at all, though they are part of the Precinct Centre group.

The busy road bisecting the site and the variety of building styles and materials militate against coherence or a natural centre. The most characterful part is *Waterhouse*'s original quad and his subsidiary courtyard behind, though parking in both places detracts from the collegiate atmosphere. The only area with a sense of peace and space is w of Oxford Road between the Precinct Centre and the Museum where vehicles do not penetrate and there are trees and expansive lawns.

The University of Manchester area extends from Booth Street East and Booth Street West, N side, to Cambridge Street on the w, Upper Brook Street on the E and Denmark Road to the s. Since the 1980s there has been overspill on to the w side of Cambridge Street. Roughly speaking, to the w are Arts, to the E the Sciences. There are two Walks, the first covering the Waterhouse quad and its environs, mainly buildings in the first generation, the second covering the later buildings in a sweep from N to s.

Walk 1. The Waterhouse Quad and its Environs

Owens College appointed *Alfred Waterhouse* in 1869 and building began in 1870. The buildings are arranged around a quadrangle on the w side of Oxford Road with a subsidiary courtyard behind, to the w. The plan, different from today in many ways, was exhibited at the Royal Academy in 1872. Work was not completed until 1902 (*Paul Waterhouse* finished things off), but the buildings of the quad form a convincing whole in style, form and massing. The idiom was aptly described at the time as modern Gothic. They are of stone, in alternating narrow and wide masonry courses as at the town hall (*see* Major Buildings), with steep tiled roofs. Many of the buildings have exposed timber roofs in the upper rooms. There is economy and practicality of plan and construction, which is largely on the *Dennett & Co.* fireproof system. In 1896 *The Builder* thought the irregular appearance suggestive of spontaneous growth over time, but attention was paid to the overall appearance of the scheme as the individual elements were added, and massing according to the demands of function and visual effect would have been Waterhouse's aim, rather than historicism. In the oblique view from the

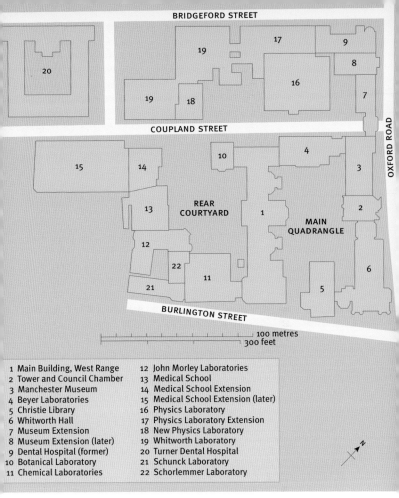

BRIDGEFORD STREET

COUPLAND STREET

REAR
COURTYARD

MAIN
QUADRANGLE

BURLINGTON STREET

OXFORD ROAD

100 metres
300 feet

1 Main Building, West Range
2 Tower and Council Chamber
3 Manchester Museum
4 Beyer Laboratories
5 Christie Library
6 Whitworth Hall
7 Museum Extension
8 Museum Extension (later)
9 Dental Hospital (former)
10 Botanical Laboratory
11 Chemical Laboratories
12 John Morley Laboratories
13 Medical School
14 Medical School Extension
15 Medical School Extension (later)
16 Physics Laboratory
17 Physics Laboratory Extension
18 New Physics Laboratory
19 Whitworth Laboratory
20 Turner Dental Hospital
21 Schunck Laboratory
22 Schorlemmer Laboratory

72. Walk 1. The Waterhouse Quad and its Environs.

N along Oxford Road the buildings are drawn together by the rhythm of buttresses, the dominant tower accentuated on the N side by a stair-turret, with the lower tower of the Whitworth Hall at the s end of the range acting as punctuation. The views down the streets on either side of the quad, Coupland Street (N) and Burlington Street (s), are also carefully managed.

It has not been possible to devise a straightforward Walk around the buildings because if the chronological order of building is completely disregarded the development of the site cannot easily be conveyed. In consequence there is some chopping and changing between the main quadrangle and Oxford Road.

We start in the main quadrangle. The w range (1) was the first to be built, along with the Chemical Laboratories and Medical School behind (for the two latter, *see* below), all completed by 1874. The building originally served teaching as well as administrative functions. It is quite low and intimate in scale. The outline with projections and recessions and the skyline are nicely varied. Polygonal entrance bays flank a central pavilion, and there is variation in the wings on each side and in the detail, for example the differently stepped lancets of the entrance bays expressing the presence and direction of the staircases within. Having two entrances reduced the amount of internal traffic. Inside, each staircase has a stone arcade with granite piers on both levels dividing it from the corridors.

The next phase was the N part of the range along Oxford Road and the N side of the quad, including the Museum and Beyer Laboratories, 1883–7. Now this was a building for a new university, so everything had to be grand. Waterhouse was equal to the challenge. From Oxford Road the high tower, fronting the block containing the council chamber (2) is crowned with one of Waterhouse's steep pyramid roofs. There is a bay window to its right with geometrical tracery, housing the main staircase. On entering you find yourself in vaulted spaces of E.E. character. The fascinating staircase, with its glimpses into subsidiary upper caged-in staircases, one of them treated as an oriel, has similarities with the main stair of his Manchester town hall (*see* Major Buildings). The double-height landing and corridor are spanned by a bridge reached from one of the subsidiary staircases which leads to the oak gallery of the council chamber. Apart from this gallery, which runs the full length of the E side of the room, and a marble **relief** showing Socrates by *Harry Bates*, 1886, the room is not as ornate as might be expected. Display was concentrated on the grand staircase approach, which also serves the Whitworth Hall to the s and the Museum to the N.

73. University of Manchester, main staircase in the tower (1883–7).

The **Manchester Museum** (3) was built to house the collections of the Manchester Society of Natural History and the Manchester Geological and Mining Society, which were transferred to Owens College in 1867. All is firmly utilitarian, with tripartite windows, of no period character whatever. Full-height buttresses set up a rhythm and extend above the eaves, ending in pyramidal caps. At the N end on the corner of Coupland Street there is a slightly projecting gabled block flanked by polygonal stair-turrets rising from second-floor level. The interior has a double-height ground floor and an excellent upper floor with wide galleries on two levels, reached by a cleverly designed iron stair which divides at the first level for access to the lower gallery, then turns back on itself as a bridge over the void, before continuing to the top level. The attached former **Beyer Laboratories** (4) (for which we must return to the quad) on the N side of the quad steps purposefully into the space, a grid of windows lighting the labs with a tall stone flèche providing the only

74. Oxford Road elevation by Alfred and Paul Waterhouse (1883–1902).

decorative incident. The interior is arranged so that zoology students could move easily between the collections in the Museum and their laboratories.

The S range of the quad, the **Christie Library**, (5) 1895–8, was the gift of Professor Richard Copley Christie. Another essay in free non-historicist Gothic, more relaxed than the Oxford Road frontage, with ranges of big dormers connected by arches. The stair projection on the W side was originally to have beside it a bridge link to the W range. The

75. University of Manchester, aerial view of the main quadrangle looking s.

stone cantilevered stair rises the full height of the building. Double-height upper room, with two arcades of alternatingly round and octagonal stone piers, and paired windows with detached inner shafts.

The range along Oxford Road to the s of the entrance tower consists of an archway to the quad and then the **Whitworth Hall**, (6) started 1898 and completed by *Paul Waterhouse* in 1902. The rhythm established with the Museum is answered in the full-height, flat-topped buttresses which frame high Perp windows. At the end is a large arched entrance, then on the corner of Burlington Street towers flank the gabled end bay of the hall with its great Perp window. The towers have magnificently sheer expanses of wall, relieved at the top by arcading, friezes and polygonal turrets. Upper-level seven-bay hall with a mighty hammer-beam roof, each truss springing from a detached stone pier.

The remaining parts which extend N from the Museum along Oxford Road are the **Museum extensions** by *Paul Waterhouse* of 1911–27, the last part finished by *Michael Waterhouse*. First there is a bridge link over Coupland Street. This has been raised and widened to improve links with the original Museum as part of a (so far successful) remodelling by *Ian Simpson Architects*, 2000–2, which will include a new entrance block on the N side of Coupland Street. Next a pavilion (7) with buttresses and upper turrets to the bays at each end continuing the vertical accents of the earlier part of the range. Perp motifs with a steep lead roof and charming flèche, two tall storeys with transomed windows below and traceried windows above (the back incidentally is very different from the front: brick with stone dressings). There follows a lower link and then the latest part, (8) a five-storey block framed by full-height polygonal turrets, mirroring in general appearance the end block of the original Museum building, but with different detailing.

The Museum extension is attached to the pre-existing former

Dental Hospital, (9) on the corner of Bridgeford Street, designed by *Charles Heathcote & Sons* in 1908. It is pretty, but a mismatch with the great sequence of Waterhouse buildings along Oxford Road. Brick with much stone, of five bays only, Edwardian Baroque, with a semicircular half-domed porch.

The rear courtyard, immediately w of the main quad, can be reached by returning to Coupland Street and walking w to the rear of the main quad (affording the opportunity of examining its carefully handled N elevation). The buildings are given their original names here, but most are in new uses. They are by Waterhouse with additions by Paul Waterhouse. The rear of the original 1873 building takes up the E side of the courtyard, simply and crisply treated, with a range of dormers linked by window strips to light the attics. Attached on the N side is the **Botanical Laboratory**, (10) 1911 by *Paul Waterhouse*. This is also crisp, but more ornate, with a big gable to the left containing a large arched window and a two-storey oriel to the right. The remaining buildings of the quad are stripped Gothic of 1871–1909, all of buff brick with stone dressings, chosen no doubt to harmonize with the pale stone of the main quad. Chimneys, pinnacles, turrets and flèches create a picturesque roofscape. On the S side are the **Chemical Laboratories**, (11) 1871–3, the elevation to the courtyard very simply treated (for Burlington Street side *see* below). Attached to the right is the relatively ornate **John Morley Laboratories,** (12) by *Paul Waterhouse*, opened in 1909, with a pretty stair-tower and an angled bay with large multi-paned windows. Beside it the **Medical School**, (13) opened in 1874, and to the right an extension of 1882–3. (14) Finally another extension (15) was added to the w in 1891–4 along Coupland Street. This is stepped out, with entrances in a corner tower with a tall pyramidal roof, which forms an incident in views w down the street.

Coupland Street is crowded on the N side with buildings and extensions of different dates, mostly in red brick. The principal elements are as follows, identified by their original names. Starting at the E end the **Physics Laboratory** (16) by *J. W. Beaumont* 1900–1. Stone dressings, transomed windows and an elaborate entrance. Beaumont collaborated with Professor Arthur Schuster in the interior arrangements. Behind it an extension (17) of 1912, also by *J. W. Beaumont*. The self-effacing **New Physics Laboratory** (18) 1930–1 by *Percy Scott Worthington* follows, attached by a later link to the **Whitworth Laboratory** (19) of 1909, by *J. W. Beaumont*, with two orders of pilasters. Another part of this building faces Bridgeford Street. The **Turner Dental Hospital**, formerly the Dental School, (20) by *Hubert Worthington*, 1939–40, is quite plain, with curved corners and horizontal emphasis given by white stone bands. It was completed by a fourth S range in 1951–2; additions of the 1990s are in matching style.

Walking S around the Medical School extension brings us out on the w end of Burlington Street. First on the N side is an oddity, the **Schunk**

Laboratory, (21) dated 1871. This was the distinguished chemist Dr Schunk's personal laboratory, brought from Kersal in Salford in 1904 and re-erected by *Paul Waterhouse* as a mirror image of the original. It is of the same buff brick as its neighbours, suggesting that this material may have been substituted for the original in the rebuilding. The neighbouring polygonal laboratory of 1904 has attached at the rear the **Schorlemmer Laboratory,** (22) by *Alfred Waterhouse*, opened in 1895. Finally the s side of the Chemical Laboratories (11) has buttresses echoing the s side of the original building of the main quad, the tumbled-in brickwork aptly acknowledging the change from stone to brick.

Walk 2 can be joined by returning to Oxford Road and heading N to the Precinct Centre which spans the road s of the junction with Booth Street East and Booth Street West.

Walk 2. The Later Buildings of the University of Manchester

The start is at the N end of the complex with the **Precinct Centre.**(1) By *Wilson & Womersley* in association with *H. Thomas*, University Planning Officer, 1970–2. It was conceived as the key building of the 1967 plan, though it was not the first one to be put up. The University promoted it as a commercial development, but although the offices were all let within two years, the shop units were never fully taken up. Red brick and red tiles spanning Oxford Road. On the upper level shops are ranged around two interconnected squares with glazed tent-like roofs. An upper-level walkway to the RNCM (*see* p. 135) crosses Booth Street West to the N. Only the E side of the Centre works, with co-ordination and connection with other buildings. Set back from the road, SE, and reached from a generous sweep of steps **St Peter's House** (2) by *Cruickshank & Seward* in matching red brick and tile, was part of the original scheme. It incorporates St Peter and its chaplaincy and, on the upper walkway, a small chapel, top-lit and simply treated. On the SW side there is a ramp, conceived as a temporary measure pending development on this side of the road.

The **Federal School of Business and Management** now occupies much of the Precinct Centre. The postgraduate School of Business building, (3) attached to the W of the Precinct Centre was designed *c.* 1972 by *Cruickshank & Seward* who were persuaded to match the existing style. In 1994 the University and UMIST decided to merge their departments of business, management, accountancy and policy research, and facilities were concentrated in and near the existing Business School. Parts of the E side of the complex were taken over and remodelled and new build-

76. Walk 2. The Later Buildings of the University of Manchester.

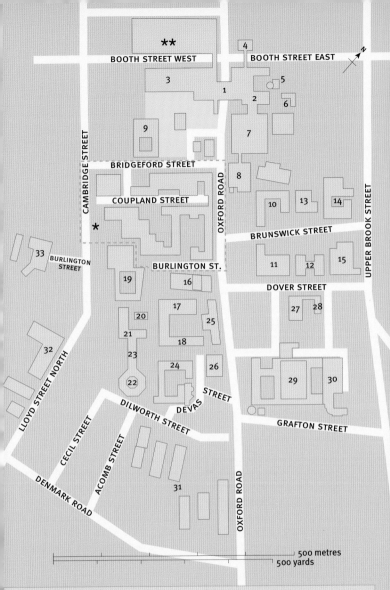

BOOTH STREET WEST ✱✱ **BOOTH STREET EAST**

CAMBRIDGE STREET

BRIDGEFORD STREET

COUPLAND STREET

OXFORD ROAD

✱

BURLINGTON STREET

BURLINGTON ST.

BRUNSWICK STREET

DOVER STREET

UPPER BROOK STREET

LLOYD STREET NORTH

CECIL STREET

ACOMB STREET

DILWORTH STREET

DEVAS STREET

GRAFTON STREET

DENMARK ROAD

OXFORD ROAD

500 metres
500 yards

N

1 Precinct Centre	17 Faculty of Arts
2 St Peter's House	18 Faculty of Arts (extension)
3 Federal School of Business and Management	19 John Rylands University Library
4 School of Management	20 Stephen Joseph Drama Studio
5 School of Accounting and Finance Lecture Theatre	21 Mansfield Cooper Building
6 Career Services Unit	22 AQA Building
7 Computer Centre	23 AQA Building (extension)
8 Mathematics Building	24 Humanities Building
9 Architecture and Planning Building	25 Students' Union
10 Williamson Building	26 Academy
11 Simon Engineering Laboratories	27 High School for Girls (former)
12 Electrical Engineering Building	28 Social Science and Economics Building
13 Roscoe Building	29 Stopford Building
14 Schuster Building	30 Biotech Building
15 Chemistry Building	31 Whitworth Park Student Accommodation
16 Moberly Tower, Staff House and Refectory	32 Science Park
	33 McDougall Sports Centre

✱ See University of Manchester, Walk 1, the Waterhouse Quad and its environs

✱✱ See Royal Northern College of Music

ings were put up. The **School of Management** (4) by *ORMS*, 1997–8, lies on the N side of Booth Street East. In a revival of the 1960s ideal, it is connected to the Precinct Centre at upper level by a footbridge. A stone-clad base contrasts with glazed upper floors, expressing the interior arrangement of offices above teaching rooms and lecture theatres.

On the S side of the street, attached to the E side of the Precinct Centre, is a white drum with approaches at two levels, very well integrated into its surroundings. It contains the 400-seat **lecture theatre** of the School of Accounting and Finance, (5) based on a concept of 1996 by *Hodder Associates* (but carried out through a design and build arrangement). A short detour S brings us to the **Career Services Unit**, (6 and illus. 31) offices of an independent company offering a nationwide careers service. *Hodder Associates* won the competition in 1995. The L-shaped building is carefully related to its surroundings. Three storeys, rendered white, with strong forms and patterns of projection and recession, solid and void. The E side has a projecting linear office range with window slits at the first floor; to the right is the windowless gable of the adjoining range above an offset ground-floor glass window bay; finally a two-storey porte-cochère of white slabs at right angles to one another marking the entrance around the corner on the N side.

Returning to the Precinct Centre upper level, the walkway continues S past St Peter's House into the upper part of the **Computer Centre** (7) by *Building Design Partnership* in association with *H. Thomas*, opened in 1972. Three storeys, 250 ft (76 metres) square, at the time one of the largest computer science centres in the country. A big aggressive box of brick piers and vertical window strips. The walkway leads to an upper paved piazza with Perret-style demi-columns and a central rectangular pool with a fibreglass sculpture designed to move in the wind. The extension of 1988 on the E side houses information-technology laboratories. Continuing S the walkway becomes a dismal corridor but leads to one of the most interesting buildings of this group, *Scherrer & Hicks*'s **Mathematics Building**, (8) 1967–8. The general massing had to follow the Wilson & Womersley proposals which decreed that this should be the main vertical element of the scheme and link ground-level and high-level circulation. It was the first building erected after publication of the plan and remains the tallest of the University buildings. A sixteen-storey tower standing on one corner of a three-storey podium with cantilevered lecture theatres. Concrete-framed, with brick facing. The tower is assertively composed of free cubic shapes stepping vertically and horizontally. Tall piers enclose a ramped stair leading to the recessed entrance at first-floor level, i.e. in the expressionist brutalist style of the moment. In the podium courtyard a **sculpture** by *Michael Yeomans* looks like an organic growth attacking the walls.

Architecture and Planning Building, (9) Oxford Road W side, is almost opposite the Maths tower but set well back behind Waterloo Place (*see* Outer Areas, Chorlton-on-Medlock, p. 318) on the edge of a

77. Mathematics Building, Oxford Road, by Scherrer & Hicks (1967–8).

grassy enclave. By the building's then inhabitants, Professors *N. L. Hanson, R. H. Kantarowich*, with *M. C. Schonegevel & G. Skacel*, opened in 1970. Grey concrete with grooved ribs acting as a giant order. The top part bulges out and there is a recess at the s end and answering projection at the N end, this with removable panels to receive upper level walkway links to unrealized buildings to the E and w. Inside there is a large attractive courtyard with pools and a **sculpture: Head of Ra** by *Barbara Hepworth*, 1972, on loan from the Hepworth Estate.

Back on Oxford Road is a group of 1957–67, designed around the monumental w–e axis of Brunswick Street which had been proposed by Worthington. Most are set well back from the line of the road. With two exceptions they are by *Harry S. Fairhurst & Son* (i.e. *H. M. Fairhurst*), of brick with copper-clad ribs and roofs. Starting at the N corner of Brunswick Street: the **Williamson Building** (10) with a big sun relief by *Lynn Chadwick*. Opposite, s side **Simon Engineering**

Laboratories. (11) Immediately E the pattern is broken by **Electrical Engineering** (12) by *J. S. Beaumont*, 1953, frankly Neo-Georgian at this late hour. Opposite, a breath of fresh air, the **Roscoe Building**, (13) by *Cruickshank & Seward*, 1964, lecture theatres and classrooms gathered together in one building following the principle of their Renold Building on the UMIST campus (*see* p. 124). White concrete, with a six-floor glass façade. Not a building of great individuality but one of the best in the area. To the E two more by *H. M. Fairhurst*: the **Schuster Building**, (14) N side, physics and astronomy departments. Here there is variation with a polygonal chapter house of a lecture theatre attached to the left of the entrance, the copper-clad roof crowned by an abstract **sculpture** by *Michael Piper*. Opposite, s side, the **Chemistry Building,** (15) with big circular reliefs at the entrance by *Hans Tisdall* representing the elements.

78. The Elements (detail) by Hans Tisdall (*c.* 1967). Chemistry Building entrance, Brunswick Street.

We return to Oxford Road and Waterhouse's quadrangle, w side, where Walk 1 can be joined. To the s **Moberly Tower** (a hall of residence), **Staff House** and **Refectory** (16) by *J. S. Beaumont*, 1960–5, characterless and deplorably unsubstantial next to Waterhouse. The relief panel on the N side is by *Mitzi Solomon Cunliffe*. There are plans to alter this part and remove the tower altogether. The **Faculty of Arts** (17) by *Percy Scott Worthington* 1911–19, lies to the s, set well back from Oxford Road. The *Architectural Review* in 1920 expressed its approval of the choice of style 'which accords admirably with present-day progress and development'. Red brick and Portland stone, symmetrical with a classical stone portico. Projecting entrance with two Roman Doric columns and projecting wings. The entrance leads to a noble hall, top-lit, with Ionic columns and a coffered barrel roof, which Worthington was to re-create on an even grander scale for his Masonic Hall (*see* Inner City, Walk 3, p. 249). Stately corridors lead off to the E and w, top-side lit by semicircular windows in circular openings, with on each side tall arcades of openings for offices etc. To the w a brick addition with sash windows erected by *H. M. Fairhurst* in the 1950s to designs by *Sir Hubert Worthington*, who was too busy to do it himself. The white concrete and Portland stone extensions at the rear (s) and running E from the w wing (18) are additions of *c.* 1970 by *Cruickshank & Seward*, Corbusian external stairs and a curving rooftop pavilion containing a library, the interior of which is an exciting space with big circular rooflights and very narrow vertical window slits on one side only.

The paved area fronting the Arts Faculty gives the building space and links with connected open areas to the w. On the w side the **John Rylands University Library,** (19) 1935–7, is by *Percy Scott Worthington*. Symmetrical, presenting a dignified and orderly façade to the square. Portland stone below and red brick and stone dressings above, with pairs of vertically linked windows and projecting bowed end bays. The L-shaped rear (w) extension is a self-effacing addition by *Sir Hubert Worthington* of the mid 1950s. Attached to the N at the E end of **Burlington Street** is a large red brick four-storey extension with a new main entrance by *Dane, Scherrer & Hicks* opened in 1982. Four roof projections create a distinctive outline, which closes views w along Burlington Street.

To the s of the library the **Stephen Joseph Drama Studio** (20) occupies a former German Protestant church, a small low-key affair of stone with lancets probably of the mid or late 1860s. Immediately s the large brick **Mansfield Cooper Building** (geography department) (21) is by *Cruickshank & Seward*, 1975–7. This is attached on the s side to the AQA (Assessment and Qualifications Alliance) building, formerly the Joint Examination Board, (22) not strictly a building put up by the University of Manchester. It is by *Playne & Lacey*, 1962. Octagonal, and with a pointed roof ending in a nice lantern. Altogether it is an intimate building, as befits its function. The octagonal shape suited the fact that the core of the building had to be one large packing room for examination papers. The extension (23) to the N, by the *Playne Vallance Partnership*, was erected *c.* 1975. This is joined to the Mansfield Cooper Building by an attractive linking block clad in timber planks with variously horizontal, slanting and zigzag window strips, by *Short Ford Associates*, 1999 (illus. 79).

To the E behind the Arts Faculty is the **Humanities Building** (24) 1961–7 by *G. G. Baines* of *Building Design Partnership*. A building of some power. It is of brown concrete, bush-hammered, with the verticals of the frame projecting in front of the wall. Low left addition with abstract concrete reliefs designed by *William Mitchell* of the sort which were so overdone at that time. This brings us back towards Oxford Road and the **Students' Union** (25) w side, 1953–6 by *J. S. Beaumont*, stone faced and stodgy, given a revamp in 1999. Also fronting Oxford Road, to the s, the 1980s **Academy**, (26) a big shed used for student entertainments and events.

79. Linking block by Short Ford Associates (1999) between the Mansfield Cooper Building and the AQA building extension.

Now we cross the road and retrace our steps to **Dover Street**, which runs E. The former **High School for Girls**, (27) s side, by *Mills & Murgatroyd*, 1881–6, is now the Department of Economic Studies and the Department of Government Faculty Administration. Red brick heightened by a few touches of stone and red terracotta and an eye-level animal carving at the entrance, in the sort of Northern Gothic established by Waterhouse and Thomas Worthington as a civic style a decade before. The tall pyramidal roof echoes Waterhouse's University buildings. Next to it the **Social Science and Economics Building** (28) by *Cruickshank & Seward*, 1966–7, white concrete, with a core clad in dark grey brick, the windows boxed out in canted surrounds. Each projecting panel expresses the presence internally of a staff room.

The **Stopford Building** (29) is reached by returning to Oxford Road and turning s past the Church of the Holy Name of Jesus (*see* Outer Areas, Chorlton-on-Medlock). This is the Medical School, by *H. S. Fairhurst & Son*, in association with University Planning Officer *H. Thomas* 1969–72. A huge building stretching E from the street frontage, the largest medical school in Europe of its day, sited here for convenient communication with the adjacent teaching hospitals (*see* Outer Areas, Chorlton-on-Medlock). Four storeys, brown brick, crowned with a concrete frieze to a design by *Antony Hollaway*. On the roof ranks of copper-clad ventilators. Linked to it on the E side is the **Biotech Building** (30) fronting Grafton Street. By *Fairhurst Design Group* completed 1999, reminiscent of the American architect Richard Meier with sparkling white cladding in the style introduced to Manchester by Mills Beaumont Leavey Channon's 1990 Siemens Building in Didsbury, q.v. *Manchester and South-East Lancashire* (forthcoming), but executed without their flair. The front has a big angled entrance and attached single-storey café, but the E side is poorly resolved. It contains laboratories designed for advanced biomedical and biological research projects.

Whitworth Park Student Accommodation, (31) Oxford Road w side a little to the s, by *Building Design Partnership* 1973–4. Low blocks in traditional materials with roof sections sloping down to the ground following the original street pattern and creating a pleasant domestic atmosphere, a reaction against the big accommodation blocks of the previous decade. A row of shops, cafés, etc. was erected as a second phase on the E side, fronting Oxford Road.

Outliers

Science Park (32) w side of Lloyd Street North. A group of unremarkable 1980s and 90s buildings erected as a joint initiative between the University and the private sector.

McDougall Sports Centre (33) Burlington Street. 1885 by *J. R. Hillkirk*. This originated as a Drill Hall of the Third Manchester Rifle Volunteers. It was converted to a physical education centre for the University in 1939 by *J. S. Beaumont*.

University of Manchester Institute of Science and Technology (UMIST)

This is part of the University but remains an autonomous body dealing direct with the University Grants Committee. It started as a successor to the Mechanics Institute which became a municipal college. New buildings were erected s of the C19 buildings on Sackville Street from 1962 and the area was incorporated into the *Wilson & Womersley* 1963–7 Educational Precinct Plan (*see* pp. 105–6). The 1849 MSJ&AR viaduct cuts across the precinct of the Institute, with older buildings on the N side of it and most of the newer to the s lying on low ground in a loop of the (culverted) Medlock, w of London Road.

We start with the earliest part, to the N, with the front to Sackville Street, built for the Municipal School of Technology by *Spalding & Cross*, 1895–1902. (1) A splendid expression of municipal pride and confidence. It is a grand composition in the Loire style, looking larger than its five storeys, with a gabled gatehouse-type entrance bay flanked by octagonal turrets and a big arched portal. Brick with red sandstone, lavishly decorated with tawny-red terracotta panels with Renaissance motifs by *Burmantofts*. The prominent dome on the Whitworth Street side houses an observatory, the gift of Frances Godlee. The deep plan consists of rooms in four blocks along the street frontages, with superimposed halls at the centre flanked by light-wells faced in white glazed brick.

Interior. The foyer is lit by a glazed entrance screen with stained glass, part of an extensive and attractive scheme by *W. J. Pearce*. Stairs with terracotta balustrades lead to the lower hall, an impressive space with large square piers clad in terracotta following the theme of the exterior, decorative terracotta panels in the window reveals, and large five-light transomed windows. The main staircase lies to the rear of the hall. This too is elaborate, with a chunky balustrade clad in brownish terracotta. The upper hall has a vaulted ceiling encrusted with plasterwork. The enormous extension, separated by a courtyard behind, was designed in 1927, by *Bradshaw, Gass & Hope*, but only completed in 1957, a gross anachronism by then. Red brick and much yellow terracotta, Norman Shaw gables, and a high set-back top at right angles.

80. University of Manchester Institute of Science and Technology (UMIST).

1 Main Building
2 Chandos Hall
3 Renold Building
4 Barnes Wallis Building
   and Wright Robinson Hall
5 Staff House
6 Moffat Building
7 Chemical Engineering
   Pilot Plant
8 Jackson Street Mill
9 Mathematics and
   Social Sciences Building
10 Ferranti Building
11 Pariser Building
12 Faraday Building
13 George Begg Building
14 Paper Science Building
15 Weston Building

To the s of the building a park with **sculptures**, most with a scientific or technological theme, for example **Technology**, parabolic metal cables, 1989, by *Axel Wolkenhauer* and beneath a railway arch, **Archimedes** by *Thompson W. Dagnall*.

Chandos Hall by *Cruickshank & Seward* (in charge *W. A. Gibbon*), 1962–4, (2) overlooks the gardens from the E. Fifteen storeys with ribbed white concrete walls, and a roomy glass staircase tower on one side. The windows of the rooms are units, not parts of bands, and they are not over-large. For 160 students, each floor designed as a unit with study bedrooms and a common room with a kitchen. This was a response to

81. Etched glass at the entrance to the main UMIST building, Sackville Street, by Spalding & Cross (1895–1902), showing the building itself.

research showing that smaller groupings within large halls of residence helped to foster friendship and a sense of community. On the s side of the viaduct is a pleasant elevated walkway. Many of the railway arches are open so there is a visual link between the old and new areas. The post-war buildings have a sense of purpose lacking in most of their contemporaries at the University. This is largely owing to the confidence of those designed by *W. A. Gibbon* of *Cruickshank & Seward*. Corbusier and Niemeyer influences are evident. We start at the heart of the complex where a turfed precinct forms a little square reached from the viaduct walkway by a handsome flying staircase descending in two arms. Part of the c19 cast-iron structure of Havelock Mills (dem., *see* topic box, Introduction p. 15, and City Centre, Great Bridgewater Street) has been reconstructed at the base. To the w the **Renold Building** by *W. A. Gibbon*, 1962, (3) a six-storey tower on a two-storey base, a building of lecture theatres with one for 500, two for 300, six for 140, and twelve smaller ones. The idea was to provide a central facility for rooms that would otherwise be dispersed amongst separate departmental buildings, a new initiative in British academic planning at that time. Generous transparent stair-tower on the nw side. The e face is a folded white concrete wall with angled window strips lighting the lecture theatres. The entrance hall is impressive, on two levels with Perretesque columns and a stair. In the lower hall **mural: Metamorphosis** by *Victor Pasmore*, 1968.

To the e **Students' Union** (Barnes Wallis Building) with the **Wright Robinson Hall**, (4) a podium with a fifteen-storey tower of residence behind, part of one integrated plan and erected in 1963–6 by

82. UMIST Campus. On the right, Renold Building (1962), on the left, Wright Robinson Hall (1963–6), both by W. A. Gibbon of Cruickshank & Seward.

W. A. Gibbon. It is all in white concrete with shuttering marks. The site had been designated for this use in the Campus Development Plan and the scale and form relate to the earlier Renold Building and Chandos Hall (*see* above) by the same architects. The Union building is supported on free-standing columns, finished to give a fluted effect like those of the Renold Building. They create a loggia at the sw entrance and s side. Vertically stabbing roof erections like funnels give light to the stairs.

Staff House (5) on the s side of the square by *Thomas Worthington*, 1960, extended 1968, slotted in behind the mill building (*see* below). An uncompromising frame of big squares, four storeys with a loggia on two sides with Perretesque piers. On the s side, abutting the mill, is a friendly semicircular stair-tower in brick. E of the Union and Renold Buildings the unremarkable brick **Moffat Building** (Ophthalmics) of 1967. (6) Behind, to the E a blocky sculptural boundary wall by *Antony Hollaway*, *c.* 1965. Prefabricated textured concrete panels slotted into concrete columns. It was designed to have grass growing on it and gradually to blacken as atmospheric deposits were laid down. It extends s as far as the excellent **Chemical Engineering Pilot Plant** by

83. Chemical Engineering Pilot Plant, UMIST Campus, by H. M. Fairhurst of
H. S. Fairhurst & Son (1966).

H. M. Fairhurst of *H. S. Fairhurst & Son*, 1966. (7) Engineering brick s,
glass N, boldly dividing the building into two halves. The glass part
is open through four storeys and crowned by a contrastingly solid-
looking cooling plant hovering above the roof. This part is designed for
students to erect their own large-scale experimental rigs. In the other
part services, and single- and double-height laboratories.

To the w **Jackson Street Mill** (Chemical Engineering), (8) a large,
brick mid-C19 cotton-spinning mill, utilitarian in design apart from an
unusually ornate Italianate entrance bay. The building was converted to
chemistry laboratories in just six months by *H. S. Fairhurst & Son*, in
1959. It all had to be done cheaply and quickly. s of this **Mathematics
and Social Sciences** (illus. 29), by *W. A. Gibbon* of *Cruickshank &
Seward*, 1966–8, (9) a fifteen-storey tower block, and a landmark – it is
the highest and most noticeable building of the complex. A subtle composition with careful grouping of the blocks which have huge brutal
expanses of precast shuttering. The two vertical circulation blocks
extend above the main roof level. Attached to the E of the tower is a
two-storey lecture-theatre block, windowless except in the circulation,
continuing the brutal vocabulary of bare concrete. Attached on the sw
side of the main building the **Ferranti Building** (Electrical Engineering),
(10) by the same architects. A low three-storey reinforced concrete
block, with at the w end a High Voltage Laboratory, a stark box clad in
ribbed aluminium. It was positioned to the s to admit the maximum
amount of sunlight to the grassed area in the angle of the buildings.
Here a **sculpture** if it can be called that, pleasing and appropriate
though it is: **Insulator Family**, three high-voltage ceramic insulators supplied by *Allied Insulators* of Stoke-on-Trent, installed in 1987. To the NW
the **Pariser Building** (Civil, Structural and Mechanical Engineering);

H. M. Fairhurst, 1963, (11) brick with copper cladding. The interior, as with all of Fairhurst's laboratory buildings, was designed to offer the greatest possible flexibility. The low building attached to the E is the Hydraulics Laboratory. Opposite, the **Faraday Building** (Chemistry), also by *H. M. Fairhurst*, 1967, (12) concrete and quite extensive. The abstract patterning of the concrete surfaces was designed by *Antony Hollaway*. There is a high slab, a bridge across Sackville Street, and a four-storey part. The E part is for undergraduates, the w part for graduates, and in the bridge there is a library, originally designed as a link between the two. The entrance opposite the Pariser Building is arcaded with a coffered roof. In the first two entrance bays, covering the whole of the rear walls, textured **mosaics** entitled The Alchemist's Elements, by *Hans Tisdall*, 1967.

To the w, also by *Fairhursts*, of similar date, the **George Begg Building**, 1974 (Mechanical Engineering), (13) with huge basement laboratories incorporating engine cells and an upper part with drawing offices, lecture rooms, etc. Fronting the E side of Sackville Street, just to the N, is the 1960s Paper Science Building. (14) Opposite is the **Weston Building**, (15) 1991 by *Downs & Variava* with extensions completed in 2000 by *Halliday Meecham*. Conference centre with lecture rooms and student residences. Big, dull brick blocks with pitched roofs and no memorable features whatever. What a come down after all the 1960s bravado.

For the Sugden Sports Centre *see* MMU, p. 134; the Federal School of Business and Management *see* University of Manchester, Walk 2, and the Languages Department *see* Outer Areas, Chorlton-on-Medlock, Walk 2.

Manchester Metropolitan University

The John Dalton College of Technology, the College of Commerce and the Regional College of Art were merged as Manchester Polytechnic in 1970. University status came in 1990. Spread over seven different sites, it is one of the largest universities in the country. The main buildings in central Manchester occupy the area N of the University of Manchester between Oxford Road (E), Cambridge Street (W), Rosamond Street West (S) and Chester Street (N). For the Aytoun Buildings, originally the College of Commerce site, *see* City Centre, Whitworth Street. The centre of the site is Grosvenor Square.

Grosvenor Square was designated a cultural centre in the City of Manchester Plan of 1945 and confirmed as the main campus for the city's colleges in the 1967 *Wilson & Womersley* plan for the educational precinct (*see* pp. 105–6). Buildings of the John Dalton College of Technology and the College of Art were already established in the immediate area (*see* p. 131, below). *Sheppard Robson* were appointed architects for the new polytechnic in 1971, with *Gordon Taylor* in charge of the project. Their Development Plan of 1972 identified sites for new buildings around the square, of which only the College of Art building and the former town hall (both now the Grosvenor Building, *see* below, p. 131) were to be retained, along with the recently completed St Augustine (*see* Outer Areas, Chorlton-on-Medlock, Churches). The city council was already in possession of large parcels of land in the area, partly as a result of acquisitions for the construction of the Mancunian Way (*see* Outer Areas, Chorlton-on-Medlock, Walk 2) which divides the All Saints area from the College of Technology buildings to the N. The plans were never fully realized and more of the existing buildings around the square were retained and converted. The effect is pleasing in variety.

To the N of the Mancunian Way on the W side of Oxford Road, the **Faculty of Technology**, (1) a descendant of the Mechanics' Institute and Municipal College of Technology. The first building of 1966 by the *City Architect's Department* is a conventional tower with a glass stair attached. The extension of 1974 is by *W. Heppell, City Architect's Department*. Five storeys, all but the ground floor with continuous windows with slanting

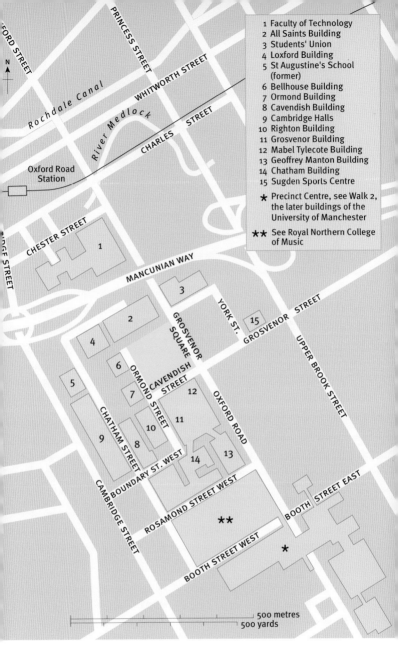

1 Faculty of Technology
2 All Saints Building
3 Students' Union
4 Loxford Building
5 St Augustine's School (former)
6 Bellhouse Building
7 Ormond Building
8 Cavendish Building
9 Cambridge Halls
10 Righton Building
11 Grosvenor Building
12 Mabel Tylecote Building
13 Geoffrey Manton Building
14 Chatham Building
15 Sugden Sports Centre

★ Precinct Centre, see Walk 2, the later buildings of the University of Manchester

★★ See Royal Northern College of Music

84. Manchester Metropolitan University.

glazing bars angled upwards from the concrete frame, somewhat in the manner of the GLC's Pimlico School of 1966–70. To the w single-storey engineering workshops of similar date have a jaunty stepped roofline. The main entrance is recessed back from Chester Street. Beside it a

bronze **statue** of John Dalton by *William Theed* after *Chantrey*, 1855,
moved from Piccadilly in 1966.

Grosvenor Square, the heart of the campus, if it can be called that,
lies immediately s of the Mancunian Way, w of Oxford Road. It is known
as All Saints, after the church which stood there until it was demolished
following war damage. A pleasant park has been created on the site.

The **All Saints Building** (2) by *Gordon Taylor* of *Sheppard Robson*,
opened in 1978, takes up the whole of the N side, housing the Arts Library,
offices and administration. Brownish-red brick, with parts of three,
four and five storeys. It has a relaxed look and it works well in an understated way. The entrance to Oxford Road was remodelled by *Mills
Beaumont Leavey Channon* in 1999–2000 and exhibition spaces created
in the ground-floor reception area. On the opposite side of the road the
Students' Union, (3) opened in 1980, is also of brownish-red brick.

The **Loxford Building** (4) adjoining the All Saints Building to the w
was designed by *City Architects* in 1974. It was the first of a series of
multi-purpose buildings on the site, combining teaching suites with
accommodation. Brick with eleven-storey towers with angled window
bays to the accommodation units, windowless service towers, and a
three-storey lower part.

The former **St Augustines School** (5) lies w of the square on Chatham
Street. Low brick buildings of the mid 1960s leased by the polytechnic
from the Roman Catholic Diocese of Salford in 1983.

The **Bellhouse Building**, (6) (Ormond Street, w side), on the w side
of the square. A town house built in 1831 for the Bellhouse family, the
most successful building contractors in Manchester of the day. Only the
façade is original. Three storeys with a central entrance and a pedimented window above. It was converted *c.* 1910 by *Thomas Worthington
& Sons* for the Manchester Ear Hospital but became offices in 1987.

Ormond Building, s, (7) on the corner of Cavendish Street. The site was originally occupied by a house built in 1796 for the cotton manufacturer Samuel Marsland whose mill can be seen on Cambridge Street nearby (*see* Outer Areas, Chorlton-on-Medlock, Walk 1). The present building, by *Mangnall & Littlewood*, opened 1881 as Offices of the Poor Law Guardians and a Registry Office and was taken over by the polytechnic in 1970. Two storeys with a basement, ornate in red brick with stone dressings. The building gathers itself up towards the Cavendish Street corner where there is an octagonal upper-floor oriel surmounted by a turret with an elongated dome and cupola. The roofline is varied here by a balustraded parapet and ornate paired chimneys linked at the top with pediments. The **interior** has a top-lit stair with upper and lower arcades of granite columns, and a large top-lit hall. The windows on the N side show allegorical scenes of Charity. Ranged along Chatham Street to the w and straddling Cavendish Street, the **Cavendish Building**, (8) *Sheppard Robson*, 1978, similar in style to their other buildings here, is another multi-purpose building for teaching and accommodation. It replaced a Congregational chapel of 1848 by Edward Walters. The view w down Cavendish Street is continued by the entrance to one of the courtyards of **Cambridge Halls**, (9) self-catering student accommodation, by *Cruickshank & Seward*, 1998. The buildings occupy the space between Chatham Street and Cambridge Street to the w. Overpoweringly bright red brick four-storey blocks with service towers crowned by concave caps.

The **Righton Building** (10) occupies the s corner of Cavendish Street and Ormond Street. Built as a draper's shop, named and dated 1905 in a raised parapet over the entrance, and taken over in 1970. White glazed brick and buff terracotta, two storeyed, with a partially altered lower floor and long upper-floor ranges of pedimented transomed windows alternating with oriels.* It has probably the best preserved Edwardian **shop interior** in the city. There are two light-wells, with a common gallery, reached by the original Jacobean-style stair. Both levels have cast-iron columns with attractive foliated capitals. Balustrades around the wells have Art Nouveau ironwork, and the roof of the larger has iron trusses with pierced spandrels.

The **Grosvenor Building** (11) (Faculty of Art and Design), two buildings: the original Regional College of Art building to the w, the Chorlton-on-Medlock Town Hall and Dispensary to the E. First the College of Art building, 1880–1, designed by *G. T. Redmayne*. The college began as the School of Design in 1838, renamed the School of Art in 1853, which became a sectional department of the Royal Manchester Institution; in 1892 it became the Municipal School of Art. It is a remarkable building. Gothic and symmetrical, with a central entrance, but take the period details away and you have Mackintosh's Glasgow School of Art of 1898,

*According to Terry Wyke the use of white glazed brick on one of the walls was required to respect ancient lights, perhaps laying the basis for the decorative scheme.

86. Grosvenor
Building,
Cavendish
Street. Former
town hall and
dispensary by
Richard Lane
(1830–1).

i.e. an ornate treatment of the centre but otherwise all frank large studio windows. The entrance has a moulded arched head, richly carved spandrels and a little three-light oriel above flanked by circular tourelles with conical caps. This is flanked by three arcaded bays and one continuous strip of north-light studio glazing across the roof. At each end gabled wings have large simply treated upper windows with pointed heads. By 1880 women formed part of both student and teaching bodies, and a separate studio for female students served by a segregated stair was part of the original design. At the back is an excellent extension of red brick and orange terracotta, dated 1897. It is by *J. Gibbons Sankey* and has three plain gables and one tier of terracotta E.E. two-light windows with angels in the tympana designed by *W. J. Neatby*, the head of the Architectural Department at *Doulton's*. The interior has three linked top-lit studio/exhibition halls at upper level separated by corridors with round-headed terracotta arcades with more beautiful Art Nouveau motifs in the capitals and spandrels, by Neatby again. Unfortunately

87. Extension to the Grosvenor Building by J. Gibbons Sankey (1897), with terracotta designed by W. J. Neatby.

they have been treated carelessly, there is some damage and parts have been painted. Various extensions were made in the early C20.

Next the former Chorlton-on-Medlock Town Hall and Dispensary. It is dignified by being set back from the line of the street. By *Richard Lane*, 1830–1, nine bays wide, with a Greek Doric pedimented portico based on 'Doric Portico in Athens' from Stuart & Revett's *Antiquities of Athens*. Severity is relieved only by lion masks and Lane's hallmark wreaths in the frieze. The functions of the Chorlton Police Commissioners who operated from the town hall part of the building were taken over in 1842. A variety of uses followed before it was taken over by the School of Art, though the trustees of the dispensary did not sell their part of the building until 1952. The façade only survives.

Adjoining, on the corner of Oxford Road, the **Mabel Tylecote Building** (Drama Department), (12) by *City Architect's Department* 1973, originated as a purpose-built college of adult education. It was designed to link in with the high-level walkways of the *Wilson & Womersley* plan (*see* pp. 105–6). Oversailing upper floor of exposed concrete, brick lower part with concrete ribs. It was taken over by the Metropolitan University in 1991.

Geoffrey Manton Building (Humanities), (13) 1996–9 by *Sheppard Robson*, fronts Oxford Road to the s. A ground-floor glass screen gives views of the atrium. The principal entrance is from a courtyard on the w side. At the corner there is a full-height triangular tower, from which a glass-sided first-floor level bridge connects with the Grosvenor Building. An entrance beside the tower leads to a large atrium with a tubular-steel roof. The generosity of the space and the views from the different levels give an open airy feeling, at the cost of some rooms lacking natural light.

88. Geoffrey Manton Building, Oxford Road, by Sheppard Robson (1996–9).

Student activities are concentrated on the lower floors, where there are lecture theatres, exhibition spaces, etc., with staff offices above.

To the w another bridge of unexpected geometrical shapes, with hexagonal roofs to each section, connects the 1897 College of Art extension building diagonally with the well-composed **Chatham Building**, (14) the Faculty of Art and Design. Nine-storey block by the *City Architect's Department (S. G. Besant Roberts)* of 1966–71. Straightforward bands of glass and white panels and a lower part to the w.

The **Sugden Sports Centre** 1996–7 by *Downs & Variava* (15) was a joint project with UMIST. It lies to the E on Grosvenor Street, N side.

Royal Northern College of Music

Oxford Road and Booth Street West

The Royal Manchester College of Music was founded in 1893 and had as its first principal Charles Hallé. In 1972 it merged with the Northern School of Music, which began as a private music school formed by Hilda Collens in 1920 and became a public institution in 1943.

Premises for the institution were built on Oxford Road and Booth Street West by *Bickerdike, Allen, Rich & Partners*, 1968–73. A concrete rectangle only two storeys high, the top solid except for window strips, double-height spaces below, slightly recessed behind tall stilts. On the s side glazed bays to the right light the original foyer and the stair. It was designed to accommodate high-level walkways linking with surrounding buildings, but only the one to the Precinct Centre, s (*see* the University of Manchester, Walk 2), spanning Booth Street West, was built. The others are truncated at the ends of the deck on the E side of the building, pointing to unrealized projects. The impressive interior has expansive double-height spaces and auditoria served by a very generous stair

89. Royal Northern College of Music, Booth Street West, by Bickerdike, Allen, Rich & Partners (1968–73).

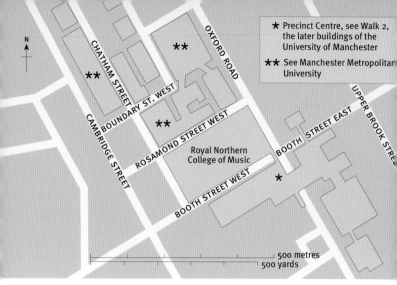

★ Precinct Centre, see Walk 2, the later buildings of the University of Manchester

★★ See Manchester Metropolitan University

CHATHAM STREET

OXFORD ROAD

★★

★★

CAMBRIDGE STREET

BOUNDARY ST. WEST

ROSAMOND STREET WEST

★★

Royal Northern College of Music

BOOTH STREET EAST

UPPER BROOK STREET

BOOTH STREET WEST

★

500 metres
500 yards

90. Royal Northern College of Music.

rising majestically on the s side of the building. An extension with a new entrance was added on the w side by *Mills Beaumont Leavey Channon*, 1997–8. A library and rehearsal block incorporates soundproof practice rooms constructed as isolated boxes within the building structure. The relative solidity of this part, faced in granite and grey brick in similar tones to the original building, contrasts with a double-height glazed entrance block which links the extension to the original building.

City Centre

Streets are listed alphabetically. For Major Buildings see p. 43–102.

City Centre

The central area of Manchester, s and se of the medieval town, was developed in the C18 and then intensively rebuilt as the civic and commercial centre in the C19 and C20. Its streets are so rich architecturally that they need to be described individually. Principal public buildings are described on pp. 43–102; others are under the relevant streets.

The area is bounded on the w side just short of Deansgate, on the n side by Market Street, Piccadilly Gardens and Piccadilly, on the e side London Road, on the s side Whitworth Street West, Granby Row and the boundary with Chorlton-on-Medlock (*see* map pp. 140–1). In the following account streets are arranged alphabetically; for those interested in particular themes the following can be especially recommended: C18 relics: St Ann's Square; C19 warehouses: Charlotte Street, Oxford Street, Portland Street, Princess Street; early C20 warehouses, Whitworth Street, Granby Row; banks, insurance companies, etc.: Cross Street, King Street, Spring Gardens; recent architecture: Barbirolli Square, Windmill Street.

Albert Square

Created when the town hall (*see* Major Buildings) was built on the old town yard. The roughly triangular shape of the square and town hall site originated in field boundaries shown on Casson & Berry's 1746

91. Detail of Casson & Berry's 1746 map showing the site of Albert Square and the town hall.

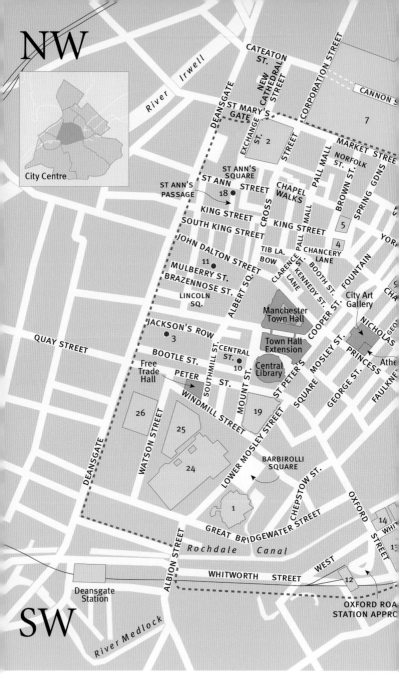

City Centre

River Irwell

CATEATON ST.

NEW CATHEDRAL STREET

CORPORATION STREET

CANNON S

DEANSGATE

ST MARY'S GATE

EXCHANGE ST.

2

MARKET STREE

7

ST ANN'S SQUARE

ST ANN STREET

ST ANN'S PASSAGE

18

CHAPEL WALKS

CROSS STREET

KING STREET

NORFOLK ST.

PALL MALL

BROWN ST.

SPRING GDNS

KING STREET

SOUTH KING STREET

PALL MALL

5

4

YOR

JOHN DALTON STREET

TIB LA. BOW

CHANCERY LANE

MULBERRY ST.

11

CLARENCE ST

BOOTH ST.

COOPER ST.

FOUNTAIN

CHA

BRAZENNOSE ST.

ALBERT SQ.

KENNEDY ST.

City Art Gallery

LINCOLN SQ.

JACKSON'S ROW

3

Manchester Town Hall

NICHOLAS

GEO

QUAY STREET

BOOTLE ST.

CENTRAL ST.

SOUTHMILL ST.

Town Hall Extension

MOSLEY ST.

PRINCESS

Ath

Free Trade Hall

PETER ST.

10

MOUNT ST.

Central Library

ST PETER'S

SQUARE

GEORGE ST.

FAULKNE

WINDMILL STREET

19

26

WATSON STREET

25

LOWER MOSLEY STREET

BARBIROLLI SQUARE

CHEPSTOW ST.

OXFORD STREET

24

1

GREAT BRIDGEWATER STREET

14

WHIT

ALBION STREET

Rochdale Canal

13

Deansgate Station

WHITWORTH STREET

WEST

12

OXFORD ROA STATION APPRO

River Medlock

92. City Centre.

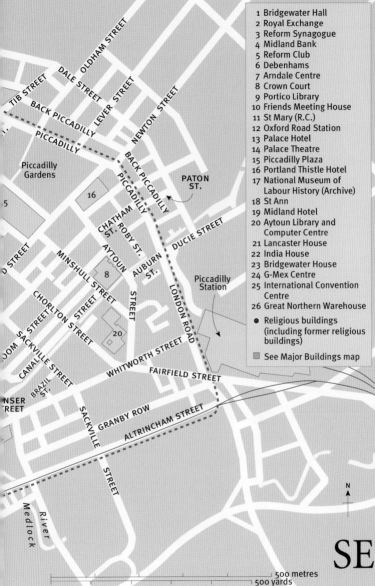

NE

1 Bridgewater Hall
2 Royal Exchange
3 Reform Synagogue
4 Midland Bank
5 Reform Club
6 Debenhams
7 Arndale Centre
8 Crown Court
9 Portico Library
10 Friends Meeting House
11 St Mary (R.C.)
12 Oxford Road Station
13 Palace Hotel
14 Palace Theatre
15 Piccadilly Plaza
16 Portland Thistle Hotel
17 National Museum of
   Labour History (Archive)
18 St Ann
19 Midland Hotel
20 Aytoun Library and
   Computer Centre
21 Lancaster House
22 India House
23 Bridgewater House
24 G-Mex Centre
25 International Convention
   Centre
26 Great Northern Warehouse
● Religious buildings
   (including former religious
   buildings)
▣ See Major Buildings map

SE

map. Only the s side can make any claim to be a worthy foil for the town hall. On the left corner at the junction with Mount Street, Nos. 20–21 is quite ornate Gothic by *G. T. Redmayne* for the Scottish Widows Fund Life Assurance Society, dated 1872. Redmayne, a pupil of Alfred Waterhouse, makes use of motifs such as tourelles and tall traceried windows echoing his master's town hall, diagonally opposite. It was highly praised as an example of small-scale street architecture in the C19, for example by the *British Architect* in 1881 and *The Builder* in 1896. Beside it, No. 17 **Carlton House** is free European Gothic with three-storey oriels crowned by gabled dormers, 1872 by *Clegg & Knowles*. The usual variation of window heads but more ornate than their contemporary warehouses (e.g. No. 101 Portland Street, q.v.). Also by them is neighbouring No. 16 **Albert Chambers**, 1873. Venetian Gothic, with arched window heads springing from giant pilasters and a busy frieze at the top, crowned by spiky battlements.

Memorial Hall, on the right corner, 1863–6 by *Thomas Worthington*. An awkward site with its longer side to Southmill Street, but Worthington was equal to the challenge. Brick and stone and decidedly Venetian Gothic with ranges of traceried windows (Ruskin's fifth order of the *Stones of Venice*) lighting the hall on the topmost floor. The detailing is good and the subtlety of the polychromy was achieved by careful choice of materials. Worthington had returned from his second tour of Italy in 1858, and this reflects what he had absorbed. The hall was erected to commemorate the secession in 1662 of Nonconformist clergy, and the ground floor and basement were let separately to generate income.

Lloyds House pokes its nose into the s w corner of the square. Designed in 1868 by *Speakman & Charlesworth*. Gothic, a relatively early use of the style for a warehouse. The focus is at the corner entrance with an open colonnade of paired granite columns supporting an octagonal tower with a tall pyramidal roof. It was probably the city's first purpose-

Venetian Gothic

Publication of John Ruskin's beautifully illustrated *The Stones of Venice*, 1851–3, heralded widespread adoption of European, and particularly Venetian Gothic form, in English architecture. Ruskin promoted a style with emphasis on contrasting, differently coloured materials, pointed arches, columns with foliated capitals, and elevations of flat character. The warmth, colour and lively detail contrasted with early Victorian Gothic Revival architecture which was largely informed by English medieval precedent. In Manchester Alfred Waterhouse was the main promoter of Ruskinian Gothic architecture, but two of his early and

influential designs have been lost – the Assize Courts of 1859–64 (for the salvaged sculptural scheme, *see* Inner City, Walk 3, Crown Square) and a sugar warehouse of 1855–6, which was based on the Doge's Palace in Venice. Polychromatic buildings with tall Northern Gothic roofs enriched with polished granite and stone carving became part of the street scene in Manchester in the 1860s and 70s. Thomas Worthington's Police Courts (*see* Minshull Street) and Edward Salomons' Reform Club (*see* King Street) are good examples and the style seen in developed form in Waterhouse's town hall. It was also applied to commercial warehouses by firms such as Clegg & Knowles, for example their Nos. 66–68 Fountain Street (*see* pp. 157–8).

94. Watercolour of arch masonry from John Ruskin's *The Stones of Venice* (4th edn, 1886).

built packing warehouse, becoming a model for the building type (*see* topic box, Introduction p. 24). The w side of the square has little to offer apart from No. 1 in Portland stone, by *Percy Scott Worthington c.* 1919. Tall with a narrow curved front to the square and giant Corinthian pilasters. On the N side (Princess Street) Nos. 1–7, offices and shops by *Pennington & Bridgen*, 1877. Tudorish Gothic, in soft red brick with stone dressings, enlivened by delicate traceried parapets and terracotta panels. Beside it Nos. 9–21 by *Waddington, Son & Dunkerly*, 1902, is stone faced and much grander, elaborate at the top with a conglomeration of gables and turrets.

Albert Memorial, in the square, by *Thomas Worthington*, his first

95. Albert Memorial, Albert Square, by Thomas Worthington (1862–5).

big success and his first important Gothic work. The idea came in 1862 when the mayor offered to present a statue of the prince by *Matthew Noble* to the city provided that a suitable protective cover was supplied. Worthington's design has the statue on a high base, protected by a Gothic canopy with open corner pinnacles, steep gables and a spire. It is based partly on sketches made in Pisa of Santa Maria della Spina, a favourite of Ruskin, combined with elements taken from St Mary, Nantwich,* which Worthington had drawn when he was a pupil in the office of Henry Bowman. The carving is by *T. R. & E. Williams* of Manchester. The base has bands of heraldic panels, the upper canopies contain statues representing Art, Commerce, etc. The armorial bearings of the Prince Consort feature prominently. It was designed a little earlier than Scott's Albert Memorial in London† but some twenty years after the canopied monument to Walter Scott by George Meikle Kemp in Edinburgh.

Also in the square **statues**: John Bright by *W. Theed*, 1891, white marble; Gladstone by *Mario Raggi*, 1878, bronze. Oliver Heywood, by *Albert Bruce Joy*, 1894, marble; Bishop Fraser, by *Thomas Woolner*, 1888, bronze with reliefs. **Fountain** by *Thomas Worthington* erected in 1897 to commemorate Queen Victoria's Diamond Jubilee, restored and returned to this position from Heaton Park in 1998. Hexagonal with three basins, the uppermost like a dainty font, with a bronze dolphin on top and winged beasts below by *John Cassidy*.

*As Nicola Smith has shown, *Burlington Magazine*, 123, April 1981.
†Gilbert Scott's design for the London Memorial was accepted on 22 April 1863.

Albion Street

On the E side the façade of a canal-side warehouse of 1869 by *Mangnall & Littlewood* with unusual cast-iron traceried windows. The office behind, by *Provan & Makin*, 1991, has full-height gabled bays to the canal, looking like loading slots. The basement colonnade of squat columns is continued beyond the building with broken columns.

Aytoun Street

Named for Roger Aytoun, who acquired the Minshull estates in this area in 1769. In 1770 the surrounding streets were laid out in a grid and sold for building (*see* topic box, Introduction p. 12). **The Grand**, NE side, started as a warehouse of 1867–8 by *Mills & Murgatroyd* and was converted to an hotel by them in 1883. Stone, Italianate, rusticated ground floor, two upper floors linked by a giant arcade and two more floors above. Conversion to flats has ruined its proportions by giving it two extra storeys. Further S, NE side a seven- and eight-storey apartment block under construction, 2001. On the same side the former Employment Exchange was designed 1936 by *David Thomson* for the Office of Works, but work was suspended until 1948 when *E. H. Montague Ebbs* took over. Brick, thin and cheap.

Barbirolli Square

By *RHWL Partnership*, 1990s, as the setting for the Bridgewater Hall. Set back from Lower Mosley Street, new buildings overlook a canal basin, created by re-opening a branch of the Rochdale Canal and part of the Manchester & Salford Junction Canal (*see* below). **Sculpture** by *Kan Yasuda*, 1996, Touchstone, a big, smooth, sensuously curved pebble of marble (illus. 32 and 96). Standing on the S side the **Bridgewater Hall**, by *RHWL Partnership*, 1993–6, the first auditorium of its size to be built as a free-standing structure since the Royal Festival Hall in 1951. The aim was to connect visually with the centre of town, but it does not really succeed in doing this. Moreover it is diminished by the bulk of the very offices on the other side of the square (*see* below) which provided part of the financial package. Set at an angle to the street it has a transparent prow pointing towards Albert Square and the town hall. Angled bays on the canal side house function rooms and foyers, etc. To Lower Mosley Street a glazed stair projection juts out from a stepped wall clad in silver-coated aluminium panels. Finally there is a semicircular plant tower with tiers of glass planks. The building is of some constructional interest and the interior is impressive. GERB vibration isolation bearings, developed to protect buildings in earthquake zones, are used to insulate the foundations from the superstructure. Here, used for the first time in a concert hall, they shield the building from the vibrations of the traffic and trains. The undercroft is an impressive sight with silver service ducts snaking through the space. The (surprisingly small)

96. Bridgewater Hall, Barbirolli Square, by RHWL Partnership (1993–6).

GERB units, metal boxes with transparent panels revealing rows of springs, are sandwiched between huge white concrete piers.

Interior. A tier of airy galleries with foyers and bars on four floors enjoys views between levels and out over the city and the canal. The underside of the auditorium sails into the space through four floors, a white inclined plane adorned with rippling enamelled and painted steel strips designed by *Deryck Healey*. Doors to the auditorium are of flamed bronze in bronze patinated surrounds giving a hint of opulence and creating a sense of occasion and anticipation, which is not disappointed. The auditorium seats 2,400, and was designed in consultation with *Arup Acoustics*. It combines the traditional shoebox plan with the vine-yard format of terraced seating of the Berlin Philharmonic. The seating is grouped to create a sense of intimacy, and the seats are ingeniously contrived to reflect sound equally whether occupied or empty. The visual focus is the striking arrangement of the (functioning) silver-coloured pipes of the huge *Marcussen* organ behind the podium. In contrast to the whites and blues of the foyer, colours are muted, with oak floors and cherry-veneer acoustic boards. Tall piers support a heavy concrete roof structure but its density is counterbalanced by the height of the space and by the steel tensioning structure which doubles as a lighting rig.

Nos. 100 and 101 Barbirolli Square loom over the N side of the square. Overscaled office buildings, also by *RHWL Partnership*, 1998–9. Designed as a pair and faced in pale grey granite and reflective glass. Each has a corner drum and tower, No. 100 with projecting curved bays on each side and No. 101 with answering recessions with balconies. The hard landscaping of the open space and huge glittering office blocks give the scene an alien transatlantic look, soon dispelled by the Manchester weather.

Manchester & Salford Junction Canal 1836–9. This ran between the branch of the Rochdale Canal beside Barbirolli Square and the Irwell near the w end of Quay Street. It opened in 1839. It was ⅝ m. (1 km.) long with seven locks, a storage reservoir, two pumping houses and a *c.* 500 yard (450 metre) tunnel. The project was a failure partly because of the enormous costs and partly because the Irwell was connected to the Bridgewater and Rochdale canals by a shorter and more convenient route in 1838. The E part between Lower Mosley Street and Watson Street was closed and backfilled when Central Station was built. In 1898 the remaining w part received a boost when the Great Northern Railway Goods Warehouse (*see* Windmill Street) was constructed incorporating an interchange with the canal which allowed goods to be transported to and from the railway via the Irwell and the Ship Canal. It was officially abandoned as a navigation in 1936.

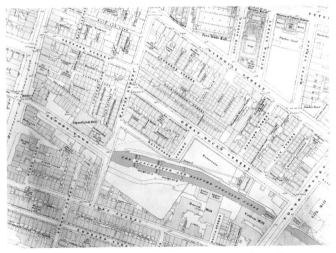

97. The Manchester & Salford Junction Canal as shown on the Ordnance Survey map (surveyed 1849).

Bloom Street

Part of the late C18 Aytoun development (*see* Aytoun Street and topic box, Introduction p. 12). The interest is on the E side. From the N, No. 11, by *Pennington & Bridgen*, 1889, for the Globe Packing and Shipping Company. A severe stripped palazzo, not at all like their usual work. Further s opposite the coach station (*see* Portland Street) and cast into shadow by it, a range of small offices and warehouses, the best, No. 17, Albert House, of 1903 by *Mills & Murgatroyd*. Red sandstone, fine red brick and terracotta, with Art Nouveau detailing. Further s beyond Sackville Street there are some plain early C19 houses of two and three storeys.

Booth Street

NW end, at the junction with Pall Mall, No. 1, N side, was built 1846–7 for R. H. Greg & Co. by *R. E. Whittaker*. A large palazzo warehouse on an island site, the half-basement vermiculated, ground-floor ashlar, the rest brick with stone dressings. Important as an example of fireproof construction applied to a warehouse, with cast-iron columns and beams and brick jack arches. Manchester warehouses seldom adopted this form, preferring to stick to the cheaper option of timber floors. *The Builder* in 1847 described it as 'presenting a model for this class of buildings'. Opposite, **Clarence Chambers**, 1906, by *Royle & Bennett*, red sandstone with sparing decoration, converted to flats 1999–2000. Next, on the same side, two buildings by *Edward Salomons*. No. 6 **Massey Chambers**, of 1872, ornate Renaissance style, symmetrical, with a parapet with a central pedimented dormer supported by putti. Salomons liked a lot of surface decoration, and it is generally used judiciously. The piano nobile features carved heads (one veiled) with foliate surrounds in the spandrels of the windows. Its more robust neighbour, Nos. 8–10, is the former **Manchester and Salford Trustee Savings Bank** opened in 1874. Three storeys, rich carving and rounded mouldings to the ground floor marble bands and cambered window heads. Tall piano nobile with graceful windows and carved arched window heads, all the windows of the top floor in elaborate architraves. For the Scottish Provident building, *see* Brown Street.

Brown Street

On an island site, between Chancery Lane and Booth Street, the seven-storey **Scottish Provident** building, by *Cruickshank & Seward*, 1971, with an aggressive look given by the closely set slits to the ground floor. Opposite, in contrast, the delightful Nos. 46–48, the former Brook's Bank, by *George Truefitt*, dated 1868. At the corner an intricate openwork iron crown tops a three-storey semicircular oriel. The beautifully crisp carving is by *Williams & Mooney*. Further s, on the E side, the sober mid- to late C19 **Chancery Chambers**. Its stone rusticated base, brick upper floors and heavy top cornice are echoed in simplified form

98. Nos. 46–48 Brown Street (formerly Brook's Bank) by George Truefitt (1868).

in the attached office building around the corner in Chancery Lane, by *Hamilton Associates*, 1994. Less self-effacing, the octagonal corner entrance bay with glazed turret to Spring Gardens.

Canal Street

runs along the w side of the Rochdale Canal from Princess Street to Minshull Street. Little of the early c19 remains, except in the modest scale of some of the buildings. In the late 1980s and 90s many were converted to clubs and café bars, e.g. in the s part No. 46 **Manto's**, converted in 1989 by *Benedict Smith Architects*. The balcony suspended from a row of laminated timber struts rearing up from the roofline is a later addition.

Central Street

N side. A big four-storey palazzo warehouse of *c.* 1865, so similar in style to No. 109 Princess Street (q.v.) by *Clegg & Knowles* that it must also be by them.

Chapel Walks

On the N side **Old Half Moon Chambers**, by *Speakman & Charlesworth*, 1870. The first two storeys are ornate with entertaining animal carvings and grouped arched windows. Further E **Tudor House** by *Barker & Ellis*, 1889, is brick below and elaborate half-timbering above. On the corner with Pall Mall a palazzo-style warehouse of *c.* 1868 looks like a typical *Clegg & Knowles* effort.

Charlotte Street

On the N side **St James House**, a slab and podium of 1964 by *Gunton & Gunton* is on the site of St James, consecrated in 1786 and demolished in 1928 (*see* topic box, Introduction p. 11). The s side has one of the very best and most complete ranges of mid-C19 purpose-built commercial warehouses. Built between *c.* 1850 and *c.* 1860, all are by *Edward Walters*, in his personal and highly influential interpretation of the palazzo style. With one exception each occupies a block with access to the loading

99. Detail of No. 10 Charlotte Street (*c.* 1856–8).

bays from the side streets. All are of fine quality brick dressed with stone, of five storeys over a basement. What matters in all is the conscientious and discriminating decoration, the amount of which depended on the purse of the client. From the E: No. 36, *c.* 1855–60, has a rusticated stone plinth and ground-floor windows with segmental heads, the entrance to the right. Above, grouped windows with round heads, the storeys divided by dentilled sill bands. Heavy cornice surmounted by a parapet and big corniced chimneys at the corners. Next No. 34, *c.* 1855. The simplest, the entrance offset to the right. Round-arched openings to the ground, segmental above, stone sill bands, and quoins. The keystones of the ground-floor windows are linked to the sill band above. Now a block is skipped and Nos. 14–16, *c.* 1855–60, is richer. The ground floor and basement in stone are linked in a continuous arcade with central paired doors. Second-floor windows have alternating segmental and triangular pediments and along the eaves a staccato rhythm of chimneys.* The corner is splayed and rusticated, the cornices nicked and the corner chimney angled to the splay. Finally, No. 10, the most ornate, *c.* 1856–8. Combined sills and pediments and crisp detailing create a sophisticated interplay between vertical and horizontal.

For the Portico Library *see* Mosley Street.

Chatham Street

s side, on the corner of Roby Street, a freestyle composition with Arts and Crafts touches with an attractive understated entrance front and a rooftop playground. By *F. B. Dunkerly*, dated 1910, built for the Manchester and Salford Boys' and Girls' Refuges and Homes Society and used as a base for messenger boys who were trained to run errands at nearby Piccadilly Station to earn their keep.

Chepstow Street

Facing the junction with Great Bridgewater Street **Canada House**, a ten-bay, six-storey warehouse fronted in pale orange terracotta. 1909, by *W. & G. Higginbottom*. The rear is a glazed screen with full-height octagonal piers. Inside there are some original interior features, e.g. the glazed corridor screens of the offices along the front. **Chepstow House**, to the SW, is a former packing warehouse (now flats) built in 1874 for Samuel Mendel by *Speakman, Son & Hickson*. The usual corner turret and a long façade with the openings grouped and treated differently to give variety.

Chorlton Street

Near the E end, N side, two former canal warehouses. First No. 47 **Minshull House**, probably mid-C19 with later additions to the rear and left. Canal warehouse with a huge rusticated semicircular arched

---

*Some of the chimneys were probably unheated flues acting as ventilators.

entrance (now infilled) in a slightly projecting central bay flanked by tall round-headed openings. To the rear on the former Grocer's Company Coal Wharf (now a car park), there is a jetty at first-floor level. The interior has rows of cast-iron columns, and on the upper floors an impressive system of tie-rods and struts for the overhanging upper floor. Next, No. 45, a mid- or later C19 warehouse. Beside it a lock house straddles the canal. It was rebuilt, probably in the early C20. On the other side of Canal Street there is a late C18 block with upper work-shop windows at the back and a stable in a rear courtyard. Finally near the junction with Portland Street a seven-storey office building, **Arthur House** by *Cruickshank & Seward*, 1962, conspicuous for the use of white concrete favoured by the firm at that time.

Clarence Street

A minor street linking Princess Street with Booth Street. On the w side dull late C19 red brick offices suddenly come to life with a cluster of stone three-storey semicircular oriels on the Bow Lane corner, which were added in 1895.

Cooper Street

continues Fountain Street. **Cooper House**, w side, by *Essex Goodman & Suggitt*, 1972. Moulded precast slabs form strong horizontals between inset window bands. The ground floor and central angled glass service tower are recessed. Opposite, No. 9 **Waldorf House** was designed by *W. Mangnall* for the Freemasons in 1863. Masonic emblems proliferate and there are richly carved Venetian Gothic motifs, rows of pilasters and niches with statues, but the elevation is crowded and the details fail to cohere.

Cross Street

linking Albert Square to Market Street is lined with large C19 and C20 commercial buildings, several by *Charles Heathcote*. For the Royal Exchange *see* Exchange Street, and for Nos. 1–7 Princess Street on the E corner of Albert Square *see* Albert Square. At the s end, w side, early C20 insurance offices in *Charles Heathcote*'s blocky and vigorous Baroque, of red sandstone with grey granite. A good example of this architect's skill at handling corner sites. **Bow Chambers**, opposite, offices and shops of 1869 by *Speakman & Charlesworth*, has showy polished granite columns to the ground-floor shops. **Steam Packet House** (w side), nothing special, but the Portland stone elevations have carvings of jolly tritons, fish and shells. By *Grace & Farmer* with *Oakley & Sandbill*, 1927. Neighbouring Nos. 62–68 **Eagle Star House**, on an island site, is by *Charles Heathcote & Sons*, 1911, not large, with rounded corners and nice Edwardian Baroque motifs convincingly and firmly controlled, one of

101. Eagle Star House, Cross Street, by Charles Heathcote & Sons (1911).

the best of his city centre buildings. Opposite (E side) on the corner with King Street is No. 37, 1895, also by *Charles Heathcote* in a Renaissance mode for the Northern Rock Building Society. The corner is handled well but the overall effect is rather bland. On the other corner **Lloyds Bank**, completed in 1915. *Heathcote* again, overpowering and richly Baroque, in Portland stone. The carvings and statuary are by *Earp*,

Hobbs & Miller. The banking hall is resplendent in coloured marbles and a big glazed barrel vault.

Mr Thomas's Chop House, w side, dated 1901. A sudden, almost comical change of scale. One narrow bay only, three storeys with an attic. Red brick and buff terracotta with Art Nouveau motifs. The corner entrance, two-storey oriel and elaborate crowning gable combine with lively effect. A striped chimney creeps up the exposed side of the neighbouring building towards the air. This part was originally a shop and offices, designed by *Mills & Murgatroyd*, the chop house was the part behind facing on to St Ann's churchyard, and is also dated 1901, designed by *Woodhouse & Willoughby*. The same pale terracotta, the detail different but still Art Nouveau. Some of the original scheme of pale green, dark green and cream glazed tiles remains inside. Next, **Hanover House**, w side, built as a Conservative club 1875–6, by *Robert Walker* with *Horton & Bridgeford*. Italianate with richly carved tympana of the windows contrasting effectively with smooth ashlar walls. On the nw corner of St Ann Street **Alliance House** by *Heathcote & Rawle*, *c.* 1890. All in stone in eclectic style.

The **Observatory** on the e side dominates this part of Cross Street as well as views from St Ann Street. An office block by *Holford Associates*, 1995–7, taller than anything else on the street, nine storeys and an attic part. Stone and brick grids appear to float in front of the glass façade. On the site was the **Cross Street Chapel** (Unitarian), built 1693–4, destroyed during the Second World War and replaced during the 1950s. A new **chapel** was built within the ground floor of the office block, the design by *Edwina Wilson* of Holford Associates in consultation with the congregation. To the right a hall with separate street access, to the left the entrance to the chapel, in a splay at the corner. The meeting room is a double-storey drum with foyer and corridor curving around it. Inside is a circular colonnade of cylindrical piers. Pale colours predominate with fittings of sycamore, including a lectern and communion table by *Gary Olson*, pale orange marble floors and smooth and roughcast wall finishes. Windows in the upper part of the drum allow the interior to be viewed from the upper corridors at the back.

Commercial Buildings further n, more offices and shops of *c.* 1868 by *Walters Barker & Ellis*. Walters had retired by this time and so had nothing to do with this rather lacklustre composition. The interest is in the introduction of European Gothic motifs with ranks of grouped windows and variation in the form taken by the window heads.

Exchange Street

is physically and visually part of St Ann's Square (q.v.). It now links with New Cathedral Street, a pedestrian route running n to the cathedral (*see* Major Buildings). Exchange Street was laid out in 1777 to link the square with the market place.

The **Royal Exchange** has a grand classical Edwardian exterior of 1914–21 by *Bradshaw, Gass & Hope*; within is a radically modern theatre by *Levitt, Bernstein Associates*, of 1976, refurbished after the 1996 bomb.

The Lord of the Manor Sir Oswald Mosley built the first exchange in 1729, not far from the (long gone) medieval courthouse and town hall, just to the N of the present building. He built it 'for chapmen to meet in and transact their business' as a sort of indoor extension to the market. It was the only large assembly room in town at the time and consequently became a venue for theatrical performances and meetings, including meetings of the Court Leet. It was replaced by a new Neoclassical building on the E side of Exchange Street by *Thomas Harrison* in 1806–9, enlarged by *Alex Mills* in 1847–9, then replaced by *Mills & Murgatroyd* in 1869–74 before the present building came. Membership rates had been introduced in 1809, and subscriptions were quickly taken up. Trading was never restricted to textiles and cotton, though they always predominated, and members were not required to deposit a sum of money as a surety. Initially business was transacted between the owners of the businesses – mill and warehouse owners, importers, finishers, etc. – but before long trading was left to their representatives – managers, agents and salesmen. Decline came not just through slumps in trade but also through the advent of new communications and the rationalization of many little businesses into large conglomerates, though trading continued until 1968.

The building remained empty after closure in 1968 until 1973 when it was used to house a temporary theatre by the Sixty-Nine Theatre Company. Their use of the space follows a line of succession from Elizabethan circular playhouses to Sir Tyrone Guthrie's improvised theatre instituted in 1946 in the Assembly Hall of the Church of Scotland, Edinburgh, and subsequent buildings at Stratford, Chichester and Sheffield. The idea of creating a permanent structure in the building followed from what had initially been seen as a stop-gap. The theatre group themselves came up with the initial ideas and *Richard Negri*, who was subsequently appointed as designer, produced a detailed model. *Levitt, Bernstein Associates* were chosen as architects with *Max Fordham & Partners* and *Ove Arup* as engineers. The building was completed in 1976. *Levitt, Bernstein Associates* came back to carry out the necessary repair works and introduce improvements after severe damage caused by the 1996 bomb.

The present building had to cater for eleven thousand members and boasted of being the largest place of assembly for trades in the world. It takes up the whole of the E side of the street and part of St Ann's Square. All in stone, with giant columns and pilasters and a round angle tower at the corner. In rebuilding after war damage the hall was truncated. Entering the building is a theatrical experience in itself. A glass lift (part of the 1990s improvements) brings one to the entrance of the enormous

102. Royal Exchange, Exchange Street, by Bradshaw, Gass & Hope (1914–21). Theatre pod (1976) and refurbishment (1996) by Levitt, Bernstein Associates.

hall, with giant columns and three glass domes. Beneath the largest, central, dome and suspended from the four central columns is a tubular steel theatre-in-the-round, a high-tech 'Lunar Module' (as it was soon christened). The design is ingenious. The four piers support welded tubular steel trusses spanning 98 ft (30 metres). Secondary trusses then span between the two main ones so that a square is formed. Within the square the theatre is seven-sided – so that the tiered banks of seats are not directly opposite one another. The hall retains its sense of spaciousness, more so since the recent refurbishment. Intruding shops and stalls were swept away and rationalized, new sulphur-plasma lighting brought in and a colour scheme dominated by blues and pinks introduced. The domes were reglazed and swathes of colour splashed on the upper glazing and glass entrance doors, to designs by *Amber Hiscott*. The theatre module was refurbished and modernized with new heating, lighting, ventilation and seating. The roof was raised to incorporate these and other technical improvements, but the result is not greatly different in appearance. A new studio theatre was created from rooms on the w side of the hall.

Acresfield, w side, refaced by *David Backhouse*, 1986. Shops and offices with garish coloured and mirrored columns and pediments. More interesting is the rear of the building where there is a tiered glass projection to gather light from the small courtyard. Beside it **Kings Court**, by *J. Seymour Harris*, curves gracefully around the corner to balance the Royal Exchange. The date is 1956 but the style still pre-war.

Fairfield Street

Outlying, E of the London Road junction, the **Star and Garter** pub, dated 1877, is brick with Queen Anne touches and panels with sunflower designs. w of the junction, s side, a temperance coffee house, by *Charles Heathcote*, for the Coffee Taverner's Company, 1902. Plain, red brick, with big gables. The N side is taken up by the police and fire station (*see* London Road) and the remaining s side by large early C20 commercial warehouses.

Faulkner Street

The **Chinese Imperial Arch**, a traditional design built by Chinese craft workers in 1987, straddling the street close to the junction of Nicholas Street, proclaims that we are in Manchester's Chinatown. The E side is lined with former commercial warehouses. Nos. 41–43, by *Thomas Fish Taylor*, 1846, is Grecian, with an absurdly high stone base and attached Doric columns supporting a pediment – hopelessly incorrect, but done with such panache that it is difficult not to like it. Warehouses of more conventional design follow. Nos. 45–47, probably 1840s, and adjoining No. 49, *c.* 1850, are similar in style, both brick with stone dressings. On the corner with Nicholas Street No. 55 is a big brick job by *Clegg & Knowles*, 1870. Unlike their usual warehouse style of the 1860s and 70s, the verticality is emphasized by giant pilasters. On the same side Nos. 59–61 was a mid-C19 milliner's shop and workshop. A central door in a stone surround with fancy pilasters is flanked by large shop windows in stone architraves. At the top, above a bracketed cornice, there is an attic workshop with a continuous range of windows. On the other (w) side there is a variety of smaller mid- to late C19 warehouses.

Fountain Street

is a continuation of Cooper Street (q.v.). It is crowded with a variety of recent buildings, none exceptional. Of the C19 survivors Nos. 66–68 on

103. **No. 46 Fountain Street by Thomas Worthington (1852–8). Drawing by Anthony J. Pass.**

the corner of Booth Street is a colourful Venetian Gothic affair by *Clegg & Knowles*, dated 1868 in warm red brick with sandstone dressings. No. 60, by *Ratcliffe Groves Partnership*, 1992, clad in pale stone, has a very prominent gracefully curving eaves cornice. Beside it an extension to Alfred Waterhouse's No. 60 Spring Gardens (q.v.) by *Cullearn & Philips*, 1988–9. Waterhouse's forms are picked up and simplified so that it slots into place unobtrusively. The best building is No. 46, w side, by *Thomas Worthington* for Overseers' and Churchwardens' offices in 1852 with the two top floors added in 1858. Each floor is treated differently and there is a range of œil-de-bœuf windows in stone frames in the attic. Towards the N end of the street where the back of Lewis's Department Store (*see* Piccadilly Gardens) dominates the E side the **Shakespeare** pub, opposite, is a curiosity. It was rebuilt in 1923 by *W. Johnson & Sons* incorporating parts of a demolished building from Chester. Some of the carving and bargeboards, as well as the crude caryatids of the tympanum over the entrance, are probably authentic C17 work, the rest mock timber framing.

George Street

At the N end, w side, the former telephone exchange, **Rutherford House**, built by the *Ministry of Public Buildings and Works* in 1967. A disciplined elevation of six storeys. Slim vertical ribs front a white grid with the horizontals stressed by dark strips. To the s, E side, a mid-C19 stone warehouse on the corner of Charlotte Street, sometimes attributed to *Walters*. Texture is carefully controlled, the rusticated basement is punch-dressed and the ground floor channelled and given emphasis by scrolled keystones which double as brackets to a cornice. Four storeys above, with ranks of windows between superimposed pilasters. Further s on the corner of Nicholas Street No. 33, a warehouse of red brick with stone dressings, by *J. P. & I. Holden*, 1845. Adjoining to the s, Nos. 35–37, another warehouse, this time of stone, probably 1840s. Nos. 39–41, adjoining, is by *Walters*, *c.* 1845 for Salis Schwabe. It is all fronted in stone, rusticated ashlar below and (unusually) coursed rubble above, the upper windows in quoined surrounds. George Street continues on the other side of Princess Street. On the corner of Dickenson Street a banal eight- and nine-storey apartment block, opened 2001. No. 63 is a well-detailed palazzo warehouse of *c.* 1857. The quality of the design has led some to attribute the building to *Walters*.[*]

Granby Row

An area of imposing Edwardian warehouses and the centre of Granby Village designed by *Halliday Meecham*, 1989. Existing buildings were converted into flats and new blocks of flats added in imitation Edwardian warehouse style. This was the first large-scale experiment in warehouse conversion and purpose-built apartment blocks in the city centre. **Orient House** by *G. H. Goldsmith*, *c.* 1914, is one of the most extravagant, six storeys with attics, of white faience with a giant Ionic colonnade. The back and part of the side are exposed showing the steel frame with glass curtain-walling. Beside it **Granby House** (Nos. 61–63), is also by *Goldsmith* but of 1908 and completely different in spirit and style. Red brick with Portland stone dressings and Art Nouveau motifs. The gabled corner bays are framed by polygonal piers giving a faintly Elizabethan accent.

Great Bridgewater Street

Attached to the Tootal Broadhurst, Lee & Co. building (*see* Oxford Street) **Lee House**, s side, is the eight-storey base of a proposed seventeen-storey tower. It is by *Harry S. Fairhurst & Son* with *J. H. Sellers*, 1928–31 and one of the very best of the interwar buildings in the centre. The steel frame is clad in fine, small brownish bricks in delicately ribbed panels between canted window bays. The bronzed multi-paned glazing was removed in a late C20 refurbishment, so some of the subtle surface interplay has been lost. Doors and loading bays in Portland stone surrounds with understated Art Deco mouldings; similar mouldings to attach the rail at the top. It was designed so that additional storeys could be added. Further w on an island site the jaunty early C19 **Peveril of the Peak** pub holds its own thanks to a refurbishment of *c.* 1900 when the whole of the street elevations were cased in coloured tiles. The interior is good too, with small rooms and coloured glass screens. The street curves w along the line of the Rochdale Canal. Opposite the Bridgewater Hall (*see* Barbirolli Square) and alongside the Rochdale Canal an office

[*]Dr A. V. Cooper attributes it to *J. Pickard*.

block, erected 2000, and a 1990s hotel. They replaced the early C19 Havelock Mills, a sad loss. Further w, s side, the **Britons Protection** pub is early C19 revamped in the 1930s, with much interior decoration of that date.

Jackson's Row

On the s side the **Reform Synagogue**, 1953 by *Eric Levy* with *Peter Cummings*, built to replace a synagogue in Cheetham Hill destroyed during the war. Reddish brown brick. Set back from the street and approached by a flight of steps, the central entrance with a range of small windows above is flanked by thin piers. On each side, breaking forward, slightly lower bays have tall narrow window strips. **Interior.** Galleries, including a choir gallery behind the ark, clerestory lighting. Oak furnishings – **ark** where the torah scrolls are kept, with a marble surround. In front of this a **bima**, from which the torah is read. Ground-floor windows have unusual figurative **stained glass** by *C. Lightfoot* of Manchester, 1953, to designs by *John Bradshaw*, showing biblical scenes. Those on the E side are deprived of light by an extension.

John Dalton Street

Laid out in 1844 as a link between Deansgate, w, and Cross Street, E. Starting at the Cross Street end, N side, first the brick horizontals of the **Bank of Ireland** by *Peter Black & Partners*, 1977, then **Grange Court**, by *Fairhurst Design Group*, 1991, an overblown office building with swept concave sides filled by huge bowed projections. On the s side No. 16, a five-storey polychromatic Italianate office building of 1865 by *Edward Salomons*. Red and blue brick with stone dressings. All the windows are in groups of three, those to the second and third floors with slender barley-twist columns. The ground floor has stone pilasters with panels and incised decoration. It was incorporated into **Trinity Court**, offices and shops by *Stephenson Architecture*, 1991–2, a superior façade job, in

105. Atrium of Trinity Court, John Dalton Street, by Stephenson Architecture (1991–2).

the quality of the new spaces and in the treatment of old work too. The façade only was retained and part of the ground floor converted to a colonnade using the original stone pilasters. New shops are set back to the left with the entrance to the offices to the right. The office accommodation is in two blocks divided by an impressive and generous atrium pouring light into the heart of the building, with a stair which starts as stone and changes to steel at upper level. Finishes are in limestone and marble.

Kennedy Street

runs parallel to Booth Street. It has an air of neglect. No. 6 by *J. W. Beaumont*, 1885, is distinguished by attractive carving with sunflower motifs. The most notable building is the delightful **Manchester Law Library** by *Thomas Hartas*, 1884–5. This is the home of one of the oldest provincial law libraries, founded in 1820. Venetian Gothic, only three bays, each divided into three again with richly traceried and strongly moulded frames to the openings. An oriel marks the first-floor reading room, steps lead up to the entrance on the left, recessed behind a traceried screen. Three floors with two main staircases. The entrance foyer has the entrance to the library itself to the left and a top-lit staircase leading up to second-floor rooms, which could be let separately, and also to the first-floor reading room. The ground floor housed a circulating library (now with C20 furnishings). The other staircase leads to the first-floor reading room which has most of the (slightly rearranged) attractive original fittings. The ceiling has moulded wooden ribs, the wooden cornice a frieze with pierced quatrefoils. Tall bookcases have cresting and slender detached shafts, some placed at right angles to the wall making separate bays. Arched upper screens have open cusped arcading, rising from piers placed against the bookcase ends. Stained

glass by *S. Evans* of Birmingham includes roundels with judges in wigs.

Most of the rest of the library's neighbours are in a regrettably parlous condition. Nos. 28–30, probably of the 1870s, is plain but for the solemn bearded heads on the ground-floor keystones. Nos. 32–34 by *Pennington & Bridgen c.* 1875 has an upper row of transomed windows with traceried ogee heads and coved eaves with pargetted motifs like Japanese pies, though they are treated as suns, not sunflowers. No. 36, by *Nicholson & Mottram*, 1878, uses strongly moulded elements to impress itself upon the street. Stone, Gothic, with an oriel rising from the first floor to end as a gabled dormer. At the N end of the street two late C18 houses which are now pubs.

King Street

Described by an American visitor in 1777 as the best built of Manchester streets: 'long and sufficiently wide; most of its houses noble'. The s part has kept its Georgian proportions but only two buildings of that date survive. Most of the rest date from the later C19, including attractive examples of retail architecture. They are not large, generally of three or four storeys only, with varied narrow frontages, some with delicate cast-iron window arcades. It is on the N part that there is real excitement.

The start is at the w end near the junction with Deansgate. On the s side, Nos. 8–14 offices and shops, by *Clegg & Knowles*, 1875. Two office entrances survive between the new shopfronts, each one different, each with fine carved detail. Opposite, Nos. 15–17, by *Maxwell & Tuke*, 1902, high and elaborate, all in half-timbering. The various dates which appear on the building refer to events in the history of the firm which occupied it, Goodall & Co. who were agents and furniture manufacturers for the Century Guild. For Old Exchange Buildings on the N side, *see* St Ann's Square.

Nos. 35–37, N side, is a five bay brick house, originally with wings, built in 1736 for Dr Peter Waring, which became a bank in the late C18. Its interior has gone and the wings replaced by 1990s glass shop fronts. Beside it Nos. 39–43 is an ambitious mid 1990s design by *Buttress Fuller & Allsop*, incorporating the arched entrance to the bank. A lower part of red and buff stone cladding and glazed upper storeys recessed behind a colonnade of circular piers. At the rear a circular glazed turret with iron balcony railings resembling the top of a lighthouse. No. 56, opposite, has early C18 origins, though you would hardly know it to look at the façade with its C20 shutters and upper balconies.* Further along, s side, No. 62 is by *Pennington & Bridgen*, 1874, with its original Shap granite front. Gothic, but lacking the delicacy of much of their other work.

King Street continues E of Cross Street. (For Lloyds Bank and the former Northern Rock Building Society premises *see* Cross Street.) The wider top part leads into the otherwise crowded banking and financial quarter. It was residential in the C18, and by the early C19 many lawyers lived and practised here, with banks coming soon after. s side, *Waterhouse*'s minor but unmistakable **Prudential Assurance** building of 1888–96, red brick and terracotta, the top part shorn off and the ground floor now opened out for shopfronts.

No. 82, s side, is the former **Branch Bank of England** by *Charles Cockerell*, 1845–6. The bank had been given the right to establish branches in 1826 as compensation for its loss of monopoly of joint-stock banking. Cockerell succeeded John Soane as the bank's architect in 1833. He was asked to supply plans for new buildings for branches in Manchester,

107. Branch Bank of England (former), King Street, by Charles Cockerell (1845–6).

*The interior retains C18 panelling and early C18 plasterwork (Statutory List).

Liverpool and Bristol in 1844. The Manchester design is the earliest and most expansive, though the general spirit is the same. Only five bays with giant attached columns and a crowning motif of an aedicule window in an arch which pushes up the pediment. The pediment is three bays wide, and in this part the lower windows are large and arched with a recessed tripartite arrangement with lunette over. They correspond to the banking hall. Cockerell uses one of the simplest of Greek orders, from the Temple of Apollo at Delos, which he had employed at Oakley Park, Salop. Inside, a tunnel vault leads to a saucer dome, continuing as another tunnel vault. The dome stands on four cast-iron Tuscan columns with pierced capitals. The King Street entrance is an early c20 insertion* and the original arched opening on the w side of Pall Mall was reinstated in 1995 when the building was reduced to the status of an entrance foyer to the office block behind, by *Holford Associates*. This is too large and high, of fifteen storeys, with a tired broken pediment motif on top.

Still on the s side, beside the bank on the E corner of Pall Mall, Nos. 84–86 was built in 1841–2 by *Richard Lane* 'after the example of the Monument of Thrasyllus' as he put it, for the Manchester and Salford Savings Bank. Savings Banks were philanthropic in origin and designed to encourage thrift in the working classes. The Manchester Bank was founded in 1818 and this was its first purpose-built premises, erected at a time when many Savings Banks were being built, but a relatively early (if mutilated) surviving example nevertheless. The ground-floor continuous arcade with polished granite trim is a rebuilding of 1904 by a deferential *Charles Heathcote* for the Sun Insurance Company. The upper part, of sandstone ashlar, is indeed closely based on Stuart & Revett's illustration. Giant pilasters and laurel wreaths in the frieze, surmounted by a pedestal.

Next **Ship Canal House**, s side, by *Harry S. Fairhurst*. It was one of the tallest office buildings in the country when it was erected in 1924. Portland stone with a basement and five storeys over, then a classical colonnade of paired columns with two more floors, this topped with a statue of Neptune. Finally an attic, well set back from the main façade. **Atlas House**, 1929, by *Michael Waterhouse*, is squashed up next to it on the corner of Brown Street. Opposite (N side), two of the city's most interesting commercial buildings of the 1960s. The first is the former **District Bank** by *Casson, Conder & Partners*, 1966–9. It is only six storeys high, entirely faced with granite, vertically ribbed, and that is a relief after all the raw concrete and tinny curtain-walling of many of its contemporaries (for example the Norwich Union Building, a little further E on King Street, by *T. P. Bennett & Son*, 1959–60). The general shape is a slab set back from the streets and at its two ends irregular octagons elongated at right angles to the slab. On the ground floor the

*Perhaps by Blomfield who designed (demolished) extensions to the rear in 1904.

Greek Revival Architecture in Manchester

Manchester was to the fore in adopting the classical architecture of Greece, as opposed to Rome, for public buildings. The appreciation of Greek architecture had grown during the later C18, as more adventurous travellers, including many architects, began to include Greece and Asia Minor (modern Turkey) as part of the Grand Tour. Those without the means to travel could consult published architectural surveys, notably James Stuart and Nicholas Revett's four-volume *The Antiquities of Athens* (1762–1816). The early C19 saw the erection in Manchester of three distinguished Greek buildings by *Thomas Harrison*: the Portico Library, 1802–6 (*see* Mosley Street), the Theatre Royal, 1803 (burnt down 1844), and the Exchange building (demolished 1872). The popularity of the style was confirmed by its use for Manchester's first town hall, of 1819–34 by *Francis Goodwin*, which stood at the corner of King Street and Cross Street, an outwardly magnificent building which used the Ionic order of the Erechtheum in Athens. *Charles Barry* and *Charles Cockerell* were among the architects who visited Greece; Barry's Royal Manchester Institution (now City Art Gallery, *see* Major Buildings) and Cockerell's Branch Bank of England in King Street are both strongly personal interpretations inspired by Greek ideas. *Richard Lane*'s Friends Meeting House (*see* Mount Street) and Chorlton-on-Medlock Town Hall and Dispensary (now Grosvenor Building, *see* Academic Institutions, Manchester Metropolitan University) are more typical of the style as generally practised in early C19 Britain.

108. Monument of Thrasyllus, *The Antiquities of Athens* (1762–1816).

areas between the slab and streets are filled in, and there are here also canted projections, just as the roof is canted. The impressive banking hall is no more, lost during a conversion to shops, 2000. Next to it No. 55 **Pall Mall Court**, by *Brett & Pollen*, 1969 for London Assurance Ltd. Strongly modelled and striking with tall angled service towers, that to the street with a single window slit. The lower part is tiered, with ranks of boxed-out windows. Cladding throughout is bronze patinated aluminium, and blue-bronze Staffordshire brick or mosaic.

The **Midland Bank**, s side, on an island site at the top (E end) of the street. It is the King of King Street, the major work in Manchester of

Sir Edwin Lutyens in collaboration with *Whinney, Son & Austen Hall*, who took care of the practical side. Carving was by *J. Ashton Floyd* of Manchester. Designed 1928, erected 1933–5. It is a nearly square block and treated as such, with the upper motifs identical on all four sides. The two angle porches are in King Street, and the entrances all have pilasters which die away and disappear, as at his Midland Bank on Poultry in London. The elevation steps back and contracts and the tops of the centre motifs have French pavilion roofs. Sheer walls with simple openings contrast with the texture of the lower entrances and the upper stages. The proportions are ingeniously calculated, as Lutyens in his later years adored to do. The top stage is two-thirds of the stage from the obelisks to the next set-back, and that middle stage is two-thirds of the bottom stage. Also the walls above the first-floor sill have a very slight batter: 1 in. in every 11 ft (2.5 cm. in every 3.35 metres). The banking hall could not be sky lit, so Lutyens gave it arcading on all four sides and wooden galleries much as in Wren churches. The galleries have large arched windows to let enough light in. The Delhi Order, with bells, which Lutyens devised for the Viceroy's House in New Delhi (1913–29), is used.

Opposite, the **Reform Club** by *Edward Salomons*, 1870–1, his best city-centre building in his romantic interpretation of Venetian Gothic and one of the largest surviving provincial clubhouses in the country. The street elevation is symmetrical, but it is the verticality of the corner oriels surmounted by graceful turrets and the external expression of the internal spaces which one notices. The two-storey hall on the piano nobile has a range of large windows, matched in the soaring oriels, that

109. Midland Bank, King Street, by Sir Edwin Lutyens in collaboration with Whinney, Son & Austen Hall (designed 1928, erected 1933–5).

110. Reform Club (former), King Street, by Edward Salomons (1870–1). Carving by T. R. and E. Williams to designs by Robert Pollitt.

at the centre with a balcony. Beneath is a fanciful portal, richly adorned with carving including large winged beasts, a motif repeated with variations amongst the lively foliage carving of the frieze. Ironwork balconies have springing flower motifs and there are carved plaques with allegories of the Arts on the E turret and Sciences on the W turret, designed by *Robert Pollitt* and carved by *T. R. & E. Williams*. The ground floor of the interior was originally let as offices, apart from the entrance vestibule, and it has been split into different units. It is of two periods, one contemporary with the exterior, the other of 1910 by *Maxwell & Tuke* who converted some of the rented ground-floor offices for use by the club. To the first period belong a fine staircase running up the full height of the building from a spacious entrance hall, the grand main dining room two storeys high on the piano nobile (now entered from the side and used as a restaurant) and an enormous billiard room, running the whole length of the building, in the roof – this part now offices. Of the second phase the best surviving rooms are the magnificent ground-floor lavatories with marble basins and marble panels in the ceiling, now used as a stock room for a shop.

Lincoln Square

On the S side of Brazennose Street between Albert Square (E) and Deansgate (W). **Brazennose House**, N side, by *Leach Rhodes & Walker*, 1964. Designed as three linked buildings to avoid a long unbroken façade to the public space. In the square a **statue** of Abraham Lincoln by *George Grey Barnard*, 1919. Presented to the city of Manchester by Mr and Mrs Charles Phelps Taft of Cincinnati, Ohio. It had been destined for Parliament Square in London as a symbol of Anglo–American unity but the American Commission of Fine Arts considered it insufficiently reverent and ruled in favour of a copy of the figure by Augustus Saint-Gaudens at Lincoln Gardens, Chicago.

London Road

Opposite Piccadilly Station is an enormous (former) **police and fire station**. By *Woodhouse, Willoughby & Langham*, 1901–6, winners of a competition judged by Waterhouse. The building incorporates a coroner's court which is still in use. It was a magnificent municipal showpiece, now shamefully neglected, the detail blurred by a thick layer of dirt. A huge near-triangular block is ranged around a courtyard used for drill. As well as all the usual facilities there was accommodation for thirty-two firemen and their families and six single men. The style is neo-Baroque in red Accrington brick, tawny terracotta and brown faience, with Hawksmoorish turrets as part of a picturesque skyline. A high offset tower forms a landmark. To London Road there is a wide arched entrance to the yard and an upper Ionic colonnade. The elevation is symmetrical except at the corners, to the left there is a squat domed turret, to the right a small upright turret crowned with a flame motif. The

111 & 112. Police and fire station (former), London Road, by Woodhouse, Willoughby & Langham (1901–6). Terracotta by Burmantofts, sculptural and architectural modelling by J. J. Millson.

terracotta is by *Burmantofts*, and the sculptural and architectural modelling by *J. J. Millson* symbolizes the various functions of the building through allegorical representations of Courage, Vigilance, Justice, Truth, etc. Watching birds perch around the tower and there are four figures around each of the two turrets. Relief panels on themes of fire and water are placed high up on the principal London Road elevation. Paired figures recline over each of the four main entrance doors in the manner of Michelangelo's Night and Day in the Medici chapel in Florence (illus. 21). Similar figures over the second-floor window spandrels. The classically inspired figures are generous and solid, clothed in flowing drapery, with a hint of Art Nouveau attenuation.

Further N, W side, just beyond the line of the Metrolink, the battered late C18 **Coach and Horses** pub has ranges of workshop windows in the N elevation.

Lower Mosley Street
For the Bridgewater Hall *see* Barbirolli Square.

Market Street
Originally a lane leading from the medieval market place out into open country. By 1741 it was built up as far as the s side of Piccadilly. It was widened in 1821–2. Its present function as a principal shopping street had been established by the mid C19.

At the E end on the N side Nos. 109–127 **Rylands Building** (Debenhams), completed 1932, by *Harry S. Fairhurst & P. G. Fairhurst.*

Terracotta

Terracotta and faience are ceramic wares in blocks or slabs, and the terms apply to the unglazed and glazed forms respectively. The material was widely used from the late C19, and mass-production techniques led to domination by large firms such as *Burmantofts* of Leeds and *Doulton* of Lambeth, London, whose wares were used all over the country thanks to the efficiency of late C19 transport. As well as being durable and cleanable, terracotta and faience are relatively resistant to the effects of smoke and soot, and so especially suitable for use in cities. Their popularity as facing materials for buildings reached its peak in Manchester during the opening decades of the C20. The bright, clean, colourful façades stood in striking contrast to the cloaks of soot worn by even the most distinguished of their neighbours. The Refuge Assurance Building (Palace Hotel), with rich exterior decoration by Doulton (*see* Oxford Street), the Midland Hotel (*see* St Peter's Square) and the sophisticated warehouses of the Lloyds Packing Company (*see* Whitworth Street) with terracotta and faience by *Burmantofts* were all highly visible advertisements for the variety of colour, decoration and finish available. Some of the most elaborate schemes, such as the former Municipal School of

113. Detail of terracotta angel from the Grosvenor Building, Cavendish Street, Manchester Metropolitan University, designed by W. J. Neatby (1897).

Technology (*see* Academic Institutions, UMIST) and the London Road police and fire station (*see* London Road), both by *Burmantofts*, were municipal enterprises. One of the most innovative uses of faience was for the former YMCA (*see* Peter Street), which was built using the *Kahn* system of reinforced concrete. Here the *Burmantofts* faience was built up as an outer shell before the concrete was poured in and rammed into dovetailed recesses in the slabs. Other examples of note include the slab faience panels of the town hall extension (*see* Major Buildings) by local Lancashire firm *Shaws of Darwen*, the Church of the Holy Name of Jesus (*see* Outer Areas, Chorlton-on-Medlock) where terracotta blocks by *Gibbs & Canning* were used for the interior, including the vaulting, and the delightful interior and exterior scheme designed by *W. J. Neatby* of Doulton for the extension to the Regional College of Art (now part of the Grosvenor Building) at Manchester Metropolitan University (*see* Academic Institutions).

114. Rylands Building (Debenhams), Market Street, by Harry S. Fairhurst &
P. G. Fairhurst (completed 1932).

The largest wholesale textile warehouse of its day in the city. The
frontage is over 230 ft (70 metres) long. Stripped classicism in Portland
stone with huge corner turrets turned from the frontage at an angle of
forty-five degrees. Elevations are enlivened by ornamental metalwork
and zigzag patterns in stone. The remainder of this side is dominated
by the **Arndale Centre** (1972–80, *Wilson & Womersley*) which occupies
a 15 acre (6 hectare) site. The unlovely tile-clad Arndale tower is a landmark, and the whole was designed as an inward-looking block with long
blank frontages except on Market Street. For the w side, to Corporation
Street, *see* Walk 2. There is more variety on the s side. After the bulk of
Lewis's Department Store (*see* Piccadilly), some late c19 and early c20
commercial buildings. The only really notable building is No. 70, of
c. 1825. All that survives is the upper part with giant unfluted Ionic
columns. It was evidently competing with the (long gone) Cunliffe &
Brook's Bank of 1824 which stood nearby and sported superimposed
Doric and Ionic colonnades. It was built (by whom?)* for the short-
lived Thomas Crewdson & Co. Bank and occupied by the Bank of
Manchester from 1829. The plain painted brick building beside it, with
stone sill bands and a bracketed cornice, is another early c19 survivor.
New shops behind the façades of these buildings were designed by
Stephenson Bell, 2000. **Stephens Buildings**, on the corner with Brown
Street – a Waterhousish effort. Of *c.* 1896 by *Booth & Chadwick* in very
fine red brick, red terracotta and red sandstone. Perky corner turret and
richly decorated shaped gables.

*Richard Lane would be the obvious candidate, but the detailing does not seem like his
work.

Minshull Street

Starting at the w end, s side, a big vaguely Italianate warehouse by *Clegg & Knowles*, 1872, not their best effort. The austere No. 10, **Minshull House**, a warehouse probably of the 1860s or 70s, is much more effective, in a no-nonsense way. Stone basement and ground floor and brick above with ranks of flat-headed windows. Then the former City Police and Sessions Courts in 1867–73 by *Thomas Worthington*, now part of the **Crown Court**. For its other buildings *see* Inner City, Walk 3, pp. 248–9. The building is informed by Worthington's absorption of Ruskinian principles and his knowledge of European Gothic. *See* topic box, p. 143.

115. Crown Court, Minshull Street, by Thomas Worthington (1867–73), with extension to Aytoun Street by James Stevenson of the Hurd Rolland Partnership (1993–6).

The design has a vigorous urban quality imparted by the flat areas of brickwork, deeply recessed openings and bold outline. There are parallels with his designs for the town hall competition, submitted in the same year. The site is awkward and the asymmetrical composition with corner tower and central campanile chimney turns this to advantage – Worthington had initially planned the tower as the central axis (cf. his Nicholls Hospital, now Ellen Wilkinson High School, Outer Areas, Ardwick and Beswick). Orderly rhythm is given by the ranks of tall closely set windows and, as at Nicholls Hospital, decoration becomes more concentrated at the top in the stonework of the chimney with its spiky gargoyles and the corner tourelles and open arcading to the tower. Owls top the elongated finials to the gables. The carving by *Earp & Hobbs* includes fierce beasts placed at eye level at the entrances, as Ruskin would have liked. Worthington's design for the Assize Courts in Manchester was criticized for poor circulation, and he learnt from his mistakes. The separation of different users was achieved by placing pairs of court rooms on each side of an open courtyard, each separated from its neighbour by offices and flanked on two sides by corridors.

The extension to the Aytoun Street side is by *James Stevenson* of the *Hurd Rolland Partnership*, 1993–6. Adapting a complex building to suit the even more complex requirements of a modern crown court presented a formidable challenge. Worthington's forms are simplified for the new work, which echoes the tall windows and gables. The courtyard was glazed over and four new court rooms inserted into the ground floor, where there had been public areas and holding points for defendants beneath the courts. Two more new courts were sited in the extension. The atrium provides views of the Worthington tower and chimney and is the hub of the separate circulation routes. There is an open deck for the public and separate glazed walkways for jurors and the judiciary. The **stained glass** of the jury walkway is by *Lavers Barraud & Westlake*. It was moved from the former judges' rooms and copied where necessary to provide a complete scheme. The three figures of Moses, St Michael and Solomon symbolize Law, Justice and Wisdom.

Worthington's court rooms have been preserved with relatively few alterations and c20 suspended ceilings were removed in the refurbishment. They have panelled roofs, pierced for ventilation, and high windows framed by ornate pilasters. The pitch pine furnishings effectively combine open, glazed and blind Gothic arcading.

Mosley Street

Named for the Lords of the Manor who laid out this and the streets in the immediate neighbourhood in the early 1780s (*see* topic box, Introduction p. 12). It quickly became one of the most elegant streets in town, but after *c.* 1840 became a premier site for warehousing. The attraction was the proximity to the Exchange. More waves of development after the war swept away almost all of the warehouses and the street is now lined with banks, offices and commercial buildings. Starting at the Piccadilly Gardens end, on the w side (for No. 10 Mosley Street, *see* Piccadilly), Nos. 14–16 **Cobden House**, an early work of *Edward Walters* and his first Manchester commission, for Richard Cobden. It was built in 1839 and can claim to be the first palazzo-inspired warehouse in the city. Brick with stone dressings with emphasis reserved for second-floor windows. The ground floor is a restoration. On the N corner with York Street Nos. 24–30, 1898 for the Mercantile Bank of Lancashire by *J. Gibbons Sankey*. Portland stone, upper Ionic colonnades and corner turrets set back in stages above entrances which have paired Doric columns with open pediments supported by atlantes. The modelling and detail start to go freestyle towards the top. Next the buildings of the **Royal Bank of Scotland**, between York Street and Spring Gardens. The first block is by *Walters*, his last great work, for the Manchester and Salford Bank in 1862. Walters' assurance shines

116. Royal Bank of Scotland, Mosley Street, by Edward Walters (1862) with extensions by Barker & Ellis (1880s) and Harry S. Fairhurst & Son (1975).

through. Two-storey rusticated giant pilasters below, so that the pedimented piano nobile windows are on the second floor. Here giant angled pilasters point to the pinched-in corners of the very emphatic cornice which is topped by a balustrade punctuated by big stone urns and corner chimneys. The top part draws the whole composition together, balancing the strength of the ground-floor rustication. To the left of the lower entrance block a matching extension of the 1880s by Walters' successors, *Barker & Ellis*. The latest extension, 1975, *Harry S. Fairhurst & Son*, has simply treated openings palely following the C19 rhythms. The same firm also did the expensive looking No. 45 on the other (E) side for the headquarters of Williams and Deacons Bank (now Royal Bank of Scotland offices) in 1963–5. A tower on a podium, all clad in dark green marble and light green granite. On the podium a tree with its own watering system.

At the corner with Charlotte Street is the noble and unassuming **Portico Library**, 1802–6, the only surviving work in the city of *Thomas Harrison*. Promoters of a scheme for a combined newsroom, circulating library and reading room visited the Athenaeum in Liverpool in 1799 or 1800. This may have been how they came into contact with Harrison whose Lyceum was built there 1800–4. The Portico is Manchester's earliest Greek Revival building and it incorporates a partially intact Soane-inspired interior. To Mosley Street a pedimented central loggia has four unfluted Ionic columns, based on Stuart & Revett's drawings of the Little Temple on the Illisus (*see* topic box p. 165). On the side to Charlotte Street a rank of attached columns and

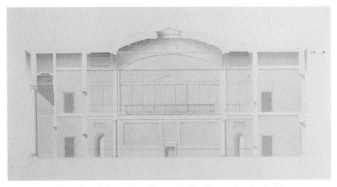

117. Sectional drawing of the Portico Library, Mosley Street, drawing by Thomas Harrison (1802–6).

ground-floor windows with alternating flat and pedimented heads, all done in finely finished Runcorn stone. The steps up to the Ionic portico and the recessed entrance emphasize the exclusive nature of the club, but they lead to a disappointing pub conversion. The ground floor was the newsroom, and there was an open well with a galleried first floor. This was closed in and floored over in the C20. The library upstairs is preserved (*see* illus. 15), and is now reached from a side entrance. Here the space is dominated by a Soanic dome (unfortunately with coloured Victorian glass), and segmental tunnel vaults to E and W. Harrison presumably knew Soane's Bank of England, and he may have had contact with Soane through his membership of the Architects' Club. The library and its fittings are intact, and the library continues in use.

On the same side No. 75 is by *H. A. J. Darlow* of *Watney, Eiloart, Inman & Partners*, 1964–6, Portland stone with boxed-out windows in a chequer pattern. Opposite was the Milne Buildings, a warehouse of *c.* 1850,* demolished for **Eagle Star House**, by *Cruickshank & Seward*, 1973, with aggressive horizontals in concrete and glass, now due for demolition itself.

Mount Street

Nos. 2–4 is a Gothic building by *Pennington & Bridgen*, 1874–6, built for the Queens Building Society. Crocketed gable with tourelles and a statue of Queen Victoria beneath a canopy. The corner entrance (to Central Street) is flanked by a lion and a unicorn on pedestals, with an elaborate two-storey oriel above. **Friends Meeting House**, at the S corner with Central Street, 1828–31 by *Richard Lane*. This has presence, partly because it is given space and dignity by being well set back from the

---

*Described in the 1969 edition of the *Buildings of England: South Lancashire* as 'the most startling warehouse in Manchester' for its design of superimposed giant orders.

118. Friends Meeting House, Mount Street, by Richard Lane (1828–31).

street front with generous steps up to the entrance, and partly for the restraint and purity of the design. Five bays with a three-bay portico of attached unfluted Ionic columns after the example of the Illissic temple from Stuart and Revett's *Antiquities of Athens*. (*See* topic box, p. 165.) The rest is mainly brick, the side elevations with projection and recession articulated by stone pilasters and sill-bands. The Doric interior was altered by *Alfred Waterhouse* 1861–4 and gutted during the c20. In the roof the remains of Lane's mechanism of retractable shutters survive, designed to allow the men's and women's meeting rooms to be thrown together when required.

Mulberry Street

St Mary (R.C.). Of 1848 by *W. G. Weightman & M. E. Hadfield*, the second being the Catholic church specialist in the firm. It is built on the site of a chapel which was erected in 1794 in an area which had become a notorious slum by the c19. The design is a modification of one by Hadfield published in the *Rambler*, which had so infuriated Pugin that he wrote a pamphlet to denounce this and other churches. He said (among many other equally defamatory remarks) that it 'shows to what depth of error even good men fall, when they go whoring after strange styles'. The choice of Rhenish Romanesque was both anti-Puginian and novel, and probably reflects the imagination of Hadfield's young assistant George Goldie. It had few immediate Catholic progeny, though Goldie later developed the style in Ireland. The early use of structural polychromy is notable, though this applies only to the exterior. There was no hesitation in painting the columns inside to resemble marble. The building is of red brick, with sparing use of pale sandstone. There

119. St Mary (R.C.), Mulberry Street, by W. G. Weightman & M. E. Hadfield (1848).

is a richly carved portal and a sw tower with Rhenish helm roof.* The arches over the windows are banded in red and yellow sandstone, as is the surround to the wheel window. Lombardic frieze to the gable of the nave and second stage of the tower. In contrast to this the **interior** is basilican, with six bays of painted columns and tall round-arched clerestory windows. Exposed timber roof, with a lantern to provide additional light. A w gallery incorporates an **oratory** on the s side with linenfold panelling, an altar and reredos and a glazed screen to the gallery.

The interior is dominated by an array of marble and Caen stone statuary (now partially painted), in architectural settings. The scheme is attributed to a *Mr Lane* of Preston. It was introduced after the building opened, replacing painted figures, and shows how Catholic iconography moved away from the strict medieval precedent Pugin preferred. In the centre the high altar below an elaborate sculptural scheme with the Virgin, attended by various saints. On the left side, a side altar of marble and Caen stone with a Pietà; on the right, Shrine of Our Lady, with the Virgin in marble. **Font** with baptismal scenes. **Stations of the Cross** by *Norman Adam* installed in 1995. **Stained glass**. The best is a late C19 brilliantly coloured window showing the Virgin. Attached to the right side of the church the **presbytery**. Red brick and painted

*The only surviving English medieval parallel is at Sompting, Essex.

stone, with churchy window to the ground floor and an oriel over. The unspoilt interior has an impressive full-height top-lit staircase and a door leading to the oratory in the church.

Nicholas Street

No. 16, by *Alfred Waterhouse*, 1872–5, larger and later than its other warehouse neighbours. Elizabethan details with gables and chimneys, creating an eventful roofline in contrast to all the Italianate cornices hereabouts. Brick with stone dressings, six storeys with the upper three slightly recessed between the gabled end bays. Inside an open-well top-lit stair acts as a ventilation shaft.

Norfolk Street

At the junction with Brown Street No. 10, the former **Palatine Bank** by *Briggs, Wolstenholme & Thornley*, 1908–9. Great circular corner towers with conical roofs, round-headed ground-floor openings and an upper arcade on the Norfolk Street side, a giant colonnade to Brown Street. Detailing includes crowstepped gables, battlemented parapets, and dog-tooth ornament, all looking rather odd in Portland stone. Further w, s side Nos. 2–6 was the **Northern Stock Exchange** by *Bradshaw & Gass*, 1907. Edwardian Baroque, with a low orderly three-storey façade of Portland stone. **Interior** (converted to a restaurant in 2000). The entrance on the left leads to a richly decorated anteroom lined with fantastically striped pink and green marble. Beyond, a magnificent hall with a dome supported at the corners by pilasters clad in sensuous green and cream marble. On the s side to the street, the arcading incorporates lunettes. Bulky plasterwork festoons and wreaths in the spandrels. On the w side the former reading room, now opened out and used as a bar, and a marble-lined smoke room.

Oxford Road Station Approach

runs sw from the corner of Whitworth Street West and Oxford Street to **Oxford Road Station**, 1958–60. One of the most remarkable and unusual stations in the country both for the architectural form and the technological interest. It is sited high on the 1849 MSJ&AR viaduct. An inverted timber prow rears up over the station entrance, part of a roof formed by a series of three prefabricated timber shells on huge laminated timber beams. More curved beams support curved platform canopies with lines of portholes. The use of timber is continued with the booking office, café and the seating. The design is by the Midland Region architectural team (project architect *Max Clendinning*) with engineer *Hugh Tottenham* of the Timber Development Association who developed the technique of using laminated timber to create conoid shell roof forms. This was not the Midland Region's only experiment with timber shell technology but it is the most architecturally dramatic, and it is an important example of the deployment of timber to achieve large roof

120. Oxford Road Station, Oxford Road Station Approach, by the Midland Region architectural team (project architect Max Clendinning) with Hugh Tottenham (1958–60).

spans incorporating clerestory lighting. In this instance the fact that the lightness of the structure reduced foundation loads was a consideration.

Oxford Street

has some of Manchester's more spectacular offices and warehouses. We start at the s end and the boundary with Chorlton-on-Medlock marked here as elsewhere by the looping Medlock and 1849 railway viaduct. **Little Ireland** lay to the w within a loop of the Medlock, a notorious slum described by Kay, Engels and others. Nothing is left of this but some of the factories survive to the w (q.v. Outer Areas, Chorlton-on-Medlock).

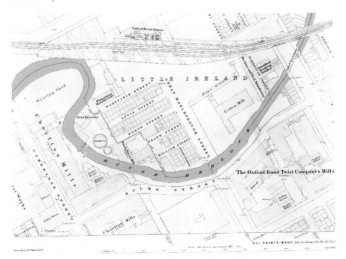

121. Ordnance Survey map of Little Ireland (surveyed in 1849).

The **Palace Hotel** at the corner of Oxford Street and Whitworth Street began as offices for the Refuge Assurance Company. Built in three phases: No. 1 building, by *Alfred Waterhouse*, 1891–5 at the corner of Whitworth Street; No. 2 building by *Paul Waterhouse*, 1910–12, doubling the Oxford Street façade and linked to No. 1 building by a 217 ft (66 metre) clock tower over the new entrance; No. 3 building, 1932 by *Stanley Birkett*, doubling the Whitworth Street façade. Clad with imperishable pressed brick and dark red terracotta (by *Doulton*) only relieved by the grey granite of the tower base and orange terracotta at its top. The decoration is of the Northern Italian c16 type. A powerful effect is achieved by the richly textured side blocks set against the sheer mass of the tower when seen in foreshortened perspective. The sheer back elevations are faced with white glazed brick and are almost devoid of ornament – in their way almost as spectacular.

The **interiors** show equally imperishable and highly wrought materials (*see* topic box p. 170). *Burmantofts'* faience and glazed brick in butterscotch shades are used for No. 1 building, with characteristically muted stained glass and excellent ironwork. The richest display is reserved for the corner entrance, now blocked. Apart from the entrance and stair, the whole ground floor, including the glassed-over light well, was one vast open business hall. On the third floor is the panelled former boardroom suite. No. 2 building employs a wider palette, including greens and copper shades, and more bulgy forms. It incorporates a

sumptuous full-height marble and bronze staircase. No. 3 building is similar to No. 2 but red tiles are substituted for faience. Here is another vast interior space, this time at basement/river level. It was the staff dining room, but was provided with a sprung dance floor and fully equipped stage. The building proved versatile enough, despite the omnipresent Refuge logos, for successful conversion to an hotel (by *Richard Newman*) which opened in 1996. MH

The **Palace Theatre** on the corner with Whitworth Street, E side, by *Alfred Darbyshire*, 1891, altered by *Bertie Crewe* in 1913. It is clad in ugly beige tiles added in 1956, but the splendid auditorium was retained. There is a dome over, and on each side of the proscenium arch, two tiers of boxes with atlantes and caryatids and a pedimented Ionic colonnade. There are two tiers of curved balconies. The elaborate plasterwork is an exuberant mixture of classical and Egyptian motifs. A refurbishment and restoration of 1981 by *Smith & Way* improved circulation and backstage facilities. Beside it on the same side **St James's Buildings** by *Clegg, Fryer & Penman*, 1912–13 for the Calico Printers' Association. High and broad and all Portland stone: Baroque. So big that it can only be seen obliquely. A tower, rising from a broken pediment, crowns the central entrance block, and the entrance itself, as if more emphasis was needed, has a silly 1990s canopy. The entrance hall is the most opulent of surviving Manchester warehouses. Apart from the elaborate plaster ceiling with its deep dome, it is all of marble: grey- and white-clad walls, green columns and a sumptuous stair with black handrail and cream and brown balustrade. All internal areas were lined with patent fireproofing cement and beneath the marble cladding the stair is of reinforced concrete. Opposite, No. 56, the almost equally impressive offices of textile manufacturers **Tootal Broadhurst, Lee & Co.**, 1896–8 by *J. Gibbons Sankey*, are large too, in red brick striped with orange terracotta, but comparatively classical. Polygonal corner towers frame an arcade with giant Corinthian columns. The theme is continued in the long elevation to the s side of Great Bridgewater Street. The **interior** has been refitted, keeping on the stairs a war memorial by *Henry Sellers*: a frame of layered coloured marbles with a niche (from which the bronze figure was stolen) above a cream marble panel on which the names are recorded.

Picture House of 1911 by *Naylor & Sale*, further N and on the w side. One of the earliest purpose-built cinemas in the city centre, retaining something of its original form, though the ground floor has been horribly ruined and the tower over the entrance removed. Orange terracotta and red brick with segmental gablets punching through the balustraded parapet. The long elevation to Chepstow Street is punctuated with upper bullseye windows. On the other (N) Chepstow Street corner, a 1980s toy Georgian office development is fronted by **Princes Buildings** (Nos. 18–28 Oxford Street), built as offices, shops and warehousing by *I. R. E. Birkett* in 1903. Only the terracotta-clad façade is left, but this has verve with a row of tall chimneys linked by a sweeping curved parapet. The detail is Art Nouveau. Opposite the inter-war **Odeon** by *F. T. Verity & S. Beverly*, with flattened pilasters and stylized capitals above garish tiles. The remainder of Oxford Street is dominated by the ponderous Portland stone **Peter House**, by *Ansell & Bailey* of 1958, on the w side. Opposite is the unattractive **Elisabeth House** of 1971, by *Cruickshank & Seward*.

Paton Street *(formerly Booth Street)*

A minor street linking Piccadilly with Dale Street. On the s side, Nos. 2–4 are late C18 houses with crude pedimented doorcases. They are part of the block which includes No. 97 Piccadilly (q.v.). No. 13, on the s side and the corner of Back Piccadilly, a late C18 two-bay three-storey brick house with cellar and area railings. Neighbouring No. 15 was added

126. Paton Street (formerly Booth Street) as shown on Bancks & Co.'s map (1831).

after 1794. Adjoining it is slightly later No. 19, still three storeys, but of three bays and taller because the storey heights are much more generous. Lastly and latest of all, a brick building on the corner of Dale Street, probably an 1840s warehouse.

Peter Street

The name is for St Peter's Field, and the site of the 'Peterloo' massacre, *see* topic box. Here is also the site of one of the city's most important civic buildings, the Free Trade Hall (*see* Major Buildings). The rest is an eclectic mixture of buildings of different dates and styles. Starting from the St Peter's Square end, on the NW corner with Mount Street **Television House**, a straight curtain-walling job by *J. E. Beardshaw & Partners*, 1959–60. Opposite, s side, **St George's House**, the former YMCA

Peterloo

Popular radicalism in post-Waterloo England was fuelled by economic hardship and informed by the philosophy of Tom Paine. Manchester moved to centre stage in the story on 16 August 1819, when tens of thousands of marchers descended on St Peter's Field, in the area where the Free Trade Hall now stands, to hear the radical leader Henry Hunt. The meeting was one of a series in the campaign for universal suffrage, annual elections and other reforms. Most people, in response to Hunt's exhortations, were armed only with banners and flags, but even by the most conservative estimate (reported numbers vary between 30,000 and 150,000) it was a huge crowd. Manchester had never seen a meeting on this scale before, and the magistrates watched with rising anxiety as more and more people arrived. They had taken the precaution of stationing the military at various strategic points around the town, and when it was decided to arrest Hunt they called in the Manchester Yeomanry, led by Hugh Hornby Birley (*see* Outer Areas, Chorlton-on-Medlock, Walk 1, topic box), to assist. Sabres were drawn and violence erupted. With the arrival of the 15th Hussars the meeting was quickly and bloodily dispersed, leaving several dead and hundreds injured. Each side blamed the other for starting the violence, but the brutality of the attack was undeniable and news of the 'Peterloo Massacre' spread quickly, fuelled by suspicions of an establishment plot to demoralize and discredit the radicals. When the poet Shelley heard he swiftly revised 'The Mask of Anarchy' to honour the victims and their cause. Peterloo became the most famous event in the history of popular struggle for political reform in C19 England.

There is a large body of research on Peterloo. For recent contributions *see Manchester Region History Review* vol. 3, 1, 1989, a special issue devoted to the subject.

127. St George's House (former YMCA), Peter Street, by Woodhouse, Corbett & Dean (1907–11).

designed in 1907, completed 1911, by *Woodhouse, Corbett & Dean*, winners of a competition with rules enjoining competitors to bear in mind the architectural quality of the other Peter Street buildings. They seem to have come together just for the competition, but the result was felicitous. A great solid block of a building, of reinforced concrete construction using the *Kahn* system. The cladding is brown and buff *Burmantofts* terracotta with very shallow projections (*see* topic box, p. 170). The front is not symmetrical. The central entrance is a big semicircular arch. To the right undulating, slightly projecting bays on each side of a recessed lunette, simpler treatment to the left, the whole drawn together by a big bracketed cornice. Restrained and judicious use of ornament, including a copy of Donatello's St George in a niche. The incorporation of swimming baths, gymnasia and other sports facilities can be traced to New York prototypes, in particular the Brooklyn YMCA, 1885, and West Side Branch YMCA, 1897 by Paris & Schroeder, which was illustrated in *Architecture and Building* in the same year. Like these the Manchester building had a gymnasium with an oval running track around it and a swimming pool, in this case on the top floor, but everything was unfortunately removed when the building was converted to offices in the 1990s.

On the same side, w, the **Theatre Royal** (now the Royale night club) dated 1845 and built on the site of Thomas Harrison's 1803 theatre which burnt down in 1844. This incarnation is by *Irwin & Chester*, altered inside by *Edward Salomons* in 1875. A splendid classical composition in stone, one of the best examples of theatre architecture surviving anywhere in England from the first half of the c19. Projecting entrance

bay with giant recessed portico with Corinthian columns and pilasters. A central semicircular arch breaks through into the gable above. Steps up to the (altered) entrances, the central one surmounted by a pedimented niche with a statue of Shakespeare after the Westminster Abbey example by Peter Scheemakers. Flanking bays have tall pedimented first-floor windows with balconies. A debt is surely owed to Cockerell, whose Branch Bank of England was being erected at the same time (*see* King Street). On the N side a pair of warehouses, both erected *c.* 1868, on the corners of Southmill Street. No. 47, E side, is by *Walters Barker & Ellis*. A typical palazzo of the date, red brick with stone dressings, the ground floor altered. On the other corner **Harvester House** by *Clegg & Knowles*, stone-faced, five storeys, with the usual tall ground-floor arcade. The windows on first and second floors are pedimented. Still on the N side and set back from the street line, **Petersfield House**, 1965 by *Howitt & Tucker*. Six storeys, clad with precast concrete panels. Beside it No. 49, offices by *Mills Beaumont Leavey Channon*, 1992 with a bowed front above a recessed entrance with a single cylindrical column at the corner.

Further W, on the S side beside the Free Trade Hall, No. 44, by *Fairhurst Design Group*, 1988–90, offices; a stone-clad grid with a pediment on top and upper storeys recessed behind. Its neighbour, Nos. 38-42 **Fourth Church of Christ, Scientist**, is an intelligent conversion of 1950s Portland stone offices by *OMI Architects*, 1998. The interior has a remarkable double-height auditorium rising from the basement in

129. Fourth Church of Christ, Scientist, Peter Street, by OMI Architects (1998).

which white walls form planes, cut away and recessed to form a complex but uncluttered light-filled interior. To one side of the dais a load bearing column and beam form a cross, screening subsidiary spaces beyond. A gallery gives visual and physical connection with the foyer and stair, where the outside world is drawn in through large windows in the Watson Street elevation. On the N side, the **Albert Memorial Hall**, for the Manchester and Salford Wesleyan Mission. 1910, by *W. J. Morley* of Bradford, who won the limited competition. It was probably one of the largest Methodist halls in the country when it was built. It is just approximately churchy in some details, with a mixture of Gothic and Baroque elements. Octagonal turret with a domed top, all clad in yellow *Burmantofts* terracotta, with quite sparing decoration including sunflower motifs. (See topic box, p. 170.) The ground-floor rooms included lecture halls, classrooms, etc. Decorative plaster ceilings have been preserved in the pub conversion. The basements were used for social-work activities. A tile-clad foyer has stairs leading up to the huge (disused) upper hall, which seated more than two thousand, with horseshoe gallery and rostrum with an ornate organ case. Upper arcades of cast-iron columns have decorative spandrels.

The SW part of Peter Street was opened out as part of the scheme by *Leslie Jones Architects* for the conversion of the Great Northern Warehouse (*see* Windmill Street). A square was laid out in 1999 on the site of the goods yard which served the warehouse. A café on the corner of Watson Street is triangular, with the long side to Peter Street where it comes to a startlingly acute angle. Between café and warehouse are gardens with water features and a circular amphitheatre. On the Deansgate corner the former goods yard walls have been furnished with a tower which does not seem to serve any purpose beyond punctuating the corner.

Piccadilly

forms the approach to the town centre from Piccadilly Station (*see* Inner City, Walk 1a). Starting from the station end, E side, **111 Piccadilly** (formerly the Rodwell Tower), 1963–6 by *Douglas Stephen & Partners*, concrete with an eighteen-storey tower and a lower part. The construction is interesting for the building had to span the canal with large piers. Visually it reflects the influence of Louis Kahn's Medical Research Building, Philadelphia, with its boldly articulated uprights. The concrete has worn badly and there have been successive facelifts. Spanning the canal on the other side is the **Malmaison Hotel**, incorporating the Joshua Hoyle Warehouse by *Charles Heathcote*. It was built in 1904 using a completely rigid steel frame, clad in brick, terracotta and faience. The splayed corner bay containing the main entrance is crowned by a turret and flanked by gabled and turreted bays. The elevation to Auburn Street has a stair-tower with staggered windows. The new hotel entrance on Piccadilly is marked by a spiky raked and angled canopy linking the original building with a smooth bowed block which wraps around circular and square glass towers. This part and the conversion are by *Darby Associates*, completed in 1998. A further extension to the N is under construction, 2001.

No. 107, E side, is offices and warehousing, by *Charles Heathcote*, dated 1899. Typical Edwardian Baroque with gable and round angle turret, and with alternatingly blocked columns, but distinguished by subtle asymmetry in the elevations and robust muscularity. It has an iron frame and concrete floors. Simpler linked warehouse behind, being converted to flats, 2001. Dwarfed by its neighbour, No. 97 is a late C18 inn, the only survivor on Piccadilly of the buildings shown on Green's 1794 map. Stuccoed, with doorways with Doric columns and pediments. On the other side No. 12, **Barclays Bank**, an individual and powerful classical

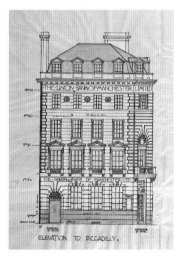

130. Barclays Bank, No. 12 Piccadilly, drawing by Percy Scott Worthington (1911).

essay by *Percy Scott Worthington*, for the Union Bank, dated 1911, strongly modelled in Portland stone. On the other, w side, No. 93, late C19 **Caxton Buildings** has a narrow brick frontage enlivened with tiles. Nos. 77–83, dated 1877, conventional eclecticism up to the eaves, but then the architects (*Clegg & Knowles*) suddenly go in a completely different direction – unless we are looking at later additions. It is certainly unlike their other buildings. There is a wide band of richly moulded fruit and foliage motifs, then a variety of oversized sculptures and gargoyles, topped by a timbered gable and the obligatory corner turret. Beside it Nos. 69–75 is Venetian Gothic, probably 1870s, with the entrance bays at each end given emphasis and the doorways with ornately carved consoles. Next the **Prince of Wales Buildings**, probably of the 1850s, has a rusticated ground floor and a range of upper windows with alternating segmental and triangular pediments.

Piccadilly Gardens

A wide square with the gardens in the centre. This was the site of the Manchester Royal Infirmary, erected in 1755 on the edge of the C18 town and demolished in 1909. Sir Oswald Mosley gave the land on condition that it should remain in public use. Prior to this the area was known unromantically as Daub Holes, for the clay pits here. These were transformed into a canal with fountains. The gardens were laid out with an esplanade on the N side by *Joseph Paxton* in 1854, partly to provide a setting for statuary. The present gardens on the site of the demolished hospital have little to recommend them, and a new layout to a design by

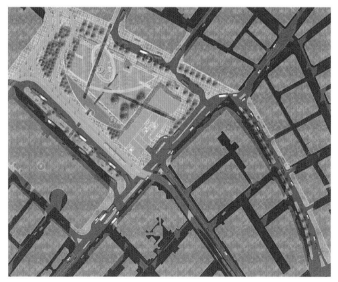

131. Visualization of the forthcoming changes to Piccadilly Gardens to a design by Tadao Ando.

132. Piccadilly Plaza, Piccadilly Gardens, by Covell Matthews & Partners (1959–65).

Tadao Ando is under construction at the time of writing. An elongated pavilion will be sited on the s side and new axes created, with water features and trees. Less welcome is the new commercial block to be erected on the E side, in spite of Lord Mosley's injunction, and the possible loss of the esplanade and dispersal of the **statues**, described here (from the w) although they are likely to be moved to other locations in the square, or elsewhere. Sir Robert Peel by *Marshall*, 1853, bronze with two bronze allegories below; Watt by *Theed*, 1857, a copy of Chantrey's statue at Westminster Abbey. Then the Queen Victoria Memorial (illus. 20) by *Onslow Ford*, 1901, with a stately and dignified seated bronze figure against a Baroque architectural background of Mazzano marble. On the other side a niche with a figure representing Maternity, on top a bronze of St George and the Dragon. Wellington by *M. Noble*, 1856. Public opinion favoured an equestrian statue but Noble's figure shows the Duke as an elder statesman. There are four supporting figures and four bas-reliefs. On the E side of the gardens a group by *John Cassidy*, 1907, representing Humanity adrift in the sea of life. Cassidy was a graduate of the Manchester School of Art and this was the first outdoor, non-portrait example of the new sculpture to be acquired by the city.

On the s side of the square, **Piccadilly Plaza** by *Covell Matthews & Partners*, 1959–65, to be remodelled and reclad by *Leslie Jones Architects*, 2001. Built on the site of warehouses destroyed in the war, a huge commercial superblock consisting of three buildings linked by a podium, more exciting than architecturally valuable. The **hotel** is a high slab parallel to Piccadilly, cantilevered out on a sloping underside, creating a very powerful effect when viewed from the side. The low restaurant projects towards Piccadilly and has three funny little roofs. The slab is stressed horizontally. The high office slab, twenty-four storeys high, **Sunley House**, has not got that horizontal emphasis. Also it stands at right angles to Piccadilly, and has towards it a wall decorated with relief designs derived from circuit boards, with just one long window slot. It is sheer on each side except for a little row of canted bays at the very top. The third element, **Bernard House**, at the corner of Mosley Street, with its stabbing-out roof, is to be replaced with a building of bland appearance. The group, instead of reading together, has always looked desperately disparate. It completely fails to take any account of its surroundings, but the sheer confidence and scale impress. What will be made of it in the remodelling remains to be seen.

On the older w side of the square No. 10 **Mosley Street**, 1836–8 by *Richard Tattershall* for the Manchester and Salford Bank: stone, with giant Corinthian columns on a high base bizarrely decorated with triglyphs. Then **Lewis's** Department Store, here from the 1870s. The original building was replaced by a huge untidy Baroque pile of 1915 by *J. W. Beaumont & Sons*, at that time the biggest store in the provinces rivalling the attractions of London shops. Extension of 1929, by the same architects. On the N side, from the w: No. 1 **Piccadilly**, by *J. Lynde* of 1879, a jolly incident on the corner of Tib Street with corner turret and upper bays articulated by short iron columns framing canted windows. It is the only one of his iron-framed buildings to survive. To the E the remains of a café of 1910, by *W. A. Thomas & C. Heathcote*, with Moorish detailing in white faience. No. 11, right, by *P. Hothersall*, 1922, was a cinema. Portland stone with giant pilasters and a balustraded parapet. Further along **National Westminster Bank** of *c.* 1930 by *J. Hembrow* of *Mills & Murgatroyd*. A nicely austere frontage of Portland stone with stylized Ionic pilasters and a row of solemn lions. Sparing ornament above, culminating in an attic sporting big cartouches and a cornice with lion masks. In 1932 *The Builder* described it, rather extravagantly, as 'one of the newest and most important [buildings] in Manchester'. No. 47 is a stuccoed late C18 survivor, diminutive beside its neighbours. No. 49, the former J. P. & E. Westhead & Co. warehouse, probably built 1846–7, is a severe palazzo in red brick with stone dressings; two great stone arched loading entrances at the rear on Back Piccadilly. Nos. 51–53, dated 1904, and Nos. 59–61, dated 1907, two versions of the same design by *W. & G. Higginbottom* separated from each other by a rather dull 1870s effort. **St Margarets Chambers** on the corner of Newton Street, 1889 by *Heathcote & Rawle*, has tall, ornate shaped gables and a wide carved stone frieze. Note the carving in the gable facing the square.

Portland Street

runs along the E side of Piccadilly Gardens and then continues SW to Oxford Street. It is a street of great C19 warehouses, still impressive, despite intrusions caused by demolitions and war damage which have robbed it of the canyon-like effect seen in Princess Street. No. 1, by *Gordon White & Hood*, 1974, a large brown glass block, canted at the top, sits uneasily beside the most distinguished buildings of the square, three former home trade warehouses all designed by *Edward Walters* between 1851 and 1858 in his accomplished palazzo style. He was designing the warehouses on Charlotte Street (q.v.) at about the same time, but here there was room – and the funds – for larger, more impressive buildings, all in stone. They make an imposing group, each one with fine, deeply cut carved detail. Nos. 3–5 and 7 are now the **Portland Thistle Hotel** and No. 9 offices. The façades only survive. Beginning with No. 9 on the corner of Aytoun Street, 1851–2, four storeys, rusticated ground-floor arcading and a central entrance. Second-floor windows with segmental pediments; balustraded parapet. No. 5, to the left, 1852, has five storeys with attic and basement and a ground-floor arcade. The two upper storeys are linked by giant pilasters. The proportions have been damaged by the additions above the cornice. The best of the group is Nos. 3–5, added in 1858, a refined version of No. 7, with more assurance and *élan* than its neighbours. It was designed when Walters was occupied with the Free Trade Hall (*see* Major Buildings), cf. the ground-floor arcade with spandrel carving. The horizontal stress of the rank of second-floor pediments is balanced by the verticality of giant pilasters linking to the floor above. This and the integration of sill with lintel, the whole united by the controlling forces of cornice and quoins, marks it as a product of Walters' maturity.

133. Nos. 3–5 Portland Street, by Edward Walters (1858).

Continuing sw down Portland Street, the dull former **County Hall**, se side (by *Fitzroy Robinson & Partners*, 1973). Next the **Britannia Hotel** (illus. 17 and 134), formerly Watts Warehouse, king of the home trade warehouses, a vast and ambitious affair of 1851–6 by *Travis & Mangnall*. S. & J. Watts was the largest wholesale drapery business in Manchester and the owner James Watts typical of the city's new mercantile princes, a self-made man who espoused the free-trade cause. His warehouse aptly encapsulates the spirit of self-confidence mixed with a touch of brashness. The length is twenty-three bays or *c.* 300 ft (90 metres), the height nearly 100 ft (30 metres). There are four roof towers but the ranges of gables between and on top of the towers shown on c19 engravings have been lost. The general outline resembles the Fondaco dei Turchi in Venice. Each of the six floors is given a different treatment ranging from Italian Renaissance to Elizabethan, culminating with wheel windows in the roof towers. This fantastic mixture is held together by an orderly rhythm and the confidence of the composition, so it is more than just a curiosity. The building had four large internal wells and a system of circulation which segregated customers, staff and porters. Inside, the original sumptuous staircase is preserved, as are the generous landings with their ornate cast-iron columns. In the entrance foyer a **First World War Memorial** executed in 1921. The Sentry (illus. 28), by *C. S. Jagger*, a strongly expressive bronze. A soldier with a rifle similar to the figures on his Royal Artillery Monument in London (1921–5). The watching figure aptly suggests both vigilance and contemplation. Opposite, and part of the same memorial, a stone plaque designed by *Hubert Worthington* recording the names of the dead. Also a Second World War memorial – the Risen Christ – by contrast weak and lacklustre.

On the nw side, **Bank Chambers** by *Fitzroy Robinson & Partners* of 1971. Podium faced with granite, rough below and polished above, supporting two towers clad in granite and Portland stone. Further s, se side, **St Andrews House**, a twenty-one storey slab, behind it a bleak bus and coach station, due for refurbishment 2001, beneath a multi-storey car park, all part of one scheme by *Leach Rhodes & Walker*. The tower is a straightforward job constructed in 1962 using a fairly new technique – a continuous climbing shutter and a tower crane to lift and position precast sections, so avoiding the need for scaffolding. The neighbouring No. 55 is a curtain-wall slab of 1959–61 by *E. Norman Bailey & Partners*. On the other (nw) side, No. 73, a former warehouse at the corner of Nicholas Street by *Pennington & Bridgen*, 1873. The style is becoming eclectic and Italian Gothic motifs are employed. Greatest emphasis is reserved for the piano nobile where the window surrounds are elaborate. Beside it a group of modest buildings gives an indication of late c18 scale. The rows of attic windows in some of them show that they were either designed or converted to accommodate workshops. The tall intruder in the middle of the block with its large windows is by *J. M. Porter*, 1883. Two little pubs in this row have partly original

134. Britannia Hotel (formerly Watts Warehouse), Portland Street, by Travis & Mangnall (1851–6).

interiors. The **Circus** (No. 86) has a bar in the entrance hall, grained matchboard partitions, and bench seating, an almost miraculous survival considering the tiny scale of it all.

On the corner of Princess Street is No. 101, the former **Pickles Building** (now the Princess Hotel). By *Clegg & Knowles*, *c.* 1870, stone with a corner entrance, and Continental Gothic motifs; in the eclectic style adopted by the firm at this time. The composition has been damaged by the loss of the tall chimneys at the eaves. Grouped windows of

135. Princess Street looking NW towards the junction with Portland Street.

diminishing size create an orderly rhythm, but with no indication of a piano nobile. Good carved decoration, as on all their buildings of this period. It is by *Simpkin & Stewart*, working to the architects' own designs. For Portland House on the other corner, *see* Princess Street. The whole of the remaining SE side has more big late C19 warehouses, all of red brick with stone dressings, all exhibiting more or less elaborate treatment of the openings. Together they create a powerful effect. The ground floor and basement of Nos. 113–115 were converted by *Hodder Associates*, 1998, for CUBE (Centre for Understanding the Built Environment); exhibition galleries with a bookshop and lecture theatre. Everything was stripped back to bare brick, timber beams and cast-iron columns, used as a backdrop for white screens and panels of opaque glass which admit diffused light. Generous stair to the lower level, set beneath an existing light-well bringing light down to the basement.

The **Behrens** building is the last in the sequence on this side. A long four-storey warehouse built for multiple occupation with a rounded corner to Oxford Street, by *P. Nunn* for Louis Behrens & Sons, *c.* 1860. The giant arcade creates a relentless rhythm, linking first and second floors and extending unbroken for twenty-three bays. The corner entrance leads to (converted) offices with Doric columns and a coffered ceiling. The late C19 buildings opposite have been demolished and their neighbours demolished behind façades. They made an important contribution to the street scene and should not have been allowed to go. A new hotel and health club by *Leslie Jones Architects*, 2000–1, will fill the space.

Princess Street

The most impressive Victorian street of the city. Like Portland Street it is lined with commercial warehouses, but here more survive and there are long unbroken sequences. Few are without interest and almost all keep within a single scale, having four or five storeys over a half-basement. In general they occupy a block each and most date from the 1860s onwards. A high proportion are by *Clegg & Knowles*, or by *Charles Clegg* alone, the leading firm for warehouse architecture of the late 1860s to the 1880s. Some have been converted to flats, and several are in the process of residential conversion, 2001. The buildings are so tall and close to the edge of the street that it is only possible to see them from the opposite side, so several blocks will be described sequentially to avoid crossing and recrossing this busy thoroughfare.

We start at the junction with Mosley Street. (For Princess Street NW from here *see* St Peter's Square and Albert Square.) Beside the Athenaeum (*see* Major Buildings, City Art Gallery) the earliest warehouse in the sequence is No. 83, on the corner of George Street. By *Travis & Mangnall*, *c*. 1847, with round-headed windows and an arcaded ground floor and basement. *The Builder* described it in 1847 as 'perhaps the best ware-house erected in Manchester since our previous visit' (in 1845) but it looks heavy-handed compared with its near contemporaries on Charlotte Street and its more refined neighbours opposite. Then as far as Portland Street mainly over-restored C18 or early C19 houses. On the w side Nos. 14–16, *c*. 1875, take the corner with Mosley Street gracefully; brick with stone dressings and a balustraded parapet. The corner is given emphasis by balconied first-floor windows. Next Nos. 18–24, Dugdale's ware-house, *c*. 1877–8, sandstone, in a free European Gothic style, with a hint of polychromy in the polished shafts to the upper-floor windows. The most striking feature is the open arcaded parapet and tall chimneys. It

136. A typical warehouse by Clegg & Knowles, No. 109 Princess Street (1863–4).

has all the hallmarks of *Clegg & Knowles*. Next Nos. 26–30 by *C. Clegg*, 1883 with a sandstone ground floor, brick with sandstone dressings above, corner oriels and two sets of paired entrances with consoles and broken pediments. No. 34, by the same architect, is also of 1883. Here there is a Tudor flavour with octagonal brick piers topped with stone pinnacles flanking tall gables. Over the central entrance a florid crocketed surround. On the N corner of Portland Street, occupying an island site, No. 36 is by *Clegg & Knowles*, 1880–2. Stone, in a variation of their usual eclectic style of the time. Note the elevation to Faulkner Street: no less rich, but the rhythm changes, with the openings grouped more closely, to suit the relative narrowness of the street.

Continuing SE of Portland Street, first the E side. After the Pickles Building (now Princess Hotel) on the corner (*see* Portland Street), No. 101 by *Clegg & Knowles* again, 1869, in the earlier version of their palazzo style. Brick with stone dressings, a high stone rusticated half-basement, a cornice above the ground floor, and first-floor windows emphasized with alternate flat and pedimented heads, all crowned with the usual emphatic cornice, here with paired brackets. On an island site, No. 103 is the former **Mechanics' Institute** of 1854–5 by *J. E. Gregan*. The institution had been founded in 1824 and this building was commissioned to replace premises on Cooper Street which had become too small. This refined palazzo was Gregan's last work. After his death in 1855 construction was supervised by *W. R. Corson*, with whom Gregan had trained in Scotland. It set a standard for the scale of the commercial warehouses which were to follow, but the nobility and purity of the

137. Mechanics' Institute (former), No. 103 Princess Street, by J. E. Gregan (1854–5).

design sets it apart from its neighbours. The proportions, with three tall storeys with a basement and blind attic storey, also contrast with the five-storey norm for the warehouses. Brick with stone dressings, central entrance and first-floor windows with segmental pediments. The site is awkwardly shaped and the parallelogram plan is stepped at the sides to make maximum use of the space and light. The arcaded first-floor windows on the Major Street elevation mark the position of the lecture hall. The interior has been altered, but the elegant entrance hall remains, and a full-height cantilevered stone staircase with an ironwork balustrade rises at the rear. It now houses archives of the National Museum of Labour History.

Nos. 105–107 is by *Clegg & Knowles*, 1871, a variation on their usual formula, this time in buff brick. No. 109, also by them, 1863–4, resembles No. 101. The New Union Pub beside the canal has early C19 origins.

Now for the w side. **Portland House**, on the corner of Princess and Portland streets, is a huge eclectic effort by *Pennington & Bridgen*, 1887, red brick, with pale stone bands and hipped gables with finials. Squashed up beside it No. 46a **Langley Buildings**, *c.* 1895 by *W. Waddington*, with a corner entrance with a ship's prow over it. The remaining buildings on this side as far as the canal are all late C19 variations of similar materials and scale.

The **bridge** over the Rochdale Canal has a separate footbridge to one side with a late C19 cast-iron parapet. Just beyond, w side, a departure from the Italianate norm with No. 74 (now part of the Dominion Hotel), 1880 by *Corson & Aitken*. Scottish Baronial style with angle

138. Manchester House, No. 86 Princess Street, by I. R. E. Birkett (1906–9).

tourelles and dormers with paired chimneys. A solid design accentuated by stone dressings and header bond brick. Corson was a Scot who trained in Dumfries, but his foray into Scottish style was not emulated by anyone else in Manchester. At the corner of Whitworth Street, the former Dominion House, now part of the hotel, by *I. R. E. Birkett*, 1893.

Across Whitworth Street, on the E side, the former premises of Morreau and Spiegelberg, by *C. Clegg*, 1912. Arcaded below with slightly projecting bays above, topped with a range of big shaped gables. On the other side two quite splendid early C20 packing and shipping warehouses, No. 82 **Asia House** and No. 86 **Manchester House**, by *I. R. E. Birkett*, 1906–9. Six storeys with attics and basements, essays in Edwardian Baroque stylishly executed in brownish red sandstone and pink bricks. No. 82 has an exceptionally rich entrance hall and stairwell lined with veined marble and green and cream faience, with designs of trees and Art Nouveau stained glass. It is a good example of the warehouse type, designed for multiple occupation by shipping merchants and furnished with offices with secure self-contained warerooms behind with the accommodation arranged in two blocks on either side of loading bays. The company running the warehouses provided portering, making-up, packing and despatch services carried out by their own staff in the basement and sub-basement with access to the loading bays.

139 & 140. Asia House,
No. 82 Princess Street, by
I. R. E. Birkett (1906–9).

Sackville Street

runs SE from Portland Street across the Rochdale Canal. Warehouses, all of *c.* 1870: No. 27 on the NE side has a door with an ornate overlight. SW side, between the Rochdale Canal and Brazil Street, nicely detailed Nos. 42–44 is by *Pennington & Bridgen*. Its neighbour No. 46 has an entrance in the splayed corner. Further S, beyond Whitworth Street, some large early C20 warehouses.

St Ann's Square

was laid out in 1720 on Acresfield, the site of an annual fair from the C13 until it moved to Knott Mill in 1823. The square represented the first major development away from the medieval centre around the cathedral. It was a select residential area, shown on a 1741 engraving with formal rows of trees.

St Ann, 1709–12. The church was founded by Lady Ann Bland née Mosley who obtained the necessary Act of Parliament in 1708 and built her church as a Whig and anti-Jacobite alternative to the high church Tory faction centring around the collegiate church. The design was probably by *John Barker* (cf. his St Alkmund, Whitchurch, Shropshire), executed by a local builder/architect. Purple-red Collyhurst sandstone with much patching. The W tower looks blunt, but it had originally a three-stage cupola, removed *c.* 1800 and replaced by the upper stage of the tower. Six-bay sides with two tiers of round-headed windows and coupled pilasters above and below, the lower ones fluted with Corinthian capitals. Apse with giant Corinthian pilasters and carvings in the frieze including cherubs of startling crudity compared with the graceful, if somewhat stiff, carving of the capitals (note the rainwater head immediately to the right of the apse treated as a Corinthian capital). The Baroque door on the N wall was added by *Waterhouse*, who restored and

141. St Ann, St Ann's Square (1709–12).

142. St Ann, St Ann's
Square. Wrought
ironwork pulpit rail
(*c.* early C18).

remodelled the church 1887–91. **Interior**. Waterhouse's interventions were remarkably restrained and sensitive. At the E end the apse was panelled, a platform inserted and altar and reredos added. The carved design of cherubs and swags in the panelling above the altar is copied from the Grinling Gibbons original in the choir of St Paul's Cathedral (the church was for many years attributed to Wren). Three galleries were retained but the Tuscan columns supporting them are replacements, only the slim upper columns are original. s chapel and N vestry. Waterhouse retained many furnishings including – **communion rail**. Partially original with beautiful scrolling wrought-ironwork. – **Pulpit**. Three-decker with angle columns and marquetry panels. Waterhouse gave it the right proportions by sinking it into a well in the floor. – **Pulpit rail**. Early or mid-C18 work, probably by the same hand as the altar rails. – **Font**. Shaped marble polygonal bowl with baluster stem, the gift of Francis Latham, dated 1711. – **Box pews**, remodelled but with the original brass plaques. s chapel: some original reset woodwork. – **Pew** with carved foliated panels. – **Altar table** with a dense array of columnar balusters on urn bases. – **Stained glass**. In the apse a scheme by *Frederic Shields* made by *Heaton, Butler & Bayne*. Figures in rich Germano–Swiss architectural surrounds, in pale tones. Shields had designed glass and mosaics for Waterhouse's chapel at Eaton Hall, Cheshire, during the mid 1880s. Other windows are mostly by Heaton, Butler & Bayne as well, of a variety of different dates but with unity of style. N side, E, three painted figures, St John, St Peter and St Matthew, of the 1760s by *William Peckitt* of York from the demolished St John, Byrom Street (*see* Inner City, Walk 3, p. 253, and topic box, Introduction p. 11). Upper windows are plain. In the s chapel an unusual etched abstract Art Deco design, in memory of Hilda Collens who founded the Northern School of Music in 1920.

Winter's Buildings, E of the church, is a big colourful mixture of brick, stone and terracotta, by *J. W. Beaumont*, 1901. To the s the rear of Nos. 39–43 King Street and Mr Thomas's Chop House (*see* Cross Street) form interesting points on the little enclave around the church. **Old Exchange Buildings**, a red sandstone block dated 1897 by *Royle & Bennett* s of the church, incorporates **St Ann's Passage**, leading through to King Street, with ornate pilasters to the passageway. On the SE side of the square the St Ann Street corner is graced by the urbane No. 25, now the **Royal Bank of Scotland**, built in 1848 for Benjamin Heywood's bank by *J. E. Gregan*. It is one of the finest of the palazzo-inspired buildings in the city, three storeys, of pale sandstone, beautifully finished. Care was taken to place the stone on its natural bed and so avoid premature decay. The rusticated ground floor has arcades of windows, on the upper floor pedimented windows have balconies. The corner is taken with a generous splay. The lower brick-built manager's house on St Ann Street is a more simply treated palazzo, with a splay to Cross Street drawing the composition together. It is linked to the main block by the single-storey entrance, an arrangement recalling the Palazzo Pandolfini in Florence, successfully relating the smaller scale of the domestic premises with the noble proportions of the bank. Beside it to the left Nos. 17–23, later C19, has ornate plasterwork decoration which has been extensively replaced by fibreglass. Next, on the corner of Old Bank Street, **Old Bank Chambers** (Barclays Bank) is of Portland stone with a very narrow corner splay with relief sculpture. By *Harry S. Fairhurst* for Manchester Liners, *c.* 1925. For the Royal Exchange, *see* Exchange Street. On the w side of the square there are some late C18 or early C19 houses, generally quite plain, though Nos. 6 and 20 have nice stuccoed decoration.

143. Royal Bank of Scotland, St Ann's Square, by J. E. Gregan (1848).

Statues in the square: Richard Cobden, by *Marshall Wood*, 1867, bronze; Boer War Memorial by *Hamo Thorneycroft*, 1907, a rifleman protecting his wounded comrade. Also a **fountain** with a fanciful bud of red granite on a dark stone drum by *P. Randall-Page*, 1995.

St Peter's Square

St Peter was built on the edge of the town in 1788–94 by *James Wyatt* and demolished in 1907 (*see* topic box, Introduction p. 11). On the site a

144. St Peter (demolished), St Peter's Square, by James Wyatt (1788–94). Engraving by J. Fethergill.

memorial garden designed by *L. C. Howitt* and dedicated in 1949, which incorporated a Portland stone cross by *Temple Moore* unveiled in 1908, commemorating the church, and the Portland stone **cenotaph** by *Lutyens*, 1924, similar to the Whitehall one; a pylon in diminishing stages with a figure of the Unknown Soldier draped in a greatcoat on top. As a public space the square does not work and the lack of coherence is exacerbated by the visual mess and physical barrier created by the Metrolink stop and the graceless stanchions for overhead wires. **Statues**: at the N end, opposite the rear of the town hall, **Messenger of Peace** by *Barbara Pearson*, 1986, bronze, whimsical stylized female figure with doves. Opposite the town hall extension, **Struggle for Peace and Freedom** by *Philip Jackson*, 1988, bronze, a group of linked figures.

The **Midland Hotel**, 1898–1903 by *Charles Trubshaw* for the Midland Railway, stands on the s side – a vast and varied affair, red brick and brown terracotta, with the French touches of, e.g., the Russell Hotel in London. Louche and undisciplined, but so confident as to be an essential part of the Manchester streetscape. The exterior is clad in several varieties of polished granite and generous quantities of *Burmantofts* faience (*see* topic box, p. 170) in which the company's wyvern emblem features prominently. The huge mass is hollowed out by two light-wells, like the town hall, but there is none of the town hall's logic of design or circulation. The interior has lost a good deal of its opulent detail but it is still possible to identify the Winter Garden and Octagon which, together with the saucer-domed corridor linking the hotel with the (former) route to Central Station (*see* Windmill Street), make up the chief reception area. Upstairs the Lancaster Suite has bold Jacobean plasterwork and panelling and a canted and angled oriel overlooking one of the light-wells. The Adamesque Derby Suite has some very handsome and probably genuine c18 doors and doorcases, wainscotting and chimney-piece. The magnificent Concert Hall is lost, its presence indicated today by just a stained-glass window by *George Wragge* in a lower corridor, and the four tympana on the Whitworth Street façade depicting the Arts by *E. C. Spruce*. MH

On the N side of the square (Princess Street) a row of late Georgian houses with doorcases all looking greatly restored. Nos. 73–75, Gothic, polychromatic and strongly, almost crudely, textured, is by *Ernest Bates* of 1868.

South King Street

parallel to the S part of King Street, is a backwater preserving some attractive late c19 cast-iron shopfronts along the N side. No. 41 and No. 19 are the best and most complete.

Southmill Street

W side, **Police Headquarters**, 1937 by City Architect *G. Noel Hill*. The Portland stone front is in stripped classical style with a rusticated ground floor and two lower projecting bays flanking the central entrance, seeming to owe a debt to Percy Scott Worthington's Masonic Hall of 1929 (*see* Inner City, Walk 3, p. 249). The part behind is all in pale brick around a big courtyard entered from Bootle Street.

Spring Gardens

From the junction with Mosley Street there is an intriguing glimpse of Lutyens' Midland Bank (*see* King Street). At the junction with Fountain Street on the left corner, S side, an office building by *Edward Walters*, 1851, with a splayed corner to Spring Gardens. Four storeys and added attic storeys. Rusticated stone below, red brick above, with pedimented second-floor windows which have sills integrated with the lintels of the windows below. On the right corner, N side, No. 49, a former warehouse by *Clegg & Knowles*, 1879. A disciplined and satisfying composition in stone with curved corners to Fountain Street and Concert Lane. On the left corner, N side, Nos. 60–62 is a former warehouse of 1881–3 by *Alfred Waterhouse*. Pale stone laid in his favoured alternating narrow and wide courses of, e.g., the town hall. Splayed corner with an octagonal turret, the ground floor rusticated with a continuous arcade of openings. For the extension *see* Fountain Street.

The street curves around to the right (for Chancery Chambers *see*

145. Lancashire and Yorkshire Bank (former), Nos. 43–45 Spring Gardens, by Heathcote & Rawle (1888–90).

Brown Street). Here a group of imposing bank and insurance buildings closes the view E along King Street. No. 47 was built in 1881 for the Commercial Union Assurance Society by *Charles Heathcote*. Renaissance with richly decorated dormers and a turret to the corner. The exploitation of this awkward site shows that Heathcote's considerable skill was already well developed. The adjacent Nos. 43–45 of 1888–90 was the premises of the Lancashire and Yorkshire Bank, by *Heathcote & Rawle*. Free Renaissance, not yet the fully blown Baroque Heathcote is best known for. Stone, the first two storeys rusticated with a window grid recessed between rusticated piers. A tall Baroque turret gives emphasis to the principal entrance bay, on the left side, and then the roofline shapes diminish in size with smaller shaped gables. The huge and splendid banking hall, with twin saucer domes, polished granite columns and marble-lined walls, retained some of the original furnishings, such as the customer writing cubicles on the left side, when converted to a pub. Adjoining it is No. 41 curving around the corner of York Street. Stone, built for the National Provincial Bank by *Alfred Waterhouse*, 1888–90 and not at all Gothic. The style might be called free German Renaissance, with its variety of gables. The stone front curves round and is in high relief, thanks chiefly to very prominent brackets for balconies and pediments. The banking hall is no more.

On the corner of York Street, opposite, is *Charles Heathcote*'s superb former **Parrs Bank** of 1902. His usual bold Edwardian Baroque, with Art Nouveau motifs in the ironwork. All of red sandstone with an angle dome and corner entrance. The arched windows have paired Doric columns between, supporting nothing more than big scrolled brackets. The banking hall (now used as a pub-restaurant) is amongst the most opulent of any of the date surviving in Manchester, and for that matter, in London. First a foyer in mahogany with Ionic columns framing the doors, then the sumptuous banking hall, with green marble walls and Ionic columns. The ceilings are encrusted with richly moulded plaster-

work, and some of the original stained glass survives in the windows.
Now there is a change in character as the street continues N. On the w
side **Amethyst House**, a large office block by *Howitt & Tucker*, 1973.
Beside it the **Post Office**, by *Cruickshank & Seward*, opened 1969. Three-
storey podium block and an eight-storey tower with stone cladding.
Inside, the upper walls are lined with bold fibreglass relief panels.
Glossy **Tootal House** opposite is by *John Ratcliff & Associates*, 1982.
Gloomy **Lowry House**, by *Arthur Swift & Partners*, 1975–6, dominates
this area with its 190 ft (58 metre) tower.

Tib Lane

is a little street between Cross Street and Booth Street. On the s side
No. 10 is a late C18 former town house. Next, and almost as narrow, but
of four storeys over a tall basement, a jewel-like warehouse of 1876, by
Smith & Heathcote in Italian Gothic style. Stone with a richly carved
entrance to the right and grouped windows, treated differently on each
floor. A little further to the E another (altered) building of late C18 origin.

Watson Street

For the Great Northern Warehouse *see* Windmill Street.

Whitworth Street

One of the great Manchester streets, the w part as impressive as Princess
Street but of the next generation. We start at the E end. For the
University of Manchester Institute of Science and Technology (UMIST),
s side, *see* Academic Institutions. On the N side, at the junction with
Aytoun Street and Chorlton Street, is the Manchester Metropolitan
University Aytoun Campus. This was the site of the College of Commerce
which joined with the College of Art and the John Dalton College of
Technology to become Manchester Polytechnic in 1970. University
status came in 1990 (for a fuller history and the other central Manchester

147. Aytoun Library and Computer Centre (Manchester Metropolitan University), Whitworth Street, by Mills Beaumont Leavey Channon (1993).

buildings, *see* Academic Institutions). A twelve-storey tower and podium clad in grey precast concrete by *S. G. Besant Roberts*, the City Architect, 1966, was the college's first purpose-built premises. In front, and linked by a two-storey glass entrance block, the impressive contrast of **Aytoun Library and Computer Centre** by *Mills Beaumont Leavey Channon*, 1993. It has an irregular plan, made to fit the site, and a sinuous form following the curve of the street and echoing the lines of Gateway House (Inner City Walk 1a, p. 217) which forms a backdrop to views to the N E. Five storeys, clad in shining white powder-coated aluminium panels. Inside, a ramp sweeps up from the entrance foyer and turns back to the first floor.

Shena Simon School, N side, on the corner of Chorlton Street. By *Potts & Pickup*, opened in 1900 as Manchester Central School. Red brick and orange and buff terracotta with a tall polygonal corner turret. The building fronts a small park facing Sackville Street, but despite this luxury in an otherwise crowded area, the architects could not rise to the challenge; the elevation has a variety of shaped gables and other Renaissance detailing but is straggly and unimaginative. In the **Park**, sculpture: **Beacon of Hope** by *Warren Chapman* and *Jess Boyn-Daniel*, 2000. Steel column with incised and pierced designs dedicated to those affected by HIV/AIDS. This and the nearby Canal Street area has come to be known as the Gay Village. On the N side, at the corner with Sackville Street a big warehouse of c. 1880, dwarfing pedestrians with a massive plinth of punch-dressed stone. Each of the wide windows has a central square-section cast-iron pier. Beside it there is a gap with only low walls and an entrance left to commemorate No. 42, the late C19 premises of Somerset & Co. On the other side a range of big ware-houses, all of a height, all of the late C19 or early C20, all of red brick.

Individually they are not outstanding but the visual coherence and massing is a vital part of the street scene.

Lloyds Packing Warehouses dominate the remaining part of the street s of the junction with Princess Street. The company was formed in 1896 through mergers, giving it a virtual monopoly over the packing trade. By 1926 it was packing and despatching one third of the foreign cotton trade of Lancashire. The warehouses here were built in response to the boom in trade and confidence following the opening of the Manchester Ship Canal in 1894, when easy access and efficient loading facilities were essential. The huge buildings are steel-framed and built to high-quality fireproof specifications. Terracotta and faience fronts contrast with the rear elevations where the steel frame is exposed and glazed. The architect, who was the leading expert in the design of these advanced warehouses, was *Harry S. Fairhurst*. First **Lancaster House**, built in two phases between 1905 and 1910. Edwardian Baroque, of red brick and orange terracotta. It is the scale which impresses rather than the detail. The first phase was the section to the w alongside Whitworth Street. The second phase, on the corner of Princess Street, is more elaborate, with an ornate four-storey corner turret. Premises for the Union Bank were incorporated from the beginning in a ground-floor suite of rooms reached from a corner entrance. The neighbouring **India House**, 1906 is also Edwardian Baroque. Between them the entrance to the rear yards, with a lovely arching ironwork gate with an Art Nouveau style lamp hanging from the upper part. Both buildings were converted into flats in the 1980s. Opposite, backing on to the Rochdale Canal,

148. Lancaster House, Whitworth Street, by Harry S. Fairhurst (1905–10).

Canal, **Bridgewater House**, 1912, typically ambitious business architecture of its time, granite below, white faience above, with a ripple of canted bays. Eight storeys with attics and basements. Probably the most advanced building of its type when it was erected. Fairhurst's design revolutionized the business of loading and unloading of goods, and here twenty-six lorries could be dealt with simultaneously using a drive-through system.

Whitworth Street West

continues w of Oxford Road. The **Corner House** (s side) is a complex of cinemas and exhibition space formed from a cinema of 1910 which had been used as a store for many years. *The Millard Partnership* and *Fletcher Priest Architect*s undertook the conversion in 1985. The cinema opposite with the curved corner is part of the complex. By *P. Cummings*, 1934–5, refitted in 1998 by *David Chipperfield* who clad the upper part with green glass strips, lit from behind at night, and introduced a spacious foyer. On the N side, beside the canal, a large (154-unit) residential development by *Mills Beaumont Leavey Channon*, under construction 2001. From this point the MSJ&AR viaduct follows the s side of the street. Further w the **Green Room Theatre**, inaugurated in 1987, is accommodated within two of the arches. The painfully sparse entrance and front of house was transformed in two phases between 1992 and 1996 by *Ian Simpson Architects*. A little farther w, the **Ritz**, a dance hall built in 1927–8 with a white faience front sporting trophies with musical instruments. It was one of *Cruickshank & Seward*'s early commissions. Not far beyond, on the same side, another white-faience-clad block is a warehouse of 1914, by *Harry S. Fairhurst* again. The arches of the viaduct open out as the junction of Albion Street is approached, and items of gasworks machinery have been arranged within the arcade. On the gasworks site to the s in landscaped grounds **Grand Island** by *P. Shuttleworth* of *Building Design Partnership*, 1991. A great square office block clad in purple-grey panels with a central atrium, heavy-looking because of the client's requirement to reduce solar gain. On the opposite side of the street the former Haçienda Club, opened in 1982, now being converted to flats. The club was the first of its type in Europe and it attracted people from all over the country when it first opened.

Windmill Street

N side: attached to the rear of the old YMCA (*see* Peter Street) an office block by *Essex Goodman & Suggitt*, 1973, with uncompromising full-height window strips. The **G-Mex Centre**, formerly **Central Station**, stands high up on the s side. It was Manchester's fourth railway terminal, erected 1875–80. *Sacre*, *Johnson* and *Johnstone* were the chief engineers of the three companies that came together as the Cheshire Lines Committee to undertake the project. They were the Midland, the Great Northern and the Manchester Sheffield & Lincolnshire Railway. The huge

149. G-Mex Centre, Windmill Street, by the Cheshire Lines Committee (1875–80), converted by Jack Bogle of Essex Goodman & Suggitt (completed 1986).

wrought-iron and glass train shed is in the form of a segmental vault, spanning 210 ft (64 metres), only 30 ft (9 metres) less than St Pancras. There are eighteen main arch frames, the gables are double arches, giving fifteen bays. Arches are linked by latticed purlins carrying intermediate ribs. Beneath the shed is a vast brick undercroft with intersecting tunnel vaults. This was used for storage and there were wagon lifts from the adjacent goods sidings. The exposed front was to be hidden by an hotel or offices, but instead low waiting rooms and offices were built, and the Midland Hotel, opposite (*see* St Peter's Square), was not started until 1898. Closure of the station came in 1967. The future of the building was secured when the Greater Manchester Council acquired control of the site in 1978 and the building was converted to the Greater Manchester Exhibition and Events Centre, or G-Mex, by *Jack Bogle* of *Essex Goodman & Suggitt*, and opened in 1986. The shed ends were glazed on the inside of the structural ironwork and the scruffy frontage buildings removed and replaced with low glazed foyers. The roof, which had already been replaced in 1950, was reclad in aluminium and the undercroft repaired and converted for car parking.

Immediately right of G-Mex, to which it is linked at the rear, the **International Convention Centre** by *Stephenson Bell* and *Sheppard Robson*, 1999–2001, occupies a site which slopes down to Watson Street to the w. A glass foyer on two levels fronts Windmill Street and wraps around an 800-seat stone-clad auditorium, shaped like a scallop shell in plan, which rises above the entrance with an angle jutting out to the street. A multi-purpose hall at the rear (s) is separated from the auditorium by a taller service stack. It sits well with its neighbour, but the proposed fourteen-storey block alongside it to the right along Watson Street will surely be too high and cut off all the views of the Great

150. International Convention Centre, Windmill Street, by Stephenson Bell and Sheppard Robson (1999–2001).

Northern Warehouse (*see* below). The appearance and character of this area will be further changed by extensions to the Free Trade Hall (*see* Major Buildings).

The w side of the junction of Windmill and Watson Streets is the site of the gargantuan **Great Northern Warehouse**, opened in 1898. It was planned by *A. Ross* of the Great Northern Railway with consulting engineer *W. T. Foxlee*. It is a hugely impressive block, much larger than its five storeys would suggest, of blue brick below, red brick with blue brick dressings above, and lettering in white brick at the top. Steel stanchions, each one capable of bearing a load of 650 tons (660 tonnes) with longitudinally riveted wrought-iron girders, support arched brick fireproof floors. It acted as a railway, road and canal interchange. The Manchester & Salford Junction Canal (*see* Barbirolli Square) *c.* 40 ft (12 metres) beneath ground level was reached by shafts. The future of the building was uncertain for many years. Eventually the carriage ramp and viaducts serving the upper level goods station were removed as part of a conversion of 1999–2000, and it is to be incorporated into an extensive leisure complex by *Leslie Jones Architects* (*see* also Peter Street) and deprived of its monumental isolation by the new buildings to the s stretching the full length of Watson Street to Great Bridgewater Street. For all its ambition, the new block between the warehouse and the new building fails to do its job of visually linking the two. There is an abrupt change in plane and materials, and fiddly detail. The new building, under construction at the time of writing, aims for a tough industrial look.

Winser Street

beside the Rochdale Canal. **Electricity Station**, opened in 1901. Red brick, sandstone dressings, with giant round-headed arches with keystones. The large octagonal chimney is a local landmark. It was powered by four steam engines each driving a 1,800 kw direct current British Westinghouse generator. At this time the plant was one of the most

151. Great Northern Warehouse, Windmill Street, by A. Ross of the Great Northern Railway, with W. T. Foxlee as consulting engineer (1898).

compact in the country reflecting the limitations on space in this crowded warehouse district. It was one of the earliest combined heat and power stations in the country, providing steam heating for many of the nearby warehouses.

York Street

On the N side the rear of the Piccadilly Plaza with entrances to the offices and a spiral car ramp. On the s side No. 26, *Leonard Stokes's* former telephone exchange, *c.* 1909. Freestyle, an original and subtle design with gently canted bays of fine red brick, in places laid in herringbone pattern, with blue brick banding and sparing white faience decoration. Further w beyond the junction with Mosley Street the scene is dominated on the N side by the large Postmodern **Royal & Sun Alliance**, by *Cassiot & Ashton*, 1993, with an incongruous flattened pediment. Opposite, and set back from the street line, **York House**, an eleven-storey tower by *Leach Rhodes & Walker*, 1973, with their characteristic alternating dark brick and slim white strips.

The Inner City

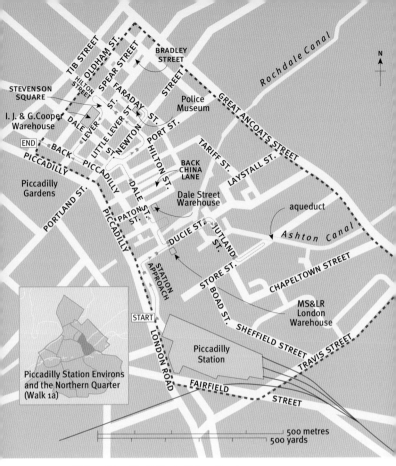

N

TIB STREET

OLDHAM ST.

BRADLEY
STREET

HILTON
STREET

SPEAR STREET

STREET

Rochdale Canal

STEVENSON
SQUARE

FARADAY
ST.

Police
Museum

GREAT ANCOATS STREET

I. J. & G. Cooper
Warehouse

LEVER
ST.

LITTLE LEVER ST.

NEWTON
ST.

PORT ST.

DALE
ST.

HILTON ST.

TARIFF ST.

LAYSTALL ST.

END

BACK
PICCADILLY

PICCADILLY

BACK
CHINA
LANE

Piccadilly
Gardens

PORTLAND ST.

PICCADILLY

DALE
ST.

PATON ST.

Dale Street
Warehouse

aqueduct

Ashton Canal

DUCIE ST.

JUTLAND
ST.

STORE ST.

CHAPELTOWN STREET

STATION
APPROACH

START

LONDON ROAD

Piccadilly
Station

BOAD ST.

SHEFFIELD STREET

MS&LR
London
Warehouse

TRAVIS STREET

Piccadilly Station Environs
and the Northern Quarter
(Walk 1a)

FAIRFIELD

STREET

500 metres
500 yards

152. Walk 1a. Piccadilly Station to Oldham Street.

Piccadilly Station Environs and the Northern Quarter

This Walk covers the area NE of the central part of town, known as the Northern Quarter. It contains the area between the centre to the SW, Ancoats to the NE and Shudehill to the NW. The Walk is split into two, the first covering the SE part, with the station and canals, the second covering the area W and NW of Oldham Street.

The area N of Piccadilly was largely open countryside until the late C18. Most of the land belonged to Sir Ashton Lever of Alkrington, who began selling it in large blocks to developers *c.* 1770 (*see* topic box, Introduction p. 12). Some buildings of that period survive. A few have some architectural pretension but most are modest brick houses, some with attic workshops. Late C19 and early C20 textile warehouses, offices and other commercial buildings now crowd the streets nearest the town centre which largely retain the scale of C19 Manchester. The scale, colour and detail of some of the later buildings contrast with the utilitarian appearance of what survives from the early part of the C19. Much of the area is something of a backwater, but regeneration, initially centred on Oldham Street, started in the late 1990s with new bars, cafés and shops as well as residential conversions of warehouses and commercial premises. Around a dozen have been started or are proposed and by some estimates there will be more than two thousand new residential units in the area by 2004.

The part N and W of Oldham Street includes areas where crowded streets and narrow alleys give a flavour of how the area must have been before later C19 rebuilding. Much of this area had already been built up by the mid C18 as the town expanded E from the medieval core around the cathedral and some late C18 and early C19 houses and warehouses survive here.

1a. Piccadilly Station to Oldham Street

We start at the top of **Station Approach**, a ramp leading up to **Piccadilly Station**. The first station here opened in 1842. It was operated jointly by the Manchester & Birmingham Railway (later the London & North

153. Gateway House, Station Approach, by Richard Seifert & Partners (1967–9).

Western Railway, LNWR) and the Sheffield, Ashton-under-Lyne & Manchester Railway (later the Manchester, Sheffield & Lincolnshire Railway, MS&LR). Enlargement of the station was completed in 1866 and further extensions made 1880–3 when the present roof was installed. The LNWR 1880s extension, over a vast undercroft, lies to the s. The mutilated frontage on London Road includes the goods office entrance, Renaissance style with pilasters with fanciful ram's-head caps. Refurbishment and rebuilding of the station was undertaken in 1959–66 by the Midland Regional Architect's Office (*R. L. Moorcroft*) when new platforms were built and the 1866 offices replaced by a high oblong office block. This is to be remodelled and reclad as part of a major refurbishment of the office and concourse areas, 2000–1.

Manchester South Junction and Altrincham Railway (MSJ&AR). This was one of the first suburban railways, started as a joint venture between the two original companies on the Piccadilly Station site in 1845. The 224 brick arches of the **viaduct** run between Piccadilly Station and Liverpool Road, following approximately the route of the River Medlock and forming the visual boundary to the s side of the city centre. It was constructed in 1845–9 by the builder *David Bellhouse Jun.*, and several of the cast-iron bridges were built by his son, engineer and iron-founder *Edward Taylor Bellhouse*. The 1¾ m. (2¾ km.) structure used 300,000 cubic feet of stone (91,440 cubic metres), 50 million bricks and 3,000 tons (3,048 tonnes) of wrought iron.

Piccadilly Station has an interchange with the **Light Rapid Transport System**, in Manchester called the **Metrolink**. It was constructed by a consortium consisting of GEC (electrical, signalling, telecommunications, vehicles, etc.), *John Mowlem & Co.* (civil engineering) and *AMEC* (depot facilities). Plans for an underground railway between Piccadilly and Victoria Stations, to be integrated with the bus and rail system, failed to win Government backing in 1974. A Parliamentary Bill for a light rapid transport system was deposited in 1984. It links the existing Bury and Altrincham suburban railway lines and the route is all over-ground, running from Piccadilly Station to Victoria Station and thence to Bury, with the Altrincham route branching off in Piccadilly Gardens. Ugly traction poles support most of the overhead-line system, and obtrusive ramps at the stops damage the setting of some important buildings in the city centre (*see* St Peter's Square). The system opened in 1992 and was extended to Eccles and Salford Quays in 1999. Further extension is proposed.

Gateway House runs alongside the Station Approach ramp. An office block built speculatively as part of the station refurbishment. By *Richard Seifert & Partners*, 1967–9. A very impressive long, sweeping, undulating façade, the horizontals stressed throughout. One of the best of the 1960s office blocks in Manchester, its glittering serpentine shape well suited to the sloping site. At the base of the ramp **Ducie Street** runs NE. A former goods yard on the s side was the site of a group of four warehouses, of which the **MS&LR London Warehouse** is the sole survivor. Of 1867,

154. MS&LR London Warehouse, Ducie Street (1867).

intended mainly for bonded goods. It is a massive starkly grand seven-storey block of brick with stone dressings and small segmental-headed windows. Rail access was from the NE side, bringing wagons into the building via four sets of tracks, and road access was from the SW side. **Interior**. Fireproof construction was used, an advanced type for the day, which exploited the tensile strength of wrought iron to achieve greater spans. The cast-iron columns, those on the ground floor with base diameters of over 2 ft (65 cm.), diminish in circumference on each floor and support a grid of riveted wrought-iron box girders carrying intermediate cast-iron beams carrying brick jack-arches. There were originally eighteen internal hoists. The building was converted for mixed retail and residential uses in 2000–1.

A detour can be made from this point to the Manchester terminus of the **Ashton Canal**, built to transport coal from Ashton and Oldham to fuel-hungry Manchester (for the part to the NE in Ancoats, *see* Outer Areas, Ancoats, Canals). The Act was passed in 1792. Unlike most of the inland waterways in the North, it was for narrow boats of 7 ft (2 metre) beam. *Benjamin Outram* was responsible for the part between Great Ancoats Street and the **basin**, which lay on the S side of Ducie Street beneath the railway goods yard, where it can be seen truncated just NE of the London Warehouse. Further NE along Ducie Street the canal passes beneath the road to join the Rochdale Canal Basin to the N (*see* below). Just beyond, Jutland Street runs S to **Store Street**, which is crossed just to the N by *Outram*'s **aqueduct** (illus. 12), *c.* 1794–9. Skewed construction, derived from William Chapman's pioneering designs for the Grand Canal at Naas in County Kildare, Ireland, of a decade before. It is the earliest surviving example of the improved 'English System' of building skewed bridges, since the Irish examples and those by Jessop on the Rochdale Canal have all been demolished. Karl Friedrich Schinkel, the Prussian court architect, considered it sufficiently interesting to measure and sketch it when he visited Manchester in 1826. The Walk can be rejoined by returning to Ducie Street and continuing SW to Dale Street.

Dale Street runs NW from Ducie Street. On the E side is the **Rochdale Canal Basin**. The Rochdale was the first of the transpennine canals to be completed. By linking the Bridgewater Canal in Manchester with the Calder & Hebble Canal in Sowerby Bridge it completed the route between Hull on the E coast and Liverpool on the W. *John Rennie* assisted by *William Crosley* undertook surveys during 1791, and Crosley went on to act as engineer, with advice from *William Jessop*. After many false starts the Act was passed in 1794 and the canal was completed 1804–6.

The street entrance to the basin is via a castellated stone archway of 1822 with a tiny lodge attached behind. Attached to the left are the unassuming early C19 offices of the Canal Company. The basin is filled in and used as a car park, but two buildings survive. The first, left of the entrance, is the four-storey **Dale Street Warehouse**, dated 1806 and constructed from watershot millstone grit blocks. The initials WC on the

155. Ordnance Survey map of the Ashton and Rochdale canal basins (surveyed in 1849).

datestone suggest it may have been designed by William Crosley. It has some decorative features. The (w) elevation to the street has a slightly projecting central bay with a parapet, and there is a Venetian window in the N gable end. It is of considerable interest as the earliest surviving canal warehouse in the city which differs structurally from the warehouses of the Bridgewater Canal Basin (*see* Walk 4). It has timber floors supported by unusual branched cast-iron columns with octagonal bases. They have two struts attached to fish-bellied plates supporting timber beams. On the upper floors columns have flanges to receive shuttering for flexible division of the floor space. It is the only surviving canal warehouse of the period in Manchester to use cast-iron columns throughout. There are arched shipping holes to the E towards

156. Dale Street Warehouse, Dale Street (1806).

the basin, so that goods could be unloaded from internal wet docks.

A cast-iron and timber high breast-shot water wheel served this and a demolished warehouse to the E. Designed by *T. C. Hewes*, and installed in 1824, it survives in a subterranean stone chamber to the S of the building. On the far NW side of the basin a crumbling brick warehouse of 1836 has small windows with round heads and a range of shipping holes on the S side. (Garry Corbett reports that it was a grain warehouse with timber floors and cast-iron columns with drop holes in the floors and external hoists. The columns have sockets for shuttering, and the remains of hand pulleys for the hoists survive in the roof space.)

A scheme of 2000 for the development of the basin by *Ian Simpson Architects* proposes refurbishment of the buildings (including Brownsfield Mill, *see* Outer Areas, Ancoats, p. 282) for residential and retail purposes, reopening part of the canal basin, and building new apartment blocks.

We return to Dale Street which runs NW, lined on both sides with late C19 and early C20 commercial warehouses. No. 57, E side, 1913, in half-hearted Baroque style, has a streamlined interwar rear extension. Next to it Nos. 53–55 **Langley Buildings** of 1909 by *R. Argile* makes the most of its narrow frontage with a lively terracotta façade sporting a curved oriel and giant composite pilasters supporting a segmental pediment. Note Back China Lane, SE side, a private street for loading, with original gates. No. 56, W side, *c.* 1875, is a warehouse with a Venetian Gothic front, stone below and polychrome brick above. More warehouses follow; one of the largest, E side, is No. 35, of 1903 by *J.W. Beaumont*. Six storeys in pink terracotta and a splayed corner with upper octagonal piers with turrets. **Bradley House** sits on a triangular

157. Langley Buildings,
Nos. 53–55 Dale Street,
by R. Argile (1909).

site between Newton Street and Port Street, *c.* 1850, a late classical warehouse (five storeys, brick on a stone ground floor). The narrow elevation to Dale Street has a tripartite window with pilasters. The junction of Dale Street, Newton Street and Port Street is a good vantage point from which a variety of warehouses can be seen. On the NE side of Dale Street, Nos. 29–31 by *W. & G. Higginbottom*, 1909, is a big home trade warehouse in bright red brick with white stone dressings, earmarked for residential conversion, 2001. Opposite there is a little row of late C18 houses with doorcases. On the NW side of **Newton Street** there are two 1880s warehouses, both by *Clegg, Son & Knowles*, the first on the corner of Back Piccadilly, red brick and stone dressings, with rounded corners and prominent chimneys. Its neighbour on the corner of Dale Street is similar, though more elaborate.

Hilton Street is reached by cutting NE along Port Street beside Bradley House. A group of late C18 houses survives on the N corner. Nos. 45–47 have crude pedimented doorcases and steps from the street down to cellars. The houses extend along each side of Port Street where one or two have long attic workshop windows. Hilton Street continues NW. On the S corner of **Newton Street** No. 50 was built for a hat manufacturer by *C. Clegg & Son*, 1907. Baroque, strikingly designed to maximize light with giant three-storey glazed arcades on the three exposed sides. A short detour N to the corner of Faraday Street, brings us to the **Police Museum** in a police station of 1879, low and unpretentious in red brick. The range along the Newton Street front was rebuilt as a Weights and Measures Office later in the C19, but the station, entered from Faraday Street, retains the original charge office and windowless cells. Just to the N Baroque post

158. No. 50 Hilton Street, by C. Clegg & Son (1907).

office buildings of *c.* 1910 are being converted to flats, 2001. Returning to the corner of Hilton Street brings us to **Stevenson Square** and the site of St Clement, of 1793, demolished in the 1870s. This was the centre of a development by William Stevenson, who bought the land from Sir Ashton Lever in 1780. It now has a mixture of large textile warehouses, offices and shops of the late c19–early c20, though some look as if they have mid-c19 origins. The former premises of I. J. & G. Cooper on the s side were designed in 1906 by *John Bowden* in close collaboration with the owners. The huge home trade warehouse occupies an island site stretching through to Dale Street. The style is eclectic with tall shaped gables, all done in pressed red brick with matching terracotta and a red sandstone ground floor. On Dale Street, sw side, is an extravagant arched stone entrance with carved Renaissance and Art Nouveau motifs, while on Spear Street, nw side, the loading bay is lined with white glazed bricks.*

*The building was considered sufficiently advanced to merit a full-page description in the *Building News* in 1906. It was lit throughout by electricity, and solid steel columns diminishing in size on each successive floor were used for their superior fireproof qualities. A staff canteen catered for 400.

Lever Street leads sw towards Piccadilly, crossing Dale Street (for Nos. 69–77 *see* Outliers, below). At the junction more warehouses: the Italianate No. 20 on the NE side, by *Smith Woodhouse & Willoughby*, 1875, has arched entrances rising through two storeys with carved keystones and ironwork screens. No. 22 on the other, SE side, by *J. W. Beaumont*, 1895, has an arcaded corner entrance and a pair of large arched windows. Looking back across to the N side of Dale Street from the street corner gives a view of the frontage of the Coopers' warehouse (*see* above) and, beside it on the other corner of Spear Street, No. 3, a former millinery warehouse of *c.* 1905, red brick and yellow terracotta with Baroque touches, being converted to flats, 2001. Further s down Lever Street, opposite No. 19 **Chatsworth House**, NW side, an office block of 1975 by *Carl Fisher & Partners*, is a group of late C18 or early C19 town houses (now offices) with elegant stone doorcases and semicircular stone steps leading up to the front doors: Nos. 12–14, scribed stucco, Nos. 8–10 exposed brick.

Back Piccadilly is a narrow alley running parallel to Piccadilly from Newton Street (E) to Tib Street (W). Backtracking a little from Lever Street, the odd one out (s side) for its date and sharply contrasting scale is an early–mid-C19 warehouse with a loading slot. It backs on to No. 47 Piccadilly, of the late C18 (*see* City Centre, Piccadilly). Almost opposite the merest sliver of an early or mid-C19 house is crammed behind No. 8 Oldham Street. Further E the most notable building is **Mother Mac's** pub, probably 1870s, which crowds an absurdly steep and narrow slated turret flanked by chimneys into the tight corner to Little Lever Street. To the w the street connects with Oldham Street and the second part of the Walk.

Outliers

Laystall Street. A former warehouse of 1880 by *M. Seanor* with an extravagant front of richly moulded terracotta stands on the SE side near the junction with Tariff Street. It was built for a manufacturer of firebricks and of terracotta, for which the frontage was probably designed as an advertisement.[*] Next to it, No. 48, a cotton mill of *c.* 1830. The complex on this site includes an octagonal brick chimney rising from a square base, one of the few mill chimneys to survive in the Inner City.[†] The streets nearby retain something of their early C19 pattern, with, here and there, the bricked up ghosts of early and mid-C19 houses.

Lever Street, N part. Late C18 Manchester housing is graphically illustrated by Nos. 69–77, NW side, a row of five brick houses with pedimented doorcases backed on **Bradley Street** by the city centre's only surviving examples of one-up one-down houses. The contrast between the smart houses on the street frontage and the tiny dwellings behind is

[*]I am grateful to Steve Little for supplying these details.
[†]Shockingly demolished just as this book was going to press, summer 2001.

striking, but they were probably originally occupied by artisans, and had many advantages compared with cellars, back-to-backs, and common lodging houses which were the lot of less skilled workers. The whole range was rebuilt in 1996 so it all looks regular and new.

1b. Oldham Street to High Street

Oldham Street was one of Manchester's premier late c19–early c20 shopping streets. After years of decline regeneration has come with residential conversions and a smattering of stylish new shops and bars. We begin at the s end with a mixture of shabbily grand early c20 shops, for example Nos. 6–12, E side, with an upper Doric colonnade, which is completely outdone by Nos. 21–33, opposite, by *J. W. Beaumont*, 1914, with its grand upper Ionic colonnade. To the N is the **Methodist Central Hall**, E side, by *George Woodhouse*. The Methodist chapel in Oldham Street of 1781 was demolished in 1883 and replaced by the present hall on a different site in 1885–6. It was substantially rebuilt following war damage. The exterior is undistinguished, in a weak and flat Renaissance mode, but the site is important historically as the centre of Manchester Methodism from which a large and well-organized social services mission spread during the c19 and earlier c20.

    Smithfield Building, w side, is the former Affleck and Brown emporium, actually several separate buildings around a central courtyard, converted to flats by *Stephenson Bell* for developers *Urban Splash* in 1997–8. Shops below with flats recessed behind balconies above held together with a tight urban vocabulary of grids, though the treatment is varied to the N to express the different elements of the original buildings. Upper floors generally retain the late c19 façades. To the N more late c19 and early c20 shops and offices follow before we reach two interesting pubs. **The Castle**, E side, built in 1789, was used as a pub

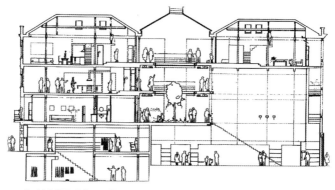

159. Smithfield Building, Oldham Street, converted by Stephenson Bell (1997–8).

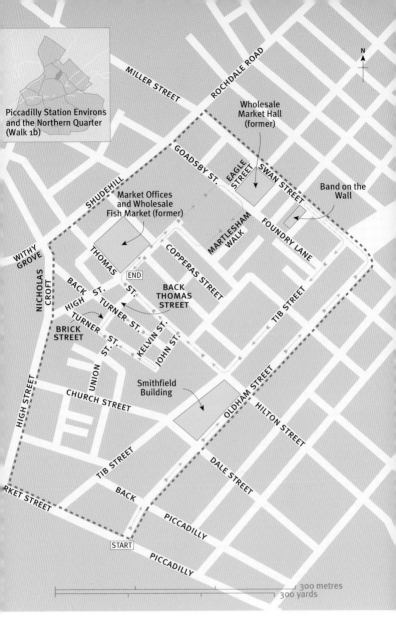

160. Walk 1b. Oldham Street to High Street.

from at least 1816. The present décor probably dates from 1897, when it was taken over by Kay's Atlas Brewery. Arts and Crafts lettering outside and late C19 plan and fittings inside. **The City**, w side, also late C18, was called the Prince of Orange from *c.* 1800. It has a good late C19 timber front with carved pilasters and fanlights with radiating bars. Above, early C19 plasterwork panels. Adjoining are the **Big Issue Offices**, an

161. Plasterwork panel on The City pub, called the Prince of Orange from *c.* 1800. This shows William and Mary arriving in England attended by Britannia, a rejoicing clergyman and angel.

imaginative conversion of a 1950s shop by *Ian Simpson Architects*, 1998. Opposite, a 1950s store is being converted and extended as a residential development by *Hodder Associates*, 2001.

There are one or two interesting buildings on **Swan Street** which runs NW at the top of Oldham Street, for those who feel equal to a detour. Nos. 2–4, N side, a former **Midland Bank**, by *J. B. Whinney*, was completed in 1922. Classical, in Portland stone, with a curved end to Oldham Road, upper Ionic pilasters and a balustraded parapet. Further NW, the entrance to **Swan Buildings**, N side, a passageway inserted into early C19 houses which has a nicely carved plaque with a swan over the entrance. Almost opposite, the altered and garishly painted **Band on the Wall**, formerly the George and Dragon, was an Edwardian music hall-pub which retains a bold ground-floor arcade outside and splendid plasterwork ceilings with pendants inside. Its neighbour, No. 11, is Ruskinian Gothic in red brick. Rejoin the Walk by returning along Swan Street and turning right down Tib Street.

Tib Street runs SW parallel to Oldham Street. It originated as a foot-path alongside the River Tib, which was culverted in 1783. The narrow street is lined with a mixture of buildings, including some later C19 warehouses. A few C18 houses survive, most of them greatly altered. Nos. 47–53, W side, had originally basement cellar dwellings and attic workshops. The (restored) workshop windows and N gable taking-in door survive. In this and neighbouring streets there are various small-scale artworks such as passages of text in the pavement and reliefs on walls, by various artists, 1996–8.

Thomas Street runs NW, but there is not much to see until Nos. 48–50, SW side, is reached. It has long ranges of upper workshop windows and a warehouse extension with its loading bay at the rear on **Kelvin Street**. This area was built up by the middle of the C18 and the maze of tiny streets here reflects the essentials of the layout shown on Green's 1794 map. A little further S on Kelvin Street, W side, Nos. 3–5 are a pair of three-storey houses of *c.* 1772–4. Beside them No. 1 is similar, and prob-ably of a similar date, but better preserved with the original entrance, cellar steps and attic workshop windows. Kelvin Street connects with **Turner Street** where there are more warehouses of different C19 dates. Turn left for No. 37, N side, another house, built in the 1760s, with a

Workshop Dwellings

In late C18 and early C19 Manchester typical city-centre housing included buildings designed to incorporate cellars and attic workshops. Similar buildings are found elsewhere, for example in Macclesfield, Cheshire, where the workshops were used for weaving silk. They can be seen as an urban parallel to C18 Pennine stone cottages with rows of upper weavers' windows. They were of brick, double pile, usually of one bay and three storeys. Sometimes they would be given a touch of class by a stone doorcase. The cellar could be used as a dwelling or workshop, or both; separate accommodation above might also be used as a shop or beer house, while the attic had long ranges of windows to light workshops for textile preparation or finishing processes such as handloom weaving and fustian cutting. Information on exactly how they were used and occupied before the 1801 census is sparse, but they were probably erected by speculators for skilled workers or artisans on good incomes. Documentary research, and the evidence of the surviving buildings, has shown they were often erected in ones and twos, with more being added as the developer could afford it. Where they survive they are usually greatly altered, but good examples can be seen in several parts of central Manchester, especially in the areas covered by Walk 1 and on Liverpool Road in Castlefield (*see* Walk 4, p. 270).

162. Attic workshop, No. 53 Tib Street (*c.* late C18).

cellar entrance and crude area railings. Next but one on this side is a utilitarian mid-C19 warehouse of four storeys and a basement. Opposite, s side, on the corner with Union Street, a range of mid- to late C19 warehouses with stone dressings and polychromatic brickwork. Turning N up Brick Street then E along **Back Turner Street** brings us to another group of much-mutilated buildings. On the s side No. 36, in header-bond brickwork, has late C18 origins, and its neighbour, No. 38, was built in the 1820s. The most outwardly interesting is No 42, a late C18 or early C19 building of four storeys and a basement and a full-height loading slot to the left, possibly a conversion of a dwelling for warehousing. Kelvin Street completes the circuit back to Thomas Street. Further W, Nos. 30–35, NE side, is a row of town houses with late C18 or early C19 doorcases placing them a cut above the humbler Kelvin Street dwellings, though the attics have workshop windows. More C18 and early C19 buildings, most of them substantially altered, can be found in the immediate area.

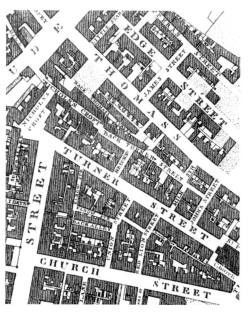

163. Turner Street, as shown on William Green's map (1794).

Thomas Street continues NW to the top of **High Street**. On the SE side a range of 1870s brick polychrome warehouses. They are not individually especially interesting but are effective as a group. They probably include those being erected here to designs by *E. J. Sherwood* in 1874. Opposite, Nos. 75–77 is a showy Venetian Gothic warehouse, *c.* 1875, sandstone and red brick, with elaborate corner entrances with big carved heads. Beside it on Thomas Street there is a similar, slightly more subdued warehouse, dated 1878.

At the NE end of High Street a number of the buildings of the former **Smithfield Market** can be found. The market grew up in the late C18. In 1846 the Corporation bought land on the SE side of Shudehill and the site expanded throughout the C19. The **Market Offices**, on the NE corner of Thomas Street, are by *Travis & Mangnall*, 1877. Three storeys, red brick with stone dressings, with an arcade of round-headed windows at first-floor level. On top a conglomeration of tall chimneys and pedimented gables crowned with urns. The bowed corners have

164. Wholesale Fish Market, High Street, by Speakman, Son & Hickson (1873). Sculpture by Henry Bonehill.

curving windows with ranks of granite shafts – a favourite Travis & Mangnall motif. Attached to the right is the eccentric **Wholesale Fish Market** by *Speakman, Son & Hickson*, 1873. It is beside the site of a building improbably described in 1849 as a cheese market and night asylum. Only the gabled brick façades and some cast-iron columns survive, though plans for incorporating these elements into a new building are in preparation (*see* below). The style is Italian Romanesque with stepped gables and prominent Lombard friezes. There is sculpture in the tympana by *Henry Bonehill* of Manchester showing scenes of fishing at sea, landing the catch and selling it on, etc. What these lack in finesse is partly made up for by their vigorous narrative qualities. Attractive ironwork gates survive, by *Hodkinson Poynton & Lester*.

To the N E, on **Goadsby Street**, the **Wholesale Market Hall**, by *Isaac Holden & Son*, dated 1857, altered 1867. Classical, in a style described by *The Builder* in 1859 as 'Roman composite'. Stone, pedimented, with pilasters incorporating bulls' heads and arched openings, some with decorative metal screens. The area in front bounded by Martlesham Walk S E, Shudehill N W, and Goadsby Street N E was a huge wholesale food market with an iron and glass roof erected by *Mr Wheeldon* of Derbyshire under the superintendence of *William Fairbairn* in 1853. It was removed in the late C20 for a car park. This is to be the site of a mixed retail, commercial and residential scheme by developers *ICIAN*. The National Embroiders Guild plans to have a headquarters building here, and some of the existing market buildings will be converted. Emphasis will be on small-scale crafts businesses, building on trades operating from the **Craft Village** in the retail fish-market building of *c.* 1895, which lies near the SE corner of the site. Glazed roof, arcaded brick sides – nothing special, but suited to the new use; craft studios and shops inserted in the 1980s. There is already a residential area just to the N, low-rise local authority housing of the late 1970s, the first public-sector housing in the centre after slum clearance and exodus in the 1960s.

High Street leads S to the centre, and Market Street. Walk 2 can be joined by proceeding N along Thomas Street to Withy Grove, which runs W to Corporation Street.

Outliers

Church Street. The W part was laid out 1741–51. Set back from the S corner of High Street, offices; a concrete podium with only a narrow horizontal slit of a window and four recessed storeys above. By *Leach Rhodes & Walker*, 1969. Next on this side a large former warehouse now called **The Coliseum**, 1928 by *Jones, Francis & Dalrymple* with a grand stone front with fluted Doric columns. On the N side a late C19/early C20 warehouse converted to flats, 2000. Beside it a multi-storey car park on the corner of Tib Street occupies the site of St Paul, consecrated 1765 (*see* topic box, Introduction p. 11), and the premises of J. & N. Philips, from which two First World War memorial plaques by *Sir Hubert Worthington* and two smaller Second World War plaques were salvaged and placed on the car park stair-tower.

High Street E side, the **Hogshead** pub, *c.* 1870, looks as if it originated as offices, perhaps by *Pennington & Bridgen*. Gothic detailing and window arcades between entrance bays with Tudor moulds over the doors.

From the River Irwell to Shudehill

Including the medieval core around the cathedral

This Walk covers the NW side of the city centre from the Irwell and the boundary with Salford on the W side, to Miller Street to the N and Shudehill to the E.

The medieval core of the city which lay near the river had become a squalid slum by the early–mid C19. Corporation Street was cut through the E part in 1848 and became a centre for warehousing. On its E side the Co-operative Wholesale Society and the Co-operative Insurance Society began building offices and warehouses from the early C20, a process which continued to the 1980s. The area wore an air of neglect for many years, but its regeneration has begun; prompted partly by the damage caused by the terrorist bomb which in 1996 exploded near the S end of Corporation Street causing severe damage to the immediate area. The urban design competition for the city centre launched in response covered not only the area damaged by the bomb but also the neglected hinterland to the N. The winners were a team consisting of EDAW, *Ian Simpson Architects, Alan Baxter Associates, Benoy* and *Johnson*

165. Late C18 view of the River Irwell looking SW from a point near present day Victoria Bridge Street.

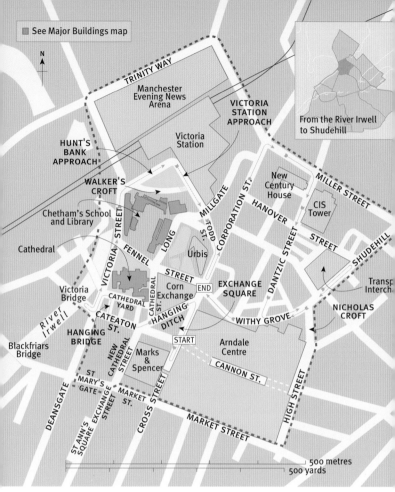

166. Walk 2. From the River Irwell to Shudehill.

Urban Development Consultants, whose proposals included linking the cathedral area with the centre by creating a new pedestrian route (New Cathedral Street, below) and new public open spaces (Exchange Square and Cathedral Gardens, the latter to a design by *Building Design Partnership*), as a focus for regeneration and development.

Corporation Street is a continuation of Cross Street (*see* City Centre). The N part was cut through a muddle of tiny alleys and courtyards in 1848, the year in which the Corporation purchased the manorial rights of the town from Sir Oswald Mosley. The aim was to connect the centre with Ducie Bridge, a principal crossing point over the Irwell to the N, achieved by clearing a route from Market Street as far as Todd Street (formerly Toad Lane) and later extending the line to Miller Street. The

167. Footbridge over Corporation Street by Hodder Associates, with engineers Arup & Partners (completed 1999).

new thoroughfare swiftly became a centre for warehousing but nothing much survives from this time. We start at the s end at the point where the 1996 explosion occurred. Here the whole area has been rebuilt keeping most of the basic street pattern. The new **Marks & Spencer** store, w side, by *Building Design Partnership*, opened in 1999. An enormous free-standing block with a central light-well and big glass screens which have alternatingly transparent and reflective qualities. Despite its size it does not dominate, thanks to the careful detailing of the elevations and respect for the cornice line of the Royal Exchange. A high-level foot-bridge over Corporation Street by *Hodder Associates*, engineers *Arup & Partners*, completed in 1999, replaces the footbridge destroyed in the explosion. It is a hyperbolic paraboloid in the form of a translucent spiralling hourglass, with triangular glass cladding panels. A solid deck was inserted instead of the proposed transparent glass surface which was considered too unnerving for users. It links with the w side of the Arndale Centre (*see* also City Centre, Market Street), but cannot bridge the stylistic gap between the classy refinement of the M&S store and the unexciting Arndale Centre frontage, with formulaic towers, by the *Ratcliffe Partnership*, completed 2000.

To the n a new public space, **Exchange Square**, by *Martha Schwarz*, 1999–2000. The shape was determined by the line of Hanging Ditch on the n side (*see* below), New Cathedral Street to the w and Corporation Street to the e. The fall of the land is taken by a series of angled terraces from the platform upon which Marks & Spencer sits. The creation of a big public space here is to be welcomed, but the scheme has been let down by gimmickry, e.g. the strange pop **sculptures** by *John Hyatt*,

1999, in the form of giant grey metal children's windmills set at different angles. The space is over-structured, so it is not possible to traverse it in all the desired directions. The lighting scheme is imaginative, however, and at the base of the terraces there is a curving linear water feature with blocks of stone rising above the water so that it can be crossed at any point.

The **Corn Exchange**, now renamed the Triangle, dated 1897 and 1903, takes up the N side of the square. It is free Renaissance, top-lit with a dome. The site is triangular and the straggly four-storey building took thirteen years to build, which must partly account for its lack of coherence. *Ball & Elce* did the brick part to Fennel Street and *Potts Son & Pickup* the rest. It suffered extensive bomb damage in 1996 and most of the comfortable Edwardian interior has gone, replaced by new retail outlets, with the general idea of galleries lit by the central dome retained. The building fronts **Hanging Ditch**, *see* topic box, a street named from a watercourse running in an arc between the Rivers Irwell and Irk, first mentioned in an early C14 property agreement, which enclosed the heart of the medieval settlement.

Cateaton Street runs w as a continuation of Hanging Ditch. The **Old Wellington Inn** and **Sinclair's Oyster Bar**, N side, are known collectively as the **Shambles** of which they were originally a part. They were modified in 1925, jacked up from the medieval street level to Shambles Square (*see* New Cathedral Street, below) in the 1970s, a process which involved the insertion of a steel framework, and finally moved here in 1998–9 as part of the post-bomb redevelopment. In their new context they have been put up in a different relationship to one another so that they form an L-shape, conveniently creating an outdoor seating area in the angle. The **Wellington Inn**, probably C17, has close-studded framing with angle braces and mullioned windows, the jettied gables decorated with lattice framing. The framing of the upper floor shows that it is a later addition. Of 1998–9 the odd rear extension which reproduces timber framing in stone cladding, and the stone linking block to the **Oyster Bar**. This was of brick, the internal timbers reused, so its origins are obscure though a C16 date has been suggested for it. In the re-erection it was decided to perpetuate painted mock timber framing. Inside mid- to late C19 bar fittings have been preserved. More important Manchester buildings have disappeared without a trace in the last decade, so perhaps the main point of this exercise will be to illustrate an enduring C20 love affair with timber framing. The buildings form the visual termination of **New Cathedral Street**, a welcome new pedestrian route, running from St Ann's Square along the w side of Marks & Spencer. Immediately w the awful 1970s Shambles Square shopping precinct has been demolished. New mixed development here is scheduled for completion by the end of 2001.

Mynshull's House further w on Cateaton Street, N side, is an engaging little building with an openwork parapet and Jacobean detailing. By

Hanging Ditch

Hanging Ditch is the outermost of three ditches encircling a promontory at the confluence of the Irwell and Irk. This was the site of the manor house of the Grelley family at the heart of the early medieval town, where the c15 buildings of Chetham's School and Library (*see* Major Buildings) now stand. The earliest reference to settlement here dates from the c13, but it is the likely site of a castle recorded in 1184, and might conceivably have Saxon origins. The line of the ditch is clearly visible in the street pattern shown in c18 and early c19 maps, and can still be divined from the curving line discernible in (from the s) Cateaton Street, Hanging Ditch, part of Corporation Street, Todd Street and Victoria Station Approach, where the line of the culverted Irk is marked by Walker's Croft. The section between Cathedral Street and the Irwell has been investigated in recent times but the exact route and origins of the remaining stretch are still conjectural. In 1997 excavations on the present site of the Shambles (above) indicated that the ditch was a natural watercourse which had been modified, perhaps in order to improve its defensive capabilities. The stream had been culverted at some point, and although partially open in the c17 it was subsequently filled in and built over.

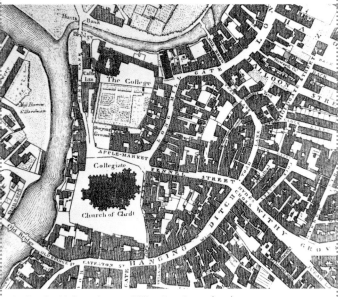

168. Hanging Ditch, as shown on William Green's map (1794).

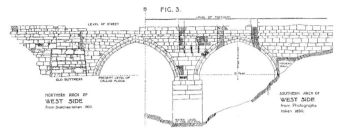

169. Hanging Bridge as shown in a pamphlet (1910) of the same name.

T. B. Elce with carving by *J. J. Millson*, dated 1890 (the basement was designed to preserve and display the E face of Hanging Bridge, *see* below, which can still be seen there). It is supposedly the site of the house of the apothecary Thomas Minshull or Mynshull (d. 1689). Cutting N along the narrow alley beside the building brings us to Cathedral Yard. **Hanging Bridge** spans Hanging Ditch between Cateaton Street (S) and Cathedral Yard (N), where it is *c.* 66 ft (20 metres) wide. Standing on top of the bridge is Hanging Bridge Chambers of 1880–1, a narrow office building with ranges of boxy oriels. The bridge formed the principal approach from the town to the parish church (now the cathedral) during the medieval period. The earliest reference to it occurs in 1343, but the present structure is probably a later rebuilding or remodelling, a likely date *c.* 1421–*c.* 1500, the period when the parish church was rebuilt. It is of coursed and dressed Collyhurst sandstone. Only one arch is visible, but both arches survive and they were drawn in the late C19 when they were exposed during building work. These drawings, combined with observations made from the basements of Hanging Bridge Chambers and Mynshull's House, have allowed a picture of the structure to be built up.* There are two Tudor arches with a central pier which has a cutwater on its E side. Irregularities in the alignment and masonry detail at the N end of the W side suggest that part of an earlier bridge may have been incorporated. The arch to the S has three stone ribs on its underside, perhaps later additions inserted to strengthen it. The sides differ from one another as well, with larger stone blocks on the E face, possibly evidence for refacing or repair. The bridge is to be incorporated into a cathedral visitor centre within the shell of Hanging Bridge Chambers, designed by *Hurd Rolland Partnership*, 2000.

Victoria Street (which was formerly known as Hunt's Bank Approach) runs N alongside the Irwell, which is crossed by **Victoria Bridge**. Of 1837–9, replacing the C14 bridge which linked Manchester with Salford. Stone, with a heavy parapet and in the middle on each side the Queen's orb on a massive Grecian scroll. A set of blocked openings to the Irwell in the road retaining wall can be seen from Victoria Bridge.

*This description is based on Dr Arrowsmith's account published by the University of Manchester Archaeological Unit, 1999.

Part of a large complex of c19 arches beneath the street, they were used in the late c19 as a copper and ironworks but can hardly have been built for that purpose. Further N beyond the Chetham's buildings (*see* Major Buildings), three railway bridges cross the street, two with cast-iron parapets decorated with a cheerful pattern of pilasters and festoons. They emanate from the nearby Victoria Station (*see* below). We turn right into **Hunt's Bank Approach**, which runs alongside the River Irk, culverted between the Irwell and Victoria Station in a series of five campaigns through the c19. This was a principal crossing-point into Manchester from the N, on the line of the Roman road to Ribchester and Carlisle. City Engineers' plans show three separate phases of stone bridges over the Irk beneath the road, perhaps including the remains of c18 and earlier bridges. On the N side the sprawling **Manchester Evening News Arena** by *Austin-Smith: Lord* with *Ellerbe Beckett* 1995–6. A huge soulless sports and entertainment complex, grafted on to the back of Victoria Station. It is clad in banded masonry with upper parts in purple-grey cladding and green glass. The constructional interest is in the use of reinforced concrete to improve sound insulation and the huge size of the roof which is spanned by a 345 ft (105 metre) steel truss. The development includes a speculative office block jutting out on to Hunt's Bank Approach, beside steps up to the entrance. To the N, on the site of the Manchester Union Workhouse, there is a multi-storey car park with circular stair-tower of glass bricks.

Victoria Station was opened in 1844 by the Liverpool and Manchester Railway and the Manchester and Leeds Railway. An L-shaped block on the corner of Hunt's Bank Approach and Victoria Station Approach. *Robert Stephenson* was the designer of the original Hunt's Bank Approach building. This is Italianate, of stone with an added upper storey and wings. The station was extended in 1864–5 and enlarged again in 1909 by *William Dawes* for the Lancashire and Yorkshire Railway Company. It was adapted during the 1990s to accommodate the Metrolink, which enters from the E side to serve a new platform before joining the line to Bury. The long stone Baroque elevation to Victoria Station Approach is unexciting, but there is attractive detail such as a glazed canopy along the street frontage, with the names of destinations and a tiled map beside the northern entrance showing the railway network. The bronze **war memorial** beneath was unveiled in 1922. Inside the Edwardian booking hall survives, also a range consisting of a first-class restaurant, domed refreshment room, and bookstall, all with gold mosaic lettering on a turquoise ground. The refreshment-room interior has walls of marble, mosaic and tiles, and the underside of the dome is richly decorated with festoons of fruit and flowers.

Todd Street is the continuation of Victoria Station Approach, running s. The area to its s is to be incorporated into the Cathedral Gardens, designed by *Building Design Partnership* and due for completion late in 2001 (*see* topic box).

170. Victoria Station,
Victoria Station Approach.
By William Dawes (1909).

The corner of Todd Street and Corporation Street is the site of
Urbis, by *Ian Simpson Architects*, 2000–1. Shaped like a rearing transparent prow and clad in textured semi-translucent glass, the entrance
from the low N end will lead to a progression of spaces through six
storeys to the tallest, S part. It is intended to include a restaurant and
café on the top floor, and a permanent exhibition 'exploring the experience of the modern city'.

The block on the E side of **Corporation Street** at the corner of
Withy Grove, is occupied by the **Printworks**, an entertainment centre
by *RTKL UK Ltd*, 1999–2000, which retains the weakly Baroque Portland
stone façade of early C20 newspaper offices and works by *A. Rangeley*.
The main interior space, depressingly, is a sort of Edwardian pastiche.
Much better is the light-hearted high-tech of its cinema. The buildings
of the **Co-operative Wholesale Society** (CWS) and **Co-operative
Insurance Society** (CIS) occupy the remainder of the E side of the
street. First the **Co-operative Bank**, 1977 by *CWS Architects*, red brick
with a deep mansard, built on a horseshoe plan. Beside it a **statue** of
Robert Owen by *Gilbert Bayes*, 1953, moved here in 1994. Next CWS
offices, Baroque, by *F. E. L. Harris*, 1905–9, with coupled giant Corinthian
columns and arcading at the top. The unbalanced look is due to the loss
of the corner domes. Then more offices, originally a bank, this time of
1928, by CWS chief architect *W. A. Johnson*. Uninspiring and severe

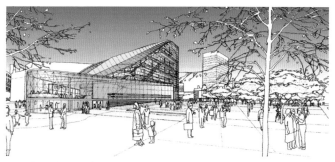

171. Urbis, Todd Street/Corporation Street, by Ian Simpson Architects (2000–1).

The Cathedral Gardens

The Cathedral Gardens will go some way to creating the haven envisaged in the 1945 City of Manchester Plan, which aimed to create an appropriate green setting for the medieval buildings here. Fennel Street and Long Millgate will be closed to traffic and green space will be extended around the cathedral. Contoured lawns and trees, planted informally and in blocks, will create a more tranquil setting for the buildings.

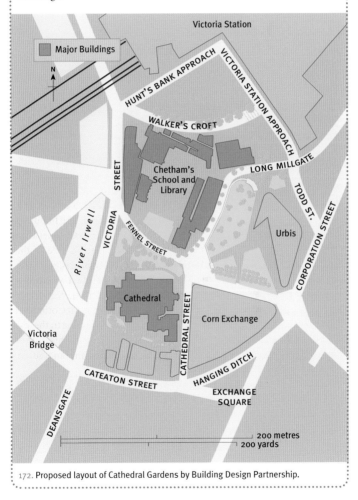

172. Proposed layout of Cathedral Gardens by Building Design Partnership.

173. CIS tower, Miller Street, by G. S. Hay of the CWS and Gordon Tait of Sir John Burnet, Tait & Partners (1959–62).

with giant upper pilasters. **Parkers Hotel**, by *Bradshaw & Gass*, 1906, on the N part of Corporation Street beyond Miller Street, started as the CIS head office. Edwardian Baroque, red brick and Portland stone, with a curved frontage to the street corner and a copper dome. A simpler stone addition to the left.

Miller Street is named for Arkwright's mill of *c.* 1782, which was sited here. It was the largest of the Arkwright-system mills built in England and Scotland and probably the first Manchester mill to use steam power to raise water to the waterwheel.

On the s side the offices of the CWS and CIS. The complex consists of a twenty-five-storey tower, a five-storey lower part, and the fourteen-storey **New Century House** to Corporation Street, a curtain-walled slab. The **CIS tower**, the best of the Manchester 1960s office blocks, done with discipline and consistency, and inspired by the achievements of Skidmore, Owings & Merrill, in particular the Inland Steel Building in Chicago, which was amongst the buildings inspected by the design team on a fact-finding trip to America. The team were *G. S. Hay* of the CWS and *Gordon Tait* of *Sir John Burnet, Tait & Partners*, the date 1959–62. When the building was being planned the CIS General Manager

174. CIS tower, Miller Street. Part of the executive suite by Professor Misha Black and the Design Research Unit.

set out three general aims. The building should add to the prestige of the Society and the Co-operative Movement, improve the appearance of the City of Manchester and provide first-class accommodation for staff. The aims were fulfilled, and continue to be fulfilled forty years on.

First the CIS tower. Steel frame and a windowless service tower of reinforced concrete clad with mosaic and rising to 400 ft (122 metres). Glass, aluminium and black enamelled steel were chosen for the exterior instead of concrete or stone, which become dirty so quickly in Manchester's atmosphere, and this decision has paid off. It remains the tallest building in Manchester and one of the most distinguished. The details around the entrance from Miller Street are the only weakness. The entrance hall is excellent, the cool spaciousness only slightly marred by a new controlled-entry system. The mural by *William Mitchell*, of bronzed fibreglass, fits perfectly with the optimistic 1960s ambience. *Professor Misha Black* and the *Design Research Unit* designed the interiors including the executive dining rooms in cherry veneer and the executive suite with teak veneer and vertical green glass strips.

New Century House is approached from an entrance forecourt from Corporation Street, with an abstract relief by *John McCarthy* on a screen wall at right angles. This should be enlivened by water, but the system has sadly fallen into disuse. The effect of the forecourt and entrance steps is spoiled by a crassly positioned bus shelter. Between the two buildings a conference hall for 1,000. *Jonathan Green Associates* and a CWS in-house team designed the interior and the figurative sculptured panels are by *Stephen Sykes*.

Dantzic Street runs s between the CIS and CWS buildings. Here and in surrounding streets other Co-op buildings including **Redfern House**, CWS offices designed in 1936 by *W. A. Johnson* with *J. W. Cropper*. The inspiration is Dutch brick modernism, a style already used for a much larger CWS building in Prescot Street, East London, by L. G. Ekins. Seven storeys with a flat roof, pale brown brick with a blue brick base. Tall service tower to the left and receding curved blocks with continuous window bands with Portland stone frames and metal casements. It is a pity that this does not enjoy a better site – the impact is

175. Redfern House, Dantzic Street, by W. A. Johnson with J. W. Cropper (1936).

partly lost to its towering neighbours and by its relationship with adjoining **Holyoake House**, for the Co-operative Union by *F. E. L. Harris*, dated 1911. Three storeys and a basement. Baroque in blue-green and cream faience cladding with an extension in similar style to the N on **Hanover Street**. Another 1930s building on the opposite side of the street seems to be a missing part of Redfern House and must have been designed by the same team.

Victoria Buildings lie further s on Dantzic Street. A triangular block of offices, warehouses and workshops by *E. J. Sherwood & R. Thomas*, 1874. Grouped windows and doorways, linked by round-headed arcades. The street continues s to Withy Grove. Opposite the car park of the Arndale Centre, remodelled in 2000. **Shudehill** runs NE. Older buildings to note are, on the NW side, No. 29, a stuccoed warehouse of *c.* 1810 with a full-width first-floor window fronted by four graceful twisted cast-iron columns, and, on the other side further to the NE, No. 46, the **Hare and Hounds** pub, late C18 origins with a remarkably complete interwar interior. The N side of the tramway is to be the site of a large new transport interchange. Designs were prepared in 2001 by *Ian Simpson Architects*, showing much glazing toward Shudehill with subtle surface interplay of transparent, opaque, facetted and angled surfaces. Beyond this, at the corner of Hanover Street, the **Smithfield** pub, built for the Lancashire and Yorkshire Bank in 1904 by *Jesse Horsfall*. Conventional apart from an attractive Arts and Crafts corner tower.

Returning s and continuing w along Withy Grove brings us back to Corporation Street (for the continuation of this street *see* Outer Areas, Ancoats). Walk 3 starts just to the w, at the bottom of Cateaton Street on Deansgate.

Deansgate and the River Irwell to Castlefield

This Walk explores the area on the w side of the City Centre to the boundary with Salford. Deansgate linked the medieval centre with the site of the Roman fort (*see* Walk 4, p. 269), and is approximately on the line of the Roman road between Chester and Carlisle. A mid-c17 map shows the n part was already built up, and expansion continued in the c18. By the middle of the c19 the s part was little more than a slum. Deansgate was widened in a process which started from the n in 1869 and new offices, shops and commercial buildings replaced the old buildings and the slums. Some c18 houses, including Manchester's best-preserved Georgian terraces, survive near the s end.

Deansgate. Starting at the n end, w side, the over large and uninspiring **Ramada Renaissance Hotel**, 1972, former offices by *Cruickshank & Seward*. A fifteen-storey tower, all in ribbed white concrete, rises above a lower part. The six-storey block on the other (s) corner of Blackfriars Street is by *Philips Cutler Philips Troy*, also 1970s, this time more self-effacing. **Blackfriars House** can be seen from here, on the s side of Blackfriars Street. By *Harry S. Fairhurst* for the Bleachers Association,

176. Barton Arcade, Deansgate, by Corbett, Raby & Sawyer (1871).

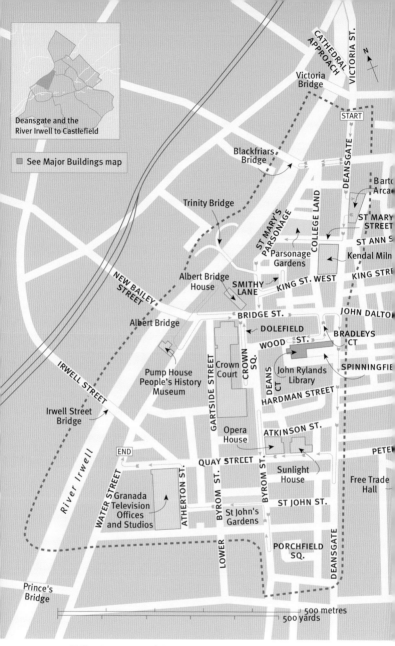

177. Walk 3. Deansgate and the River Irwell to Castlefield.

1925. Portland stone, in the crisp classical idiom favoured by the firm between the wars. A detour to the Irwell brings us to **Blackfriars Bridge**, 1817–20, replacing a footbridge. Three arches with coupled Ionic columns rise from the cutwaters. Originally the parapet had turned balusters. Back on Deansgate, w side, Nos. 62–66, **Hayward's Building**, shops of *c.* 1877. Free Renaissance with three large twin-arched first-floor windows but six smaller ones above; four storeys. By *Corbett, Sons & Brooke*, the carving by *Williams & Millson*. Opposite are **Barton's Buildings** of 1871 by *Corbett, Raby & Sawyer*. A long and thoroughly ignorant façade – the ground floor pilasters must be seen to be believed. On the first floor a cast-iron window arcade and an intricate cast-iron balcony, a hint of what is to come, for behind the façade is the **Barton Arcade** (illus. 23 and 176), a gorgeous glass and iron shopping arcade with two octagonal glass domes rising from glass pendentives. Three tiers of balconies with ornamental balustrades and mahogany handrails curve around the U-shaped arcade, which is quite narrow but very high, rising to 53 ft (16 metres). The decorative ironwork came from the catalogue of *Macfarlane*'s Saracen foundry in Glasgow. The obvious influence was the Galleria Vittorio Emanuele in Milan, which was illustrated in *The Builder* in 1868. It is the only survivor of three such arcades in Manchester, and it is probably the best example of this type of cast-iron and glass-roofed arcade anywhere in the country.

Kendal Milne's Department Store, on an island site, w side, by *J. S. Beaumont*, 1939. Unlike his usual work, or anything else in Manchester.* A sublimely monumental block with splayed corners, clad in Portland stone. In the German style of store architecture created by Messel early in the century, but stripped down. Windows are vertical strips of greenish glass blocks with a barely perceptible camber introducing subtle curves and enlivening the stark elevations with reflected light. Opposite, Nos. 83–93, the earlier Kendal's store, by *E. J. Thompson*, 1872–3. Stone, with tripartite first- and second-floor pedimented windows framed by Doric and Ionic columns, and a curved corner to King Street.

St Mary's Street runs w beside Kendal Milne's with the five-storey **Arkwright House** at the end, 1937 by *Harry S. Fairhurst*. Portland stone, with giant Corinthian columns above the entrance and an impressively long frontage with matching pilasters to **Parsonage Gardens**. This was the site of St Mary, built in 1753 and closed in 1890 (*see* topic box, Introduction p. 11). On the w side the terracotta-clad **National House**, 1905–9 by *Harry S. Fairhurst* again. The slick extension in black glass and stainless steel is by *H. M. Fairhurst*, 1968. Both were converted to flats, 2000. **St Mary's Parsonage** runs s. At an angle to the street, E side, a Venetian Gothic warehouse by *Clegg & Knowles*, 1868. Warm red brick with stone dressings and attractive details, lending colour and intimacy

*Mr Ferriday thinks it could be the work of a German émigré working in Beaumont's office.

178. Archive photograph (mid C20) of Kendal Milne's, Deansgate, by J. S. Beaumont (1939).

to this rather dark and dull thoroughfare. The dark and dull **Alberton House**, w side, is by *Leach Rhodes & Walker*, started in 1973, on the site of the town's first municipal gasworks of 1817. Beside it a footpath leads NW to the Irwell and **Trinity Bridge**, a footbridge which links St Mary's Parsonage with Salford's Chapel Wharf. By *Santiago Calatrava*, 1993–5, his first executed work in Britain and similar to his Alamillo Bridge in Seville, i.e. with a deck supported by stainless-steel cables from a sloping pylon, but much smaller in scale and correspondingly more airy and lightweight. It is white, standing out from the dark tunnel of the riverside here, with a great sense of tension and dynamism. Springing from the Salford side, the pylon is flanked by spiralling ramps and pulled at an angle towards land as it supports deck and ramps with a system of cable stays. The deck narrows and rises slightly towards the Manchester side. Anchoring the structure in Salford acknowledges the fact that it was a Salford initiative, funded by public and European grants.

King Street West. St Mary's Parsonage leads into a little square at the junction of King Street West and Bridge Street. On the N side at the corner of Smithy Lane is Nos. 31–33, mid C19 and classical, perhaps built when the street was laid out in 1842. Around the corner on **Smithy**

Lane, w side, is a severely plain early C19 coach manufactory. The front part has a loading slot, and workshops were grouped around a court-yard to the rear. Returning to King Street West and rejoining St Mary's Parsonage brings us on to **Bridge Street**, which runs between the river and Deansgate. On the N corner is **Albert Bridge House** (illus. 30), by *E. H. Banks* (Ministry of Works), built 1958–9 as tax offices. Eighteen storeys high. Set back from and at an angle to the street, which adds to its gravitas. More low blocks come forward to make a group. The high block has concrete framing and Portland stone cladding, channelled to give texture. One of the first and best of the big post-war buildings in the city. To the w, on the riverside in front of Albert Bridge House is a **statue** of the Salford MP and philanthropist Joseph Brotherton, by *Matthew Noble*, 1858, moved from Peel Park in Salford in 1986. This is a good spot for views N upriver with Trinity Bridge in the foreground and Blackfriars Bridge and the cathedral beyond. **Albert Bridge**, by *Jesse Hartley*, 1844, replaced a bridge of 1785. A single, low segmental arch of stone with pilaster terminals and curved abutments.

On the s side of the street there is a **sculpture**: Doves of Peace by *Michael Lyons*, 1986. Beside the river **The Pump House People's History Museum** is housed in a hydraulic power station by City Architect *H. Price*, 1907–9. The conversion was by *OMI Architects*, 1993–4, to accommodate part of the collection of the National Museum of Labour History. The outward form is largely preserved and best seen from the Salford side of Albert Bridge. There are two huge water tanks on each side of the central engine house, to the left is the accumulator tower. **Interior**: the engine house has an ornate cast-iron roof. This area has

179. Trinity Bridge, by
Santiago Calatrava
(1993–5).

Statuary salvaged from Waterhouse's Assize Courts is on display in the Crown Court building. Part of a full-blooded Ruskinian scheme by *Thomas Woolner*, which illustrated aspects of the history of common law, it is the largest collection of his work. The life-size figures represent kings and lawgivers. In the foyer: Matthew Hale, Thomas More and William Gascoigne. In a corridor: Ranulph de Glanville. The remainder is housed in a gallery in the basement of the building: Alfred the Great, Henry II, Edward I and Sir Edward Coke. Heads of the kings and queens have been mounted on the walls. Also preserved are the capitals from the two shafts at the main entrance, mounted on piers. These are by the *O'Shea* brothers, in the vital style of their work at the Oxford Museum. In the foliage there are scenes of traditional English punishments, including the scold's bridle, pillories, stocks, etc., as well as more terrible instruments such as the wheel (illus. 22).

been converted to a shop, café and temporary exhibition and perform-ance space. The main exhibition areas are in the former boiler house.

Returning E along Bridge Street brings us to **Dolefield**, s side, and the **Courts of Justice** in Crown Square. The square evolved from the city's 1945 plan which envisaged a processional way between the site of the town hall and riverside civic and judicial buildings. On the w side **Crown Court**, 1957–62 by *L. C. Howitt*, built to replace Waterhouse's Assize Courts of 1859–64 which were severely damaged in the blitz (*see*

180. The 1945 *City of Manchester Plan* envisaged culverting the River Irwell (fore-ground) and laying out a processional route from new law courts to a new town hall.

181. Masonic Hall, Bridge Street, by Percy Scott Worthington (1929).

topic box). Symmetrical and feebly playful. What a come-down after Waterhouse's brilliant early work. The building has a façade 289 ft (88 metres) long and is clad in Portland stone, stripped classicism with steps up to a central entrance, used only on ceremonial occasions, with a wavy canopy with eagles on top. The other entrance is in the forbidding blocky grey extension to the right, completed in 1986 by *Property Services Agency*. It houses additional courts and offices.

Magistrates' Court. The building by *Yorke, Rosenberg & Mardall*, described in the 1969 edition of the *Buildings of England: South Lancashire*, when it was about to be erected, is to be demolished. The design of the replacement has not been finalized.

Back on Bridge Street we continue E back towards Deansgate. On the s corner of Dolefield **Manchester House**, 1965, is by *Leach Rhodes & Walker*, offices, seven storeys on a podium side. Beside it is the **Masonic Hall** by *Percy Scott Worthington*, dated 1929. A monumental block in Portland stone with shallow wings, rusticated at ground-floor level. Between the wings the entrance is recessed beneath a balcony supported by big brackets. Sheer walls rise above the second-storey windows. The lower flanking wings also become sheer above the tall windows, relieved by the merest hint of fluting in upper stone panels. Inside is a splendid hall, Ionic columns and a coffered top-lit barrel-vault ceiling, recalling the entrance hall of this architect's Faculty of Arts building at the University of Manchester (*see* Academic Institutions, p. 118). Further E, s side, are the former premises of the **Manchester and Salford Street Children Mission**. By *W. & G. Higginbottom* dated 1896. Green-and-cream faience with lettering, and, above, charming panels with smiling children's heads. Attached to the rear (on Wood Street reached either from Deansgate or via Bradleys Court, a tiny alley threading through the buildings to the right), are the Mission offices and the (former) **Working Men's Church**, dated 1905. The organization, which still uses the offices here, was founded in 1869 and came to this site in 1873. It was one of the largest of the C19 charitable organizations which helped those who were excluded from official Poor Law relief or unwilling to accept the conditions of the workhouse. Back on Bridge Street again, No. 64 **Rational House**, s side, by *Samuel Davidson*, 1897, and **Kenworthy Buildings**, N side, 1902 by *Bramald & Smith*, are examples of the pleasant modestly scaled late C19 and early C20 commercial buildings to be found along the remaining stretch of the street towards Deansgate.

Halifax Building Society at the junction with Deansgate, N side, brick clad, articulated with shaped piers and recessed at the corner. By *Turner Lansdowne Holt*, 1983. It is on the site of the C19 shambles. Opposite at the N corner of John Dalton Street an office building, 1876 by *Pennington & Bridgen*: Gothic – but no longer High Victorian Gothic. The portal may still be that, but on the façade there is too much bare wall, and the rhythm is already turning Late Victorian. On the s corner of Bridge Street the mid-C19 **Sawyers Arms** adds a splash of colour with its extravagant early C20 red- and yellow-tile-clad ground floor. We turn right. Beside the pub, on the w side of Deansgate, the former **Gas Committee Showrooms and Offices** by *Edward Salomons*, 1890, very badly weathered red sandstone. Narrow three-bay frontage, three storeys with a Dutch gable on top. **Lincoln House**, E side, by *B. Johnson*, of *Holford Associates*, 1986, has pink granite piers and reflective glass. The earliest example of brash 1980s glitter in the centre. On the same side, set back, **Centurion House** by *Leach Rhodes & Walker*, 1977, eleven storeys with alternating wide and narrow vertical brick strips.

Spinningfield is a small square opposite, w side, retaining its C18 field name. The area from here down to the riverside is being redeveloped. There will be shops within the square, an hotel immediately to the s and offices, a new magistrates court and riverside apartments to

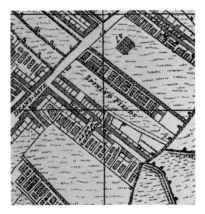

182. Spinningfield as shown on Casson & Berry's 1746 map which is oriented with s at the top rather than N.

the w. The new buildings will need to be a worthy foil for the John Rylands Library (*see* Major Buildings) which fills the N side of the square, and a suitable replacement for *J. S. Beaumont*'s spirited 1930s Northcliffe House to the s, which faces demolition.

Elliott House, Deansgate E side, 1878, is former School Board Offices by *Royle & Bennett*. Queen Anne style, red brick, red terracotta and red sandstone, and judicious use of decorative terracotta panels and carved detailing over the windows. In the corner splays, at eye level, oval windows in surrounds of beautifully carved red sandstone. Still on the E side, **201 Deansgate** by *Holford Associates*, 1995–6, pompous offices with brick and glass towers framing a cornice and single giant column. Beside them the irrepressibly cheerful Nos. 205–209, **Onward Buildings**, 1903–4 by *Charles Heathcote*, built for a federation of temperance societies, with bold stripes of red brick, pale yellow sandstone and yellow terracotta. The corners are curved and at the top there is a range of porthole-like windows and a heavy cornice. Opposite, former Government offices, 1895–6, described (with some justice) by the *Manchester Guardian* in 1895 as 'an utterly commonplace design of no interest whatever'. **Royal London House**, a big Baroque stone block by *Charles Heathcote* of 1904. Not Heathcote at his best, but the big domed turret to the corner of Quay Street is well handled.

Great Northern Railway Offices. On the s corner with Peter Street the entrance to the former goods yard of the Great Northern Warehouse (*see* City Centre, Windmill Street), then a long, remorseless, uniform range of shops and offices of *c*. 1899, stretching along the whole E side. Only one room deep, they form a screen wall to the former goods station behind. On the w side **Congregational Church House**, Baroque, Portland stone, 1909–11 by *Bradshaw & Gass*. Church-like in an English Renaissance mode, with a domed tower at one end, a rusticated basement and double-height windows seeming to imply a gallery. We return to **Quay Street** which leads w, laid out in 1735 from Deansgate to a new quay on the Irwell.

Overseas House, on the s corner of Quay Street, by *Leach Rhodes & Walker*, *c*. 1974, is another version of their 1970s formula of dark brick-clad verticals alternating with slim white piers. Beside it a striped

Edwardian Baroque job, then **No. 15 Quay Street** by *Stephenson Architecture*, 1991–2, a design of some subtlety with high-quality detailing and materials. Red brick and stone with slivers of banding in the brick as an acknowledgement of its stripy neighbour. The stone-clad attic and stair-tower to the right frame the projecting brick front. On the right a new building is being erected on the site of *Percy Scott Worthington*'s Skin Hospital, which should not have been allowed to go. Opposite, N side, **Sunlight House** is a towering Portland stone office block designed by *Joseph Sunlight* in 1932. When put up it was the tallest building in Manchester. The immense bulk is more evident from distant views than from the street, where the elevation is articulated by soaring corner towers with vertical window slits and winged angel heads designed by *J. Lenigan*. Ten storeys with four attic storeys, these set back in tiers. Inside there is a basement swimming pool (now used by a health club), part of the original design. Next on this side the **Opera House**, formerly New Theatre, 1912 by *Richardson & Gill* with *Farquarson*. Classical Mannerism in an appropriately theatrical style with an obvious debt to Cockerell, and also, perhaps, with a nod to the nearby Cockerell-inspired Theatre Royal (*see* City Centre, Peter Street). The main elevations are in imitation stone. Symmetrical, pedimented, and strongly textured with horizontal emphasis throughout given by channelled rustication. At the centre, over the entrance, three pairs of giant fluted Ionic columns, the outer pairs breaking forward to frame an arch in the tympanum which contains a fine bas-relief, The Dawn of the Heroic Age, modelled and executed by *John Tanner & Son*. The outer column pairs contain pedestals below, with the names of actors, and roundels with masks above. On each side, pilastered bays.

Behind the Opera House, on the N part of Byrom Street, E side, the former **Friends School**, built for the Quakers by *John Lowe*, dated 1886. It is rather effective in a quiet way, though marred by new windows and doors. Brick with stone dressings, hipped roof and hipped dormers, and a frieze with lettering.

Cobden House, on the s w corner of Byrom Street and Quay Street, is a large 1770s town house. The detailing of the Venetian window and plasterwork show that *Timothy Lightoler* may have been the architect, c.f. his Platt Hall of 1764 s of the city centre. Despite an unprepossessing exterior, the result of the loss of the original entrance steps and doorcase, it is the best-preserved Georgian house in the centre. Brick, symmetrical, with a slightly projecting entrance bay and a late c19 doorcase. To the rear a full-height polygonal bay has to the right a very nicely detailed stone Venetian window. The interior has been restored. Impressive entrance and staircase hall with a cantilevered stair lit by the Venetian window. All the main rooms have elaborate doorcases with broken pediments, of which one or two are original. It was built by the Byrom family and occupied by Richard Cobden from 1836 to 1850. It later became the County Court. The new building to the right is by *Stephenson Bell*, 1999. Adjoining on its right side more new work by *Elsworth Sykes*. Completed 2000, it incorporates the entrance to **Astley House**, an eleven-storey tower block of 1959 by *Leach Rhodes & Walker* (the extension to the s, of 1965, **Byrom House** is also by them). Opposite, n side, another large concrete office block, **Quay House**, by *Harry S. Fairhurst & Son*, 1964–5.

Byrom Street runs s. The Byroms had laid out a grid of streets for building by 1788, but by 1820 only around half of it had been taken up. The s end on the left side is the site of St John, 1768–9, built at the expense of Edward Byrom and the first major Manchester building in the Gothic Revival style (*see* topic box, Introduction p. 11). It was demolished 1931 and the site is now a small park. A simple stone cross com-

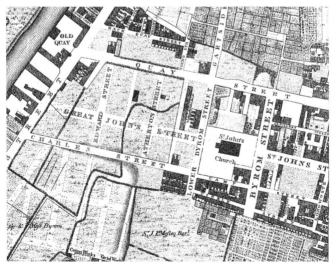

185. Byrom Street as shown on William Green's map (1794).

186. Granada House, Atherton Street, by Ralph Tubbs (1960–2).

memorates the church and burial ground. Two gravestones: Owen Owens d. 1844 and John Owens, founder of Owens College, d. 1846, a simple headstone with good lettering, erected in 1931 by the University of Manchester as a tribute to its founder. Opposite, on the right side of Byrom Street, a row of late c18 houses with charming Gothick doorcases, most of them extant by 1794. No. 31, which has been rebuilt or refaced, has attached at the rear a tiny late c19 chapel, presumably built after the house was taken over by the Convent of St Mary in the mid 1870s. To the N on **Porchfield Square**, late 1970s three- and four-storey flats, the first attempt to reintroduce private residential development to the city after the pre- and post-war clearances. Running E off Byrom Street **St John Street** has the city's most complete Georgian terraces, now used as offices, consulting rooms, etc. Of three storeys and generally of one or two bays, the houses do not form a unified scheme. The plots were taken up piecemeal during the late c18 and early c19. Some have pedimented Doric doorcases and some recessed doorcases and slim Ionic columns. No. 24, N side, is a later interloper, probably an 1840s remodelling of existing houses, five bays with a central segmental-headed doorway.

Atherton Street is reached by returning to Byrom Street and striking w across St John's Gardens. **Granada House** is by *Ralph Tubbs*, 1960–2 for the Granada Television Centre. A simple unpretentious design of eight storeys, curtain walled and topped with signage and, to one side, a spiral stair. Also part of this complex, s of the main building, the **Stage One** building (studios) uses polychromatic brick to match a restored c19 accumulator tower which was incorporated into the building. By *Building Design Partnership*, 1985. Immediately N is the the BSkyB Satellite News Studio by *Peter Shuttleworth* of *Building Design Partnership*, *c.* 1998,

The Irwell Navigation

Plans to make the Mersey and Irwell navigable as far as Manchester were made in the late C17, but nothing came of them until 1712 when the engineer *Thomas Steers* put forward detailed proposals. The relevant Act, however, was not obtained until 1720 and work did not start until 1724. The navigation was finally completed to the point at the end of Quay Street in 1736. By 1740 the navigation company had built a large quay and warehouses there, shown in plan and in two views on Casson & Berry's 1746 map. The largest warehouse is shown as a four-storey building with a loading slot and chimneys, suggesting that it was also used as domestic accommodation. One of the early C18 warehouses was still in use in 1871, according to the architect J. Corbett. He wrote: 'It has wooden galleries in front of each storey, is five storeys high, and had wooden shafting and gearing for hoisting sacks &c., worked by horses going around a capstan.' This remained the upper limit of the navigation until 1840 when it was extended as far as Hunt's Bank Approach. The rights of navigation were bought by the Manchester Ship Canal Company in the late C19 as a basis for constructing the canal.

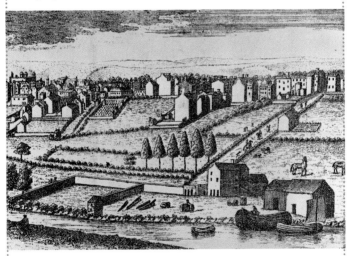

187. Quay Street and the quay. Detail of the panorama from Casson & Berry's map (1746).

glazed below, the upper part clad in cedar. To the w Coronation Street's 1960s outdoor set, a scaled-down copy of a C19 terrace with back yards, was replaced in similar style in 1981 by *Ken Moth* of *Building Design Partnership* with set designer *Denis Parkin*. For the Grape Street Warehouse *see* Walk 4, p. 268.

The former County Municipal School opposite the main Granada block is dated 1912. It has minimal Renaissance detailing and a rooftop playground with piers between the railings giving it a fortress-like look. Atherton Street brings us back to Quay Street. The greatly restored block of C18 houses on the N side was built on part of the Byrom family estate (*see* above).

Water Street at the w end of Quay Street runs alongside the Irwell. Beside the river the **Victoria and Albert Hotel**, warehouses of *c.* 1840, converted in 1991–2 by *Trafalgar House*, project architect *A. Hallworth*, retaining part of the interior structure of timber beams and cast-iron columns but not much of the character of the original buildings. On the right an (altered) mid-C19 covered quay. This area was the site of a quay built after the Irwell Navigation was completed in 1736 (*see* topic box, previous page).

Castlefield and its Canals and Railways

Castlefield was named for Manchester's Roman fort, which was located at the confluence of the Medlock and Irwell. The area's greatest importance historically and internationally lies in its substantial remains of early canal and railway structures. The pioneering Bridgewater Canal reached Castlefield in 1765, making it the hub of a transport network which attracted warehousing and industry. Interchange with sea-going vessels on the Mersey came in 1776, and, when the Rochdale Canal joined the Bridgewater Basin in 1804–6, it completed a canal route linking the w and e coasts. The railway buildings include the world's first passenger railway station and the oldest surviving railway warehouse. The area retains the most dramatic industrial scenery in the city, but fell into decline in the later c20. The purchase of the Liverpool and Manchester Railway terminus in 1978 by the Greater Manchester Council was a turning point, and Castlefield was designated an Urban Heritage Park in 1982. Revitalization was initially a slow process. The private sector took the lead in the mid 1980s, and *Building Design Partnership* was eventually asked to prepare a regeneration framework in 1993 by the Central Manchester Development Corporation. Regeneration was stimulated by grants from the European Union and other sources, resulting in new buildings as well as refurbishment of the old, and the visual excitement of the area owes something to both.

The Walk starts near the s end of Deansgate at its junction with Whitworth Street West.

Deansgate Station, e side, opened in 1849 on the MSJ&AR line. It was rebuilt in 1896. Curved to the street corner, paired corner entrances have mock portcullises and the parapet is battlemented. The **Bridgewater Viaduct** bypasses the old line of Deansgate and carries the road s beneath the railway viaduct to link with Chester Road and routes to the s. It was built in 1841 across the e end of the c18 quays of the canal basin. On the e side **Deansgate Quay**, a well-composed eight-storey apartment block by *Stephenson Bell*, 1999–2001. On the w side, right up against the s side of the railway viaduct, the former **Congregational Chapel**, 1858, is by *Edward Walters*. Brick with stone dressings, a design

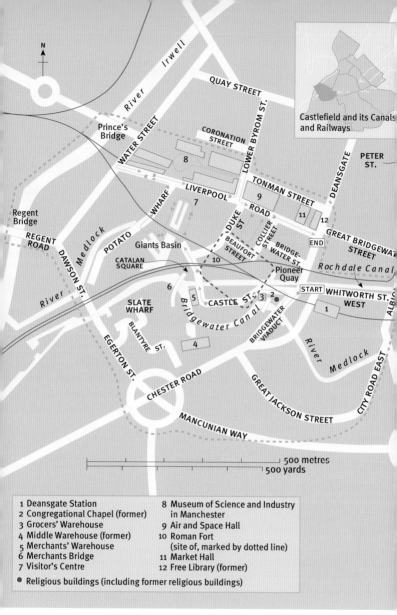

188. Walk 4. Castlefield and its Canals and Railways.

of interpenetrating temple fronts with a tall slender campanile attached to the s. The central part has an upper arcade of round-headed windows and a wheel window in the pediment. The Veneto-Byzantine style campanile has blind arcading to the first stage, with a stone arcaded belfry stage and a steep concave roof with lucarnes. It was converted to recording studios in the 1980s and the basement is used as a café bar.

The Bridgewater Canal

The Bridgewater Canal was the first modern canal in Britain, running cross-country between watersheds without relying on the courses of streams or rivers. It was built for Francis Egerton, third Duke of Bridgewater, primarily to transport coal from his mines in Worsley. The idea of a canal was not new, but the wealth, determination and acumen of the Duke, combined with the purses of his supporters and talent of his engineers, made it a reality. He was only twenty-two years of age when the first act was passed in 1759. *James Brindley* acted as consulting engineer, and *John Gilbert* was resident engineer. Although coal was being unloaded at Cornbrook, barely a mile to the s in 1763, various delays and the considerable engineering problems in harnessing the Medlock held up completion until 1765. The canal meets the river head on, and an overflow sluice here takes surplus water by tunnel (replaced in 1838) to the Giants Basin, and the point at which the river re-emerges on Potato Wharf (*see* p. 264, below). The basin and its warehouses have been described as among the most brilliant engineering achievements of the project.

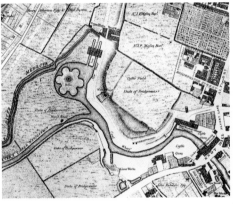

189. **The Bridgewater Canal as shown on William Green's map (1794).**

Returning N beneath the railway viaduct brings us to **Castle Street** which runs w from Deansgate. Here there are impressive views of the viaducts and skewed bridges of the 1849 railway as they cross first the street and then the Rochdale Canal, on the N side of the street. This section of the canal was originally in a tunnel, opened *c.* 1840. The narrow arm, running N alongside Pioneer Quay to a tunnel in the sandstone cliff, originated in this form *c.* 1849. The remains of buildings associated with a timber yard, including a mid-C19 chimney, lie to the w on the N side of the canal.

Castle Street overlooks the **Castle Quay**, the original terminus and coal wharf of the Bridgewater Canal basin. The sandstone cliff was cut

190. Skewed bridge, MSJ&AR Viaduct, off Castle Street (1849).

back so that coal could be heaped alongside the canal. A flight of C20 steps leads down to the wharf, where the **Grocers' Warehouse** can be seen, rebuilt in 1987 after demolition in 1960. It was built in two phases, the first completed in the early 1770s, over an existing canal arm of *c.* 1765 which was part of Brindley's system for hauling coal up the sheer sandstone face to Castle Street.* Boats were taken into a tunnel driven directly into the sandstone cliff from which 8 cwt. (406 kg.) coal buckets were raised more than 20 ft (6 metres) to street level using a water-powered crane to lift them up a shaft. What can be seen is the recon-structed front wall of the warehouse, with round-headed windows in stone surrounds. The left archway leads to Brindley's tunnel, with side shafts housing a replica waterwheel and hoist. The other archway is for a second wet dock, added before 1807. The building had a brick spine wall running along the main axis and timber floors. By 1793 it had been extended to the E, but instead of a spine wall, cross walls from the front to the back of the building facilitated easier movement of goods from quay to road. Brindley's original tunnel extended to the N, running on the line of the canal arm at Pioneer Quay, which reused the tunnel (*see* above). Early C19 plans show that the tunnel was extended at some time to a point on the N side of Bridgewater Street.†

On the s side of the wharf, up against the Bridgewater Viaduct, the **Quay Bar** by *Stephenson Bell*, opened in 1998. Café bars became popular in the city during the 1990s, and this was the first to be completely

*For a detailed description and analysis of Brindley's hoist and the Grocers' Warehouse see V. I. Tomlinson in *Transactions of the Lancashire and Cheshire Antiquarian Society*, vol. 71, 1961.
†I am grateful to Dr Arrowsmith for these details.

purpose-built. Double-height bar with slightly angled full-height fins
to the canal, these clad in metal, with recessed glass walls between. The
layout was derived from the organic geometry of spiral shells. The white-
coated accommodation block and a slimmer service-tower rise above
the main part. A walkway from the Bridgewater Viaduct slices into the
N side of the building.

A path runs w along the quay, where Castle Street can be rejoined
near the Merchants' Warehouse. Alternatively returning up the steps to
Castle Street gives a closer view of **Eastgate** (N side). A well-detailed office
conversion of an 1870s warehouse by *Stephenson Architecture*, 1992, made
a landmark by the water tower which is topped by a light. Continuing
w alongside the quay brings the magnificent **Middle Warehouse** into
view across the basin to the s. The enormous five-storey brick structure
was built 1828–31. A giant blind segmental arch houses two arched shipping holes and paired round-headed windows alternate with loading
slots on each side. Substantial remodelling in the early C20 resulted in
the loss of much of the original interior. It was probably at this time that
the roofline was altered. It was converted to flats and offices in 1988,
when the gabled heads to the loading slots were reinstated. The street

Early Transport Warehouses in Manchester

The conventional basic design of early warehouses, with brick load-bearing walls and timber floors supported by timber posts, was quickly adapted at Castlefield to suit the new circumstances. Rather than simply acting as safe storage, the warehouses were part of the transit system, which could involve moving goods some distance vertically from water to road level, a problem already encountered in the navigation warehouses on the Irwell. The incorporation of wet docks allowed barges to enter the building directly from the canal via shipping holes for unloading inside, a system which relies for maximum efficiency on the constant water level of the canal, unaffected by the tidal and seasonal fluctuations experienced by river navigations and seaports. It necessitated the elimination of tall masts from the barges, which were designed for sails but already used for towing. The first known example of an internal dock was in the Grocers' Warehouse, of the early 1770s, where the building was erected over an existing canal arm. The earliest surviving example in Manchester is the 1806 warehouse on the Rochdale Canal basin on Dale Street (*see* Walk 1, p. 218), though in some other respects this is unlike the Castlefield warehouses. Another adaptation was the use of transverse cross walls instead of a spine wall along the axis of the building. This facilitated movement of goods between quay and road, and the introduction of transverse docking bays may have contributed to this change.

continues to follow the line of the basin and curves to the N. Here on the w side is the brick **Merchants' Warehouse**, dated 1825, the oldest surviving warehouse of the basin. The repair and refurbishment in 1995–7 was by *Ian Simpson Architect*s. Brick, three storeys to the street, four to the canal. To Castle Street loading slots alternate with two-window bays, the windows small with round heads. To the canal, paired central shipping holes with supplementary loading slots on each side. Inside it has transverse walls dividing it into six bays. The renovation was achieved by placing services in slim glass blocks on each of the gable-ends. Light was brought in by means of a slot cut through the floors, lit from the roof, and by glazing the loading bays. Part of the king-post timber roof structure and some of the hoisting machinery have been preserved. Stables, E of the warehouse, were converted to a pub by *Stephenson Architecture* in 1992.

A narrow C18 bridge carries Castle Street over the Rochdale Canal just as it flows into the Bridgewater Canal Basin. Beside it lock No. 92 and a late C19 lock house. To the E the canal is crossed by the elegant understated **Architect's Footbridge** by *Ian Simpson Architects*, 1996, a slender span formed by a stainless-steel frame clad in red sandstone. To

193. Merchants Bridge, by Whitby Bird & Partners (1996).

the w the **Barça** café bar by *Harrison Ince*, 1996, is built into the 1849 viaduct arches facing on to **Catalan Square**. A wilful design with an angled sandstone wall punching through the rear and front elevations and a curved upper canopy over the entrance to a balcony. The **Merchants Bridge**, 1996 by *Whitby Bird & Partners*, crosses the canal in a curving sweep here. The white-painted steel structure is stabilized by a cantilevered sickle arch, and is wider at mid span than at the ends to give space for pedestrians stopping to look at the views. The inspiration was Calatrava's Ripoll Bridge in Gerona. To the w on the other side of the basin, **Slate Wharf**, 1990s apartment blocks. Brick, pitched slated roofs, designed to match the materials and scale of the older buildings.

Castle Street continues N beneath an impressive array of railway viaducts, which are best appreciated from the N side of the basin and will be described from that viewpoint, *see* p. 264. We are now following a canal arm which served the *c.* 1790 Staffordshire Warehouse, demolished in 1950. The basin was reopened in the early 1990s as part of a scheme by *DEGW* who designed the stepped spectator stand, sheltered by Hopkinsesque canvas tents, which overlooks the canal arm from the E, and the **Visitor's Centre** of 1993 above the basin to the N on Liverpool Road. Blue tile-clad tower and an angled steel roof, rising above a rear service block clad in white tiles. The end bay is glazed to give views of the basin. Beside it (E side) an undistinguished apartment block by *Gleeson*. The adjacent plot has been earmarked for another block. Along the other (w) side of the canal is the YMCA, called the Y hotel, by *David Lyons Associates, c.* 1990, with an attached sports complex. Pitched roofs, polychromatic brick, bright red trimmings, an attempt to fit in with the character of the area which does not really come off. A walk s along the edge of the basin beside the YMCA brings us to the YHA's **Castlefield Hostel** by *Halliday Meecham*, 1995. Two simple brick boxes with barrel roofs set at an angle to each other with a low two-tier curved glazed entrance part in the angle. Understated and suited to the environment, unlike its neighbour, the contrastingly extravagant **Visions Centre**, by *Malcolm Seddon*, 1999–2000. Three and four storeys with an upcurved roof furnished with a glazed spine and a folksy collection of green funnels. It is reached from **Potato Wharf** by crossing the **Giants Basin**, designed by *Brindley* to take outflow from the canal into the River Medlock, which emerges from a tunnel on the other side of the road. It was originally a huge clover-leaf weir but it was subject to flooding and had to be modified in the late C18 or early C19.

The **railway viaducts** span the canal basin to the s and this vantage point affords the most memorable view. In the foreground the two which ran to Central Station (*see* City Centre, Windmill Street) of *c.* 1893 and *c.* 1877. They march across the basin supported by huge castellated steel columns; the earlier part is otherwise of brick, the 1893 addition cast-iron throughout. They frame a view of the MSJ&AR viaduct with an elegantly arched bridge with Gothic pierced spandrels and castellated brick piers (the other branch of this line runs immediately behind the YHA). Lowest and latest, the Merchants Bridge arcs across the water. The truncated remains of the viaduct serving the Great Northern Company Warehouse of 1898 can be seen just to the e near Collier Street.

Potato Wharf runs n to join **Liverpool Road**. The n side of the street is taken up by the buildings of the **Museum of Science and Industry in Manchester**. The museum was opened in 1983 following the purchase in 1978 of the site of the Liverpool and Manchester Railway terminus by the Greater Manchester Council. The process of restoring and converting the buildings has been a great success. The main entrance is further e on Lower Byrom Street, but starting at this end allows us to follow the historic sequence of building.

The site settled on by the Railway Company, after many setbacks, was close to the concentration of warehousing around the canals and the Irwell with easy access to Water Street and Deansgate. *George Stephenson* was the engineer. He was re-appointed after the disastrous failure of the first railway bill in 1825 when the levelling of his route was found to be inaccurate. The route he inherited had been proposed by *C. B. Vignoles* under *George & John Rennie*. The complex consists of the viaduct and bridges over the Irwell and Water Street, the passenger station, the station agent's house, and ancillary buildings along Liverpool Road. A railway warehouse of the first phase lies to the n, beyond it to the e a

194. C19 railway viaducts near Liverpool Road.

warehouse of 1880 and goods transfer shed of 1855. Dr Greene describes it as an inland expression of the Liverpool Docks, and the volume of traffic both in terms of passengers and goods had never been tackled on such a scale before.

Water Street, at the w end of Liverpool Road, is our starting point. Opposite the road junction a car park alongside the Irwell is the vantage point for viewing *Stephenson*'s 1830 stone **Prince's Bridge** over the river, which has survived with little alteration. The design was modified during construction. The two segmental arches with radiating voussoirs were built in stone, rather than brick, and erected on a slightly skewed rather than a square plan. Converging with it to run parallel across the river is the South Junction part of the 1849 MSJ&AR viaduct. Stephenson's viaduct continues in brick from this point and has alongside Water Street an animal ramp. His bridge over Water Street (*see* topic box, Introduction p. 15) was replaced by the present structure in 1904. The viaduct to the N serves the Byrom Street and Grape Street warehouses (*see* p. 268, below).

Recrossing Water Street and returning E along Liverpool Road brings us to the **passenger station** completed in 1830. It has first- and second-class entrances with separate booking offices on the ground floor, reached from Liverpool Road, and waiting rooms above which led out to the platform. The front is classical and faced in stone and stucco. The brick house beside it on the corner of Water Street is earlier, of *c.* 1810, and became the station agent's house. (The platform side of the station and the following sequence of buildings can only be seen from inside the museum, and this involves a detour E to the entrance on Lower Byrom Street, returning inside the museum precinct to the w end of the site.)

195. Liverpool Road Station (former), Liverpool Road (1830).

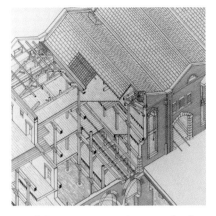

196. Sectional drawing of the original Liverpool and Manchester Railway Warehouse (1830).

The **railway warehouse**, N of the passenger station, was the first building of the complex to be completed, in 1830. It was almost certainly designed by the Liverpool architect *Thomas Haigh** and built in just five months. Three storeys alongside the railway, curving with the line of the viaduct, with rail loading at first-floor level, street-level loading at the rear. Rail wagons ran from the viaduct into the building via turntables where they were unloaded and reloaded. The internal structure is of timber, but with cast-iron columns in the basement, and brick cross walls dividing the building into compartments. Steam-powered hoists had been installed within a year as the manual system could not cope with the volume of goods. Later some hoists were converted to hydraulic operation and cranes inserted inside the ground floor. The design can be compared to river and canal warehouses, particularly in constructional features such as the use of timber floors and timber posts and transverse cross walls facilitating the movement of goods between viaduct and road. Bringing wagons directly into the building for loading has parallels with the use of internal wet docks in canal warehouses.

The restoration and refitting is by *Building Design Partnership*, project architect *Ken Moth*, in three phases over the period 1992–6. The philosophy was to keep all the accretions and to maintain an absolute distinction between these and new interventions. Even the replacement timbers have been stamped with the date of their insertion. Two glass-sided stair/lift modules rise through the structure. All the services are carried between or beneath the beams. This approach can be compared to that of a decade before when the internal structure was judged to be dispensable, or at least beyond repair, hence the loss of the interior of the easternmost bay.

The **Power Hall** is next in sequence. It was a goods transfer shed of 1855, for perishable produce, which had to be despatched on the same day. The building is a long two-bay shed running alongside Liverpool

*Dr Greene and Keith Falconer have identified unexecuted designs for warehouses at Gloucester Dock which are strikingly similar in design.

197. Aerial view of the buildings of the Museum of Science and Industry in Manchester and their neighbours. The River Irwell can be seen to the far left, the buildings of the railway terminus, left and centre, and the market halls, right.

Road, the roof hipped at each end. A central line of cast-iron columns supports the valley beams and big iron clamps secure these to the tie-beams of the queenpost roofs. The wagons entered the w side and were unloaded on the s side to road vehicles which entered from Liverpool Road. The building was opened for museum use in 1983, the alterations being largely confined to introducing limited top-lighting and glazing openings, retaining the central platform for viewing purposes.

The **Lower Byrom Street Warehouse**, 1880, is a goods warehouse served by a viaduct supported by squat cast-iron columns on stone bases. The building is fireproof with brick jack-arches and primary and secondary iron beams on large square-section columns. In the conversion for museum purposes of 1987 by *Building Design Partnership*, a full-height interior ramp was inserted and a glass-fronted lift slotted into a loading bay. *Austin-Smith: Lord* in 2000 created a new main entrance, suitably industrial in appearance, and inserted a top-floor restaurant and rear stair tower.

Beyond to the N, now part of the Granada Television site, the **Grape Street Warehouse** of 1869 is part of the group, visually and functionally. It was served by a separate viaduct across Water Street with the wagons going straight into arched openings. Red brick with blue brick dressings. The ground floor is fireproofed with brick jack-arches, riveted beams and cruciform columns. Conversion as part of the Granada entertainment complex was completed in the 1980s.

Outside the museum on **Lower Byrom Street** there are **sculptures**. Near the main entrance, a polished steel globe and cone by *Andrew Crompton*, 1988, which cleverly reflect anamorphic portraits of famous scientists painted on the pavement. To the N, positioned to catch the eye

The Romans in Manchester

Mamucium was established *c.* AD 79 on a bluff between the Medlock and Irwell, a strategic position at the meeting point of an E–W route linking the bases at York and Chester and the route N to Ribchester and Carlisle. At this time it was of timber and turf, square in plan and designed for an infantry unit of 480. After a period of abandonment a larger timber fort was built *c.* AD 160 and this was rebuilt in stone *c.* AD 200. A civilian settlement had grown up outside the fort but it is not known how long it persisted after the end of Roman rule.

from Liverpool Road, columns from Ferranti's high-voltage electricity-generating station in Deptford of 1889, erected in 1984.

Another part of the museum, the **Air and Space Hall**, lies opposite the entrance. This is housed in a market hall, called Lower Campfield Market, by *Mangnall & Littlewood*, 1876. Large, rectangular, with ornately detailed cast-iron and partly glazed roofs. It was adapted for the display of aeroplanes in 1983 by acting City Architect *E. Clark* for the City Council and taken over by the museum in 1985. The interior space is preserved with little subdivision and the volume is such that fairly large aircraft can be displayed.

Lower Byrom Street runs S back to Liverpool Road. Opposite the junction is **St Matthews Sunday School**, dated 1827 and converted to offices in the 1980s. Brick, two storeys, with an apsidal S end and windows with pointed arches and simple Y-tracery. Turning left takes us past an early C19 pub to the site of Manchester's **Roman fort** set back from the S side of Liverpool Road. The first major excavation was conducted by F. A. Bruton in 1906–7. Professor G. D. B. Jones of the University of Manchester began excavating the site of the North Gate in 1979 and work was continued by the Greater Manchester Archaeological Unit, completed in the mid 1980s (*see* topic box).

A path runs S between low walled enclosures, based on excavated plans of buildings of the *vicus* or civilian settlement. On the E side, **sculpture**. Sheep by *Ted Roocroft*, 1986. Sections of the defensive ditches have been excavated and grassed. They protected the **North Gate**, and the reconstruction of 1986 was based on the excavated foundations of the twin-portalled early C3 gateway in this position. The design was taken from European and British examples and the masonry detail from parts of the wall found during excavation.* To the SW the foundations of a granary and another part of the perimeter wall have been consolidated and reconstructed. Before leaving the site, looking E from

*The Manchester example is considered to be more historically accurate than another of similar date in South Shields. *See* R. J. Wilson, *A Guide to the Roman Remains in Britain*, 1988 edition.

the ditches in front of the North Gate gives a view of a former **police station** of the 1890s (altered) on the N side of **Bridgewater Street**. Small scale, brick with stone dressings. It included a horse ambulance station and mortuary.

Back on Liverpool Road, on the s side there is a row of altered late c18 and early c19 houses with ranges of windows lighting former attic workshops, probably the best-preserved such group in Manchester. For more details of the building type *see* topic box p. 227. Opposite there is another **Market Hall** of 1878 by *Mangnall & Littlewood*, known as Higher Campfield Market, and similar to their market now used as the Air and Space Hall. It is linked by a glazed roof to a (former) **Free Library**, by *George Meek*, 1882, fronting Deansgate. Red brick, stone dressings, two storeys. Central entrance with a big segmental pediment with strongly modelled carving. The upper floor is lit by a range of stepped triple windows, all with stone shafts, and at the top there is a pierced stone parapet and central stone pediment with the city's coat of arms in the tympanum.

Outliers

The area s of Deansgate Station in a loop of the Medlock is known as **Knott Mill**, characterized by a mixture of small-scale mid- and later c19 light industrial works and warehouses. Some of the buildings have been imaginatively converted by, for example, *Ian Simpson Architects*, *Harrison Ince* and *Stephenson Bell* for their own use and as offices, studios, etc.

Outer Areas

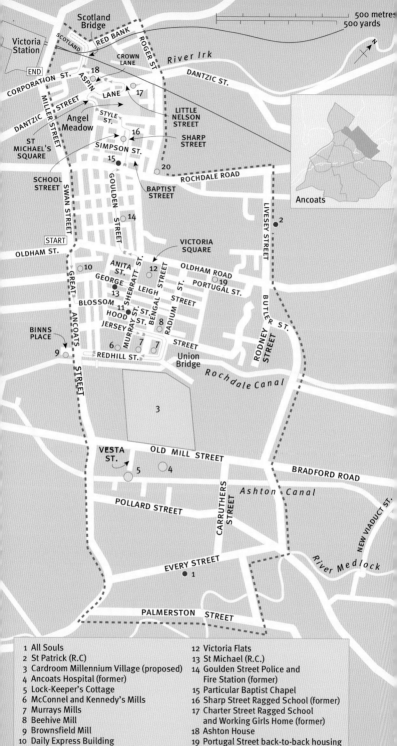

		500 metres
		500 yards

Scotland Bridge

Victoria Station

END

CORPORATION ST.

SCOTLAND

RED BANK

CROWN LANE

ROGER ST.

River Irk

DANTZIC ST.

ASPIN

18

MILLER STREET

DANTZIC

STREET

17

LANE

LITTLE NELSON STREET

SHARP STREET

ST MICHAEL'S SQUARE

Angel Meadow

STYLE ST.

16

SIMPSON ST.

15

20

BAPTIST STREET

SCHOOL STREET

SWAN STREET

GOULDEN STREET

ROCHDALE ROAD

LIVESEY STREET

2

START

OLDHAM ST.

14

GREAT ANCOATS STREET

10

ANITA ST.

SHERRATT ST.

12

VICTORIA SQUARE

OLDHAM ROAD

19

PORTUGAL ST.

GEORGE

13

LEIGH STREET

BENGAL ST.

RADIUM STREET

BUTLER ST.

BLOSSOM

11

HOOD

JERSEY

6

MURRAY ST.

8

7 7

STREET

RODNEY STREET

BINNS PLACE

9

REDHILL ST.

Union Bridge

Rochdale Canal

3

VESTA ST.

5

OLD MILL STREET

4

BRADFORD ROAD

Ashton Canal

POLLARD STREET

CARRUTHERS STREET

NEW VIADUCT ST.

EVERY STREET

1

River Medlock

PALMERSTON STREET

Ancoats

N

1 All Souls
2 St Patrick (R.C)
3 Cardroom Millennium Village (proposed)
4 Ancoats Hospital (former)
5 Lock-Keeper's Cottage
6 McConnel and Kennedy's Mills
7 Murrays Mills
8 Beehive Mill
9 Brownsfield Mill
10 Daily Express Building
11 St Peter
12 Victoria Flats
13 St Michael (R.C.)
14 Goulden Street Police and Fire Station (former)
15 Particular Baptist Chapel
16 Sharp Street Ragged School (former)
17 Charter Street Ragged School and Working Girls Home (former)
18 Ashton House
19 Portugal Street back-to-back housing
20 Marble Arch Public House

● Religious buildings (including former religious buildings)

Ancoats*

Ancoats was largely open land until the late c18. Ancoats Hall, owned by the Byroms before becoming one of the Mosley family homes, stood in fields overlooking the River Medlock. There were no defined boundaries until 1792 when the area was designated Police District 1. Development began in the late 1780s and within a few decades the area had altered beyond recognition. It became one of the most intensely developed industrial centres in the world, and it was not just cotton spinning which took place: foundries, glass works and many other types of industrial premises sprang up alongside the mills. The pace was given impetus by the construction of the Rochdale Canal on the E side of the township. This was not completed until 1804 but the route had been finalized by 1793, and factory complexes were being established along its s part from the late 1790s, while speculators were laying out streets and building housing over the rest of the area (*see* topic box, Introduction p. 12). The existing pattern of streets conforms largely with Green's 1794 map. The grid suggests that the suburb was planned, but this is deceptive: there was no guiding hand or regulatory body, and the layout was the product of the pattern of sales and convenience of plot division by speculators. It was clear from the outset, however, that the demand was for industry and housing for the workers. Covenants attached to sales generally lacked clauses regulating nuisances, unlike the conditions pertaining to the sale of, for example, the Lever lands in the Oldham Street area (*see* Inner City, Walk 1).† The housing put up for the workers was not all shoddy slum housing, though there was plenty of this, but after the middle of the c19 even the superior housing was largely reduced to slums by overcrowding and lack of maintenance. In 1815 Ancoats was the Manchester rating district with the most cotton mills and the largest number of households. The population, swelled by large numbers of immigrants from Ireland as well as the surrounding area, rose from 11,039 in 1801 to 53,737 in 1861.

*Including Angel Meadow, *see* Walk.
†For the Ancoats estates *see* J. Roberts in *Manchester Region History Review*, vol. 7, 1993.

199. Ancoats.

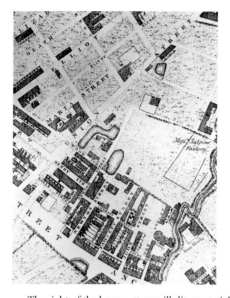

200. Part of Ancoats on William Green's map (1794), showing building plots and streets laid out for development prior to the completion of the Rochdale Canal. Union Street is now known as Redhill Street.

The sight of the huge cotton mills lit up at night by gas, with chimneys so tall they outstripped the church spires, was without parallel in the first few decades of the C19. The mills were almost invariably included in the itineraries of visitors to early C19 Manchester, some of whom evidently approached the visits in the spirit of Picturesque tourism, their descriptions dwelling on the sublime grandeur and awe-inspiring qualities of the scene. The Gothic sensationalism of the French writer Leon Faucher described the 'fogs which exhale from this marshy district and the clouds of smoke vomited forth from numberless chimneys ... you hear nothing but the breathing of vast machines, sending forth fire and smoke through their tall chimneys, and offering up to the heavens, as it were in token of homage, the sighs of that Labour which God has imposed upon man' (1844). This contrasts with the drier observa-

201. 'Manchester, Getting Up The Steam'. Manchester mills illustrated in *The Builder* (1853).

tions of Prussian court architect Karl Friedrich Schinkel who noted in 1826 that the buildings 'as big as the Royal Palace in Berlin' were erected without the benefit of an architect.

The poor social and sanitary conditions of the workers attracted the attention of a middle class appalled by the unforeseen consequences of urban industrialization and fearful of the attendant disease, lawlessness and moral laxity. The conditions were exacerbated by the cyclical depressions affecting the cotton industry; the organization of labour on seasonal and casual lines and the lack of building regulations. The response included the provision of a dispensary founded in 1828, but the shelters, ragged schools and model lodging houses which followed did not proliferate until later in the century. Cultural impoverishment was combated by the establishment of the Manchester Art Museum by T. Horsfall in 1877 (in which Ruskin took a personal interest) and Charles Rowley's Ancoats Brotherhood, founded in 1889. Horsfall was also instrumental in founding a University Settlement in 1895. Of these latter initiatives almost no physical evidence survives.* The spiritual welfare of the inhabitants was served by new churches and chapels. Many have been lost – no fewer than nine since the 1969 edition of the *Buildings of England: South Lancashire*. Of the survivors Roman Catholic churches predominate and remain in use. A preference for a Romanesque style of one sort or another is evident in surviving churches from the early C19 to the early C20 and is true also of demolished ones. Perhaps primitive architectural forms were thought to be suited to the industrial environment. There are a number of outlying churches of interest of which **All Souls**, Every Street, by *William Hayley* of 1839–40 (now used as workshops) in idiosyncratic Romanesque, is an interesting curiosity. The large Romanesque **St Patrick** (R.C.), Livesey Street, 1936 by *H. Greenhalgh*, has an associated group which includes the **Presentation Convent** (R.C.). Of 1834–6, the convent looks like a Georgian town house except for its cupola. It is said that the plans of the convent at Clonmel, Co. Tipperary, Ireland, by *Mother Magdalen Sargent*, 1828, were used. For more details of these and other outlying buildings *see Manchester and South-East Lancashire*, forthcoming.

Ancoats today has an air of dereliction and many cleared sites, but restoration of one or two of the important buildings has come after years of neglect. Regeneration has begun with a new mixed use residential and retail block planned for the site s w of Royal and Paragon Mills (*see* below), and another for which designs were prepared by *Edward Cullinan* in 2000, s e of Victoria Square (*see* below). Funds have been secured for essential repairs to the Murrays Mills complex and further repairs to St Peter, Blossom Street, with the aim of bringing the buildings back into use. The test is whether the other important mills can be saved before they crumble beyond repair. e of the Rochdale Canal the

*The University Settlement used a circular chapel of 1823 of which the truncated outer wall survives on Every Street.

202. All Souls, Every Street, by William Hayley (1839–40).

1970s Cardroom Estate was approved in 2001 as the site of a Millennium Village, part of a Government sponsored initiative to promote excellence in urban design on brownfield sites. *Urban Splash* will be the lead developer. The former Ancoats Hospital by *Lewis & Crawcroft*, 1872–4, which started as the Ardwick and Ancoats Dispensary in 1828, is within the development area.

Canals

The E side of Ancoats is crossed by two canals, the Rochdale Canal completed in 1804–6 and the earlier Ashton Canal, completed as far as Great Ancoats Street in 1796. For the history, *see* Inner City, Walk 1a, p. 218.

Rochdale Canal. A well-preserved section can be seen from Redhill Street, starting at the junction with Great Ancoats Street with Lock No. 82, and following the canal N E. A late C19 cast-iron footbridge links the towpath to Redhill Street. The next stretch gives a good view of the retaining wall of the canal and the blocked entrance to the tunnel to the former Murrays Mills canal basin (for the mills, *see* Cotton Mills, below). The wall has a parapet of huge slabs of millstone grit. At the N end of the street **Union Bridge** was rebuilt in 1903. The road bridge which runs diagonally across the canal is flanked by a separate footbridge, both with cast-iron panelled parapets. There is a spiral horse ramp with a cobbled deck on the s side.

    Ashton Canal. The s part can be reached from **Vesta Street**. A restored lock survives immediately E of Great Ancoats Street, with stone staircases flanking the lower entry. This is the first in a series of similar locks, and the next in the sequence has beside it a brick **lock-keeper's cottage** of *c*. 1800 (altered) with three storeys to the canal. Just to the E there is a towpath bridge of *c*. 1800 crossing a canal branch with a

203. Lock-keeper's cottage, near Vesta Street (*c.* 1800).

curved parapet and cobbled deck. Similar locks and a few bridges can be seen as the canal is followed N E. (On the extreme E side of the township beneath New Viaduct Street a late C18 **aqueduct** carries the canal over the Medlock.)

Cotton Mills

Ancoats contains an internationally important group of cotton-spinning mills sited mainly in the E part of the township. They illustrate the development of plan, power system, cast-iron technology and fireproof construction over a period of more than a century and include the best and most complete surviving examples of early large-scale steam-powered factories concentrated in one area. As well as the examples described below there are others in the outlying parts, *see Manchester and South-East Lancashire.*

The largest of the survivors are McConnel & Kennedy works and neighbouring Murrays Mills (Redhill Street). These are not typical. Mills of the period were generally smaller and many were designed for

Fireproof Construction

Any building constructed using timber and lit by naked flames is a fire risk, and cotton mills were especially vulnerable because of the explosive atmosphere caused by cotton fibres in the air. In the most widely used type of fireproof construction, cast-iron columns support cast-iron beams from which spring brick vaults, or jack-arches. These were covered with a layer of ash or sand and flooring of flags, tiles or floorboards. The first buildings erected using this method in England were mills in Shropshire and Derbyshire in the 1790s, followed by the Philips & Lee cotton mill in Salford in 1801–2. In some cases timber was eliminated from the roof structure as well by using lightweight trusses of cast and wrought iron. Until the design of the cast-iron beams had been perfected, structural instability and defective casting techniques were the cause of a number of collapses of fireproof mills. After improvements in the design (*see* topic box, Introduction p. 15) fireproof construction was adopted more widely and it continued in use throughout the c19. Reinforced concrete flooring was introduced in a limited way in the 1880s, as were rolled steel beams, but these materials were not widely adopted in Manchester mills until the c20. Fireproof construction was expensive and for this reason timber floors continued to be widely used, sometimes with metal or plaster cladding to give a measure of fire resistance. Heavy timber floors without joists offered some fire protection because large timbers tend to char slowly without losing structural integrity.

204. Typical c19 fireproof construction (Chorlton New Mills, Chorlton-on-Medlock).

multiple occupancy (room and power mills), rather than being purpose-built for one firm. It was partly the large size of the companies which allowed them to weather the economic storms into the c20. In the 1830s they were valued, respectively, at almost twice that of their nearest competitors out of a sample of sixty-four local mills.

205. Sketch of mills alongside the Rochdale Canal by Karl Friedrich Schinkel (1826).

McConnel & Kennedy's Mills. Redhill Street, alongside the Rochdale Canal. James McConnel and John Kennedy came to Manchester from Kircudbrightshire. Following apprenticeship to a textile machine manufacturer they set up the firm in 1791, initially to produce textile machinery. They built their first cotton-spinning factory in Ancoats in 1798 on the site now occupied by Royal Mill. (6) The firm became the largest in Manchester, employing more than 1,500 workers in 1836. Their success lay in their technological superiority to most of their rivals and their knowledge of textile machinery. They were responsible for the first successful application of steam power to mule spinning, and they were the first to build a mill in which both mules and preparation machinery were steam-powered (Old Mill, *see* Royal Mill, below). They probably established the standard Lancashire cotton-spinning mill arrangement of having the spinning mules located transversely on the upper floors, one per bay, with preparation of the cotton taking place on the lower floors. The mills were amongst the earliest to be lit by gas, with a system installed by *Boulton & Watt* in 1809.

The four main buildings on the site illustrate development from 1818 to 1913 (*see* plan p. 280). Two earlier mills were destroyed, Old Mill (1798, replaced in 1911) and Long Mill (1801–5, burnt down in 1960).

Sedgwick Mill, Redhill Street. Eight storeys, fireproof construction with tile floors. It was begun in 1818 and *William Fairbairn* took credit for planning the building with John Kennedy, fixing the position and arrangement of the machines, and calculating the 'properties and strengths of the parts'. The seventeen-bay canal-side range to Redhill Street has a very slightly projecting central seven-bay block with a parapet. (1) Eight-bay wings project to the NW at each end. (2 and 3) The courtyard was closed on the NW side by a block of *c.* 1820. (4) The three-storey internal engine house is located at the w end of the main block. It housed a 53-horsepower *Boulton & Watt* beam engine. The boiler house is in the w wing, designed for three wagon boilers. In 1865 *William Fairbairn* replaced the columns on all but the ground and first floors, an operation completed without having to stop production, so that self-acting mules could be installed.

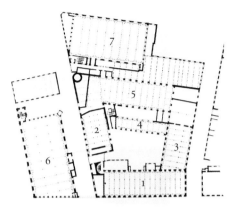

206. Plan of McConnel and Kennedy's Mills, Redhill Street (1818–1913). Plan oriented NE.

Sedgwick New Mill, (5) to the NW, is attached to the W wing of Sedgwick Mill. Built 1868. Five storeys, fifteen bays, fireproof construction incorporating improved beam design. The building was used for doubling the yarn produced in the other mills on the site.

Royal Mill (6) and **Paragon Mill**. (7) 1911–13. The drawings are signed by *Mr Porter* of the Fine Cotton Spinners Engineering Division. The former was built on the site of Old Mill. The six-storey nine-bay buildings were designed to house electrically powered mules, the electric motors were housed in external towers. The construction is of steel and concrete. There is some architectural ornament, with red brick with terracotta and stone dressings and Baroque detailing. These mills are in the first generation of those purpose-built for electricity, which was supplied by the Corporation.

Murrays Mills. Redhill Street, alongside the Rochdale Canal. The careers of brothers Adam and George Murray followed a similar path to that of their neighbours and main rivals, McConnel & Kennedy. They too

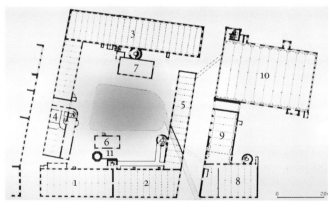

207. Plan of Murrays Mills, Redhill Street (1798–1908).

migrated from Kircudbrightshire and were apprenticed to the same textile machine manufacturer. Between 1798 and by 1806 they developed the area between Murray Street and Bengal Street into the largest mill complex in the town. The buildings are ranged around a courtyard containing a canal basin, now filled in.

Overlooking the canal **Old Mill**, (1) of 1798 is one of the oldest surviving cotton-spinning mills in the region. Its extension, **Decker Mill**, (2) of 1801–2, is attached to the right. Both have eleven bays and seven storeys. A stair-tower serving both buildings, and therefore no earlier than 1801, rises on the N side. It is of fireproof construction with a stone-flagged spiral stair and it incorporates original fire-fighting equipment in the form of a cast-iron standpipe with connections for hosepipes. Also preserved is part of the original heating system. Full-height towers on the N sides of the buildings drew heat from the boiler house or from stoves in the bases and delivered it via openings at floor and ceiling height on each level.

New Mill, (3) built 1804, lies on the far side of the courtyard, to the NW. Six storeys. Some elements of the interior construction survive in the top floor where timber beams and joists are supported by slender cruciform cast-iron columns. The original circular stair-tower is attached to the courtyard side but it has lost its fire-fighting system. The mill was powered by a *Boulton & Watt* engine in a detached house in the yard, parts of which have been incorporated into a low building (probably a blowing house) alongside the stair-tower. (7)

The E and W sides of the courtyard were furnished with narrow blocks used for warehousing and ancillary processes, (4 and 5) completed in 1806, but the Bengal Street range, NE, was demolished in the 1990s. The entrance, on Murray Street, SW, has some architectural ambition. A central stone arched entrance is flanked by stone arched doorways. Above are large tripartite windows with stone mullions on two storeys. The entrance is flanked by warehouse ranges, that to the left reduced from four to two storeys. (The right range is well preserved, with original slender cruciform columns supporting timber floors on the first three storeys, though the lowest storey incorporates T-section cast-iron beams with convex webs in the construction.) Within the courtyard a detached engine house (6) and octagonal chimney are the remains of an enhanced power system introduced to the mills c. 1870–80. Fragments of the 1802 engine house (11) are attached to this and to the stair-tower shared by Decker and Old mills.

The complex was enlarged by building E of the main complex on the other side of Bengal Street. On the corner with Jersey Street **Little Mill**, (10) 1908, replacing a building of 1820. This was one of the city's first electricity-powered mills designed to use the Corporation supply. **Doubling Mill** (8) and **Fireproof Mill** (9) were added c. 1842 and powered by a single internal beam engine. All three were connected with the main complex by tunnels beneath the road.

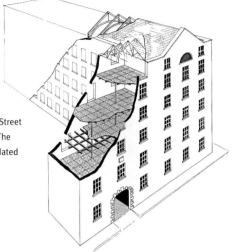

209. Beehive Mill, Jersey Street (built during the 1820s). The warehouse wing (left) is dated 1824.

Beehive Mill. Between Jersey Street, Radium Street, Bengal Street and an infilled arm of the canal on the N side. Two blocks of the 1820s with later extensions. The building was a room and power mill, i.e. designed for multiple tenancies.

The earliest part is an L-shaped block of five storeys and thirteen original bays to Radium Street with three bays to Jersey Street, s. It was extant by 1824. There is a later C19 two-bay extension at the N end of the Radium Street front. A lunette flanked by two conventional windows in the s gable, to Jersey Street, lights the attic. The (modified) three-storey engine house is in the N end bay of the original building, as was the original entrance which gave access to an internal circular stair-tower which wrapped around the chimney. The mill was affected by serious fires in the C19, so the internal construction may not be original. It has heavy timber floors without joists and cast-iron columns with compression plates at the top to spread the load. This is one of only two surviving examples of this form of construction to survive in Manchester, the other being at nearby Brownsfield Mill (*see* below). The roof has unusual trusses of timber and cast iron designed to maximize the usable attic space.

The attached warehouse wing on Jersey Street is dated 1824. A stone arched entrance leads to a yard behind. The building is a sophisticated example of a rarely surviving form of fireproof construction in which interlocking cast-iron beams supported by cast-iron columns form a grid which receives huge stone flags. In this method of construction the T-shaped beams are inverted in order to receive the flags. The earliest

208. McConnel and Kennedy's Mills (left) and Murrays Mills (right), Redhill Street (1798–1913).

210. Beehive Mill, Jersey Street. The warehouse wing of 1824 has a form of fireproof construction in which grids of cast-iron beams support stone flags.

known examples are at Armley Mill, Leeds (1810), at Stanley Mill, Gloucester (1813), and at the Royal Dockyards in Chatham and Devonport, where Edward Holl was also using the method in 1813. The roof structure is of advanced design and similarly devoid of timber: cast-iron trusses are held under tension by wrought-iron ties. Holl was using similar roofs at Chatham Dockyard and *William Fairbairn* used this type of roof from 1825 onwards, including at his own (demolished) workshops in Ancoats. There is no evidence that he was involved in the construction of Beehive Mill, but he may have contributed to the roof design or known of it.

Like so many buildings in the neighbourhood, Beehive Mill seemed destined to slow decline, but a conversion in 1996 by *Provan & Makin* gave it a new lease of life. The building houses offices, a club and rehearsal studios and teaching suites, but all of the important structural elements are intact.

Brownsfield Mill. Binns Place, on the sw side of Great Ancoats Street. Constructed *c.* 1825 as a room and power mill, i.e. for multiple occupancy, L-shaped with blocks of six and seven storeys. A circular external stair-tower in the angle of the blocks is wrapped around a chimney. The construction is of heavy timber floors without joists (for the other Manchester example *see* Beehive Mill, above). The building is of conventional design for the date, with an internal engine house, but it is unusually complete and well preserved. There is a shipping hole to a branch of the Rochdale Canal on the w side. There are plans to restore and convert it as part of the redevelopment of the Rochdale Canal Basin (*see* Inner City, Walk 1a, p. 220).

Walk. Oldham Street to Corporation Street

The Walk covers the s part of Ancoats nearest the city centre and includes the Angel Meadow area. It connects with Inner City Walks 1 (at the top of Oldham Street) and 2 (on Miller Street) and ends at the junction of Corporation Street and Miller Street.

Great Ancoats Street. We start on the corner with Oldham Street, N side. Here a pub of *c*. 1850 (disused in 2000) has tall transomed Gothic windows. The largest and most striking building not only on the street frontage but also of its type in the city is the **Daily Express Building**. By *Sir Owen Williams*, 1939, following the example of his Daily Express in London (1931). His one other Express Building, of 1936, was built in Glasgow. An all-glass front, absolutely flush, with rounded corners and translucent glass and black glass. The top floors are set back in tiers. A little turret at the left corner. The printing presses were in the triple-height press hall, a most impressive sight from the street, particularly when lit up at night. The building has been extended four times. Williams himself was responsible for the 1960 extension on George Leigh Street behind. He allowed for an extra two storeys, added in 1979 by *Rosenberg & Gentle* together with three more floors suspended over the road separating the two blocks. Further extension followed in 1983, the form still rounded, but clad in channelled steel. These two extensions are being converted to flats and integrated work and living modules. In 1993–5 *Michael Hyde & Associates* converted the main building to offices. Their extension to Great Ancoats Street, left side, is seamless, on the site of property which could not be obtained in 1939. Since the conversion views into the press hall have been obscured by reflective film.

211. Daily Express Building, Great Ancoats Street, by Sir Owen Williams (1939).

212. St Peter, Blossom Street, by Isaac Holden & Son (1859).

Methodist Women's Night Shelter (illus. 24) neighbours to the E, on the E corner of George Leigh Street. By *W. R. Sharp*, opened in 1899. Four storeys on a narrow site with an oversailing timbered attic storey and an oriel to Great Ancoats Street. There was a coffee tavern on the ground floor, and the rest was divided between a night shelter, a home for women needing 'further care and discipline' and a home for domestic servants, who were being offered an alternative to the moral perils of the lodging house.

Continuing E and turning N along Blossom Street brings us to the former premises of the Manchester Fish & Meat Salesman Ice Co. Ltd of *c.* 1870. The ice plant, which also supplied the local Italian community's ice cream trade, has gone, but the main building has been saved from dereliction and awaits a new use. Just beyond, SE side, is **St Peter**, 1859 by *Isaac Holden & Son*. Italian Romanesque with round-headed openings throughout. It was built for a newly created parish made necessary by the population explosion. It seated 1,350. After years of dereliction the exterior was restored in 1998–9, and a new use is being sought. Red brick with dressings of white brick and some yellow sandstone. Nave and apsidal chancel under one concave-sided roof. Continuous upper arcading, pierced with paired and triple clerestory windows. Lower aisles and gabled transepts with triple windows. Big NW campanile in three stages with paired belfry windows and blind arcading above, topped by a (restored) upper part with a concave-sided roof. The big blunt forms and curving apse and roof make an impressive picture. The **interior** has largely been lost, but the 'superb' plaster ceiling described in this series in 1969 has been taken down and is to be reinstated. Five lofty bays with slender octagonal cast-iron columns with foliated caps with volutes, the roof divided into bays by four elegant trusses of cast iron with enriched spandrels. Part of a w gallery survives. Three large ornate metal gasoliers have been removed for conservation.

Behind the church, on **Hood Street**, is the remains of the **Methodist Men's Hostel** by *J. Gibbons Sankey*, dated 1903. Its sheer size gives some idea of the demand for decent lodgings and the strength of Methodist commitment to social service. It is not wholly utilitarian either, with buff and brown terracotta banding and a central pedimented entrance bay flanked by turrets which were formerly domed. It had lodgings for weekly boarders, day lodgers and casuals, accommodated in cubicles, each with its own window.

A detour can be made here to see some of the more important **cotton mills** (*see* p. 277) via Murray Street, which runs s e from the n end of Hood Street, to Jersey Street for Beehive Mill. Continuing s e along Radium Street leads to Redhill Street and Murrays Mills and the McConnel & Kennedy complex alongside the Rochdale Canal. Rejoin the walk by returning to Blossom Street.

The area bounded by Blossom Street, George Leigh Street, Sherratt Street and Bengal Street is to be the site of a new mixed-use development planned to start in 2001. To the n w of the site **Victoria Square** is reached by turning n from Blossom Street along Sherratt Street. A vast slum replacement of 1897. The Corporation sponsored a competition won by *Spalding & Cross*. The result is a five-storey block with an inner courtyard or square round which balconies run on four levels. The iron railings show at once that the architects wanted to do more than was

213. Victoria Square, by Spalding & Cross (1897).

strictly necessary without at all going elaborate. The eighteen-bay front to Oldham Road has indeed good brickwork, a middle gable with some terracotta and Dutch side-gables. The sides of the block are stock brick with large segmental-headed windows in pairs alternating with small round windows in pairs. It originally comprised 235 two-room and 48 single-room flats, all paired on each side of a communal lobby with a sink and water closet. The turrets contained communal laundries and drying rooms. This initiative did not do the slum dwellers any good since they could not afford the rents and had to move to squalid conditions elsewhere, but it was the first municipal housing in Manchester and it is still occupied and in public ownership.

The adjacent block fronting **Oldham Road** was built at the same time, with shops and dwellings above, while behind there is more municipal housing of the same period on **Anita** (formerly Sanitary) **Street**, this time in the form of modest terraces, designed as one- and two-room flats. The neighbouring terraces on **George Leigh Street**, which runs parallel to the SE, were three-bedroom houses, the only element of the scheme to conform to the moral ideal for housing – i.e. allowing for separation of parents and children of each sex. These were far too expensive for working-class families at the time, but like their neighbours on Anita Street, they are still occupied and in public ownership.

St Michael (R.C.) lies to the SE. Founded in 1858, though the present façade looks later, perhaps c. 1870–80. Yellow sandstone, paired lancets flanking a central entrance, bell opening over. The façade was altered and truncated when the church behind was demolished and replaced in the mid C20. It may be by *Corbett, Son & Brooks* who did the neighbouring **school** in 1879. *O. C. Hill* extended the school and added a **clergy house** in 1887. The school is workaday Gothic and the clergy house is enlivened by a traceried doorway. These two buildings are now used as offices and a hostel.

Retracing our steps, and continuing further NE brings us to **George Leigh School**, 1912. Red brick with emphasis concentrated in tall corniced chimneys and tall, slightly projecting entrance bays. Note the rooftop playground.

Goulden Street is reached by crossing Oldham Road at the end of Sherratt Street. This part of Ancoats has a mixture of warehouses and works mainly of the late C19 and early C20. Some were produce stores serving nearby Smithfield Market (*see* Inner City, Walk 1b, p. 228). On the NE side is the disused **police and fire station** by *J. G. Lynde* for A division. A forceful, even monumental, design of c. 1870. A high windowless façade has a giant blind arcade topped by a pediment, all in stone. The rest is brick. Within the courtyard a tall channelled chimney. Mounted police were stationed here and the complex included stables. Lynde is better known for police stations in a workmanlike Gothic, but something more akin to a stronghold was required in this notoriously lawless area.

214. Police and fire
station (former),
Goulden Street,
by J. G. Lynde
(c. 1870).

Rochdale Road is reached by continuing NW. The **Particular Baptist Chapel**, Rochdale Road, is by *J. Wills & Son*, dated 1907. It is the successor to a chapel erected slightly to the N on Baptist Street through the efforts of the minister John Sharp in 1789, replaced under the ministry of William Gadsby in 1823. The present building is brick with pale faience dressings, Arts and Crafts style. The central gabled entrance bay is flanked by full-height octagonal piers with little domed caps, and lower battlemented wings. (Steve Little reports that the interior has furnishings salvaged from the earlier, C19, building and an immersion tank.) **Sharp Street** runs N. On the corner of Simpson Street, w side, is one of the earliest surviving buildings in the neighbourhood, i.e. *c.* 1830, a simple brick-built warehouse of four storeys with a full-height loading bay. Beside it to the right is the brick former **Sharp Street Ragged School**, founded in 1853, this building erected in 1869, an early and remarkably intact example of a purpose-built Ragged School. (It is said to retain a little-altered interior with a ground-floor partition which divided the reception class of wild street children from those who had been subdued.)

Style Street is reached by continuing N and turning down School Street. Here was the church of St Michael (1788, demolished *c.* 1951). The cleared area, which is partly paved with gravestones, is the site of the church and its graveyard sw, and the parish pauper graveyard, opened in 1787, NE. From here the land begins to fall steeply down to the River Irk. This is the heart of an area known as **Angel Meadow**, which remained one of the worst slums in the city throughout the C19. As late as 1897 a report to the Manchester Statistical Society concluded that it represented 'a grievous blot on our Municipal policy'.

The former **Charter Street Ragged School and Working Girls Home**

215. Charter Street
Ragged School and
Working Girls Home (for-
mer), Charter Street,
showing the extension by
Maxwell & Tuke (1898).

can be seen below the graveyard on **Aspin Lane**, where there is a gateway
from the graveyard. A relatively rare surviving example of a purpose-
built institution of this type, with a largely intact plan. The work of the
mission had commenced in 1847 and a school was built on the site in
1866. The range to Little Nelson Street by *Maxwell & Tuke*, dated 1891,
was an extension of the 1866 building, subsequently pulled down and
replaced by the block to Dantzic Street in 1898, also by *Maxwell & Tuke*.
The earlier part has tall channelled chimneys and top-floor oriels, the
rather plain later building one or two Baroque touches. Accommodation
was provided for servants who would otherwise have to use lodging
houses, with kitchens, laundries and individual cubicles. Some of these
features survive. Two large halls on two floors on the Aspin Lane side
served the Ragged School and mission. The changes of level inside
reflect the piecemeal building history and the exigencies of a circulation
system which separated the working girls from other users.

Corporation Street to the s branches from Dantzic Street. Near the

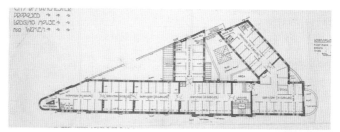

216. Ashton House, Corporation Street, by City Architect H. R. Price (1908–10).

junction **Ashton House**, a former model lodging house for women built by the Corporation 1908–10 by City Architect *H. R. Price* (a men's lodging house, far to the SE off Pollard Street, has disappeared). On an island site with a very narrow rounded NE end to the junction with Crown Lane. Red brick and cream terracotta, Arts and Crafts style. Nice details include ironwork with flower motifs, lettering in the gable to the corner with Aspin Lane and voussoirs of tiles laid on edge. It catered for 222 women, who occupied dormitories with individual cubicles and cooked for themselves in communal kitchens. **Red Bank**, the continuation of Aspin Lane, leads N beyond a railway bridge. Here the River Irk can be seen between the labyrinthine arches of the railway viaducts emanating from Victoria Station. **Scotland Bridge**, a red sandstone bridge carrying the road, is probably mid-C19 or earlier, as City Engineers' plans show evidence for at least three separate phases of construction. It seems to be on the site of a bridge shown in 1741 by Casson and Berry as well as on their reproduction of a C17 map of the town. Turning left along a street known simply as **Scotland** gives a view of the fast-flowing river as it runs over a weir and into a cavernous tunnel.

Returning to Corporation Street, which continues S into the centre of town, ends the walk. For the Parkers Hotel on the corner of Miller Street *see* Inner City, Walk 2, p. 239. Walk 2 can be joined near the junction with Cannon Street.

Outliers

Portugal Street. The battered shell of the centre's only surviving back-to-back housing. There were ten houses built in three phases in 1790–1. The block has been greatly altered, but there are plans for restoration and conversion to offices and workshops.

Rochdale Road. The **Marble Arch** by *Darbyshire & Smith*, dated 1888, is the only one of the scattered pubs in the area of architectural pretension. The interior has an unusual jack-arch ceiling with exposed cast-iron beams supported by tile-clad brackets.* Walls and ceiling of the main bar are lined with glazed bricks and tiles and a lettered frieze advertises types of drink.

*Darbyshire had considerable experience of designing fireproof cotton mills and pioneered fireproof safety theatre designs with Henry Irving.

Ardwick and Beswick

Ardwick, SE of the centre, had no manor as it was within the demesne of Manchester. The lands were acquired by the Birch family in 1636 and the estate was eventually bought by Thomas Marsland Bennett in the C19. By the late C18 houses and villas were being built and a few, mainly of early C19 date, survive around Ardwick Green. A guide of 1839 described it as a 'pleasing suburb ... ornamented by a fine miniature lake, surrounded by handsome dwellings'. It certainly is not that now. The city spread its industry and cheap housing over the area by the end of the C19, largely cleared during the 1930s and after the war. Much of the N and E part is bleak, with light industrial units cut through by busy roads. Only the w part around Ardwick Green has any cohesion and character. Neighbouring Beswick was joined with Ardwick to form a ward when Manchester was incorporated in 1838. The area was almost completely undeveloped until the mid C19, when housing and industry came. In 1945 the City of Manchester Plan proposed radical improvements, but instead of the intended low-rise housing huge tower blocks were erected in the early 1970s and demolished after barely more than

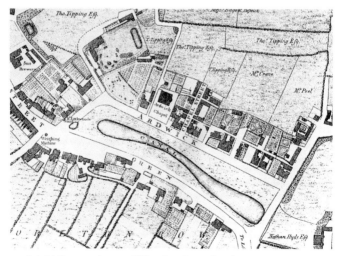

217. Ardwick Green as shown on William Green's map (1794).

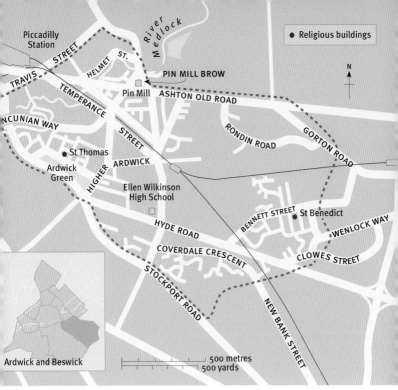

218. Ardwick and Beswick.

ten years as a result of structural failures and water penetration. New low-rise housing has followed, but there are still cleared areas to the s and a few C19 terraces survive here and there. Only the more important buildings are described. For further detail *see Manchester and South-East Lancashire*, forthcoming.

Churches

St Thomas, Ardwick Green North. Set back from the street frontage in a yard paved with gravestones. The railings have been replaced, but the columnar gateposts look C18. Built in 1741 on a small scale, widened in 1777, lengthened by two bays to the E in 1831, and provided with its W tower in 1836. The tower is the one really remarkable feature, an Italian Romanesque campanile, a type not generally favoured before the 1840s. It is in three stages above the cornice, the first with three tall blind arches pierced by slits, then a similar blind arcade, the top stage has an open arcade of the same design, capped by a shallow pyramidal roof with a projecting cornice. The architect was *William Hayley*. Brick laid in Flemish bond with flared headers and sandstone dressings including a cornice which continues around the tower. The side to the green is absolutely plain and flat. Two tiers of arched windows with Y-tracery. The only obvious exterior sign of the conversion which followed redundancy in 1978 is a pair of upper doors and fire-escape stairs at the E end. The building now houses a resources and conference centre for the community and voluntary sector. Part of the nave is preserved as a large meeting room while the aisles and galleries are used as offices. The galleries are supported by cast-iron fluted columns, but the upper columns, which were also fluted, were for some reason replaced by unfluted Doric columns during the conversion. The C18 **reredos** divides the E nave wall into three bays with fluted Corinthian pilasters supporting an entablature. The central bay is pedimented. There is a flat, deeply coffered ceiling divided into square panels by moulded ribs.

St Benedict, Bennett Street. 1880 by *J. S. Crowther*. A remarkably large church, done with panache. St Benedict is quite unlike any of Crowther's other churches. Some of the unusual features, such as the attached school and clergy house, taking the form of a presbytery, can perhaps be attributed to the input of the Anglo-Catholic Bennett family. John Marsland Bennett was a prosperous merchant who settled in Ardwick in the 1850s. When asked by the Diocesan Church Building Society in 1876 to donate a plot of land for a new church, he responded by offering to build and equip the church at his own expense. According to his son (who is credited with drawing up preliminary plans), he wanted a church which would be 'plain but massive ... it should possess a shell which would be standing years after many cheap, "dressy" churches had crumbled to ruins ... In it the Catholic Faith must be taught in all its fullness, and through the eye as through the ear.' His choice of Crowther as architect was dictated by his belief that 'to design a church demands that the architect himself shall be a true churchman.'

Crowther's scholarly approach and attention to detail is everywhere evident. With characteristic self-confidence he described the style as 'Early Geometric Decorated of the year 1245'. The building is of brick laid in header bond with terracotta and stone dressings. High N W tower with pyramid roof and tourelles at the corners. The W entrance is within an arch with clustered shafts which incorporates blind tracery above and two entrances below. Blind arcading above, then a rose window. The intended carving to the corbels and traceried door heads was never completed. On the s side there is a low aisle and single flying buttress beside the twin gables of the s chapel. The E end is a sheer cliff of brick with an enormous Geometric window above, flanked on each side by low chapels. Along the N side the N aisle is concealed by the low two-storey clergy house and the Sunday School, this now used as parish rooms. Attached to the E end of this range the vestry with paired gables and arched windows and doors, but the remaining detail looks more domestic with gabled dormers and windows under segmental heads.

219. St Benedict, Bennett Street, by J. S. Crowther (1880).

The scale mediates between the large church and the lower surrounding terraced housing.

Interior. A most dramatic and impressive space thanks partly to a
very high and elaborate hammerbeam roof. Enrichment to the top
part, in the form of angle struts, is reserved for the chancel. All exposed
brick laid in English bond with orange brick dressings and terracotta
enrichment. Narrow w organ loft with a terracotta balustrade of pierced
quatrefoils. Five-bay nave arcade with quatrefoil stone piers; the aisles
are narrow and the N aisle windows set higher than the s to gain light
from the valley between church and school. The clerestory is generously
proportioned with big Geometric windows. The three-bay raised chancel
has a high arch and is flanked by N and s chapels, both with fumed oak
panelling of 1909. The s (Lady) chapel is the more elaborate with two
shallow projecting bays on the s side. The generous NE vestries have
exposed timber roofs copied from the roof at Chetham's School and
Library (*see* Major Buildings, p. 65).

Furnishings are described topographically starting at the E end. – In
the chancel and incongruously classical, a painted **baldacchino**, introduced in the early 1960s. The accompanying reordering included removal
of the chancel screen. A mutilated part of Crowther's **reredos** survives
against the E wall. On each side Crowther's pretty ironwork **parclose
screens**. – **Lectern**, N side of the chancel steps, *c.* 1900. Stone, an angel

supports the reading desk. Designed and executed by parishioners *W. Cecil Hardistry* and *E. F. Long.* – **Pulpit**, S side of chancel steps, 1907. – **Font**, a drum with panelled tracery in the N aisle, moved there from the SW corner. – **Vestry furnishings** include very handsome cupboards and wardrobes to Crowther's design with ornamental ironwork and cresting.

Stained glass: E window, *c.* 1885. Badly faded in places. S chapel, E window, 1926. Coloured figures on a plain ground. S side E: a circular Te Deum window, 1894, probably by *Ward & Hughes.* S side W: SS Mary and Elizabeth by *T. F. Curtis, Ward & Hughes*, 1906. S aisle windows are mostly of the 1890s. They are of some quality and are probably by *Ward & Hughes.* They show saints, mostly those associated with the Benedictine order, in architectural surrounds. The odd ones out are a very good window of 1924 showing St George, and a brightly coloured window of 1935 by *M. E. Aldrich Rope.* The E rose window has a design of flowers with Marian associations. E end N side, the archangels, 1889 by *Ward & Hughes.* N side: three good windows of the 1890s, again probably by *Ward & Hughes* showing Benedictine nuns and abbesses. N chapel E window: St John the Baptist with SS Elizabeth and Zacharius, by *T. F. Curtis, Ward & Hughes*, dated 1899.

Monuments. Set into the s wall of the s chapel. Two ledger slabs of the Bennett family brought from one of the demolished c18 churches in central Manchester. Thomas Bennett timber merchant d. 1766, James Bennett timber merchant d. 1804.

Clergy house. The interior has typical Crowther joinery details. The entrance and reception rooms are at the w end with a staircase up to a long series of rooms over the school rooms. The route from the upper floor down to the vestry and the transition between secular and sacred space is marked by a change from square to arched openings, with each successive doorway becoming more ecclesiastical in appearance.

Ellen Wilkinson High School

On Hyde Road. Of 1879–80 by *Thomas Worthington*. Established as a bluecoat school called Nicholls Hospital by Benjamin Nicholls, as a memorial to his son who died prematurely in 1859 after working with the poor in Manchester. Nicholls commissioned Worthington to prepare designs in 1867 for a building to be constructed after his death, which came ten years later. It was Worthington's last major work in the city. The design is related to Worthington's Police Courts (*see* City Centre, Minshull Street) and his entry for the town hall competition, all being worked on at about the same time. Like the Police Courts it is in European Gothic style, of red brick with stone dressings. Also like them it impresses from a distance and increases in subtlety as it is approached. The architectural embellishment gradually intensifies from basement

221. Ellen Wilkinson High School, Hyde Road, by Thomas Worthington (1879–80).

to top, so apart from the entrance, reached from a flight of stone steps, the treatment is simple at lower levels. First-floor windows have delicately moulded label stops, then a range of befinialed gabled dormers strikes upwards. There are stone tourelles at the corners. The central tower is without buttresses. A machicolated stone parapet with octagonal tourelles at the corners supports a saddleback roof; tall gabled dormers with traceried windows. It is on the tower that Worthington's favourite animal carving is deployed, in the shape of heraldic beasts, though most of it has been removed. Simply planned: the entrance leads to a foyer and then an impressive hall, from which rises a top-lit stair with a cast-iron balustrade with wheel motifs. Classrooms are ranged on each side.

Original forecourt walls, gate piers and gates to Hyde Road. Late C19 and 1960s rear extensions, to the w a large addition of 1996 by City Architect *R. King*. Two four-storey classroom blocks, with angled roofs and projecting eaves; off-centre projecting brick stair-tower.

Pin Mill

Pin Mill Brow. On the site of a late C18 pin and paper factory in a loop of the (culverted) River Medlock, a fairly complete mid-C19 cotton mill complex with an engine house with distinctive arched windows and a tall brick octagonal chimney. Weaving sheds on each side of the main block with ranges of saw-tooth roofs with north-light windows are a rare survival in central Manchester.

222. Pin Mill, Pin Mill Brow (mid C19).

Cheetham and Strangeways

The township lies on the N side of the centre. The main roads are those leading N to Bury, and Bury New Road on the E side is approximately on the line of the Roman road between Manchester and Ribchester. The open farmland here was mostly part of the Stanley and Strange estates. In the late C18 industry began to encroach on the s part, and in the early C19 the area became a haven for newly wealthy merchants and professionals who built their villas on the slopes above the increasingly polluted town centres of Manchester and Salford. Manchester's Jewry were concentrated here, with poor immigrants in the low-lying Red Bank area beside the River Irk and better-off families populating the more salubrious streets to the N, which still retain signs of their presence. One of Manchester's most notable High Victorian buildings, *Alfred Waterhouse*'s Manchester Assize Courts (1859–64) stood on Great Ducie Street in front of his Strangeways Prison until it was demolished following war damage.*

The places of worship and public buildings described below are the more important buildings of the s part of the township which are fairly accessible from the centre.

St Chad (R.C.), Cheetham Hill Road, close to the former town hall. 1846–7 by *Weightman & Hadfield*. Stone, Perp, and on the way to archaeological accuracy, though window proportions and tracery detail have been varied and mixed up, not grouped to suggest different building campaigns. It could hardly be more different from their St Mary, Mulberry Street (*see* City Centre), of only a year later. All the parts are separately expressed and there are enjoyable asymmetries in the design. SW tower with a higher stair-turret, aisles punctuated by big gargoyles, nave, and lower chancel. Attached on the E side a large **presbytery** is of stone like the church, with steep gables and gabled dormers. **Interior.** Six bay nave, two bay chancel, aisles, N and s chapels, sw organ loft. C20 entrance foyer at the w end. The arcades have octagonal piers with embattled caps. The nave has a thin but complicated hammerbeam roof.

*Some of the sculpture was saved however; for this *see* Inner City, Walk 3, King Street West.

N

1 St Chad (R.C.)
2 Independent Chapel (former)
3 Spanish and Portuguese
  Synagogue (former)
4 Synagogue (former)
5 Town Hall (former) and Poor
  Law Union Office (former)
6 Free Library (former)
7 Strangeways Prison
● Religious buildings (including
  former religious buildings)

ELIZABETH STREET

NORTH STREET

BROUGHTON STREET

SHERBORNE STREET

BURY NEW ROAD

7

7

SOUTHALL STREET

GREAT DUCIE STREET

LORD ST.

CHEETHAM HILL ROAD

PARK ST.

RED BANK

ROGER ST.

River Irk

River Irwell

TRINITY WAY

Victoria
Station

CORPORATION STREET

MILLER STREET

DANTZIC STREET

Cheetham
and Strangeways

500 metres
500 yards

223. Cheetham and Strangeways.

N chapel of two bays alongside the chancel, two-bay s chapel with one bay beside the chancel and the other beside the aisle, creating the effect of a transept and allowing the chancel to be lit by two high windows on this side. **Furnishings**: mainly of various C19 dates. – Painted stone **reredos** with angels, **altar** with a Last Supper scene. – **Sedilia** with traceried heads. – Elaborate **pulpit** with much Gothic panelling and a tall pinnacled canopy. – s chapel. Very elaborate coved wooden **reredos** with angels. – **Stained glass**. E window, *c.* 1847–8, by *Barnett & Son* of York, E window N chapel by *Edith Norris*, 1956. Adoration of the Lamb, s chapel w, and St Catherine, N aisle E, both late C19, probably by the same firm. – **Monument**. Seated statue of Monsignor W. J. Canon Sheehan, rector of the church, erected by the parishioners 1906.

Independent Chapel (former), Cheetham Hill Road, at the corner of Park Street. *c.* 1840. Used as a synagogue for a while, now furniture showrooms. An excellent classical design. Ashlar, with a three-bay front with slender arched windows, a big portal, and a one-bay pediment. The side, five bays long, has giant pilasters and windows in two tiers. The end bays are blank, with banded rustication. The elegance of the design is enhanced by the approach from broad steps.

Spanish and Portuguese Synagogue (former), Cheetham Hill Road. By *Edward Salomons*, 1889, for the Sephardic Jews in what Salomons described as 'Saracenic' and 'Moresque' style, appropriately recalling the ancient architecture of Moorish Spain, and avoiding either Gothic or classical with their respective Christian and pagan associations. The use of the style for the exterior as well as the interior is quite unusual, though T. H. & F. Healey did something similar in the Bowman Street synagogue in Bradford in 1880–1.* Rescued after closure, the building is now used as the Manchester Jewish Museum, opened in 1984. It is not

224. Spanish and Portuguese Synagogue (former, now the Manchester Jewish Museum), Cheetham Hill Road, by Edward Salomons (1889).

*Dr Sharman Kadish pointed this out to me.

225. Interior of the Manchester Jewish Museum (formerly the Spanish and Portuguese Synagogue), Cheetham Hill Road, by Edward Salomons (1889).

large, and set back from the line of the street, in warm red brick with stone dressings. In the projecting entrance bay a central door framed by a Moorish arch, below an arcade of five horseshoe-headed windows. On each side are two-storey bays, windows with ogee heads below and horseshoe heads above.

The **interior** has been kept much as it was when closed in 1981 apart from the removal of seats in the ladies' gallery upstairs, where there are exhibitions. The pink and green colour scheme, with gilding, is based on what was found beneath C20 overpainting. First a foyer with the museum reception to the left, gallery staircase to the right and doors ahead leading to the main space. The open timber roof has ventilators with foliated moulding. Galleries on three sides, with an intricate iron-work parapet and cast-iron columns with fancy capitals. At the E end is a recess framed by a Moorish arch springing from paired columns, with a classical **ark**, where the Torah scrolls are kept, with paired columns and a segmental arch. The columns have gilded capitals and pink mar-ble shafts. **Bima**, from which the Torah is read, at the W end with open-work sides in Moorish designs. The bench seating with armrests is orig-inal. At the rear there is a converted **succah**, used during the festival of tabernacles, which had originally a removeable roof. **Stained glass**.

Mostly early C20. Big circular E window with a menorah, 1913. The rest downstairs show biblical landscapes and scenes, all seemingly by the same hand. Upstairs, E end: on one side the pillar of fire, on the other the pillar of cloud. Other windows have geometrical designs.

Synagogue (former), Cheetham Hill Road. By *W. Sharp Ogden*, 1889. Red brick, stone dressings, central pedimented entrance bay with an arch pushed up into it framing a circular window with a Star of David design. Flanking bays have subsidiary entrances and arcades of round-headed windows. It is set back from the street, with gate piers and stone steps up to the entrances. Altered and converted to a warehouse.

Town Hall (former), Cheetham Hill Road. 1853–5 by *T. Bird*. A sober classical composition of red brick with prominent stone quoins and a heavy bracketed eaves cornice. Two tall storeys, seven bays with a projecting three-bay centre and lower wings. Austerity is offset by the delicate iron porte-cochère in front of the central entrance. The upper hall has a semicircular end wall. Converted to offices after many years of dereliction.

Poor Law Union Office (former), Cheetham Hill Road, 1861–2. Three bays and two storeys flanked by single-storey wings. Decidedly more florid than the town hall, to which it was subsequently used as an annexe. Crowned by a cornice and balustraded parapet. The central entrance has a porch with fluted Ionic columns, the volutes linked by bulging festoons; the single-storey flanking bays have Venetian windows in elaborate pilastered stone surrounds.

Free Library (former), Cheetham Hill Road. By *Barker & Ellis*. Yellow brick and stone dressings, dated 1876 in the frieze. Above the central portal a handsome five-bay window arcade. Side bays with upper pedimented windows only; the sheer walls below increase the monumental effect. Above the cornice segmental gables on each side of a balustraded parapet. There is nothing left inside. It was damaged by fire, and like almost everything else on the main road, it is in use as a warehouse.

Strangeways Prison, Southall Street. 1866–8 by *Alfred Waterhouse*. The high minaret-chimney, actually part of the ventilation system, is a landmark. Of the rest one does not see much, except the 1990s additions and alterations (*see* below). The architectural motifs are Romanesque, with an octagonal raised centre like a North Italian cathedral or a British workhouse, in dark red brick with pale stone dressings and banding. Waterhouse took as his model Joshua Jebb's radial plan of Pentonville, in London, of the 1840s, and consulted Jebb, who was Surveyor General of Prisons, on the plans. Six wings radiate from the centre, a short entrance wing then five four-storey cell blocks. The gatehouse, now superseded by a new entrance (*see* below), is not especially conspicuous as it is overlooked by big C19 former factories. Octagonal turrets with tall pyramidal roofs flank the big entrance arch.

Extensive damage to the roof and interior during a prolonged riot in 1990 prompted refurbishment in 1991–3. The *J. R. Harris Partnership* did the work and prepared a masterplan. Later accretions were demolished, but the only original part to disappear completely was the attached Magistrates Court, originally on the sw side of the site. The main cell wings were divided into sections to improve staff and inmate access and circulation. Before the refit the impressive views along the wings from the controlling hub contrasted with the claustrophobic cells and contributed to an oppressive atmosphere. The cells were refitted and the windows enlarged. The new entrance complex, designed by *Austin-Smith: Lord* is at the angle of two new blocks, set back from the line of Southall Street. It continues the theme of banded brick, with sheer walls surmounted by glazed cladding and a cantilevered security eaves. The new security wall is also of banded brick rising from a battered plinth and topped by a curved security capping. The *John Brunton Partnership* designed new workshops, a physical-recreation centre and kitchen.

226. Aerial view of Strangeways Prison, Southall Street, by Alfred Waterhouse (1866–8).

227. Gatehouse to Strangeways Prison, Southall Street, by Alfred Waterhouse (1866–8).

Chorlton-on-Medlock

For the Universities *see* Academic Institutions.

Chorlton-on-Medlock lies to the s of the centre, s of the River Medlock, which forms the boundary. It was farmland until the late c18. The land around Grosvenor Square, formerly known as Chorlton Row, was acquired by Roger Aytoun and sold in the 1790s to Messrs Marsland, Duckworth and Cooper, who planned to create a residential suburb. The Marslands were cotton manufacturers who established large cotton mills on Cambridge Street in the sw part of the township not long afterwards (*see* Walk 1). Oxford Road was opened in 1790, running from St Peter's Square in town to Rusholme to the s, and streets and building plots were laid out in 1793–4. The Napoleonic wars prevented early development and the township had only 675 inhabitants in 1801, but by 1821 there were more than 8,000. The aims of the developers can perhaps be divined from the aristocratic names given to many of the new roads, and the fact that industrial development was controlled by restrictive covenants. The rapid development of Manchester eventually led to middle-class migration, and after the mid c19 undeveloped land was quickly taken up by cheap housing. By the 1890s the area was predominantly working class. A survey of 1904 declared: 'In no part of town have we found worse conditions prevailing among the homes of the people'. Municipal slum clearance followed later in the c20 and continued into the 1970s with the cleared areas gradually being taken over by buildings of the academic quarter. Critical to future development was the decision in 1869 to site Owens College here, followed by the erection of hospitals alongside Oxford Road to the s from the 1880s onward. The area has

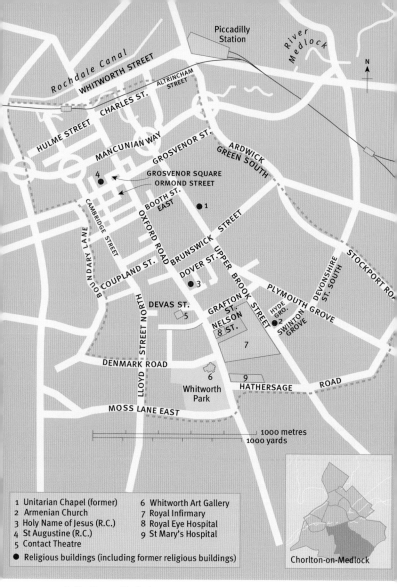

228. Chorlton-on-Medlock.

Map legend:

1 Unitarian Chapel (former)
2 Armenian Church
3 Holy Name of Jesus (R.C.)
4 St Augustine (R.C.)
5 Contact Theatre
6 Whitworth Art Gallery
7 Royal Infirmary
8 Royal Eye Hospital
9 St Mary's Hospital
● Religious buildings (including former religious buildings)

Chorlton-on-Medlock

become, as a result, dominated by academic institutions in the N part and a large hospital complex to the s, with a more mixed area, including 1970s housing estates, along the E flank.

The variety in the churches of Chorlton-on-Medlock is notable, despite many losses, among which was *Edward Walters'* dignified Cavendish Street Congregational Chapel of 1847–8, demolished as recently as 1973.

Survivors include the former **Unitarian Chapel** and attached Sunday

229. Grosvenor Square as shown on Bancks & Co.'s map (1831).

School (former), Upper Brook Street. 1836–9 by *Charles Barry*. E.E. style and much less accomplished than his contemporary secular work, but more convincing in form and detail than his earlier churches.

The **Armenian Church**, Upper Brook Street, was purpose-built for the Armenians by *Royle & Bennett*, 1869–70. A friendly low-key design in yellow sandstone. Gothic, with original simple furnishings. For more details of these and other outlying buildings *see Manchester and South-East Lancashire*, forthcoming.

Churches

Holy Name of Jesus (R.C.), Oxford Road. 1869–71 by *Joseph Aloysius Hansom*, with his son and future partner *Joseph Stanislaus Hansom*, contemporary with their Arundel Cathedral and one of their finest buildings. The elder Hansom was doubtless responsible for the daring structural design and the younger for the detail and many of the larger furnishings. The design had a steeple 240 ft (73 metres) high (based on

230. Holy Name of Jesus (R.C.), Oxford Road, by Joseph Aloysius Hansom (1869–71).

Amiens Cathedral), which remained unexecuted and the octagonal top of the tower is by *Adrian Gilbert Scott*, completed in 1928. It could not be better suited for its task. Hansom's tower is much broader than it is deep. The façade is deliberately not identical to the left and right of the tower, and on the right side is a baptistery with a conical roof. The sides and apse have flying buttresses, and along the s side low outer chapels are expressed by small gables and small windows. The e end consists of transepts, a short chancel, and a high polygonal apse with a narrow ambulatory and cross gables. Two e turrets rise where the chancel sets in. The **interior** is overwhelmingly airy, because of the extremely slim piers. The whole church is rib-vaulted using lightweight polygonal terracotta blocks (by *Gibbs & Canning*) instead of stone (*see* topic box, p. 170). Terracotta is also used as a facing material, in some places with ornamentation. Originally it was a pale honey colour but the disastrous decision to sandblast the interior in 1972 removed the original surface and lightened the colour. Vaulted narthex and w organ gallery with a very high three-bay arcade screening it. The nave has four bays, the transepts are entered by a high arch continuing the nave arcade. The chancel is very high too; its width equals that of the nave only by adding to it the ambulatory entrances, as at Gerona Cathedral in Spain. Hansom linked nave and chancel by very tall diagonal arches to soften the transition. The chancel is flanked by pairs of chapels, atmospheric spaces, with low vaulted ceilings, incorporating oculi.

Of individual motifs it may be said that the chancel and apse piers are of the French type of Chartres, Reims and Amiens, and that Hansom favoured rose windows and windows of the so-called spherical-triangle shape. Inner traceried openings are given to the clerestory and transept windows, adding to the richness. An almost theatrical drama is created through the arrangement of spaces, designed for the preaching of the Jesuits (who left in 1994); they vary between full-height and lower parts with intimately arranged chapels, concealed behind stone screens. Particularly effective is the layered effect produced by the separation of the s chapels from the nave by a pair of open traceried walls, the light shining through the oculi in the roof and through outer windows, giving the effect of caskets or reliquaries. They are mirrored on the n side by confessionals, all with fireplaces for the priests, and offices. The s chapels became the **Chapel of the Madonna della Strada** (Madonna of the Wayside), a masterpiece of *J. F. Bentley*, 1891–4. He pierced the internal buttresses to make one long space. Walls and piers were panelled in painted and stencilled wood. The wooden frontal, reredos and triptych setting of the painting are all gilt with painting by *N. H. J. Westlake*. Unfortunately structural instability resulted and the dividing walls had to be reinstated, re-creating the three original chapels, in 1997. Some panelling from the w end was taken down and put into the e chapel.

The exquisite octagonal **baptistery** at the sw corner, completed in the 1890s by the younger Hansom, has a very high vaulted ceiling with

231. Holy Name of Jesus (R.C.) by J. A. Hansom (1869–71), water-colour by Herbert Gribble.

blind arcading and lower and higher windows. It is richer in detail and different in style from the main building, using early French motifs.

Furnishings. The church has an unusually complete set of late C19 furnishings. – **High altar**, by *Joseph Stanislaus Hansom*, 1890, of the so-called Benediction Altar type, i.e. with a massive central spire to house the monstrance with the consecrated host. A marvellously detailed architectural piece with aedicules for alabaster statues of Jesuit saints, the whole carved by *R. L. Boulton* of Cheltenham. E chapels: N side N, St Joseph chapel with an ornate gilded wooden triptych altar with a scene of the death of St Joseph, probably English, and a reliquary base. By whom? Beside it Our Lady of Victories chapel with an unusual C19 Romanesque-style metal altar from France, brought here in 1872. On the S side the chapels were completed in 1885. First the Sacred Heart chapel with an altarpiece by *Charles Alban Buckler*, sculptor *R. L. Boulton*. Beside it the chapel of the Holy Souls, the altarpiece almost certainly by them also. – **Pulpit** by the younger *Hansom*, *c.* 1886, octagonal, marble with mosaic panels depicting the English Martyrs. Also by him is the alabaster **font**, *c.* 1890 with a tall oak lid, and the fine cast- and wrought-iron baptistery **screens**. An unusually large number of life-size marble **statues** of saints disposed around the interior, most of them of 1900 by *J. Alberti* who also supplied many of the plaster statues. – **Stained glass**. Mostly by *Hardman & Co.* of the late 1890s, including the five E windows and the three in the baptistery. s transept: two tall lights by *Paul Woodroffe*, a First World War memorial with Morris-like interleaving foliage.

The 1960s **chaplaincy** in Oxford Road by *Mather & Nutter* is a rather mannered design with a saw-tooth roof rising from detached piers framing the top three storeys. The ground floor is recessed behind masonry walls giving visual connection to the church, to which the chaplaincy is linked by a stone gateway. Behind, to the E on Portsmouth Street, is the **presbytery** by *Henry Clutton* for the Society of Jesus, 1874–5. An attractive design in brick with stone dressings. Domestic Tudor motifs successfully convey the relationship with the church. Single-storey stone early C20 extension to the s. Attached to the N is the (former) **church hall**, a crisp brick job by *Edmund Kirby*, dated 1892 in raised bricks, converted to a pub. To Dover Street a two-storey office part with an arched entrance on Portsmouth Street. The early C20 **school** is on the corner of Dover Street and Upper Brook Street.

St Augustine (R.C.), w side of Grosvenor Square (Ormond Street). By *Desmond Williams & Associates*. Of 1967–8, and so in the first generation of R.C. churches designed for the new liturgy. The choice of dark brick gives it an austere appearance. Load-bearing brick piers support steel trusses which are positioned to provide north light clerestories. A service projection to the left and four full-height brick piers to the right of the recessed central entrance to which steps lead up. A bell-tower rises behind from the link to low meeting rooms, chaplaincy, etc. On the projection a ceramic plaque with a star and a mitre by *Robert Brumby* is part of a unified scheme of decoration. **Interior**. Well-lit narthex, then dimness with light manipulated to heighten the effect. It is an atmospheric interior despite the spatial simplicity of the box plan. w gallery originally with seating, now housing the organ. Pairs of slim brick piers with either a chapel recess or a projecting confessional between each set, and between each pair a slit of coloured glass chips, deeply recessed to avoid distraction from the sanctuary. Free abstract designs, designed and produced by the *Whitefriars Studio*. The tones change from bluish at the w, through

232. St Augustine (R.C.), Ormond Street, by Desmond Williams & Associates (1967–8).

233. Contact Theatre, Devas Street, by Short & Associates (1999).

windows dominated by yellow, to a red scheme at the E end where a narrow glass ceiling strip casts natural daylight over a large ceramic mural in muted tones, showing Christ in Majesty by Brumby. **Sanctuary** designed so mass can be celebrated facing the congregation, white marble **altar**. White composition **font** centre N side, with aluminium lid and a ceramic inset. **Plaques** and wall-mounted light fittings by Brumby.

Arts Buildings

Contact Theatre, Devas Street. By *Short & Associates*, opened in 1999 and designed as a replacement for its 1960s predecessor by *Building Design Partnership*. The first impression is created by two ranks of fantastic chimney ventilators with a family resemblance to the architects' Queens Building, De Montfort University. Here, as there, the chimneys are part of a natural ventilation system, drawing on research by *Max Fordham & Partners*. The height and the H forms were dictated by the physics of ventilation. The building is of buff brick and the first layer of stacks is in brick, a second layer, set back, clad in zinc. Careful attention to the detail of the brickwork is everywhere apparent. The serious ecological considerations are combined with motifs expressing a punning language of theatrical forms. The round tower, for example, has something of Scott's Shakespeare Memorial Theatre, Stratford. Struts bracing the stacks are in the form of theatrical spears and the entrance is a layered, curtain-like silver screen. **Interior**. The existing auditorium and stage were retained from the 1960s predecessor but everything else, including a studio theatre, workshops and a rehearsal room, is new. Vivid colours sharply contrast with the understated tones of the exterior. The foyer curves around and invites the visitor to the ticket and information office where there is a double-height space and stairs up, or on to a café. The auditorium is entered from the rear. The stage was retained but the rest of the interior remodelled and given seating with side boxes and a parabolic seating rake.

Whitworth Art Gallery, Whitworth Park. Named for Sir Joseph Whitworth, whose bequest provided the funding. A 20 acre (8 hectare) parcel of land was acquired in 1887 and laid out as a park, within which an institute of art and industry was to be established. An existing building within it, Grove House was adapted as an art gallery. The gallery was run by a board of Governors after incorporation in 1889, and eventually handed to the University of Manchester in 1958. The competition for the new gallery building was won by *J. W. Beaumont & Sons* in 1891. Waterhouse was the assessor, and that explains the building nearly completely. It was built in phases from 1894. N, central and s galleries came first, as extensions to Grove House. Outer galleries have arcades with terracotta panels to Denmark Road (N) and the park (s). The entrance front which replaced Grove House was not ready until 1908. Jacobean, of red brick and red terracotta. Symmetrical, with two low towers and polygonal buttresses on the angle parts. A central semicircular porch has paired grey granite columns. **Interior**. Only the vestibule retains its original appearance, top-lit and lined with columns. New galleries by *John Bickerdike* were completed in two phases, 1963–4 and 1966–8. Alterations included the insertion of a mezzanine over the N and central galleries and the introduction of large windows in the s gallery giving views over Whitworth Park. A **Sculpture Gallery** by *Ahrends Burton & Koralek*, 1995, was inserted between the entrance block and the lower gallery behind, retaining the original rear exterior wall. A new angled roof appears to float above the space.

Whitworth Park. Statue. Edward VII by *J. Cassidy*, unveiled in 1913. Bronze. The king is shown in court robes with an orb and sceptre.

Hospitals

The site on the E side of Oxford Road was chosen as a successor to the city-centre location of the Manchester Royal Infirmary at Piccadilly which had been erected in 1775 and demolished in 1909 (*see* City Centre, Piccadilly Gardens). The land was donated by Owens College (subsequently the University of Manchester) who wished to improve teaching facilities for their Medical School. The Eye Hospital had already been established near the site, and St Mary's Hospital followed. The hospitals have spread over 42 acres (17½ hectares) replacing mid-C19 terraces and are due for further expansion on the site after 2002.

Royal Infirmary (illus. 26), Oxford Road. 1905–8, the great work of *E. T. Hall* who won the competition with Manchester architect *John*

Brooke. The assessor was J. J. Burnet. Vast, and in the Greenwich Baroque style, brick and much Portland stone, on the traditional pavilion plan. Of the main administration block to Oxford Road the left side was destroyed in the war. A central domed tower has an open pediment high over the entrance with a relief showing the Good Samaritan. The surviving linking block to the left is in the form of a bridge with an open walkway with a Tuscan colonnade, another block with a corner tower follows. The **chapel**, sited behind to the N, has at the w end a stone gable with an open pediment and niche. Simple oak furnishings. The E Venetian window has **stained glass** by *William Sales Arnold* of *Dudley Forsyth*, London, 1908. At the rear a **monument**, Richard Baron Howard, physician d. 1848, by *W. Theed*, dated 1853. Relief of an angel and supporter with a portrait medallion, presumably from the Piccadilly building.

Additions include an assertive brick private-patients block, dated 1936, by *Percy Scott Worthington*. Major extensions along Upper Brook Street of concrete and dark glass are by *Building Design Partnership*, completed 1992. To the E a large new ward block is by *Abbey Holford Rowe*, 2000–1, and a Clinical Research Facility on Grafton Street is by *Taylor Young Partnership*, 2000–1.

Royal Eye Hospital, Oxford Road. 1886, by *Pennington & Bridgen*. Symmetrical, in the style popularized by Norman Shaw a decade or so before, all in red brick, red terracotta and red tiled roofs. The range to Oxford Road has gabled dormers and projecting polygonal stair-towers with steep hipped roofs. High in the left end bay is a terracotta panel showing Christ healing the blind. **Out patient department** and **nurses home**, Nelson Street. Neo-Georgian by *Percy Scott Worthington*, 1937.

St Mary's Hospital, Oxford Road. 1909 by *John Ely*. Red brick and terracotta, symmetrical and mildly Edwardian. Big domed towers at each end of a range with projecting gabled bays. Slightly angled blocks to the rear. Within the body of the building the upper floor **chapel** has an ornate hammerbeam roof and original furnishings, including a font. Behind is a large extension by *Watkins Gray & Partners* 1966–70, exposed concrete, reclad in white panels c. 1990.

Walk 1. Chorlton Mills

The group of mills on the NW edge of the township is less well known than the Ancoats mills but they include important examples of early C19 fireproof construction and part of one of the earliest purpose-built rubberized-cloth manufactories in England.* The tour starts in Chester Street.

*For a full account of the mills and their owners *see* Sylvia Clark in *Industrial Archaeology Review*, vol. 2, 3, Summer, 1978.

234. Walk 1. Chorlton Mills.

Chatham Mill, (1) Chester Street, a cotton-spinning mill built in 1820 by the Runcorn Brothers, occupies the block between Chatham Street and Ormond Street, with an extension of 1823 along Ormond Street. The original six-storey block has timber floors supported by cast-iron columns, the 1823 warehousing extension is of fireproof construction. A truncated chimney is attached to the rear.

The N end of **Cambridge Street** is taken up with a group of early and mid-C19 mills and works, with an intertwined history which started with the factories of the Marsland and Birley families. There was a fleeting input from Robert Owen. Many of the buildings were eventually taken over by the Birleys, and in turn by the company they set up to produce waterproof cloth by Charles Macintosh's method, patented in 1823.

We start at the junction of Chester Street. The building between Chester Street and Hulme Street, E side, is the remains of two mills; that on Chester Street corner, **Marsland's Mill**, (2) originating in 1795, was rebuilt in 1813. The adjoining **Chorlton Old Mill** (3) was built for Robert Owen in 1795 before he moved to New Lanark. In 1803 this building was extended along Hulme Street. In 1809 it was sold to the Birley family. They immediately installed more powerful engines and a gas plant. The buildings were eventually taken over by the Macintosh works (*see*

The Marsland and Birley Families

The Marsland and Birley families are examples of industrialists who had accumulated capital during the c18 allowing them to make considerable investment and exploit the latest technology for the establishment of their mills in Chorlton-on-Medlock. The Marslands were prominent Unitarians with a flourishing cotton-spinning business in Stockport. It was probably through the liberal and tolerant circles of the Cross Street Chapel that Samuel Marsland met Robert Owen and encouraged him to set up in business with a mill next to his own. In contrast the Birleys were merchant gentry and Anglicans with a wide range of business interests. Hugh Hornby Birley, the principal figure in the development of the Chorlton Mills, was a prominent member of the group of wealthy industrialists who dominated Manchester life and politics. While Robert Owen became famous as an advocate of working-class political power, Birley achieved notoriety as the captain at the head of the Yeomanry charge at 'Peterloo' in 1819, which brutally dispersed crowds assembled to hear radical orator Henry Hunt. (The events took place on the site of the Free Trade Hall, Peter Street, *see* City Centre, topic box p. 183.) Amongst other public positions he was chairman of the Gas Board, and was involved in the locally famous gas riot of 1828, when a meeting in the town hall ended with Police Commissioners wielding chairs, fighting consumers protesting against artificially high prices. The Marslands left Chorlton in the 1840s while the Birleys and their partners and successors went from strength to strength, mainly thanks to their investment in the rubber business which outlived cotton production and continued on the site throughout the c20.

below) and partially rebuilt, late c19, reusing some cast-iron columns and beams. It is of the usual sort of fireproof construction but, as Mike Williams reports, with an unusual and ornate roof with cast-iron trusses in multiple narrow ridges. Conversion to flats came in the 1990s.

Chorlton New Mills, (4) N of Hulme Street, E side, three multi-

235. Chorlton New Mills, Cambridge Street (1813–45), in the process of conversion to apartments.

236. Aerial view of the Chorlton Mills. Cambridge Street runs diagonally across the top left side, with the Macintosh Works top left, and Chorlton New Mills, opposite them.

storey blocks built in phases for the Birley family. The first, of 1813–15, is set back from the line of the road. Six storeys and two basement storeys, fireproof construction, each floor with three rows of cast-iron columns. The original cast-iron roof has been replaced and the interior altered. It had an internal engine house, separated from the main building by a thick cross wall which incorporated the full-height ducts for the main vertical shaft and the ventilation system. The fireproof stair lay behind. Also housed within the main body of the building was a gas works. The gas was manufactured in the basement and stored in three gas holders next to the engine house on the N side of the building. A plan shows that gas was to be piped through the hollow centres of the columns but it is not certain if this potentially disastrous proposal was actually put into operation.* The next phase was the twelve-bay fireproof wing added to the s on Hulme Street in 1818. A powerloom weaving shed added to the N side has been demolished. Finally in 1845 a linking block incorporating a new engine house at the corner of Hulme Street was built. The big chimney with its ironwork strapping dates from 1853. The buildings were converted to flats, retaining the essentials of the structure, in 2000–1.

Macintosh Works w side. The Birleys built a factory to produce Macintosh's patented waterproof fabric in 1825–6. The original building on Cambridge Street (5) was demolished but the second building on the site, completed by 1838, (6) still stands on the Hulme Street corner. Attached to the w a block of 1849 (7) was built to house a vulcanization boiler. The other two additions on this side housed boilers of 1845 and 1851. The tapering octagonal chimney here is also of *c.* 1851, built for Chorlton New Mill to which it is connected by an underground flue.

*Nearby Albion Mill (demolished) used this system for at least part of its working life. The building survived into the c20.

Macintosh's Waterproof Fabric

Charles Macintosh's waterproof fabric was the first commercially successful application of rubber. It was made with a rubber solution sandwiched between two layers of cloth, and the process used naphtha, a by-product of gas production, to dissolve the rubber. It may have been this aspect of the process which interested H. H. Birley, who was interested in gas and uses for the by-products. Macintosh did not invest in the firm set up in 1824 by Birley & Kirk, with R. W. Barton, but contributed his patent, and in return received a share of the profits. The cloth was manufactured by the Birleys and the rubber solution was initially produced by Macintosh at his works in Glasgow and sent to Manchester in barrels. The many problems in refining and mechanizing the process were not fully resolved until 1830 when Thomas Hancock, who had developed his own system, was brought in to the firm. After Macintosh's death in 1843, Hancock continued to try to solve the problem of the tendency of the rubber to stiffen or melt according to changes in temperature. The answer was found not by Hancock but by a young American, Charles Goodyear, who invented the system of vulcanization which stabilizes rubber. He sent a sample to Hancock in 1844, presumably with a view to negotiating sale of the English rights, but Hancock promptly stole the recipe and patented it himself. New facilities were quickly built to put the process into operation, and it was an immediate success. By the 1850s the firm was producing over one hundred different lines with domestic, sporting, surgical and industrial applications. Eventually tyres became the main product, leading to more expansion after the First World War, but soon after the firm was taken over by Dunlop which retained a presence on the site until the close of the C20.

237. Dunlop Barrage Balloon Factory, painting by Sir Muirhead Bone, presented by Dunlop to Manchester City Art Gallery in 1946.

Interwar and post-war building reflect Dunlop's expansion in the C20.

Lastly on Cambridge Street, **Medlock Mill**, (8) *c.* 1811, on the N bank of the Medlock. A range of C19 offices fronts and follows the curve of the road, and the converted mill (Hotspur Press) rises behind. Cast-iron columns and timber beams, the variety of column types suggesting successive alterations, but the full story is difficult to divine from what little can be seen behind the partitions and false ceilings.

Walk 2. Oxford Road

The starting point is the junction of Oxford Road with Charles Street (E) and Hulme Street (w). Numbering refers to key in map, opposite.

Oxford Road on the w side has the **Dancehouse Theatre**, (1) formerly a cinema, by *Pendleton & Dickenson.* 1929–30 for Emmanuel Nove, whose initials with the date appear in the central pediment at the top. A long classical façade incorporating ground-floor shops, clad in pale cream faience with some orange faience detailing. The interior retains some authentic detail, including elaborate Art Deco plasterwork, of a richness rarely found in England, in the one surviving double-height auditorium. The cinema was advertised as the Regal Twins as it had two separate auditoria, so it was an unusually early example of a multiple-cinema complex. It was converted for theatre use in 1992. Opposite, E side, is the Manchester headquarters of the **BBC** (2) by their chief architect *R. A. Sparks,* opened in 1975. Brown brick with grubby white mosaic horizontals and ranges of unexciting brick buildings behind. Beside it to the s, and in sparkling contrast, is the **National Computing Centre**, (3) by *Cruickshank & Seward*, 1964. White concrete and white tiles. Three storeys, the top cantilevered out and crowned with angled roof projections lighting the stairs, like those on their Barnes Wallace Building (Student's Union) at UMIST (*see* Academic Institutions, p. 124). The street frontage has unfortunately been altered to incorporate shops, 2000–1. The arid gloomy undercroft which follows is beneath the **Mancunian Way** inner-city motorway which crosses the s side of the centre largely as a viaduct. The part from Chester Road (in Hulme) to Upper Brook Street (Chorlton-on-Medlock) was built 1964–7 by *City Engineers* and *G. Maunsell & Partners*. The extension to Pin Mill Brow (Ardwick), by *City Engineers*, was opened in 1992.

To the s of the motorway Oxford Road forms the E side of **Grosvenor Square**; on the E side the remains of a terrace of early C19 houses with one surviving doorcase on Sidney Street. The first inhabitants were professionals but the houses had all been converted to shops before the middle of the C19. The rest of the square was partly rebuilt for the

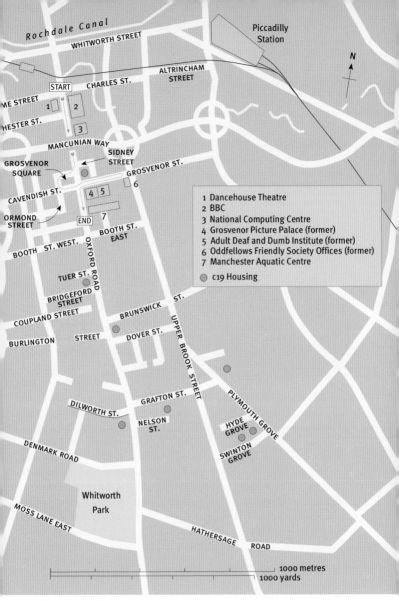

1 Dancehouse Theatre
2 BBC
3 National Computing Centre
4 Grosvenor Picture Palace (former)
5 Adult Deaf and Dumb Institute (former)
6 Oddfellows Friendly Society Offices (former)
7 Manchester Aquatic Centre
• c19 Housing

238. Walk 2. Oxford Road.

main Manchester Metropolitan University buildings (*see* Academic Institutions).

Grosvenor Street runs E from the s end of the square. The former **Grosvenor Picture Palace** (4) is on the E corner with Oxford Road. Designed in 1913 by *Percy Hothersall* and opened in 1915 when it was described grandiosely as 'Roman-Corinthian of the later Renaissance influence'. Faience and terracotta in dark green and cream shades, with

Houses and terraces for the middle classes were built during the early C19 s of Grosvenor Square as this area became more crowded and affected by industry and traffic. There are a few terraces on Oxford Road, with the survivors becoming grander to the s. To the S E, where there was still open land, some larger detached and semidetached houses were built. Some notable examples are listed below. Almost all have been converted for use as offices, flats, etc.

Nelson Street. Nos. 60–62, a pair of villas of which No. 62 was the home of Emmeline Pankhurst at the time that she founded the Women's Social and Political Union in 1903.

239. Nos. 60–62 Nelson Street (early C19).

Oxford Road. Nos. 176–188 W side. Waterloo Place between Tuer Street and Bridgeford Street: seven three-bay two-storey houses with wide arched entrances with inset Doric columns. Most have delicate fanlight glazing. Nos. 176–182 have attic additions; a low brick former school of the 1860s is attached to the rear of No. 176.

Nos. 323–333, E side, at the junction with Dover Street: a row of four quite grand three-storey stuccoed town houses. No. 323 is the largest, left, with ground-floor channelled rustication and first-floor windows with cornices. The next two have respectively a wooden porch with square pillars and a stone porch with Tuscan columns. The last, No. 333, has a recessed entrance with Doric columns.

Nos. 316–324 W side near the junction with Dilworth Street. A large detached house originally incorporating three separate dwellings. Expansive five-bay frontage set back from the street with a central arched entrance.

Plymouth Grove. A few houses survive near the NW end. No. 23, N side. Large and severely plain brick house.

No. 84, S side, dates from c. 1840 and is famous as the home of Elizabeth Gaskell who moved there in 1850. Stuccoed, with giant pilasters and a central entrance with pilasters and columns, all with capitals based on a detail from the Tower of the Winds in Athens, suggesting that *Richard Lane* may have been the architect.

Swinton Grove. Nos. 2–4, N side. Pair of brick houses at right angles to the street with full-height semicircular bays.

240. Adult Deaf & Dumb Institute (former), Grosvenor Street, by John Lowe (1878).

a domed entrance bay at the corner. It seated almost 1,000. The original canopy was removed but luckily something of the interior survives the pub conversion, including the balcony and an amount of florid plaster-work. Further E, s side, the (former) **Adult Deaf & Dumb Institute** (5) by *John Lowe*, 1878. Stone, Gothic, symmetrical with a central arched entrance. Over the doorway there is a carving of the badge used by the deaf at that time, an open hand on a book. Above this an arched recess contains a pedestal and statue of Christ healing a deaf man. There is a finely executed lettered frieze as well. The Institution had been founded in 1850, and the building was designed to offer social, religious and edu-cational services to adult deaf mutes. A little to the E, N side, there is a row of early C19 houses, most of them greatly altered. These include prem-ises which had become squalid overcrowded lodging houses by the end of the C19. No. 97, at the E end of the street, s side, is the Languages Department of UMIST, formerly the **Oddfellows Friendly Society Offices**, (6) dated 1915. White terracotta with an upper giant Ionic colonnade and a central entrance bay with a segmental pediment at the top.

Back now to Oxford Road. The **Manchester Aquatic Centre**, (7) s of Grosvenor Street, by *FaulknerBrowns* 1999–2000, was designed for use in the Commonwealth Games to be held in Manchester in 2002. To Oxford Road it presents a profile with a curving roof recalling in outline the attitude of a diver, but this side is unwelcoming and blinds prevent pedestrians seeing in. The entrance on the s side is from a new approach running N from Booth Street East. A long frontage broken by pairs of sandstone-clad piers of service and stair bays. In the centre a projecting glass screen and the main entrance. Inside one notes the asymmetrical roof shape, the shallower slope with a suspended ceiling with big rippled panels.

For the Royal Northern College of Music, Federal School of Business and Management and the University of Manchester further s *see* Academic Institutions.

Hulme

Until the late C18 this area s E of the Bridgewater Canal was largely open
land. A few Georgian villas were built in the N part of the township
around Chester Road, one of the main routes out of Manchester, and
on the E side along the Chorlton-on-Medlock border. By 1831 crowded
courts had started to spring up on the edges of the populated areas. The
boom came a little later, and by the mid C19 most of the area was packed
with terraces laid out on a gridiron plan, much of it dating from after
1844 when the Manchester Police Acts banned the construction of
houses without back yards and privies. In 1849 the *Morning Chronicle*
correspondent A. B. Reach described the new district of 'humble but
comfortable streets' as the most salubrious of Manchester's working-
class areas. By the mid C20 the area was run down, and the City of
Manchester Plan of 1945 envisaged wholesale rebuilding, mainly with
low-rise housing. Clearance did not come for another two decades, but
the 1970s deck-access flats which followed became a byword for the failures of post-war social housing. For these and their replacements, *see*

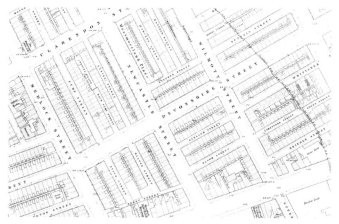

241. C19 housing in Hulme, from the Ordnance Survey map (surveyed 1844). Most of
the houses have back yards and privies, but some back-to-backs can be seen just s of
Clarendon Street on Daniel Street and Matthew Street.

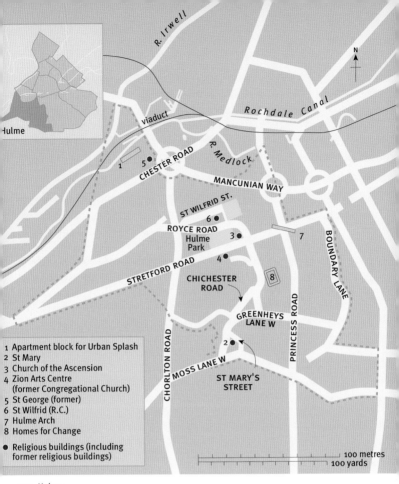

Housing, below. The N part of the township, in the St George area around Chester Road, was less affected in the 1970s, though there are some 1960s high-rise and smaller 1960s and 1970s blocks. The mixture here includes 1890s terraces on Barrack Street, built as model dwellings for NCOs by the War Office at the nearby (demolished) Cavalry Barracks. Mills and works were largely concentrated along the N border beside the Bridgewater Canal. Stimulated by the success of the new housing in adjacent Castlefield, some of these are being converted to private flats. A large apartment block by *Glenn Howells* for *Urban Splash* was built on the canal side in 2000–1.

The 1970s rebuilding imposed a new pattern on the old grid plan, except on the fringes. Stretford Road, which ran E–W through the centre, was truncated as part of a policy of separating pedestrians from traffic. This had the effect of isolating the area, which lost its main shopping street and link with the centre. The reinstatement of Stretford Road and the integration of the new housing with the road system were seen as priorities in the 1994 master plan (*see* Housing, below), which also provided for a new park, designed by *Neil Swanson*, just N of Stretford Road. This area seems destined to become a centre for the community, but the buildings of interest are scattered. The most significant architecturally are the churches. St Wilfrid is of national interest as A. W. N. Pugin's early attempt at archaeologically convincing Gothic, and St George, the most lavish of the city's surviving early C19 churches, is one of Francis Goodwin's more ambitious works for the Church Building Commission. Of the other churches **St Mary** (illus. 19), St Mary's Street, 1856–8, is *J. S. Crowther*'s earliest mature work with an exceptionally graceful spire. Part of a group with the former rectory, junior school and teacher's house. Also of note: the **Church of the Ascension**, Stretford Road. By *Maguire & Murray*, 1968–70, built for the new liturgy. The **Zion Arts Centre**, Stretford Road, is a large Congregational church of 1911, imaginatively converted in 1999–2000 by *Mills Beaumont Leavey Channon*. For more details of these and other buildings *see* the forthcoming *Manchester and South-East Lancashire*.

Churches

St George, Chester Road. By *Francis Goodwin*, 1826–8. The church lay empty for more than twenty years, and almost nothing survives inside. The search for a use that would preserve the interior volumes was finally abandoned and conversion to flats started in 2000. A Commissioners' church in fact, not only in appearance. The original cost was as much as £15,000. Ornate, decidedly pre-archaeological. w tower with diminishing pinnacles but big pinnacles on top, seemingly from the example of Hawksmoor's St Michael Cornhill. Porches set diagonally at the NW and sw angles, breaking up the box of the plan effectively, high three-light Perp windows separated by buttresses, two big E pinnacles, and a high polygonal apse. Only the latter is an unexpected motif. **Interior**: six-bay arcade of slim, soaring clustered Perp piers and an unusually well-lit apse thanks to the tall windows. The churchyard is walled, its entrances have octagonal stone piers with traceried panels.

St Wilfrid (R.C.), St Wilfrid's Street. By *A. W. N. Pugin*, 1842. A seminal building in the history of C19 church architecture, yet in striking contrast to the regeneration all around, it is in shockingly poor condition. E.E. style and memorable as a very early case of the archaeologically convincing church. The red brick exterior with lancet windows is low and massive. The parts are separately expressed, with low roofs clustering around the body of the church. The tower, never completed, is NW not w, and this end is impressively sheer, with small openings. The

243. St Wilfrid (R.C.), St Wilfrid's Street, by A. W. N. Pugin (1842). The chancel has interwar glass from the studio of Harry Clarke & Co.

structure rises from a massive stone plinth, and Pugin delights in setting back the wall surfaces and expressing points of tension, such as the corners of the tower, with flat buttresses. It all had to be done cheaply – Pugin's bane. The financial restrictions forced him to concentrate on fundamentals, but he allowed himself the touch of archaeological fun, laying his bricks in English bond, not Flemish like the hated Georgians. The s aisle has three separately gabled projections for confessionals (which Pugin so often omitted) added in the 1860s by *E. W. Pugin* who also extended the sacristies.

Interior. A conversion to offices in the 1980s was achieved by inserting a free-standing two-storey unit in the nave so that in theory the volumes could be restored, but the w end has been crudely subdivided and altered and only the chancel is preserved as open space. Six bays of octagonal piers, double chamfered arches and two-bay N chancel chapel with a round arcade pier. The s chapel has one bay, not two, to avoid the artificiality of over-symmetrical design. There is a complicated queenpost roof of domestic rather than ecclesiastical inspiration with the rood fixed in the final (E) truss. The chancel arch springs from polygonal shafts. On one side the arcade with stiff-leaf E.E. capitals and original screens to the N Lady Chapel, on the other **sedilia** and **piscina**. There is an arcade with cusped heads behind the altar, three lancets above, and finally a wheel window. – **Pulpit** set into the s side of the chancel arch and reached by a stair in the thickness of the wall which continues up to the rood-loft position, marked by a door. – **Statue**: the Virgin, *c.* 1850s. Puginesque pedestal beneath a tall crocketed canopy against the N chancel arch. In the Lady Chapel a Puginesque wooden altar and reredos. – *Pugin's* polygonal **font** has large hinges on the lockable flat lid. – **Stained glass**. E end. Rose window, with the Instruments of the Passion, *c.* 1880 and three lancets all with good interwar glass by *Harry Clarke & Co.* of Dublin. s. aisle glass *c.* 1870, much of it damaged and very badly faded. Lady Chapel glass *c.* 1920.

Hulme Arch

Stretford Road, by *Chris Wilkinson* (of *Wilkinson Eyre Architects)* and *Ove Arup & Partners*, 1997. A mighty angled parabolic arch with tension cables spanning a dual carriageway in a cutting (Princess Road). In the late C20 fashion of bridges exploiting spectacular engineering techniques for effect, here the simple form and solidity of the arch was needed for the large scale and hard urban setting. It is intended to act as a visual and physical link with the city centre, from which Hulme had been isolated in the 1970s by Princess Road and the truncation of Stretford Road.

244. Hulme Arch, Stretford Road, by Wilkinson Eyre Architects with engineers Ove Arup & Partners (1997).

245. The Crescents (demolished), by Wilson & Womersley (completed 1971). The line of Stretford Road ran E–W between the Crescents and the city centre. The curving roof of G-Mex can be seen top right.

Housing

The 1969 edition of the *Buildings of England: South Lancashire* found Hulme: 'the largest redevelopment area of Manchester, many say of England, and some Europe. At the time of writing whole blocks lie waste, streets are blocked and new streets are made.' In the interval between this and the present edition a complete housing scheme has come and gone. 3,284 new deck-access homes and fifteen tower blocks were completed in 1971. The centrepiece was four ¼-mile-long six-storey deck-access 'Crescents', constructed to designs by *Wilson & Womersley*. They

Community Architecture in Hulme

The rebuilding of Hulme is one of the most ambitious exercises in community architecture ever undertaken in Britain. The quality of urban design and lively mixture of buildings reflects tenant participation, architectural innovation, and flexibility on the part of developers and planners. Estate layout popular with housing associations, police and road-safety organizations, with groups of inward-looking houses on culs-de-sac served by a common spine road, was rejected. Those favouring models based on terraced housing facing on to the street with back alleys succeeded only through persistence, eventually rewarded by the design of the rebuilt St Wilfrid Estate N of Stretford Road by the North British Housing Association. Elsewhere community involvement had a different outcome, for example in *OMI Architects'* changeful grouping of buildings around courtyards and communal gardens on Boundary Lane. Consultation threw up predictable concerns about parking, security and the maintenance of public spaces, while the wide range of lifestyles and household structure was reflected in demand for variety and creativity in the configuration of living space. Perhaps the most surprising of the tenant-led proposals involved appropriation of features of the demolished 1970s crescents. High-density, deck-access maisonette housing with a structure of heavy precast concrete panels was radically reinterpreted by *Mills Beaumont Leavey Channon* in the Homes for Change scheme forged from intensive design workshops with tenant co-operatives who sought integration of living space with work, leisure, retail and communal facilities in a building with impeccable environmental credentials.

Further Reading: R. Ramwell and H. Saltburn, *Trick or Treat? City Challenge and the Regeneration of Hulme*, 1998.

246. Homes for Change, Chichester Road, by Mills Beaumont Leavey Channon (1999–2000).

were named, in an act of hubris, after architects Charles Barry, John Nash, William Kent and Robert Adam. Problems were apparent from the beginning, and in less than a decade this was one of the most notoriously defective and dysfunctional housing estates in Europe. Demolition began in 1991. All the 1970s deck-access housing went but some nine- and thirteen-storey towers survive amongst the new housing.

In the wake of such spectacular failure the pressure to create successful social housing was intense, and rebuilding was made possible by a successful bid for City Challenge funds in 1991. Resident participation was seen as a fundamental and an extensive consultation programme was set up. *Mills Beaumont Leavey Channon* drew up a master plan in 1994. The resulting new housing includes projects by *ECD Architects*, *Ainsley Gommon Wood*, *OMI Architects*, *Mills Beaumont Leavey Channon*, *PRP* and *Triangle*, and the North British Housing Association. Privately owned and rented accommodation is provided in a mixture of terraces, semi-detached houses and small blocks of flats around new and reinstated streets. They range in style from pastiche through quirky to frankly modern.

The showpiece of the new housing and the most striking individual element is **Homes for Change**, Chichester Road. By *Mills Beaumont Leavey Channon*, 1999–2000. The tenants opted to re-create some of the features of the system-built housing the accommodation replaces: deck-access, maisonette-type dwellings within a structure of heavy precast concrete. On the other hand, the mixture of different types of living space (fifty units in all), and integration of shops, cafés and studios into the scheme, as well as the more intimate scale, is in direct contrast to what went before. It is a four-sided four- and six-storey block around a courtyard, looking slightly haphazard, as if it has come together in an ad hoc, organic way. There are curving roofs, and cutaway walls in cream brick and render. A tall angled metal-clad stair-tower at the NW corner draws the eye upwards and directs attention to the recessions and projections of the composition. A circular brick drum punctuates the SE corner. Within the courtyard the flats have cladding of cedar planks, adding warmth, and the balconies are angled to catch the sun. The dwelling interiors could not match the Parker Morris standards of their predecessors, but they are large, and the double-height volumes are exploited to create different configurations of living space.

Excursions

This is a brief selection of buildings of national importance which are within reach of Manchester centre, including some of those singled out by Pevsner for special attention in *South Lancashire* in 1969. Most of the descriptions incorporate his assessments. More detailed discussion of the buildings and their contexts will be found in the forthcoming *Manchester and South-East Lancashire*.

The two houses, both in public ownership – one of the most interesting medieval halls in the region, and a major work of the late c18 – are a reminder that the built-up area around Manchester was countryside until the c19. The churches are outstanding examples from the Victorian, Edwardian and interwar periods, while recent architecture includes some of the most dramatic new buildings of the turn of this century which are bringing new life to the quaysides of Salford and Trafford.

Baguley Hall

Hall Lane, Baguley, Wythenshawe

The Hall lies *c.* 5 m. (8 km.) s of the centre. Buses to Wythenshawe via Altrincham Road, alight Hall Lane. The Hall is closed at the time of writing while a new use is being sought.

Baguley is an exceptionally interesting building and one of the oldest and finest surviving medieval timber-framed halls of North-West England (*see* topic box, Introduction p. 6). It was built for the de Baguleys on the site of an earlier aisled hall in the early–mid C14. Brick wings at each end, the one to the N a casing of a late medieval timber-framed wing, the other of C17 date. The timber frame of the C14 hall is a very rare example of a form in which massive planks are used, so that the uprights serve both as posts and studs. The carpentry is impressive also for the bold decorative scheme, with cusped and quatrefoil panels and cusped cross-bracing. A slight bowing of the walls, recalling Danish boat-shaped houses, is now thought to be the result of structural movement. The plank construction has parallels with pre-conquest Scandinavian traditions, but early medieval examples have also been identified in North Wales. After an ignominious career as a council store the building was acquired by the Ministry of Public Buildings and Works in 1968 and is in the care of English Heritage. Extensive excavations and restorations took place in the late 1970s.

For a description and discussion of Scandinavian parallels *see* J. T. Smith & C. F. Stell in *The Antiquaries Journal*, vol. 40, 1960, and for re-evaluation in the light of new evidence, *see* P. Dixon, C. Hayfield & W. Startin in *Archaeological Journal*, 146, 1989.

247. Excursions.

248. Baguley Hall, Hall Lane, Wythenshawe (early–mid C14).

Heaton Hall

Heaton Park, Bury Old Road

Heaton Park lies *c.* 3 m. (5 km.) N of the centre. Metrolink trams for Bury, alight at Heaton Park. House open Wednesday–Sunday April–October, grounds open all year.

Designed in 1772 for Sir Thomas Egerton, seventh baronet, by *James Wyatt*. The best house of its period in Lancashire, described by Pevsner as 'a building of refinement and elegance not exceeded in any English house of these years'. 'It is ashlar faced and exquisite in composition as well as details. The articulation of the different elements is perfect. The centre is a broad bow with Ionic demi-columns and three relief panels, and to left and right is just one large Venetian window. Then follow the links, each with a Doric colonnade of five bays ending in a pavilion with canted front.' An older house is preserved on the N side, but Wyatt was wholly responsible for the S side. The interior has a handsome sequence of rooms.

The pleasure grounds and walled park retain elements of a landscape designed 1770–3, probably by *William Emes*. There are lodges by *James Wyatt* and *Lewis Wyatt*, and a temple probably by *Samuel Wyatt*. The house and park were acquired by Manchester Corporation in 1902. Part of a Grecian colonnade from Manchester's first town hall, designed in 1821 by *Francis Goodwin*, erected beside a new boating lake in 1912. The most conspicuous landmark of the park is a 1960s telecommunications tower, NW of the Hall, and the most interesting addition is the 1955 Pumping Station on the N perimeter by *Alan Atkinson* with a sculptural mural by *Mitzi Solomon Cunliffe*.

For a full description of the Hall *see* J. Lomax, in *Transactions of the Lancashire and Cheshire Antiquarian Society*, vol. 82, 1983.

249. Heaton Hall, Heaton Park, Bury Old Road, by James Wyatt (1772).

St Francis (R.C.)

Gorton Lane, Gorton, Manchester

2 m. (3¼ km.) E of the centre. Buses to Reddish via Gorton Lane.

A major landmark in a former industrial and residential area which became little more than wasteland in the later C20. Gorton is slowly being revived by the prospect of regeneration with the 2002 Commonwealth Games and the siting nearby of the Commonwealth Stadium (*Arup Associates*, under construction 2001, *see Manchester and South-East Lancashire*, forthcoming). St Francis was closed in 1989 and sadly vandalized, but a trust has been set up for restoring and reusing the church and converting the attached plain monastic buildings. Open days are advertised locally.

One of the two churches of national importance by A. W. N. Pugin's son *E. W. Pugin*. It was built 1866–72 for the Franciscans, whose house to the right of the church was begun *c.* 1863. Red brick with generous stone dressings, late C13 style. According to Pevsner 'it was meant to be a demonstration, and it has remained a showpiece. No one could deny that it is over detailed'. The extraordinary mannered W end and vast bulk of the building with a high polygonal apse are unforgettable. The interior has a thirteen-bay nave and two-bay chancel, treated as a single tall narrow vessel, but all the furnishings have been stripped out and *Peter Paul Pugin*'s magnificent altarpiece vandalized.

250. St Francis (R.C.), Gorton Lane, Gorton, by E. W. Pugin (1866–72).

St Augustine

Bolton Road, Pendlebury

Pendlebury lies *c.* 4 m. (6½ km.) NW of the centre. Buses for Bolton or beyond via the A666, alight after Hospital Road.

The church, built 1871–4, by *G. F. Bodley*, for the local coal-mining community at the expense of Manchester banker Edward Stanley Heywood was among Pevsner's favourites. 'One of the English churches of all time. Its sheer brick exterior – no tower, one long roof – and the majestic *sursum* of its interior have never been surpassed in Victorian church building. Inspiration must have come from buildings such as Albi Cathedral and the Blackfriars at Toulouse. The tracery of the windows is Dec in the chancel, Perp in the nave as if building had gone on for half a century… The interior is of breathtaking majesty and purity. Internal buttresses pierced only right at the bottom by aisle-like passages, and arches high up from pier to pier with short transverse vaults to the window tops.' Of the furnishings, the stained glass by *Burlison & Grylls* is of special note, very individual and apparently designed and supervised by Bodley himself.

251. St Augustine, Bolton Road, Pendlebury, by G. F. Bodley (1871–4). Watercolour by the architect.

First Church of Christ, Scientist

Daisy Bank Road, Fallowfield, Manchester

1½ m. (2½ km.) s of the centre, in the Early Victorian suburb of Victoria Park. Buses to East Didsbury via Upper Brook Street, alight Daisy Bank Road.

Of 1903–4 with additions mainly of 1905–7 by *Edgar Wood*. Pevsner described it as 'one of the most original buildings of that time in England or indeed anywhere … the only religious building in Lancashire that would be indispensable in a survey in the development of c20 church design in all England. It is a pioneer work, internationally speaking, of an Expressionism halfway between Gaudí and Germany about 1920, and it stands entirely on its own in England.' The church has a steep gable with a stone chimneystack up at the top and beyond it. The portal is of cut bricks, round-arched. Two wings project diagonally from that centre; one of them is the reading room, the other the hall. Between the hall range and the church front finally is a fat, short, round tower with a conical roof. A wing containing vestries and a boardroom projects from the back of the church. The interior is equally individual and non-historicist, and without superfluous decoration. In the church the two focal points are a marble reredos panel with a cross and crown bas-relief, the Christian Science emblem, and opposite, above the main entrance, a superb Arabic style openwork organ screen.

252. First Church of Christ, Scientist, Daisy Bank Road, Fallowfield, by Edgar Wood (1903–4, with additions of 1905–7).

St Michael

Orton Road, Northenden

5 m. (8 km.) s of the centre about 1 m. (1½ km.) N of Baguley Hall. Buses from Piccadilly Gardens to Wythenshawe via Sale Road, alight Orton Road. Northenden became part of expanding Manchester between the wars.

By *N. F. Cachemaille-Day*, 1935–7. Pevsner found it 'a sensational church for its country and its day. The plan is a star consisting of two inter-locking squares. The material is brick, bare in four of the corners, with large brick windows in the other four. The intersecting arches of the windows are the only period allusion. The interior has very thin exposed concrete piers and a flat ceiling.' The plan produces a strongly centralized space, although the architect's drawings do not support the theory that he intended to place the altar at the centre. It is in the triangle facing the entrance. The stained glass is by *Geoffrey Webb*. To the right stands a low **parsonage**. The church makes it clear that the architect had studied Continental experiments. The parsonage points to Germany and Mendelsohn.

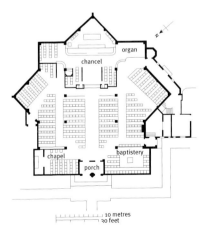

253. St Michael, Orton Road, Northenden, by N. F. Cachemaille-Day (1935–7).

The Lowry and Salford Quays

Salford Docks, which developed beside the Manchester Ship Canal, was reborn in the 1990s as Salford Quays, with commercial, leisure and residential developments. Its centre lies 1½ m. (2½ km.) w of the city centre. Metrolink trams travelling westwards, alight at Broadway.

The Lowry, an arts centre by *Michael Wilford & Partners* 1997–2000. It stands on a finger of dockland jutting into the Ship Canal. It has a nautical feel, and transparent, semitransparent and reflective surfaces attempt, not wholly successfully, to express the presence of the solid, inward-looking core of two theatres, wrapped in lighter, outward-looking spaces used as galleries, cafés, etc. The cladding of angled steel shingles suggests movement, and a huge circular funnel, with open-work at the top and clad in semitransparent gauze, anchors the building on the landward side beside the blocky entrance canopy. After the cool metallic hues of the exterior the intense colours of the interior shock. In contrast the main galleries on the second floor are dead white. They house Salford's collection of paintings by L. S. Lowry. The design of the Lowry developed substantially after the death of Wilford's partner James Stirling in 1992. Apart from the use of strong interior colours,

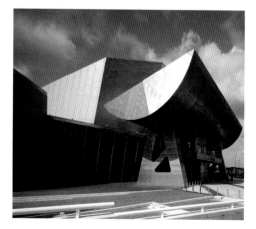

254. The Lowry, Salford Quays, by Michael Wilford & Partners (1997–2000).

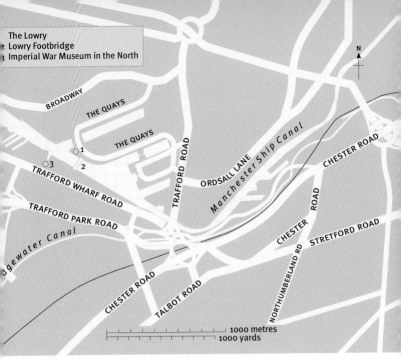

BROADWAY

THE QUAYS

THE QUAYS

TRAFFORD ROAD

ORDSALL LANE

Manchester Ship Canal

CHESTER ROAD

TRAFFORD WHARF ROAD

TRAFFORD PARK ROAD

CHESTER ROAD

CHESTER ROAD

STRETFORD ROAD

...dgewater Canal

CHESTER ROAD

TALBOT ROAD

NORTHUMBERLAND RD

N

1000 metres
1000 yards

255. Salford Quays.

there is not much here that resembles Stirling's own late style, with its Postmodern classical flavour and strongly symmetrical planning – a sign of how far Wilford has travelled in developing an architectural language of his own.

The venture was promoted by Salford City Council and its funding included substantial grants from the Heritage Lottery Fund. After the abandonment of the Stirling-Wilford master plan for the area the ambition of the scheme has not extended to the setting of the building, witnessed by the positioning of a banal multi-storey car park in the path of landward approaches and views.

Lowry Footbridge, 1998–2000 by *W. Middleton* of *Parkman Ltd*, linking the Lowry and Imperial War Museum sites. The deck, with a horizontal flash of blue in Perspex panels, is supported by an arch. At either end pairs of gantries house gravity lifts allowing it to be raised wholesale to let shipping through.

Imperial War Museum in the North

Trafford Wharf Road, Trafford Park, Trafford

1½ m. (2½ km.) w of the centre, reached by Metrolink tram to Broadway as for the Lowry.

The Manchester Ship Canal made Manchester the fourth most important British custom port, and Trafford Park, on its s side, was the first industrial estate in the world. It reached its peak in the Second World War and still has some industry. The choice of the site for the Imperial War Museum in the North will see it develop in a different direction. Funded by a consortium including Trafford Metropolitan Borough Council, which attracted European as well as private funding.

The museum by *Daniel Libeskind* was begun in 2000, with completion planned in 2002. Libeskind's first building in Britain has a design as dramatic and inventive as his proposed extension to the Victoria and Albert Museum in London, or any other of his schemes. Like the Jewish Museum in Berlin, where Libeskind has shown himself to be a master of complex internal volumes as well as external form, the building is itself a monument. Big sculptural shapes look like three huge shards, which suggest a shattered world, the pieces representing the war in the air, on land and at sea.

256. Visualization of the Imperial War Museum in the North, Trafford Wharf Road, Trafford Park, by Daniel Libeskind (2000–2).

Further Reading

There is a large body of research on Manchester's history and architecture; bibliographies and notes in the publications mentioned below will augment this necessarily brief introduction. The cathedral and the town hall both have separate suggestions for further reading which appear under the relevant entries, and footnotes draw attention to sources not mentioned here that are relevant to particular entries in the gazetteer.

General books on Manchester architecture include C. H. Reilly's short but informative *Some Manchester Streets and their Buildings*, 1924, and Cecil Stewart's *The Stones of Manchester*, 1956. His *The Architecture of Manchester: an Index to the Principal Buildings and their Architects 1800–1900* was published in 1956 and remains the only published index of this type. Short guides to the central area include P. Atkins, *Guide Across Manchester*, revised edn 1987, and E. Canniffe & Tom Jefferies, *Manchester Architecture Guide*, 1998. Recent books have tended to concentrate on architecture of the past few decades: D. Hands & S. Parker, *Manchester A Guide to Recent Architecture*, 2000, is a short guide to architecture and interior design since the late 1980s, and J. Parkinson-Bailey, ed., *Sites of the City: Essays on Recent Buildings by their Architects*, 1996, includes more extended descriptions of selected buildings of a similar period. *Manchester, an Architectural History*, 2000, by the same author, gives emphasis to post-war architecture, especially that since 1970. D. Sharp, *Manchester*, 1969, is especially useful for buildings of the 1960s, for which one of the best sources is the journal *Architecture North West*, which was published between 1963 and 1970.

There can be no better introduction to **Victorian architecture** than that which appears in J. H. G. Archer, ed., *Art and Architecture in Victorian Manchester*, 1985. This also contains a series of valuable essays including studies of the John Rylands Library on Deansgate by John Maddison, the Whitworth Art Gallery by Francis Hawcroft, the Royal Manchester Institution by Stuart Macdonald, Thomas Worthington by Anthony J. Pass and a reprint of M. Whiffen, *The Architecture of Sir Charles Barry in Manchester*, first published in 1950. For Manchester **architects** *see* J. H. G. Archer, 'Edgar Wood: a notable Manchester Architect', *Transactions of the Lancashire and Cheshire Antiquarian Society*, 73–4, 1963–4; Anthony J. Pass, *Thomas Worthington: Victorian Architecture* *and Social Purpose*, 1988, which is the only full-length published study of a Manchester architect; and C. Cunningham & P. Waterhouse, *Alfred Waterhouse, 1830–1905: Biography of a Practice*, 1992. A short article on Edward Salomons by Rhona Beenstock appears in *Manchester Region History Review*, vol. 10, 1996. The *Transactions of the Lancashire and Cheshire Antiquarian Society*, vol. 92–3, 1997, was devoted to subjects relating to the Manchester Diocese including a study of Cachemaille-Day's Manchester churches by Michael Bullen. **Commercial warehouses** *see* H. R. Hitchcock, 'Victorian Monuments of Commerce', *Architectural Review*, 105, 1949, for a review of Manchester warehouses in a wider context. A. V. Cooper 'The Manchester Commercial Textile Warehouse 1780–1914: A Study of its Typology and Practical Development', unpublished PhD thesis, four vols., University of Manchester, 1991, is invaluable. *See* also Simon Taylor, *Manchester Warehouses*, English Heritage, forthcoming.

The indispensable studies for **industrial buildings and structures** are R. S. Fitzgerald, *Liverpool Road Station Manchester: an Historical and Architectural Survey*, 1980, and M. Williams with D. A. Farnie, *The Cotton Mills of Greater Manchester*, 1992. *Industrial Archaeology Review*, 2, 1988, and *Industrial Archaeology Review*, 1, 1993, were devoted to textile mills including Manchester examples. Suggested reading also appears in the Cast-iron Technology topic box p. 15. There are numerous publications on **canals** of which C. Hadfield & G. Biddle, *The Canals of North West England*, two vols., 1970, and H. Malet, *Bridgewater: The Canal Duke, 1736–1803*, 1977, are good introductions. There is a large body of work on the Ship Canal including D. Owen, *The Manchester Ship Canal*, 1982, and P. M. Hodson, ed., *The Manchester Ship Canal a Guide to Historical Sources*, 1985.

For **public art, statuary and sculpture** *see* B. Read & P. Ward-Jackson, eds., *Courtauld Institute Illustrations Archives, 4. Late 18th & 19th Century Sculpture in the British Isles. Part 6 Greater Manchester*, 1978; D. Brumhead & T. Wyke, *A Walk around Manchester Statues*, 1990; and Terry Wyke, *The Public Sculpture of Greater Manchester*, Public Monuments and Sculpture Association, forthcoming.

The best recent **history** is by Alan Kidd, *Manchester*, 1993. L.D. Bradshaw, *Visitors to Manchester A Selection of British and Foreign Visitors' Descriptions of Manchester from c. 1538–1865* (Neil Richardson), 1987, is a very useful compendium. For the Manchester Diocese *see* A. J. Dobb, *Like A Mighty Tortoise: A History of the Diocese of Manchester*, 1978. For **Jewish history** *see* B. Williams, *The Making of Manchester Jewry 1740-1875*, 1976. For **early history** *see* S. Bryant *et al*, *The Archaeological History of Greater Manchester, Vol. 3: Roman Manchester: A Frontier Settlement*, 1987, and M. Morris, *The Archaeological History of Greater Manchester, Vol. 1: Medieval Manchester*, 1983. C. F. Carter, ed., *Manchester and its Region*, 1962, is especially useful for **medieval and early modern** Manchester; *see* also T. S. Willan, *Elizabethan Manchester*, 1980. The C17 and c18 remain a neglected subject. A. P. Wadsworth & J. de Lacy Mann, *The Cotton Trade and Industrial Lancashire 1600–1780*, 1931, and J. Walton, 'Proto-Industrialisation and the first industrial revolution: the case of Lancashire' in P. Hudson, ed., *Regions and Industries: A Perspective on the Industrial Revolution in Britain*, 1989, provide background to economy and industry, while the section on Manchester in C. W. Chalklin, *Provincial Towns of Georgian England*, 1974, is a useful exposition of late c18 development of the town. W. H. Chaloner, 'Manchester in the Latter Half of the Eighteenth Century' in *The Bulletin of the John Rylands Library*, vol. 42, 1959–60, provides an introduction to the town on the cusp of the Industrial Revolution.

The most useful **bibliographies** are by Terry Wyke. His 'Nineteenth Century Manchester – a Preliminary Bibliography' is arranged under subject headings including architecture, art, housing, canals, railway, roads, etc., and appears in a book which may be recommended in its own right, A. J. Kidd & K. W. Roberts, eds., *City, Class and Culture: Studies of Social Policy and Cultural Production in Victorian Manchester*, 1985. 'The Diocese of Manchester: An Introductory Bibliography' appears in *Transactions of the Lancashire and Cheshire Antiquarian Society*, vol. 92–3, 1997. A Manchester bibliography is published annually in the *Manchester Region History Review*, which started in 1987.

Glossary

Arch: [1] Types not shown include: *Jack arch*: shallow segmental vault springing from beams, used for fireproof floors, bridge decks, etc. *Skew*: with jambs not diametrically opposed.

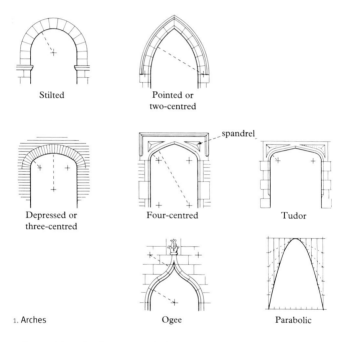

Stilted

Pointed or two-centred

Depressed or three-centred

Four-centred

Tudor

Ogee

Parabolic

spandrel

1. Arches

Atlantes (*lit.* Atlas figures): male figures supporting an entablature.

Auditory church: a church designed primarily for preaching, i.e. without a main emphasis on the altar.

Baldacchino: free-standing canopy, originally fabric, over an altar.

Brickwork: *bond*: the pattern of long sides (*stretchers*) and short ends (*headers*) produced on the face of a wall by laying bricks in a particular way. *Flared bricks or flared headers*: bricks laid as headers which are burnt darker at one end. *Tumbled-in*: with courses laid at an angle, usually perpendicular to the slope of a gable. [**2a** and **b**]

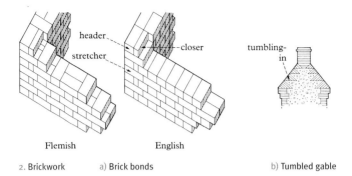

2. Brickwork   a) Brick bonds   b) Tumbled gable

Brise-soleil (French, sun break): a screen of projecting fins or slats which deflect direct sunlight from windows.

Campanile (Italian): free-standing bell-tower.

Capital: *see* Orders.

Caryatids: female figures supporting an entablature.

Choir: the part of a cathedral, monastic or collegiate church where services are sung.

Clerestory: uppermost storey of the nave of a church, pierced by windows. Also high-level windows in secular buildings.

Coffering: arrangement of sunken panels (*coffers*), square or polygonal, decorating a ceiling, vault or arch.

Collar purlin: *see* Roofs and timber-framing.

Collegiate church: a church endowed for the support of a college of priests.

Common rafter: *see* Roofs and timber-framing.

Corinthian: *see* Orders.

Crockets: in Gothic architecture, leafy hooks or knobs often used to decorate the edges of pinnacles, canopies, etc.

Crown-post: *see* Roofs and timber-framing.

Dec (Decorated): English Gothic architecture *c.* 1290–*c.* 1350. The name is derived from the type of window tracery used during the period.

Doric: *see* Orders.

E.E. (Early English): English Gothic architecture *c.* 1190–*c.* 1250.

English bond: *see* Brickwork.

Entablature: *see* Orders.

Fenestration: the arrangement of windows in a façade.

Fireproof construction: *see* topic box p. 278

Flèche (French, arrow): slender spire on the ridge of a roof.

Flemish bond: *see* Brickwork.

Garderobe: the medieval name for a lavatory.

Geometric: English Gothic architecture *c.* 1250–1310. *Geometrical tracery*: *see* Tracery.

Giant Order: in classical architecture, an order whose height is that of two or more storeys of the building to which it is applied.

Hammerbeam: *see* Roofs and timber-framing.

Helm roof: a pyramidal roof set diagonally on a tower, so that it meets the walls by means of gables.

Hoodmould: projecting moulding above an arch or lintel to throw off water. When horizontal often called a *label*.

Hyperbolic paraboloid: a special form of double curved shell, the geometry of which is generated by straight lines.

Ionic: *see* Orders.

Jack arch: *see* Arch.

Jetty: *see* Roofs and timber-framing.

King post: *see* Roofs and timber-framing.

Label: *see* Hoodmould.

Lucarne: small gabled opening, typically in a church spire.

Metope: *see* Orders.

Misericord: bracket on the underside of a hinged choir seat, which when turned up, provided support while the occupant was standing.

Mullion: *see* Tracery.

Narthex: enclosed vestibule or covered porch at the main entrance to a church.

Ogee (adjective *ogival*): *see* Arches.

Orders: [3]

Palazzo (Italian, palace): used for any compact and ornate building like a large Italian town house, usually classical in style.

Perp (Perpendicular): English Gothic architecture *c.* 1335–*c.* 1530.

Piano nobile (Italian): principal floor of a classical building, above a ground floor or basement and with a lesser storey above.

Porte cochère (French, *lit.* gate for coaches): porch large enough to admit wheeled vehicles.

Purlin: *see* Roofs and timber-framing.

Queenposts: paired upright timbers placed symmetrically on a tie-beam of a roof to support purlins (horizontal longitudinal timbers).

Reredos: painted and/or sculptured screen behind and above an altar.

Romanesque: style current in the C11 and C12. In England often called Norman.

Rood: a cross or crucifix, usually over the entry into the chancel, set on a beam (*rood beam*) or painted on the wall. The rood screen below often had a walkway along the top, reached by a rood stair in the side wall.

Roofs and timber-framing [4]

Rustication: exaggerated treatment of masonry to give an effect of strength. [5]

Scagliola: imitation marble of cement or plaster with marble chips or colouring matter.

Sephardic: pertaining to the traditions and customs of Sephardi Jews who lived in Spain and Portugal before expulsion in the C15.

Skewed arch: *see* Arch.

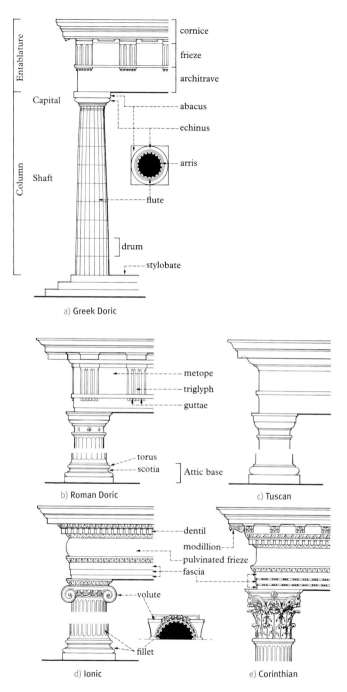

a) Greek Doric

b) Roman Doric

c) Tuscan

d) Ionic

e) Corinthian

3. Orders

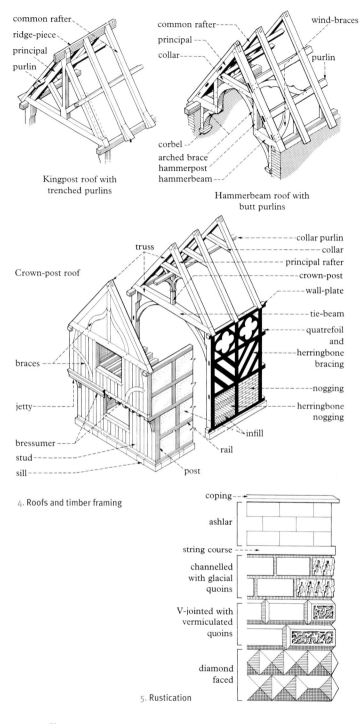

common rafter
ridge-piece
principal
purlin

Kingpost roof with
trenched purlins

common rafter
principal
collar

wind-braces
purlin

corbel
arched brace
hammerpost
hammerbeam

Hammerbeam roof with
butt purlins

Crown-post roof

truss

collar purlin
collar
principal rafter
crown-post
wall-plate
tie-beam
quatrefoil
and
herringbone
bracing
nogging
herringbone
nogging

braces

jetty

bressumer
stud
sill

infill
rail
post

4. Roofs and timber framing

coping
ashlar
string course
channelled
with glacial
quoins
V-jointed with
vermiculated
quoins
diamond
faced

5. Rustication

Spere: *see* Topic Box p. 6

Spinning mule: machine invented by Samuel Crompton in 1779 to spin yarn.

Supertransom: in tracery, a horizontal bar set well above the heads of the main window lights.

Tetrastyle: of a portico, with four columns.

Tierceron vault: a rib-vault with an extra decorative rib or ribs springing from the corner of a bay.

Tracery [6]

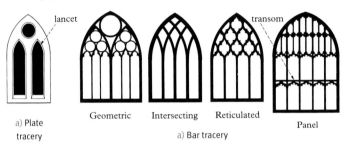

a) Plate tracery

Geometric   Intersecting   Reticulated   Panel

a) Bar tracery

6. Tracery

Transom: *see* Tracery.

Tryglyph: *see* Orders.

Truss: *see* Roofs and timber-framing.

Tuscan: *see* Orders.

Tumbled-in: *see* Brickwork.

Tunnel vault: the simplest kind of vault, in the form of a continuous semicircular or pointed arch.

Tympanum: the surface between a lintel and the arch above it or within a pediment.

Venetian window: in classical architecture, a window with an arched central light flanked by two lower straight-headed ones.

Vermiculation: *see* Rustication.

Wall-plate: *see* Roofs and timber-framing.

Index
of Artists, Architects, Patrons and Other Persons Mentioned

The names of architects and artists working in Manchester are given in *italic*. Page references in italic include relevant illustrations.

Index
of Localities, Streets and Buildings

Principal references are in **bold**; page references including relevant illustrations are in *italic*. Mills are listed by name under the heading 'mills'. 'dem.' = 'demolished'

Illustration Acknowledgements

We are grateful to the following for permission to reproduce illustrative material:

Aerofilms Limited: 197, 245
Stephenson Bell: 159, 191
Stephenson Bell/Sheppard Robson: 150
Bildarchiv Preussischer Kulturbesitz (Staatliche Museum, Berlin): 205
Whitby Bird & Partners/Peter Cook: 193
Bone family (and Manchester City Art Galleries): 237
Chris Boyles/Manchester Jewish Museum: 225
The British Architect and Northern Engineer: 47
British Architectural Library, RIBA, London: 51, 249
R. W. Brunskill/Faber and Faber: 3. Taken from R. W. Brunskill, *Vernacular Architecture: An Illustrated Handbook* (Faber and Faber, 4th edn, 2000)
The Builder: 11, 14, 18, 37, 38, 60, 71, 201
Building Design Partnership (and Manchester City Council): 172
Peter Burns/Manchester Cathedral: 45
Central Manchester Healthcare Trust: 26
Chetham's Library: 5, 8, 49, 50, 144, 165
The Conway Library, Courtauld Institute of Art: 20, 46
Co-operative Insurance Society (CIS): 173
Crown Copyright. NMR: 19, 52, 67, 110, 135, 154, 162, 196, 206, 207, 209, 210, 222, 226, 227, 236

John Donat: 179
EDAW/Tadao Ando/Ove Arup & Partners: 131
Wilkinson Eyre Architects: 244
Gee, Walker and Slater/The Home Publishing Company: 178
Len Grant: 250
Christa Grössinger: 42, 43
HarperCollins: 94. Taken from John Ruskin, *The Stones of Venice* (George Allen and Unwin, 4th edn, 1886).
Clare Hartwell: 23, 32, 53, 63, 79, 89, 122, 123, 124, 125, 128, 133, 149, 183, 252
Elain Harwood: 120
English Heritage: 1, 10, 12, 13, 15, 16, 17, 21, 22, 27, 28, 29, 30, 39, 40, 44, 48, 61, 64, 65, 73, 78, 81, 82, 83, 85, 86, 87, 93, 95, 96, 98, 99, 100, 101, 102, 104, 106, 109, 111, 112, 113, 114, 116, 118, 119, 127, 132, 134, 136, 137, 138, 139, 140, 141, 142, 143, 145, 146, 148, 151, 153, 156, 157, 158, 161, 164, 167, 170, 174, 175, 176, 181, 184, 186, 190, 192, 194, 198, 202, 203, 208, 211, 212, 213, 214, 215, 219, 221, 224, 230, 232, 235, 239, 240, 243, 246, 254
Hodder Associates/Peter Cook: 31
Trustees of the Holy Name of Jesus (R.C.): 231
Michael Hopkins and Partners: 62
Jane Kennedy/John Archer/Manchester University Press: 66. Taken from John Archer, *Art and Architecture in Victorian Manchester* (Manchester University Press, 1995).
Ian Lawson: 233
Daniel Libeskind/Torsten Seidel: 256
Manchester Central Library: 6, 7, 9, 91, 182, 187
Manchester City Art Galleries: 57
Manchester City Council: 24, 54, 55, 56, 58, 59, 70, 107, 180, 216
Manchester Evening News: 34, 35

Manchester Guardian: 41
Manchester Metropolitan University: 88, 147
Manchester Museum, University of Manchester: 75, 77
Museum of Science and Industry in Manchester: 195
OMI Architects: 129
Ordnance Survey: 97, 121, 155, 241
Anthony J. Pass: 103
Portico Library and Gallery, Manchester: 117
Hurd Rolland Partnership: 115
John Rylands University Library of Manchester: 68
St Augustine, Pendlebury, Restoration and Development Trust: 251
Parochial Church of St Michael and All Angels: 253
Andrea Sarginson: 220
Ian Simpson Architects: 171
Space Group: 33
Stephenson Architecture: 105
University of Manchester: 74
University of Manchester, Field Archaeology Centre: 4, 25, 204, 248
Prudence Waterhouse/British Architectural Library, RIBA, London/Oxford University Press: 51. Taken from Colin Cunningham and Prudence Waterhouse, *Alfred Waterhouse 1830–1905. Biography of a Practice* (Clarendon Press, 1992).
Thomas Worthington & Sons (and Manchester City Council): 130

The following illustrations were kindly loaned from private collections:

Bancks & Co.'s *Plan of Salford and Manchester with their Environs* (1831): 126, 229
A Plan of Manchester and Salford by William Green (1794): 163, 168, 185, 189, 200, 217
Hanging Bridge (pamphlet, 1910): 169
J. Stuart and N. Revett, *The Antiquities of Athens* (John Nicholls, 1762–1816): 108

Maps and plans drawn by Alan Fagan: 2, 4, 36, 69, 72, 76, 80, 84, 90, 92, 152, 160, 166, 172, 177, 188, 199, 218, 223, 228, 234, 238, 242, 247, 253, 255